CRUISIN' WITH THE HOUND

Fantagraphics Books
7563 Lake City Way NE
Seattle, Washington 98115

Editor: Gary Groth
Designer: Alexa Koenings
Production: Paul Baresh
Associate Publisher: Eric Reynolds
Publishers: Gary Groth and Kim Thompson

"My Cold War" (*New & Used Blab*, 2003)
"The Return of James" (*Blab* #16, 2005)
"The Fighting Poets" (*Blab* #9, 1997)
"The Shadow of Fred Tooté" (*Blab* #7, 1992)
"Fred Tooté Rides" (*Blab* #4, 1989)
"Mickey's Meat Wagon" (*Zap* #15, 2005)
"Fissure's Jacket" (*Zap* #13, 1994)
"The Sons of Hercules" (*Blab* #12, 2001)
"The House on Wakefield Street"
    (*Blab* #13, 2002)
"Confessions" (*Blab* #11, 2000)
"Tex's Bad Dream" (*Blab* #3, 1988)
"Wilcoxson and Nussbaum" (*Blab* #5, 1990)
"Cruisin' With the Hound" (*Blab* #8, 1995)
"Down at the Kitty Kat" (*Blab* #6, 1991)
"Carney" (*Blab* #10, 1998)
"Birth of Porn" (*Blab* #14, 2003)

"Space Case"
    (*The Comics Journal Special Edition Volume
    One: Cartoonists on Cartooning*, 2001)
"I've Seen The Best of It"
    (*The Comics Journal Special Edition Volume
    Two: Cartoonists on Music*, 2002)
"The Mandate of Heaven"
    (*The Comics Journal Special Edition Volume
    Four: Cartoonists on the Shock of Recognition*,
    2004)
"High Smile Guy In a Low Smile Zone"
    (*Blab* #17, 2006)
"Education of an Underground Cartoonists"
    (*Blab* #15, 2004)
Patriotism" (*The Comics Journal Special Edition
    Volume Three: Cartoonists on Patriotism*, 2003)

The stories in this volume originally appeared in:

To receive a free full-color catalog of comics, graphic novels, prose novels, artist monographs, and other fine works of artistry, call 1-800-657-1100, or visit www.fantagraphics.com where you may view and purchase available titles.

Distributed in the U.S. by W.W. Norton and Company, Inc. (800-233-4830)
Distributed in Canada by Canadian Manda Group (800-452-6642 x862)
Distributed in the U.K. by Turnaround Distribution (44 (0)20 8829-3002)
Distributed to comic stores by Diamond Comics Distributors (800-452-6642 x215)

ISBN: 978-1-60699-461-0

First Fantagraphics Books printing: April, 2012

Printed in Hong Kong

Cruisin' with the HOUND

Comics by **SPAIN RODRIGUEZ**

FANTAGRAPHICS BOOKS

CONTENTS

**DEBAUCHERY
& DELINQUENCY IN
BUFFALO:
An Interview with
Spain Rodriguez
by Gary Groth
97**

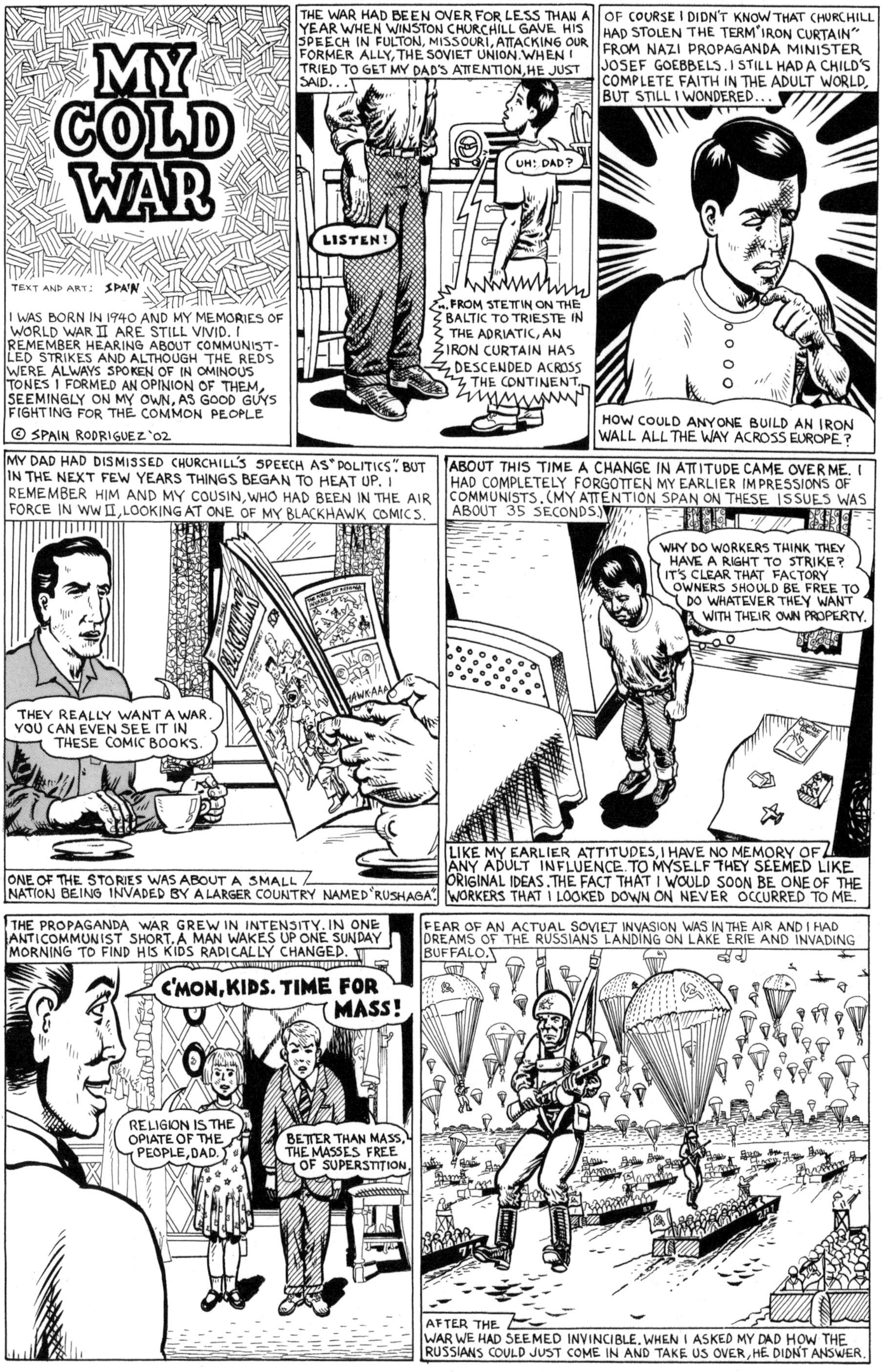

MY COLD WAR
TEXT AND ART: SPAIN
I WAS BORN IN 1940 AND MY MEMORIES OF WORLD WAR II ARE STILL VIVID. I REMEMBER HEARING ABOUT COMMUNIST-LED STRIKES AND ALTHOUGH THE REDS WERE ALWAYS SPOKEN OF IN OMINOUS TONES I FORMED AN OPINION OF THEM, SEEMINGLY ON MY OWN, AS GOOD GUYS FIGHTING FOR THE COMMON PEOPLE
© SPAIN RODRIGUEZ '02
THE WAR HAD BEEN OVER FOR LESS THAN A YEAR WHEN WINSTON CHURCHILL GAVE HIS SPEECH IN FULTON, MISSOURI, ATTACKING OUR FORMER ALLY, THE SOVIET UNION. WHEN I TRIED TO GET MY DAD'S ATTENTION, HE JUST SAID...
UH; DAD?
LISTEN!
...FROM STETTIN ON THE BALTIC TO TRIESTE IN THE ADRIATIC, AN IRON CURTAIN HAS DESCENDED ACROSS THE CONTINENT.
OF COURSE I DIDN'T KNOW THAT CHURCHILL HAD STOLEN THE TERM "IRON CURTAIN" FROM NAZI PROPAGANDA MINISTER JOSEF GOEBBELS. I STILL HAD A CHILD'S COMPLETE FAITH IN THE ADULT WORLD, BUT STILL I WONDERED...
HOW COULD ANYONE BUILD AN IRON WALL ALL THE WAY ACROSS EUROPE?
MY DAD HAD DISMISSED CHURCHILL'S SPEECH AS "POLITICS". BUT IN THE NEXT FEW YEARS THINGS BEGAN TO HEAT UP. I REMEMBER HIM AND MY COUSIN, WHO HAD BEEN IN THE AIR FORCE IN WW II, LOOKING AT ONE OF MY BLACKHAWK COMICS.
THEY REALLY WANT A WAR. YOU CAN EVEN SEE IT IN THESE COMIC BOOKS.
ONE OF THE STORIES WAS ABOUT A SMALL NATION BEING INVADED BY A LARGER COUNTRY NAMED "RUSHAGA".
ABOUT THIS TIME A CHANGE IN ATTITUDE CAME OVER ME. I HAD COMPLETELY FORGOTTEN MY EARLIER IMPRESSIONS OF COMMUNISTS. (MY ATTENTION SPAN ON THESE ISSUES WAS ABOUT 35 SECONDS.)
WHY DO WORKERS THINK THEY HAVE A RIGHT TO STRIKE? IT'S CLEAR THAT FACTORY OWNERS SHOULD BE FREE TO DO WHATEVER THEY WANT WITH THEIR OWN PROPERTY.
LIKE MY EARLIER ATTITUDES, I HAVE NO MEMORY OF ANY ADULT INFLUENCE. TO MYSELF THEY SEEMED LIKE ORIGINAL IDEAS. THE FACT THAT I WOULD SOON BE ONE OF THE WORKERS THAT I LOOKED DOWN ON NEVER OCCURRED TO ME.
THE PROPAGANDA WAR GREW IN INTENSITY. IN ONE ANTICOMMUNIST SHORT, A MAN WAKES UP ONE SUNDAY MORNING TO FIND HIS KIDS RADICALLY CHANGED.
C'MON, KIDS. TIME FOR MASS!
RELIGION IS THE OPIATE OF THE PEOPLE, DAD.
BETTER THAN MASS, THE MASSES FREE OF SUPERSTITION.
FEAR OF AN ACTUAL SOVIET INVASION WAS IN THE AIR AND I HAD DREAMS OF THE RUSSIANS LANDING ON LAKE ERIE AND INVADING BUFFALO.
AFTER THE WAR WE HAD SEEMED INVINCIBLE. WHEN I ASKED MY DAD HOW THE RUSSIANS COULD JUST COME IN AND TAKE US OVER, HE DIDN'T ANSWER.

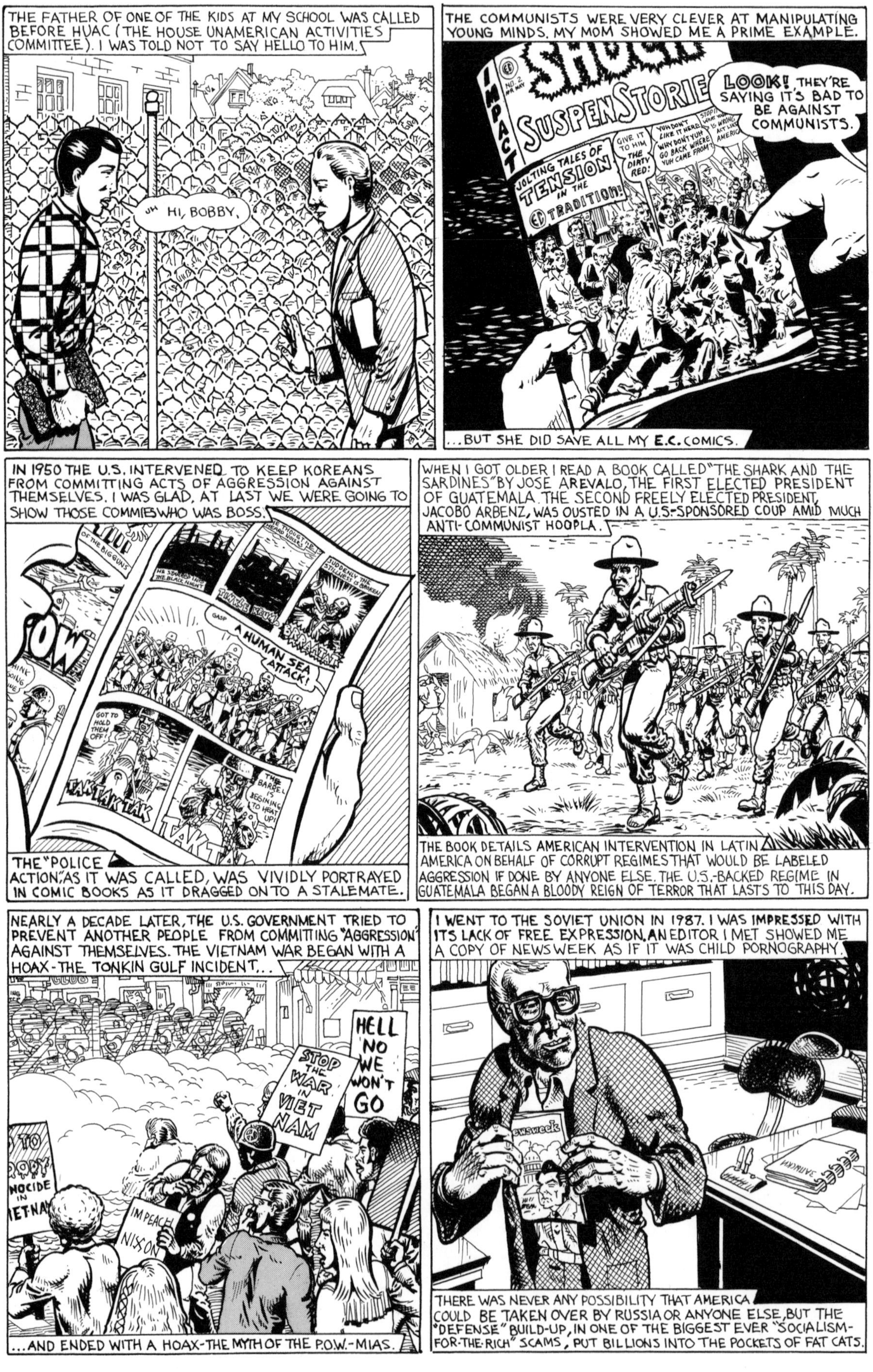
THE FATHER OF ONE OF THE KIDS AT MY SCHOOL WAS CALLED BEFORE HUAC (THE HOUSE UNAMERICAN ACTIVITIES COMMITTEE). I WAS TOLD NOT TO SAY HELLO TO HIM.
UH HI, BOBBY.
THE COMMUNISTS WERE VERY CLEVER AT MANIPULATING YOUNG MINDS. MY MOM SHOWED ME A PRIME EXAMPLE.
IMPACT
SHOCK SUSPENSTORIES
JOLTING TALES OF TENSION IN THE EC TRADITION!
GIVE IT TO HIM
THE DIRTY RED!
YUH DON'T LIKE IT HERE, WHY DON'T YUH GO BACK WHERE YUH CAME FROM?
LOOK! THEY'RE SAYING IT'S BAD TO BE AGAINST COMMUNISTS.
...BUT SHE DID SAVE ALL MY E.C. COMICS.
IN 1950 THE U.S. INTERVENED TO KEEP KOREANS FROM COMMITTING ACTS OF AGGRESSION AGAINST THEMSELVES. I WAS GLAD. AT LAST WE WERE GOING TO SHOW THOSE COMMIES WHO WAS BOSS.
GASP
A HUMAN SEA ATTACK!
GOT TO HOLD THEM OFF!
THE BARREL IS BEGINING TO HEAT UP!
TAK TAK TAK
THE "POLICE ACTION," AS IT WAS CALLED, WAS VIVIDLY PORTRAYED IN COMIC BOOKS AS IT DRAGGED ON TO A STALEMATE.
WHEN I GOT OLDER I READ A BOOK CALLED "THE SHARK AND THE SARDINES" BY JOSE AREVALO, THE FIRST ELECTED PRESIDENT OF GUATEMALA. THE SECOND FREELY ELECTED PRESIDENT, JACOBO ARBENZ, WAS OUSTED IN A U.S.-SPONSORED COUP AMID MUCH ANTI-COMMUNIST HOOPLA.
THE BOOK DETAILS AMERICAN INTERVENTION IN LATIN AMERICA ON BEHALF OF CORRUPT REGIMES THAT WOULD BE LABELED AGGRESSION IF DONE BY ANYONE ELSE. THE U.S.-BACKED REGIME IN GUATEMALA BEGAN A BLOODY REIGN OF TERROR THAT LASTS TO THIS DAY.
NEARLY A DECADE LATER, THE U.S. GOVERNMENT TRIED TO PREVENT ANOTHER PEOPLE FROM COMMITTING "AGGRESSION" AGAINST THEMSELVES. THE VIETNAM WAR BEGAN WITH A HOAX - THE TONKIN GULF INCIDENT...
HELL NO WE WON'T GO
STOP THE WAR IN VIET NAM
IMPEACH NIXON
...AND ENDED WITH A HOAX - THE MYTH OF THE P.O.W.-MIAS.
I WENT TO THE SOVIET UNION IN 1987. I WAS IMPRESSED WITH ITS LACK OF FREE EXPRESSION. AN EDITOR I MET SHOWED ME A COPY OF NEWSWEEK AS IF IT WAS CHILD PORNOGRAPHY.
THERE WAS NEVER ANY POSSIBILITY THAT AMERICA COULD BE TAKEN OVER BY RUSSIA OR ANYONE ELSE, BUT THE "DEFENSE" BUILD-UP, IN ONE OF THE BIGGEST EVER "SOCIALISM-FOR-THE-RICH" SCAMS, PUT BILLIONS INTO THE POCKETS OF FAT CATS.

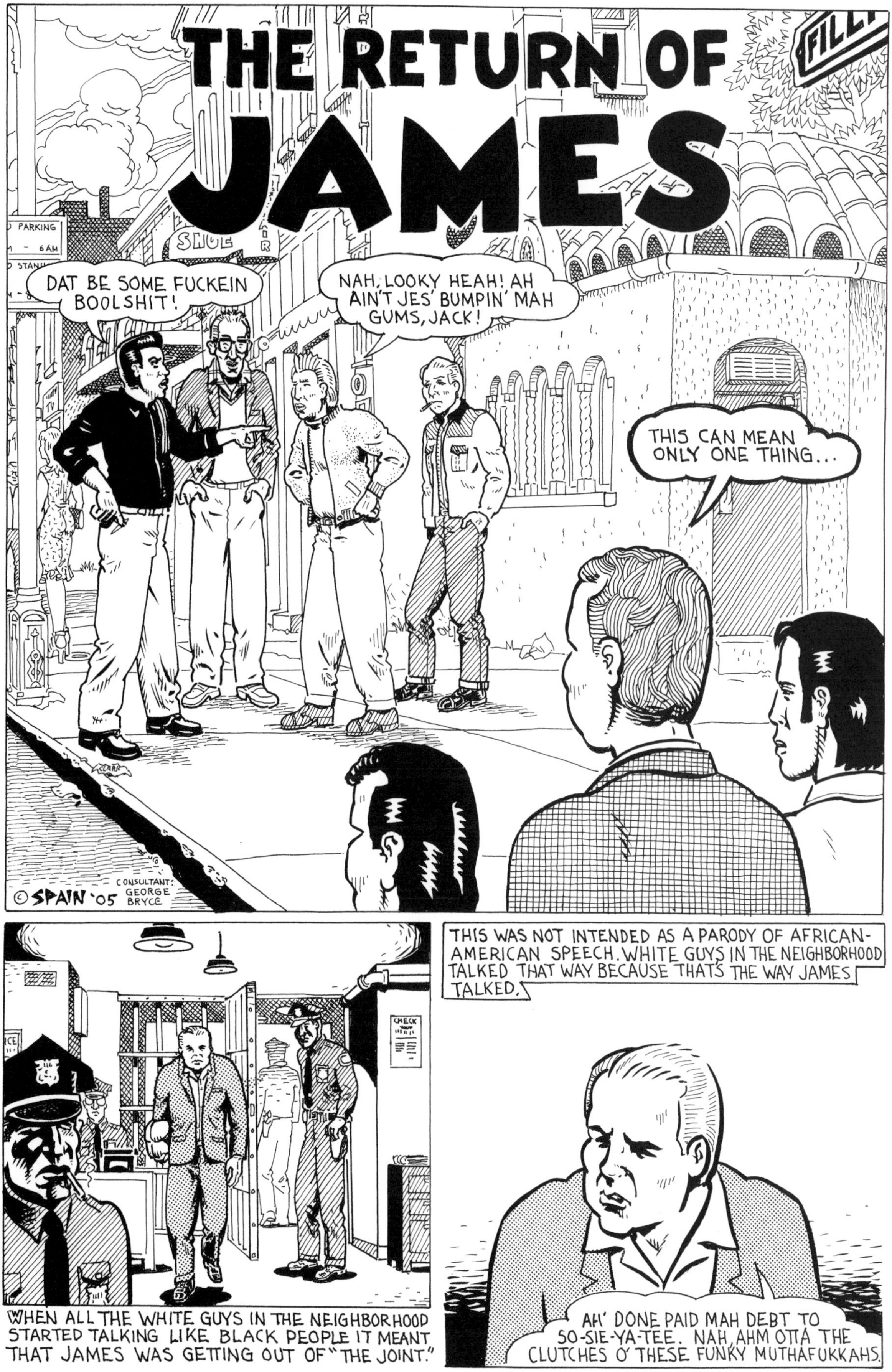
THE RETURN OF JAMES
DAT BE SOME FUCKEIN BOOLSHIT!
NAH, LOOKY HEAH! AH AIN'T JES' BUMPIN' MAH GUMS, JACK!
THIS CAN MEAN ONLY ONE THING...
© SPAIN '05
CONSULTANT: GEORGE BRYCE
WHEN ALL THE WHITE GUYS IN THE NEIGHBORHOOD STARTED TALKING LIKE BLACK PEOPLE IT MEANT THAT JAMES WAS GETTING OUT OF "THE JOINT."
THIS WAS NOT INTENDED AS A PARODY OF AFRICAN-AMERICAN SPEECH. WHITE GUYS IN THE NEIGHBORHOOD TALKED THAT WAY BECAUSE THAT'S THE WAY JAMES TALKED.
AH' DONE PAID MAH DEBT TO SO-SIE-YA-TEE. NAH, AHM OTTA THE CLUTCHES O' THESE FUNKY MUTHAFUKKAHS.

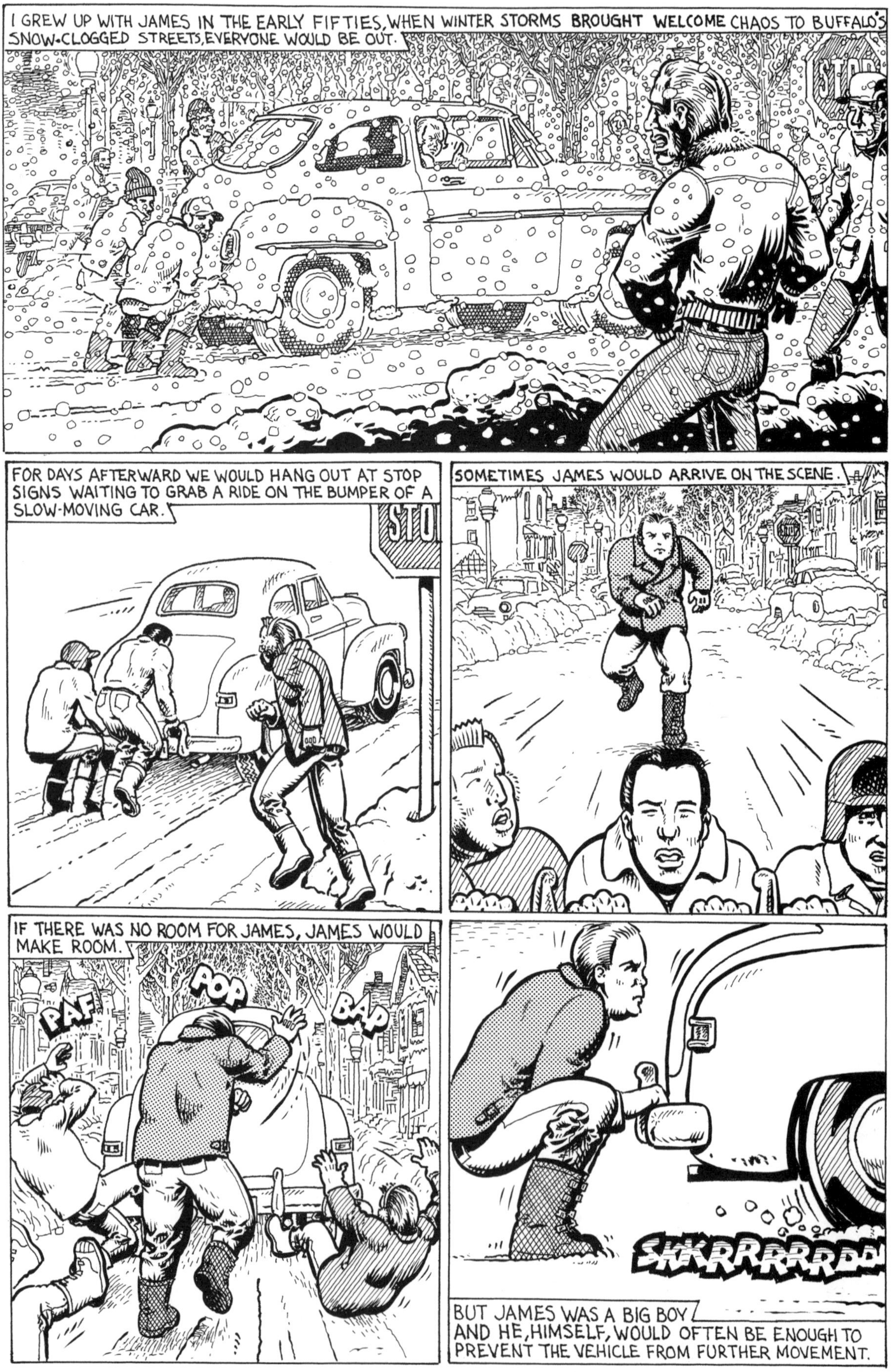
I GREW UP WITH JAMES IN THE EARLY FIFTIES, WHEN WINTER STORMS BROUGHT WELCOME CHAOS TO BUFFALO'S SNOW-CLOGGED STREETS, EVERYONE WOULD BE OUT.
FOR DAYS AFTERWARD WE WOULD HANG OUT AT STOP SIGNS WAITING TO GRAB A RIDE ON THE BUMPER OF A SLOW-MOVING CAR.
SOMETIMES JAMES WOULD ARRIVE ON THE SCENE.
IF THERE WAS NO ROOM FOR JAMES, JAMES WOULD MAKE ROOM.
PAF
POP
BAP
SKKRRRRRDD
BUT JAMES WAS A BIG BOY AND HE, HIMSELF, WOULD OFTEN BE ENOUGH TO PREVENT THE VEHICLE FROM FURTHER MOVEMENT.

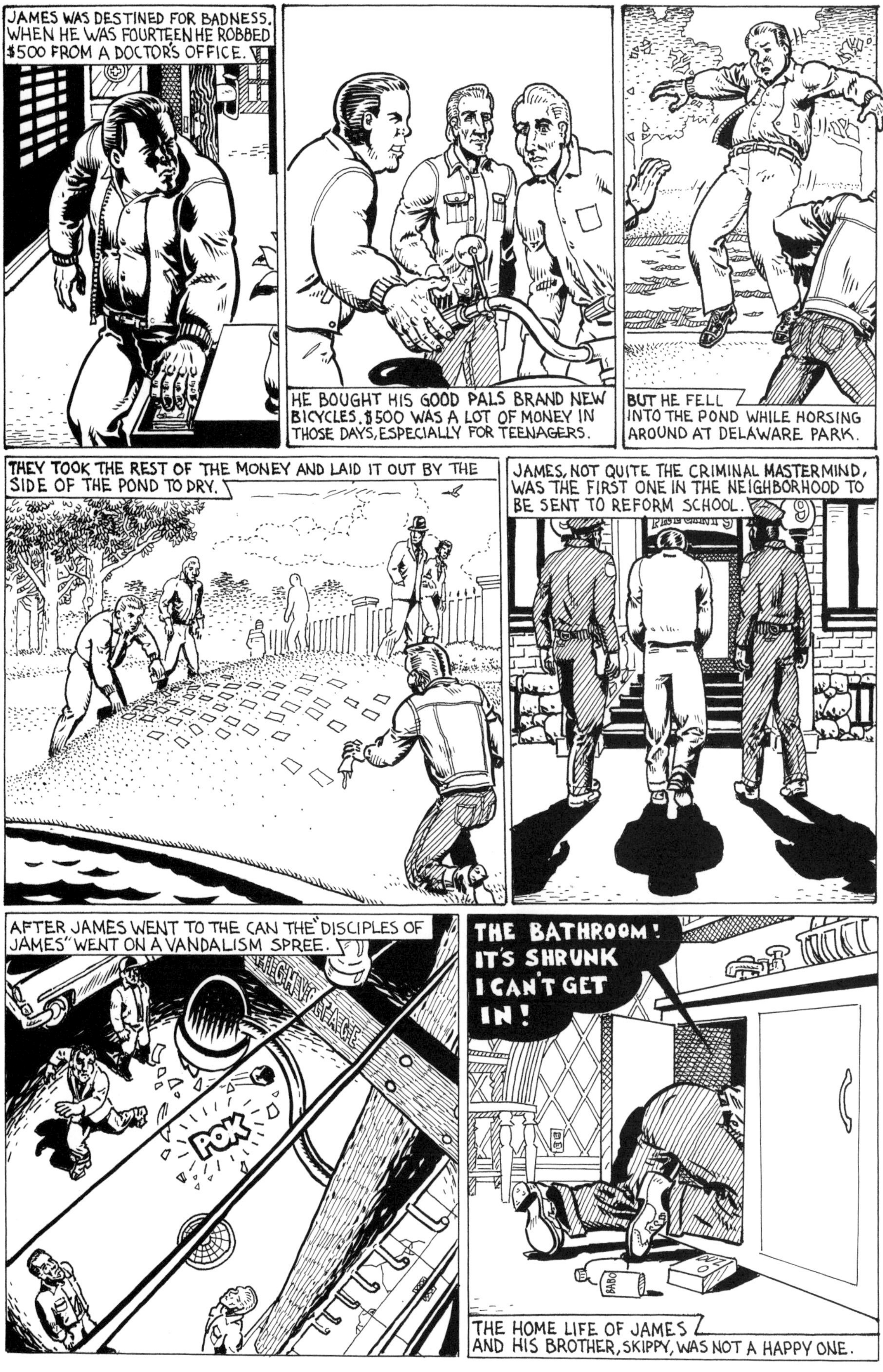
JAMES WAS DESTINED FOR BADNESS. WHEN HE WAS FOURTEEN HE ROBBED $500 FROM A DOCTOR'S OFFICE.
HE BOUGHT HIS GOOD PALS BRAND NEW BICYCLES. $500 WAS A LOT OF MONEY IN THOSE DAYS, ESPECIALLY FOR TEENAGERS.
BUT HE FELL INTO THE POND WHILE HORSING AROUND AT DELAWARE PARK.
THEY TOOK THE REST OF THE MONEY AND LAID IT OUT BY THE SIDE OF THE POND TO DRY.
JAMES, NOT QUITE THE CRIMINAL MASTERMIND, WAS THE FIRST ONE IN THE NEIGHBORHOOD TO BE SENT TO REFORM SCHOOL.
9
AFTER JAMES WENT TO THE CAN THE "DISCIPLES OF JAMES" WENT ON A VANDALISM SPREE.
POK
THE BATHROOM! IT'S SHRUNK I CAN'T GET IN!
THE HOME LIFE OF JAMES AND HIS BROTHER, SKIPPY, WAS NOT A HAPPY ONE.

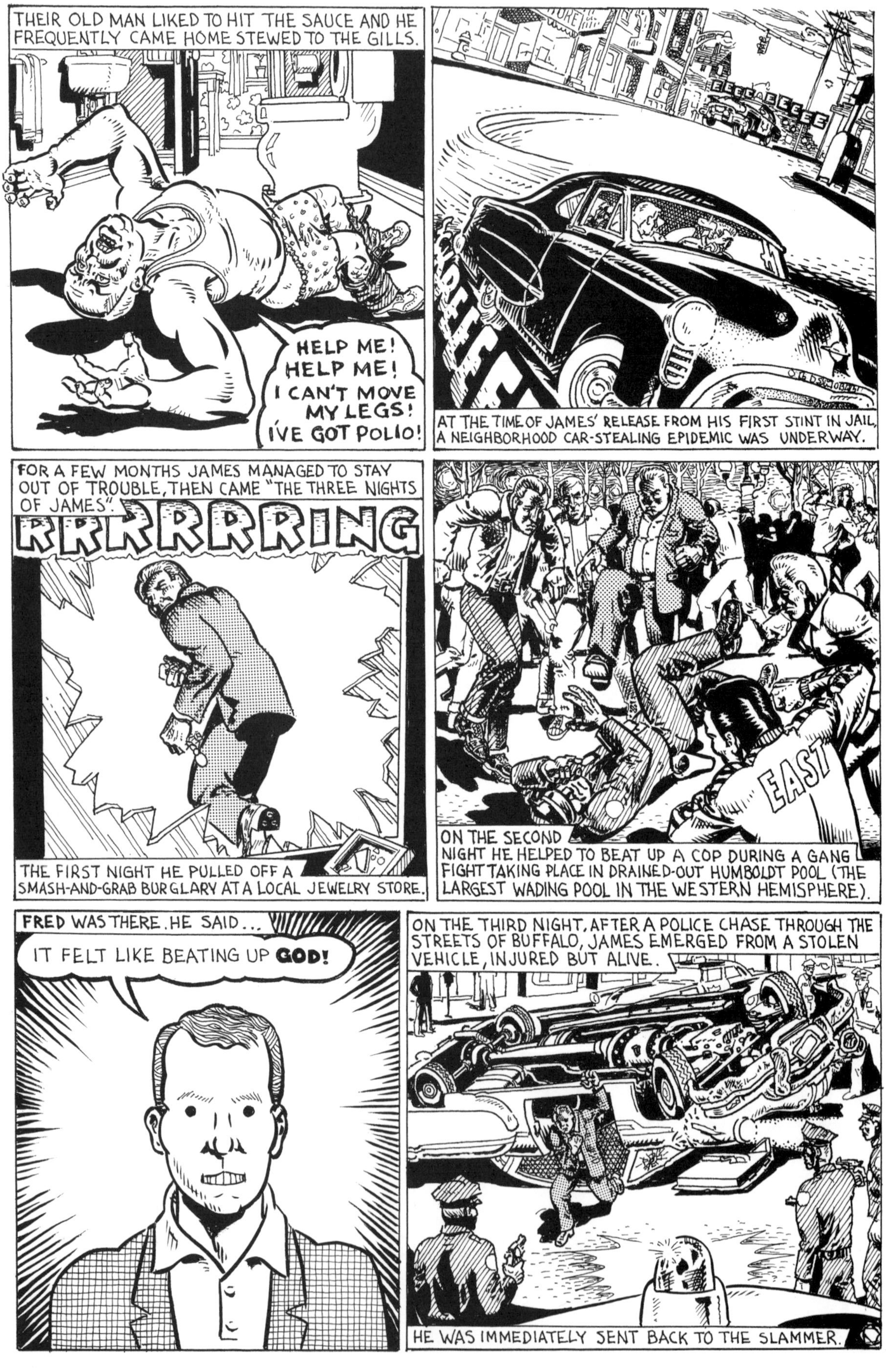
THEIR OLD MAN LIKED TO HIT THE SAUCE AND HE FREQUENTLY CAME HOME STEWED TO THE GILLS.
HELP ME! HELP ME! I CAN'T MOVE MY LEGS! I'VE GOT POLIO!
AT THE TIME OF JAMES' RELEASE FROM HIS FIRST STINT IN JAIL, A NEIGHBORHOOD CAR-STEALING EPIDEMIC WAS UNDERWAY.
FOR A FEW MONTHS JAMES MANAGED TO STAY OUT OF TROUBLE, THEN CAME "THE THREE NIGHTS OF JAMES".
RRRRRRING
THE FIRST NIGHT HE PULLED OFF A SMASH-AND-GRAB BURGLARY AT A LOCAL JEWELRY STORE.
EAST
ON THE SECOND NIGHT HE HELPED TO BEAT UP A COP DURING A GANG FIGHT TAKING PLACE IN DRAINED-OUT HUMBOLDT POOL (THE LARGEST WADING POOL IN THE WESTERN HEMISPHERE).
FRED WAS THERE. HE SAID...
IT FELT LIKE BEATING UP GOD!
ON THE THIRD NIGHT, AFTER A POLICE CHASE THROUGH THE STREETS OF BUFFALO, JAMES EMERGED FROM A STOLEN VEHICLE, INJURED BUT ALIVE.
HE WAS IMMEDIATELY SENT BACK TO THE SLAMMER.

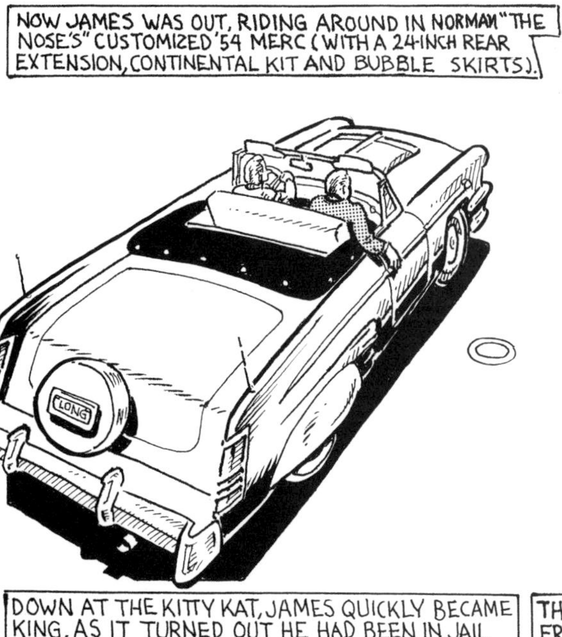
NOW JAMES WAS OUT, RIDING AROUND IN NORMAN "THE NOSE'S" CUSTOMIZED '54 MERC (WITH A 24-INCH REAR EXTENSION, CONTINENTAL KIT AND BUBBLE SKIRTS).
LONG

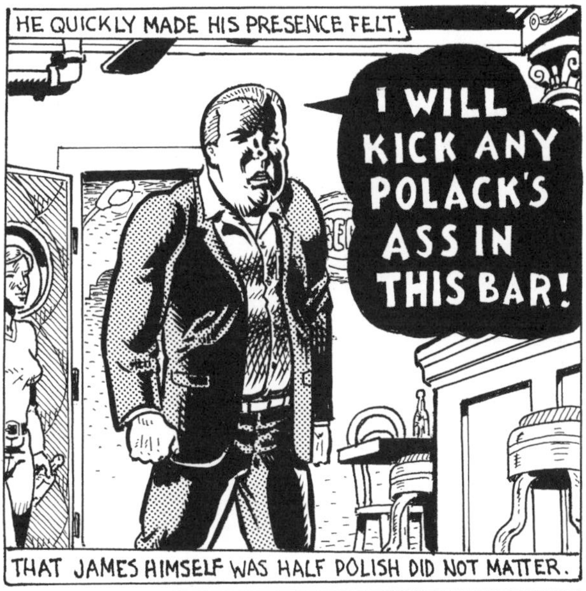
HE QUICKLY MADE HIS PRESENCE FELT.
I WILL KICK ANY POLACK'S ASS IN THIS BAR!
THAT JAMES HIMSELF WAS HALF POLISH DID NOT MATTER.

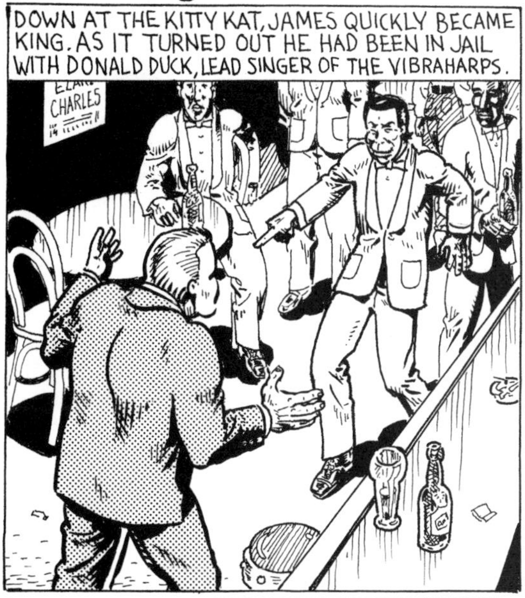
DOWN AT THE KITTY KAT, JAMES QUICKLY BECAME KING. AS IT TURNED OUT HE HAD BEEN IN JAIL WITH DONALD DUCK, LEAD SINGER OF THE VIBRAHARPS.
CHARLES

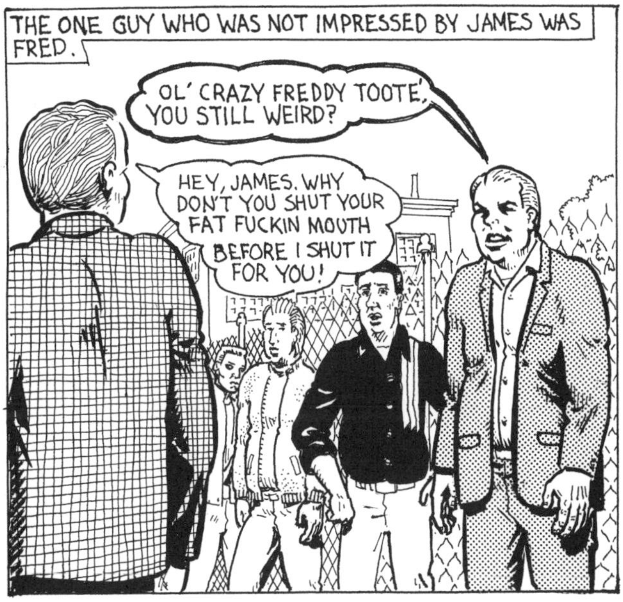
THE ONE GUY WHO WAS NOT IMPRESSED BY JAMES WAS FRED.
OL' CRAZY FREDDY TOOTE, YOU STILL WEIRD?
HEY, JAMES. WHY DON'T YOU SHUT YOUR FAT FUCKIN MOUTH BEFORE I SHUT IT FOR YOU!

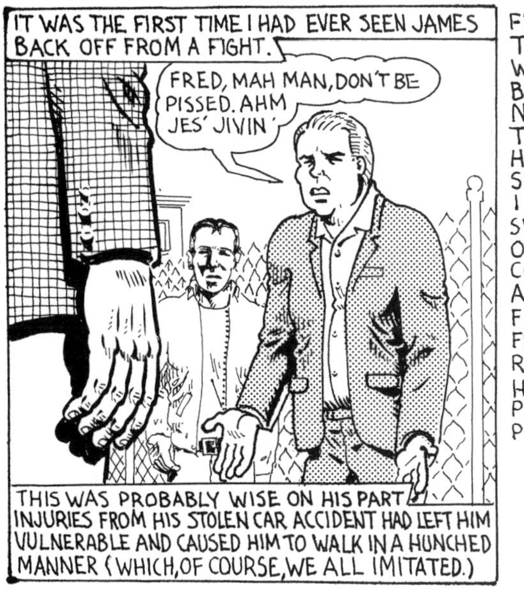
IT WAS THE FIRST TIME I HAD EVER SEEN JAMES BACK OFF FROM A FIGHT.
FRED, MAH MAN, DON'T BE PISSED. AHM JES' JIVIN'
THIS WAS PROBABLY WISE ON HIS PART. INJURIES FROM HIS STOLEN CAR ACCIDENT HAD LEFT HIM VULNERABLE AND CAUSED HIM TO WALK IN A HUNCHED MANNER (WHICH, OF COURSE, WE ALL IMITATED.)

FRED WAS ALSO THE ONLY ONE WHO REFUSED TO BECOME A "WHITE NEGRO". PERHAPS THIS WAS BECAUSE HE HAD DARK-SKINNED RELATIVES. I REMEMBER SEEING A PHOTO OF ONE OF HIS COUSINS, AN ATTRACTIVE BABE FROM JAMAICA. FRED ALWAYS REFERRED TO HER AS A POLYNESIAN PRINCESS.

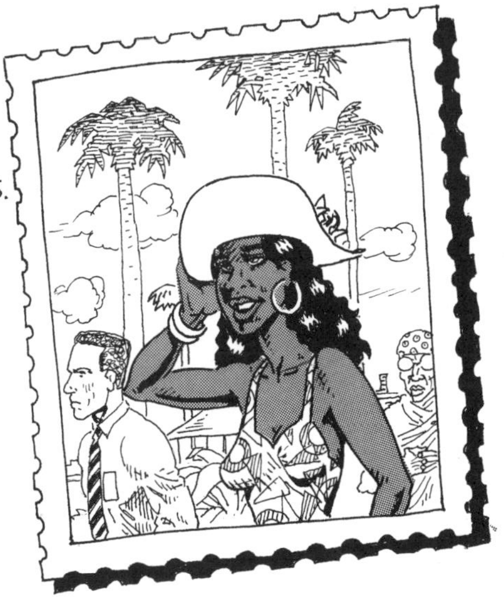

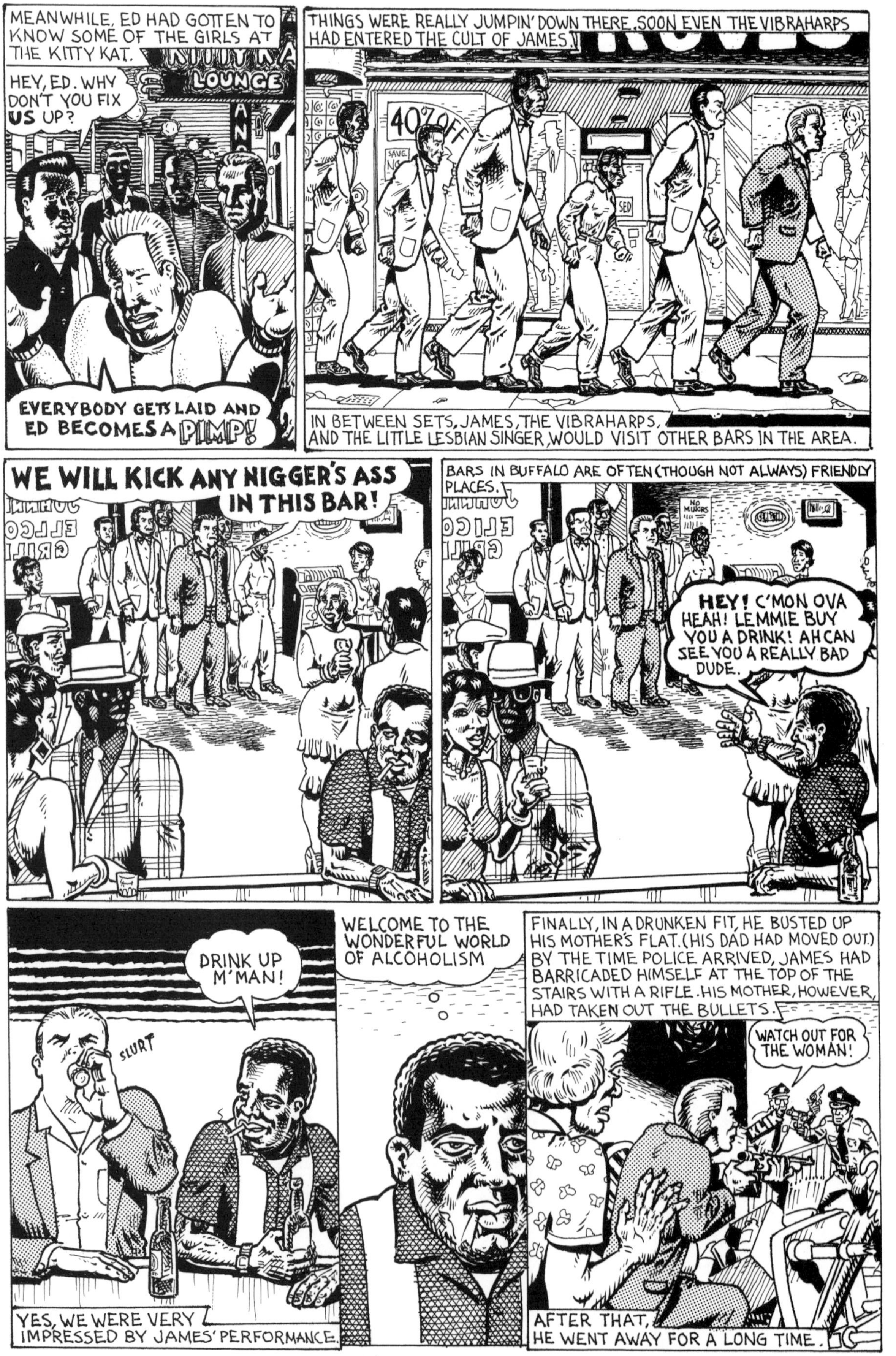
MEANWHILE, ED HAD GOTTEN TO KNOW SOME OF THE GIRLS AT THE KITTY KAT.
LOUNGE
HEY, ED. WHY DON'T YOU FIX US UP?
EVERYBODY GETS LAID AND ED BECOMES A PIMP!
THINGS WERE REALLY JUMPIN' DOWN THERE. SOON EVEN THE VIBRAHARPS HAD ENTERED THE CULT OF JAMES.
40% OFF
IN BETWEEN SETS, JAMES, THE VIBRAHARPS, AND THE LITTLE LESBIAN SINGER, WOULD VISIT OTHER BARS IN THE AREA.
WE WILL KICK ANY NIGGER'S ASS IN THIS BAR!
BARS IN BUFFALO ARE OFTEN (THOUGH NOT ALWAYS) FRIENDLY PLACES.
NO MINORS
HEY! C'MON OVA HEAH! LEMMIE BUY YOU A DRINK! AH CAN SEE YOU A REALLY BAD DUDE.
DRINK UP M'MAN!
SLURT
YES, WE WERE VERY IMPRESSED BY JAMES' PERFORMANCE.
WELCOME TO THE WONDERFUL WORLD OF ALCOHOLISM
FINALLY, IN A DRUNKEN FIT, HE BUSTED UP HIS MOTHER'S FLAT. (HIS DAD HAD MOVED OUT.) BY THE TIME POLICE ARRIVED, JAMES HAD BARRICADED HIMSELF AT THE TOP OF THE STAIRS WITH A RIFLE. HIS MOTHER, HOWEVER, HAD TAKEN OUT THE BULLETS.
WATCH OUT FOR THE WOMAN!
AFTER THAT, HE WENT AWAY FOR A LONG TIME.

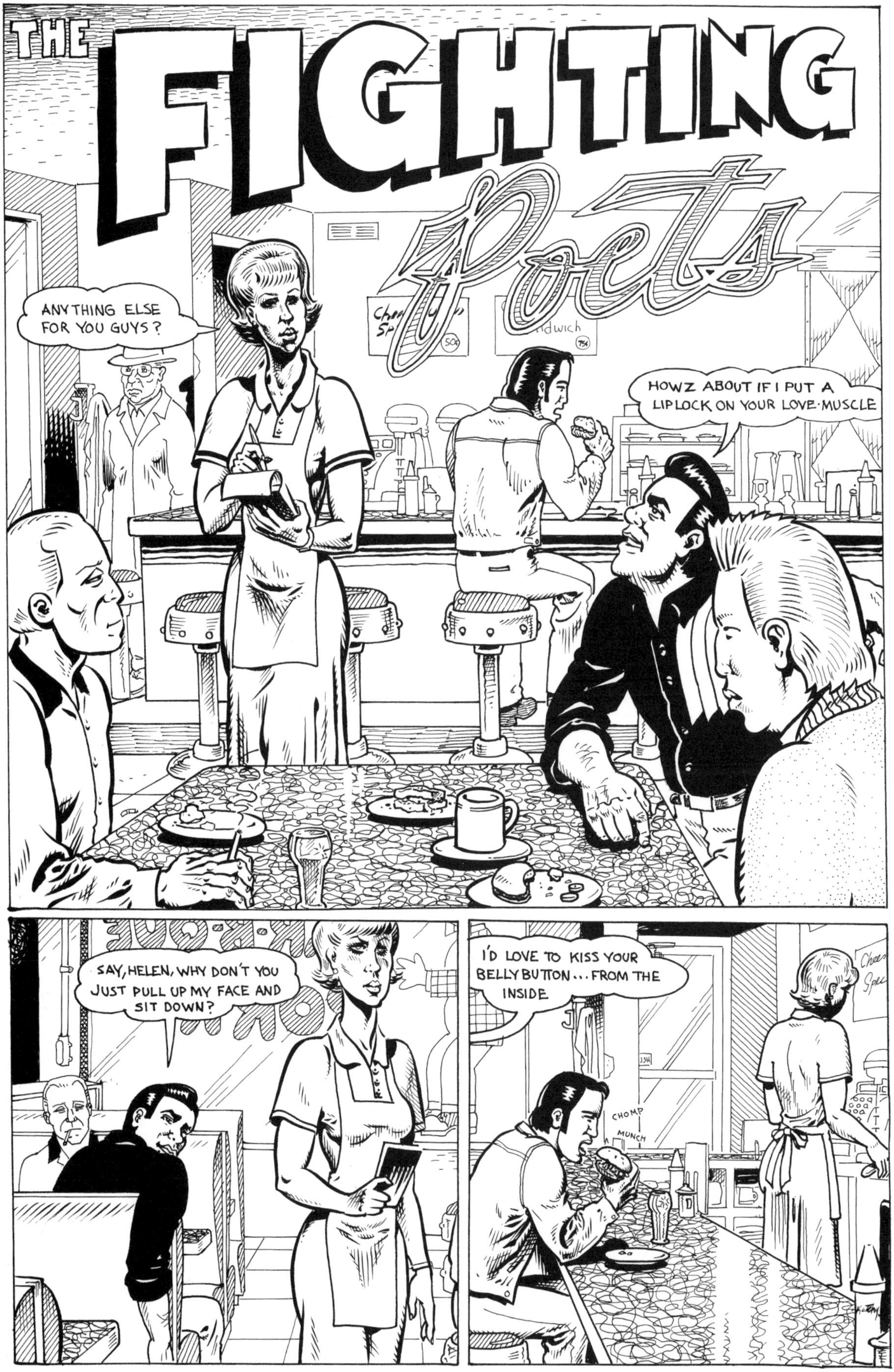
THE FIGHTING Poets
ANYTHING ELSE FOR YOU GUYS?
HOWZ ABOUT IF I PUT A LIPLOCK ON YOUR LOVE·MUSCLE
SAY, HELEN, WHY DON'T YOU JUST PULL UP MY FACE AND SIT DOWN?
I'D LOVE TO KISS YOUR BELLY BUTTON ... FROM THE INSIDE
CHOMP
MUNCH

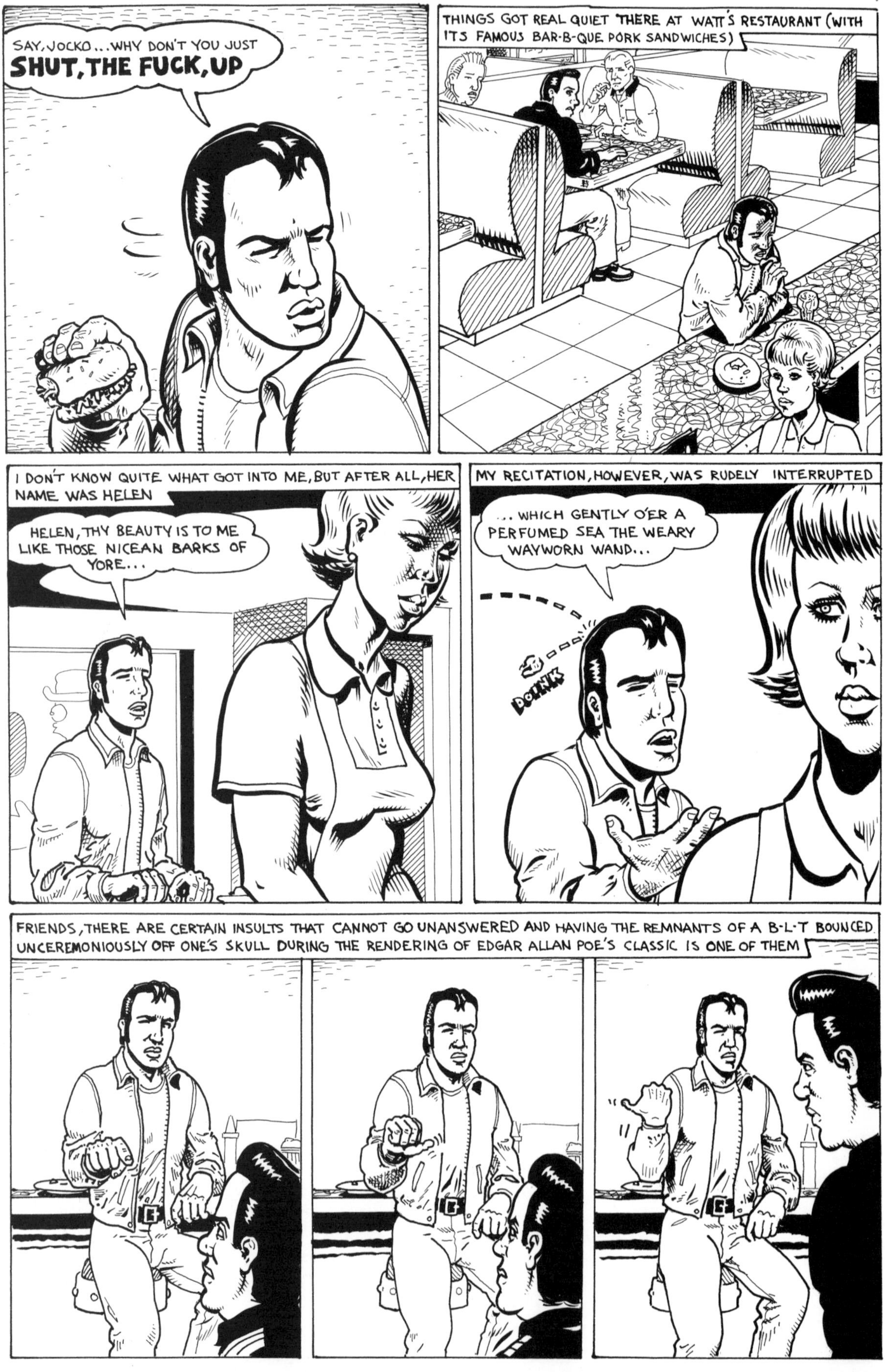
SAY, JOCKO... WHY DON'T YOU JUST
SHUT, THE FUCK, UP
THINGS GOT REAL QUIET THERE AT WATT'S RESTAURANT (WITH ITS FAMOUS BAR-B-QUE PORK SANDWICHES)
I DON'T KNOW QUITE WHAT GOT INTO ME, BUT AFTER ALL, HER NAME WAS HELEN
HELEN, THY BEAUTY IS TO ME LIKE THOSE NICEAN BARKS OF YORE...
MY RECITATION, HOWEVER, WAS RUDELY INTERRUPTED
... WHICH GENTLY O'ER A PERFUMED SEA THE WEARY WAYWORN WAND...
DOINK
FRIENDS, THERE ARE CERTAIN INSULTS THAT CANNOT GO UNANSWERED AND HAVING THE REMNANTS OF A B-L-T BOUNCED UNCEREMONIOUSLY OFF ONE'S SKULL DURING THE RENDERING OF EDGAR ALLAN POE'S CLASSIC IS ONE OF THEM

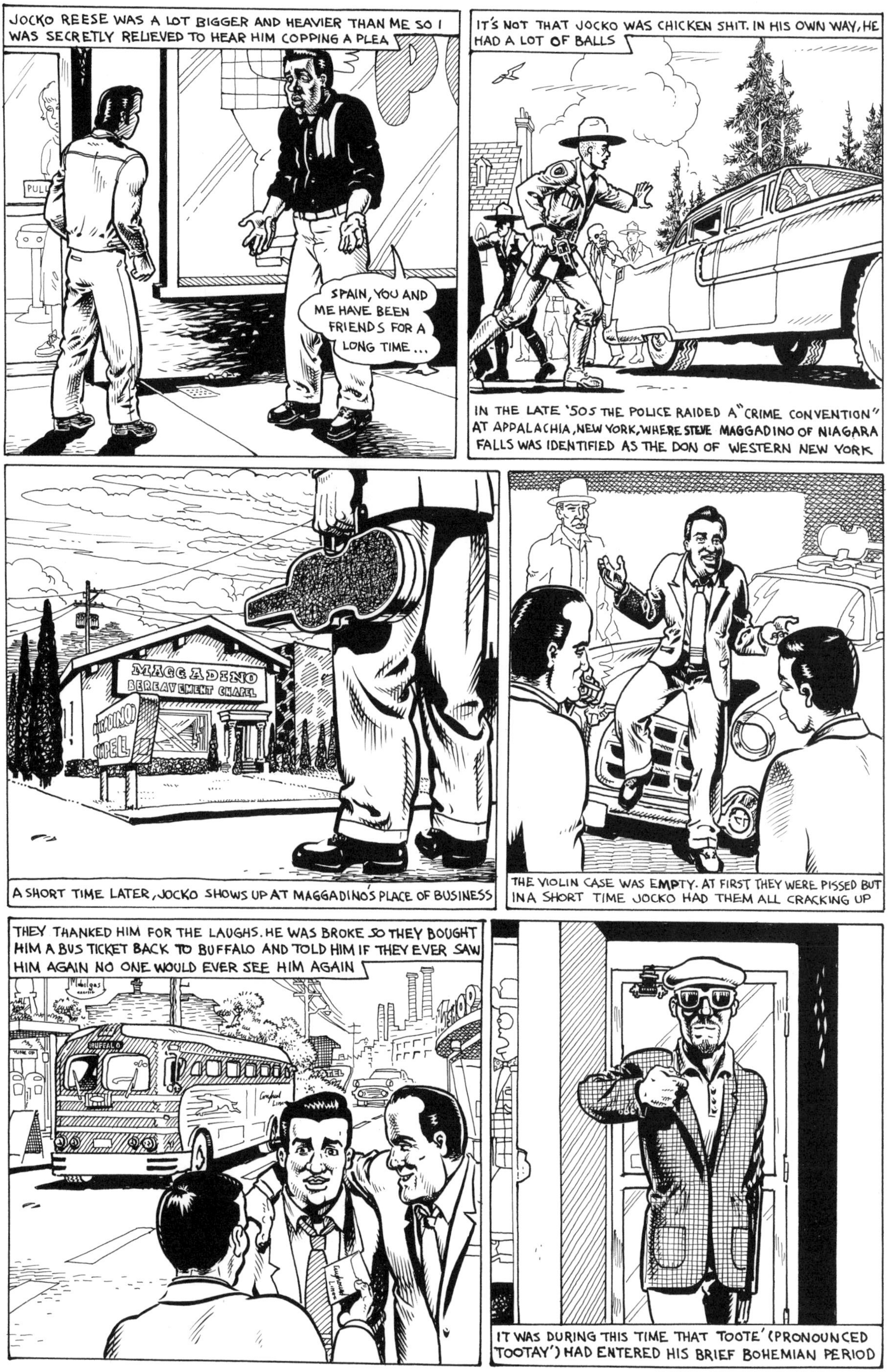
JOCKO REESE WAS A LOT BIGGER AND HEAVIER THAN ME SO I WAS SECRETLY RELIEVED TO HEAR HIM COPPING A PLEA
PULL
SPAIN, YOU AND ME HAVE BEEN FRIENDS FOR A LONG TIME...
IT'S NOT THAT JOCKO WAS CHICKEN SHIT. IN HIS OWN WAY, HE HAD A LOT OF BALLS
IN THE LATE '50S THE POLICE RAIDED A "CRIME CONVENTION" AT APPALACHIA, NEW YORK, WHERE STEVE MAGGADINO OF NIAGARA FALLS WAS IDENTIFIED AS THE DON OF WESTERN NEW YORK
MAGGADINO
BEREAVEMENT CHAPEL
A SHORT TIME LATER, JOCKO SHOWS UP AT MAGGADINO'S PLACE OF BUSINESS
THE VIOLIN CASE WAS EMPTY. AT FIRST THEY WERE PISSED BUT IN A SHORT TIME JOCKO HAD THEM ALL CRACKING UP
THEY THANKED HIM FOR THE LAUGHS. HE WAS BROKE SO THEY BOUGHT HIM A BUS TICKET BACK TO BUFFALO AND TOLD HIM IF THEY EVER SAW HIM AGAIN NO ONE WOULD EVER SEE HIM AGAIN
BUFFALO
IT WAS DURING THIS TIME THAT TOOTE' (PRONOUNCED TOOTAY') HAD ENTERED HIS BRIEF BOHEMIAN PERIOD

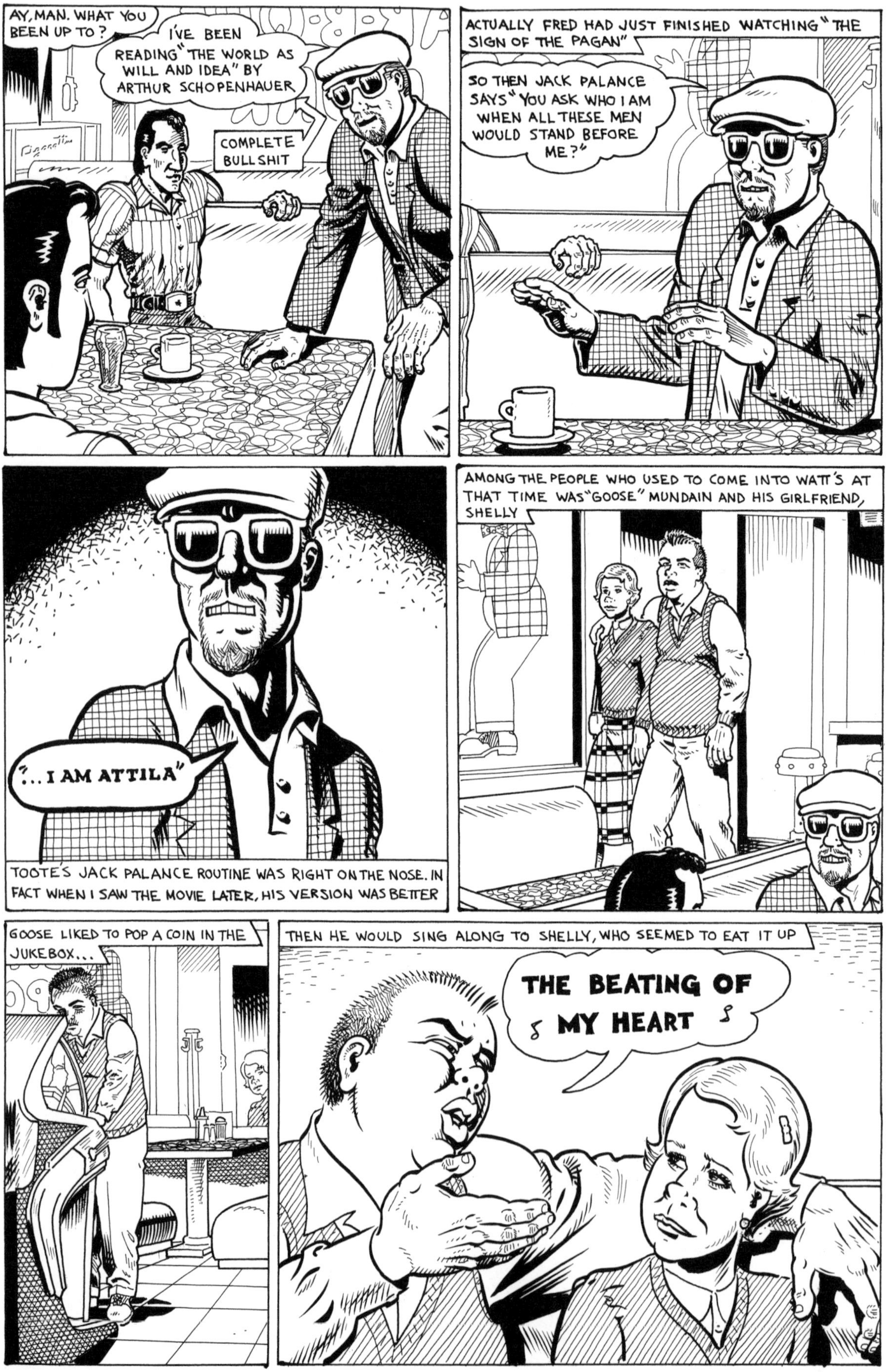
AY, MAN. WHAT YOU BEEN UP TO?
I'VE BEEN READING "THE WORLD AS WILL AND IDEA" BY ARTHUR SCHOPENHAUER
COMPLETE BULLSHIT
ACTUALLY FRED HAD JUST FINISHED WATCHING "THE SIGN OF THE PAGAN"
SO THEN JACK PALANCE SAYS "YOU ASK WHO I AM WHEN ALL THESE MEN WOULD STAND BEFORE ME?"
"...I AM ATTILA"
TOOTE'S JACK PALANCE ROUTINE WAS RIGHT ON THE NOSE. IN FACT WHEN I SAW THE MOVIE LATER, HIS VERSION WAS BETTER
AMONG THE PEOPLE WHO USED TO COME INTO WATT'S AT THAT TIME WAS "GOOSE" MUNDAIN AND HIS GIRLFRIEND, SHELLY
GOOSE LIKED TO POP A COIN IN THE JUKEBOX...
THEN HE WOULD SING ALONG TO SHELLY, WHO SEEMED TO EAT IT UP
THE BEATING OF MY HEART

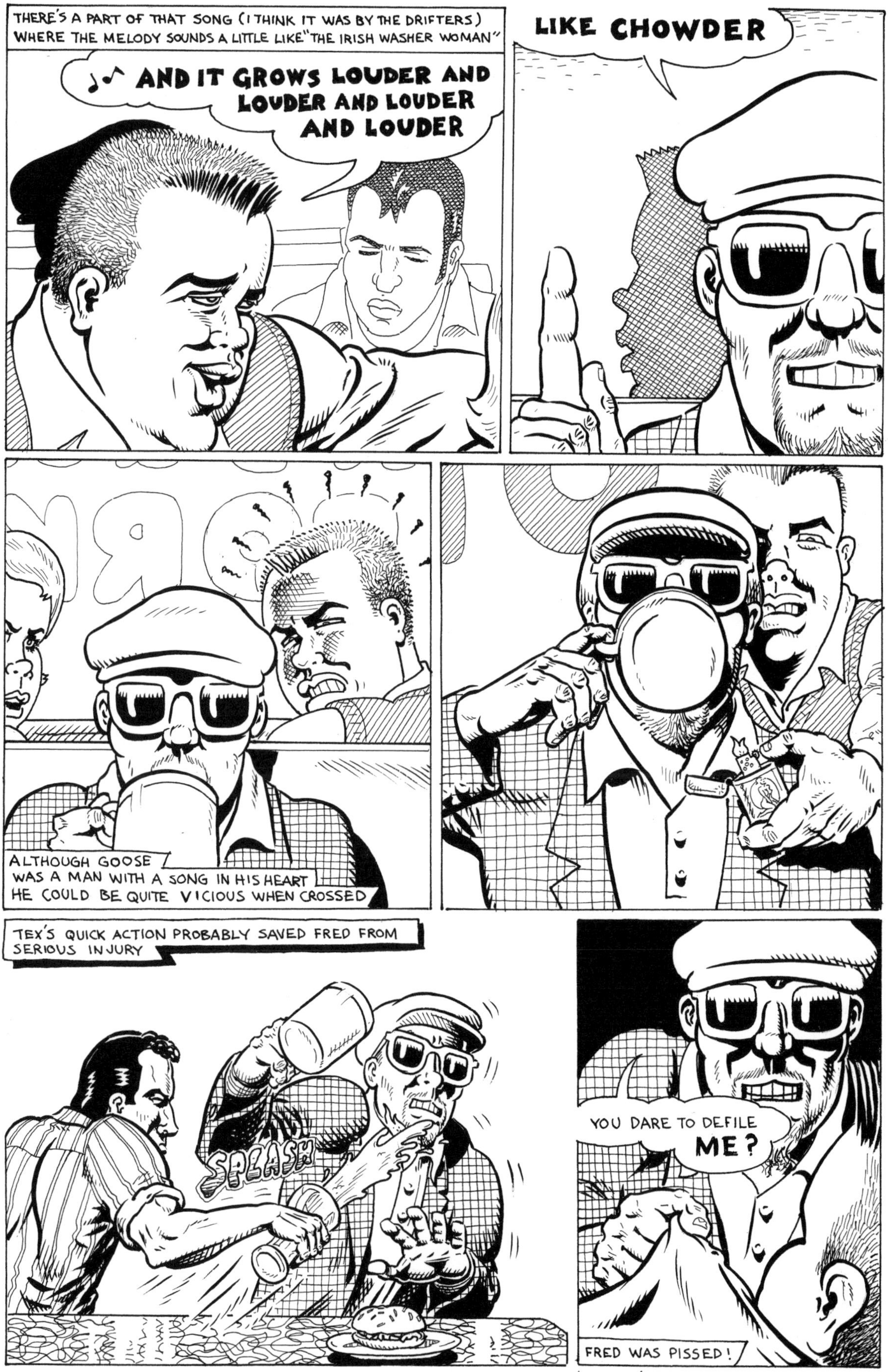

THERE'S A PART OF THAT SONG (I THINK IT WAS BY THE DRIFTERS) WHERE THE MELODY SOUNDS A LITTLE LIKE "THE IRISH WASHER WOMAN"
♪♪ AND IT GROWS LOUDER AND LOUDER AND LOUDER AND LOUDER
LIKE CHOWDER
ALTHOUGH GOOSE WAS A MAN WITH A SONG IN HIS HEART HE COULD BE QUITE VICIOUS WHEN CROSSED
TEX'S QUICK ACTION PROBABLY SAVED FRED FROM SERIOUS INJURY
SPLASH
YOU DARE TO DEFILE ME?
FRED WAS PISSED!

...67-68-69-70-71-72-73...

BRUSHA BRUSHA BRUSHA BRUSHA

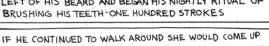
LATER THAT NIGHT TOOTE' SHAVED OFF WHAT WAS LEFT OF HIS BEARD AND BEGAN HIS NIGHTLY RITUAL OF BRUSHING HIS TEETH · ONE HUNDRED STROKES

WISK WISK WISK WISK

THUMP THUMP THUMP THUMP

BY THE TIME HE BEGAN TO BRUSH HIS HAIR (ONE HUNDRED STROKES; HE THOUGHT IT WOULD PREVENT BALDNESS) THE LADY DOWNSTAIRS BEGAN HER NIGHTLY RITUAL OF BANGING ON THE CEILING BECAUSE SHE WAS DISTURBED BY HIM WALKING AROUND AFTER 12:00

IF HE CONTINUED TO WALK AROUND SHE WOULD COME UP AND START BANGING ON THE DOOR, AT WHICH POINT HE WOULD BEGIN TO RECITE LOUDLY...

BOOM BOOM BOOM

ONCE UPON A MIDNIGHT DREARY WHILE I PONDERED WEAK AND WEARY OVER MANY A QUAINT AND CURIOUS VOLUME OF FORGOTTEN LORE...

...WHILE I NODDED NEARLY NAPPING **SUDDENLY THERE CAME A TAPPING, AS IF SOMEONE GENTLY RAPPING, RAPPING ON MY CHAMBER DOOR**

SNOW WHITE

BOOM BOOM BOOM BOOM

HE WOULD GO ON LIKE THIS UNTIL SHE FINALLY WENT AWAY. FRED TOOTE' NEVER GREW A BEARD AGAIN

END

20

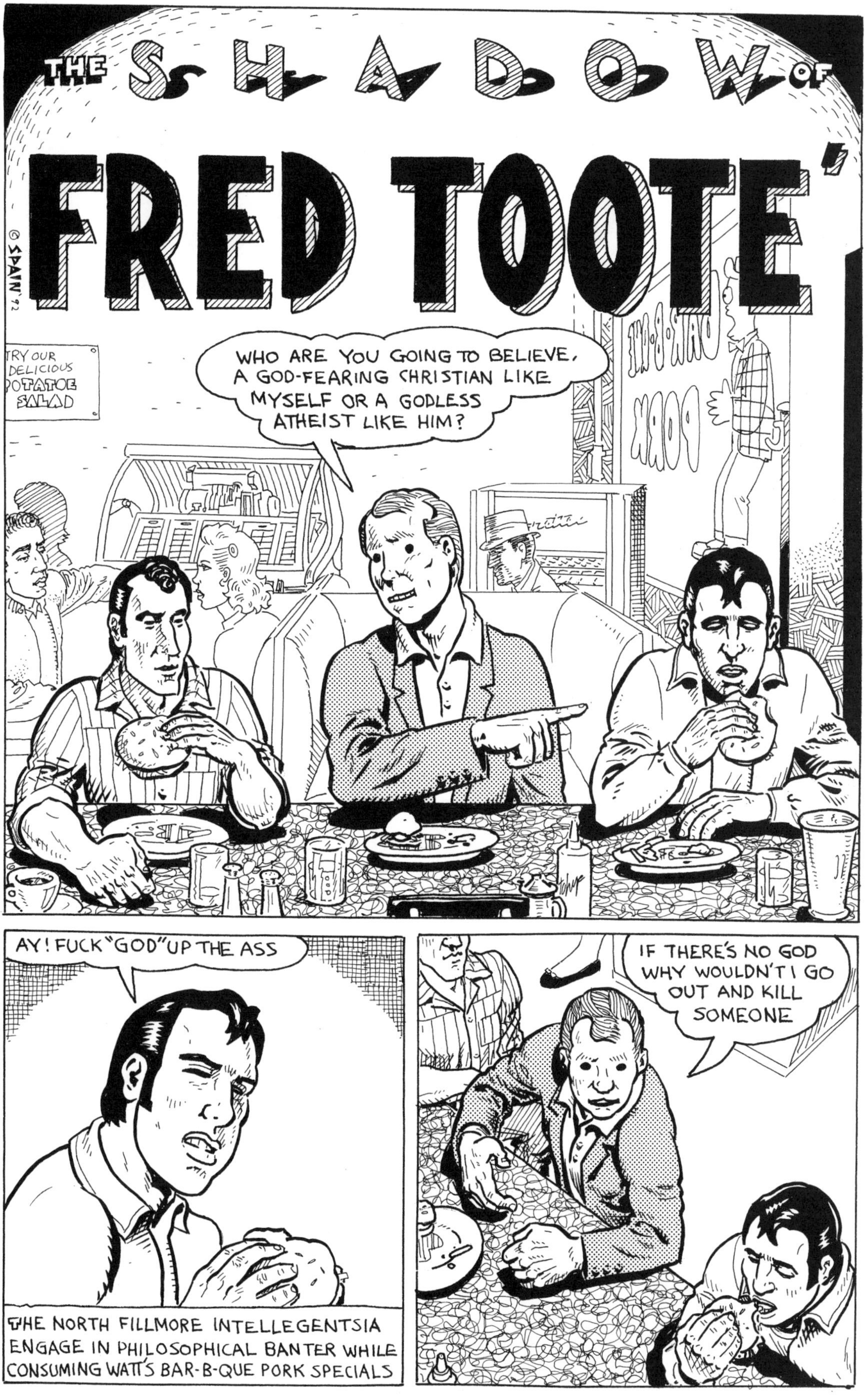
THE SHADOW OF
FRED TOOTE'
© SPAIN '92
TRY OUR DELICIOUS POTATOE SALAD
WHO ARE YOU GOING TO BELIEVE, A GOD-FEARING CHRISTIAN LIKE MYSELF OR A GODLESS ATHEIST LIKE HIM?
AY! FUCK "GOD" UP THE ASS
THE NORTH FILLMORE INTELLEGENTSIA ENGAGE IN PHILOSOPHICAL BANTER WHILE CONSUMING WATT'S BAR-B-QUE PORK SPECIALS
IF THERE'S NO GOD WHY WOULDN'T I GO OUT AND KILL SOMEONE

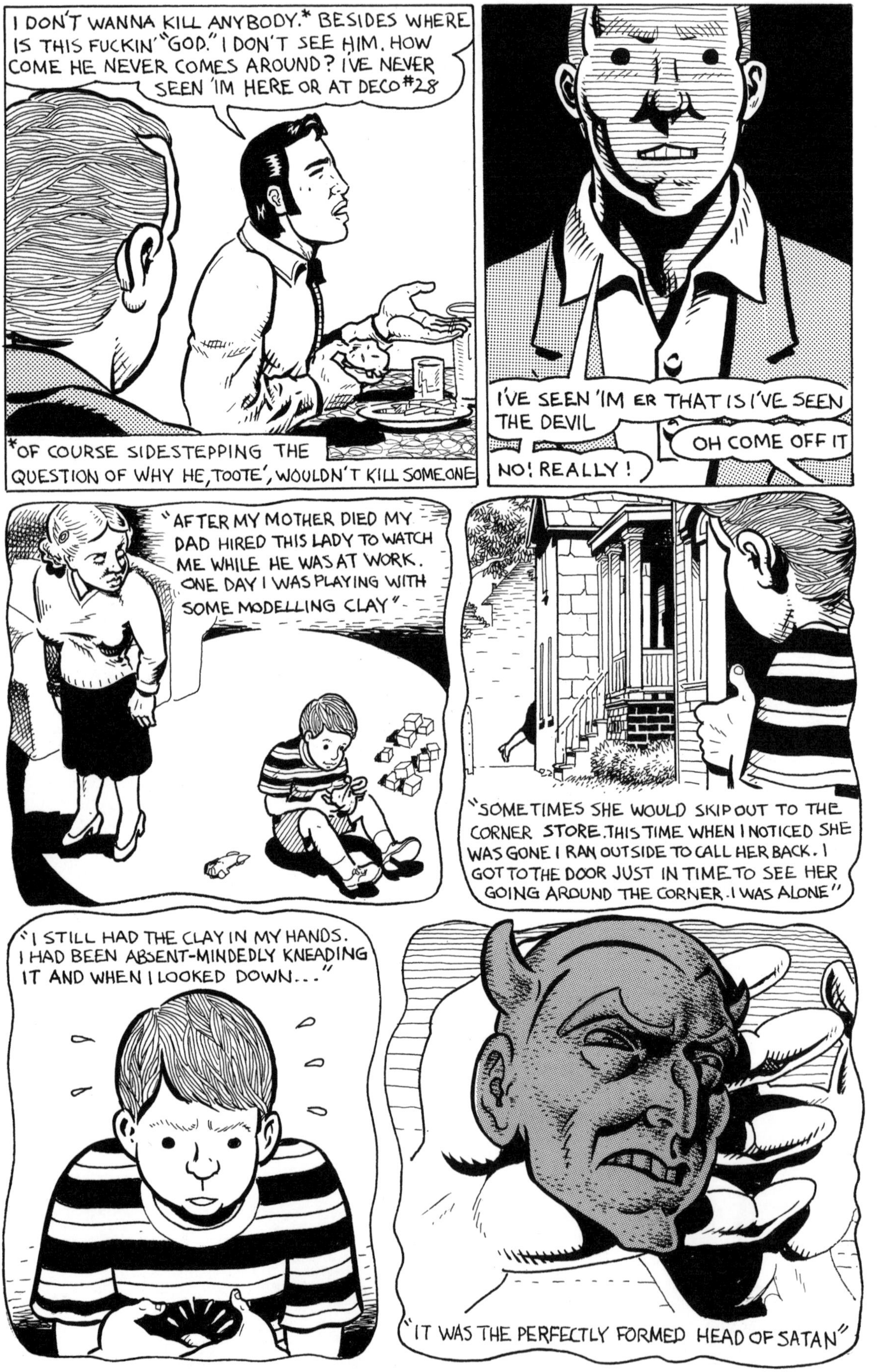
I DON'T WANNA KILL ANYBODY.* BESIDES WHERE IS THIS FUCKIN' "GOD." I DON'T SEE HIM. HOW COME HE NEVER COMES AROUND? I'VE NEVER SEEN 'IM HERE OR AT DECO #28
*OF COURSE SIDESTEPPING THE QUESTION OF WHY HE, TOOTE', WOULDN'T KILL SOMEONE
I'VE SEEN 'IM ER THAT IS I'VE SEEN THE DEVIL
OH COME OFF IT
NO! REALLY!
"AFTER MY MOTHER DIED MY DAD HIRED THIS LADY TO WATCH ME WHILE HE WAS AT WORK. ONE DAY I WAS PLAYING WITH SOME MODELLING CLAY"
"SOMETIMES SHE WOULD SKIP OUT TO THE CORNER STORE. THIS TIME WHEN I NOTICED SHE WAS GONE I RAN OUTSIDE TO CALL HER BACK. I GOT TO THE DOOR JUST IN TIME TO SEE HER GOING AROUND THE CORNER. I WAS ALONE"
"I STILL HAD THE CLAY IN MY HANDS. I HAD BEEN ABSENT-MINDEDLY KNEADING IT AND WHEN I LOOKED DOWN..."
"IT WAS THE PERFECTLY FORMED HEAD OF SATAN"

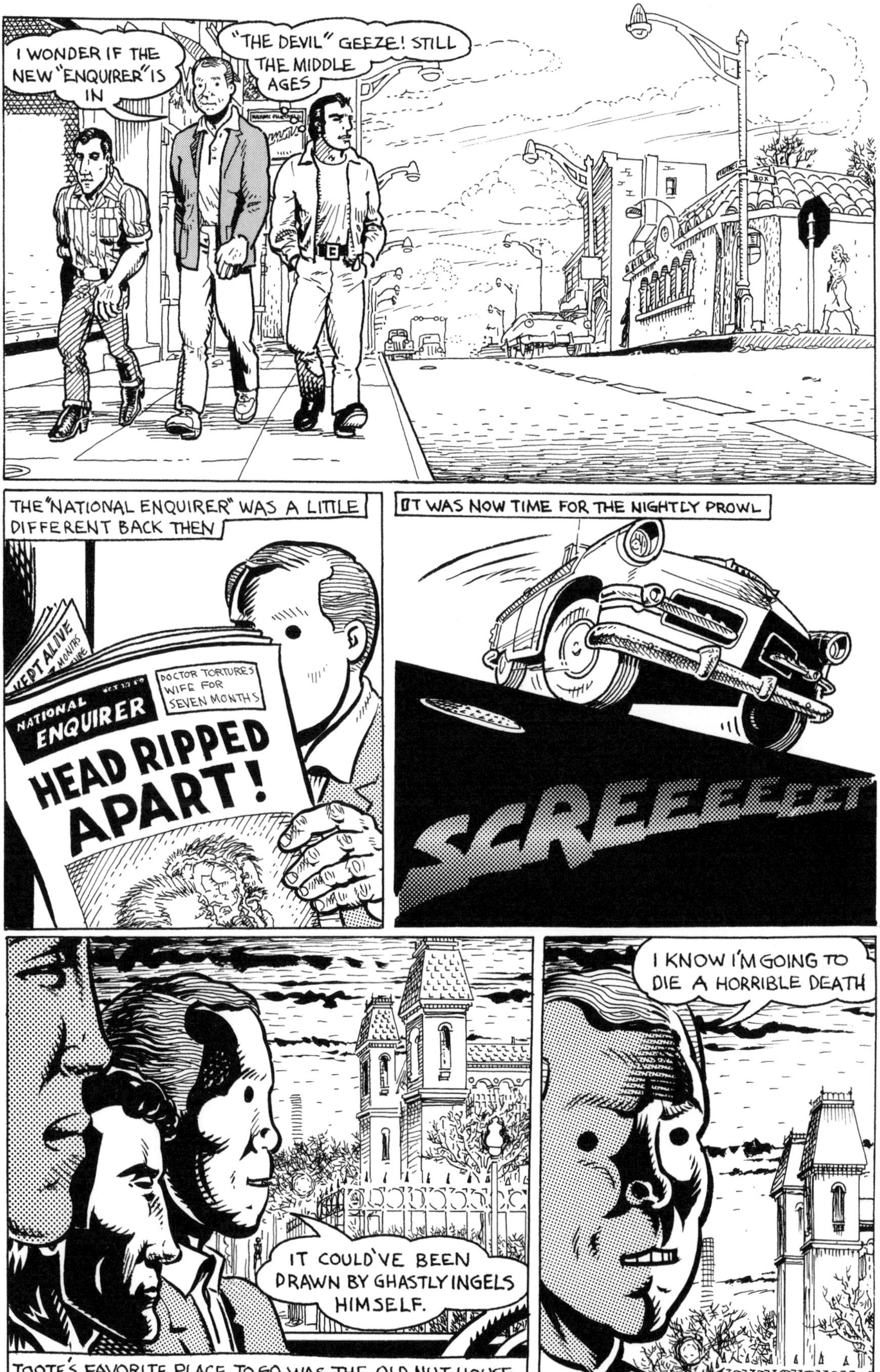
I WONDER IF THE NEW "ENQUIRER" IS IN
"THE DEVIL" GEEZE! STILL THE MIDDLE AGES
THE "NATIONAL ENQUIRER" WAS A LITTLE DIFFERENT BACK THEN
NATIONAL ENQUIRER
DOCTOR TORTURES WIFE FOR SEVEN MONTHS
HEAD RIPPED APART!
IT WAS NOW TIME FOR THE NIGHTLY PROWL
SCREEEEEET
IT COULD'VE BEEN DRAWN BY GHASTLY INGELS HIMSELF.
TOOTE'S FAVORITE PLACE TO GO WAS THE OLD NUT HOUSE ON ELMWOOD. IT NOW HOUSED THE CITY MORGUE
I KNOW I'M GOING TO DIE A HORRIBLE DEATH

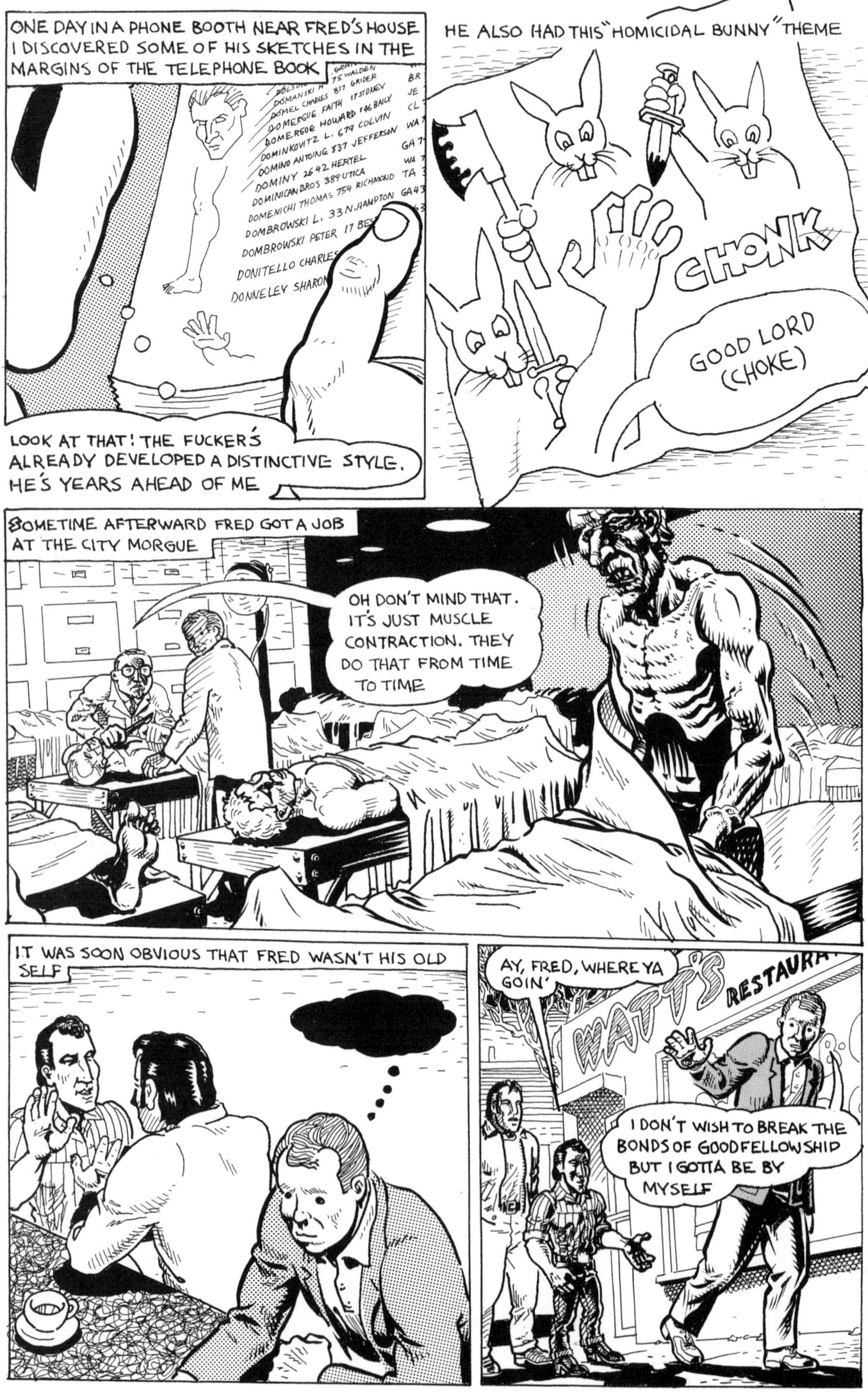
ONE DAY IN A PHONE BOOTH NEAR FRED'S HOUSE I DISCOVERED SOME OF HIS SKETCHES IN THE MARGINS OF THE TELEPHONE BOOK
LOOK AT THAT! THE FUCKER'S ALREADY DEVELOPED A DISTINCTIVE STYLE. HE'S YEARS AHEAD OF ME
HE ALSO HAD THIS "HOMICIDAL BUNNY" THEME
CHONK
GOOD LORD (CHOKE)
SOMETIME AFTERWARD FRED GOT A JOB AT THE CITY MORGUE
OH DON'T MIND THAT. IT'S JUST MUSCLE CONTRACTION. THEY DO THAT FROM TIME TO TIME
IT WAS SOON OBVIOUS THAT FRED WASN'T HIS OLD SELF
AY, FRED, WHERE YA GOIN'
WATT'S
RESTAURA
I DON'T WISH TO BREAK THE BONDS OF GOODFELLOWSHIP BUT I GOTTA BE BY MYSELF

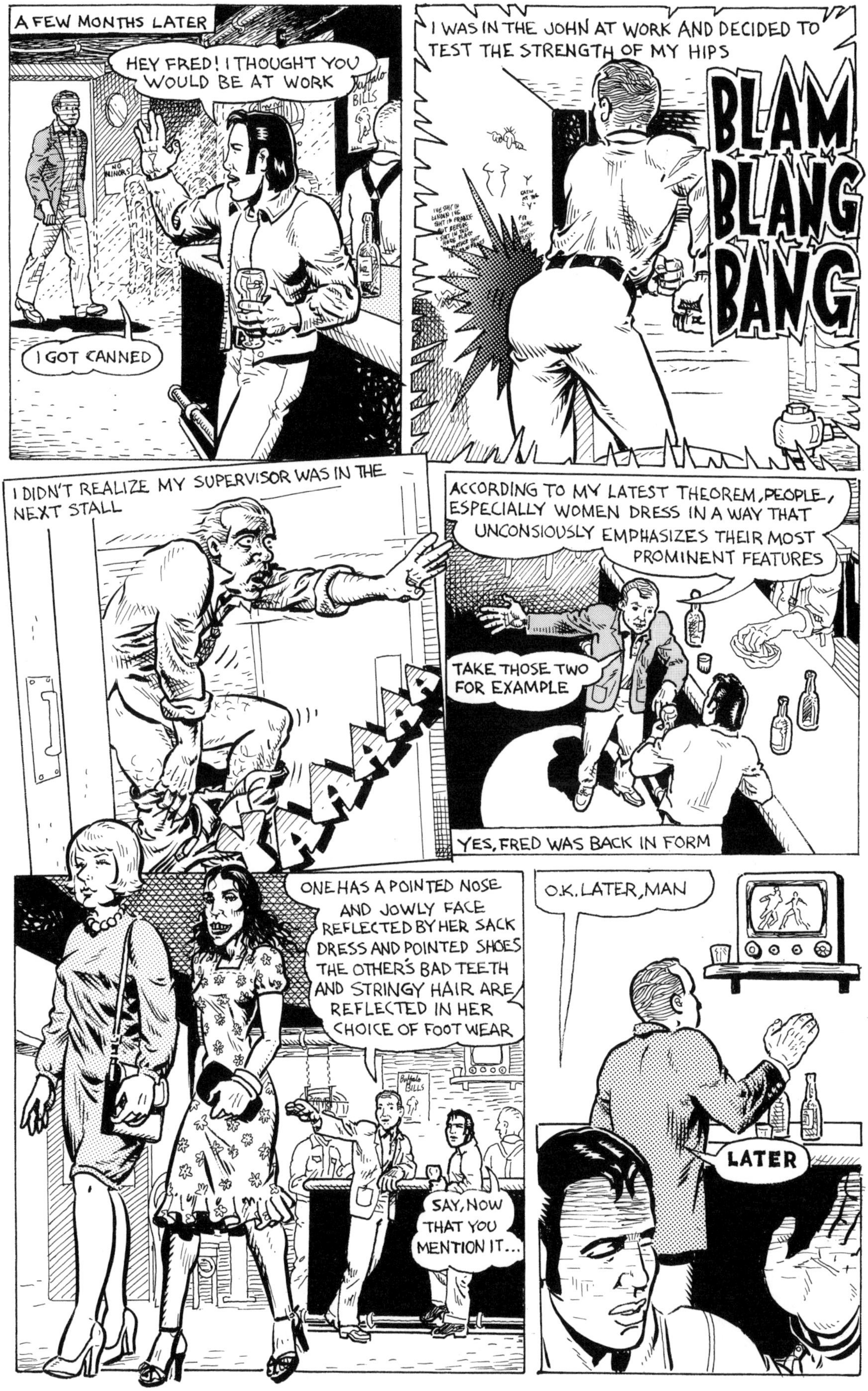

A FEW MONTHS LATER
HEY FRED! I THOUGHT YOU WOULD BE AT WORK
I GOT CANNED
I WAS IN THE JOHN AT WORK AND DECIDED TO TEST THE STRENGTH OF MY HIPS
BLAM BLANG BANG
I DIDN'T REALIZE MY SUPERVISOR WAS IN THE NEXT STALL
ACCORDING TO MY LATEST THEOREM, PEOPLE, ESPECIALLY WOMEN DRESS IN A WAY THAT UNCONSIOUSLY EMPHASIZES THEIR MOST PROMINENT FEATURES
TAKE THOSE TWO FOR EXAMPLE
YES, FRED WAS BACK IN FORM
ONE HAS A POINTED NOSE AND JOWLY FACE REFLECTED BY HER SACK DRESS AND POINTED SHOES THE OTHER'S BAD TEETH AND STRINGY HAIR ARE REFLECTED IN HER CHOICE OF FOOT WEAR
SAY, NOW THAT YOU MENTION IT...
O.K. LATER, MAN
LATER

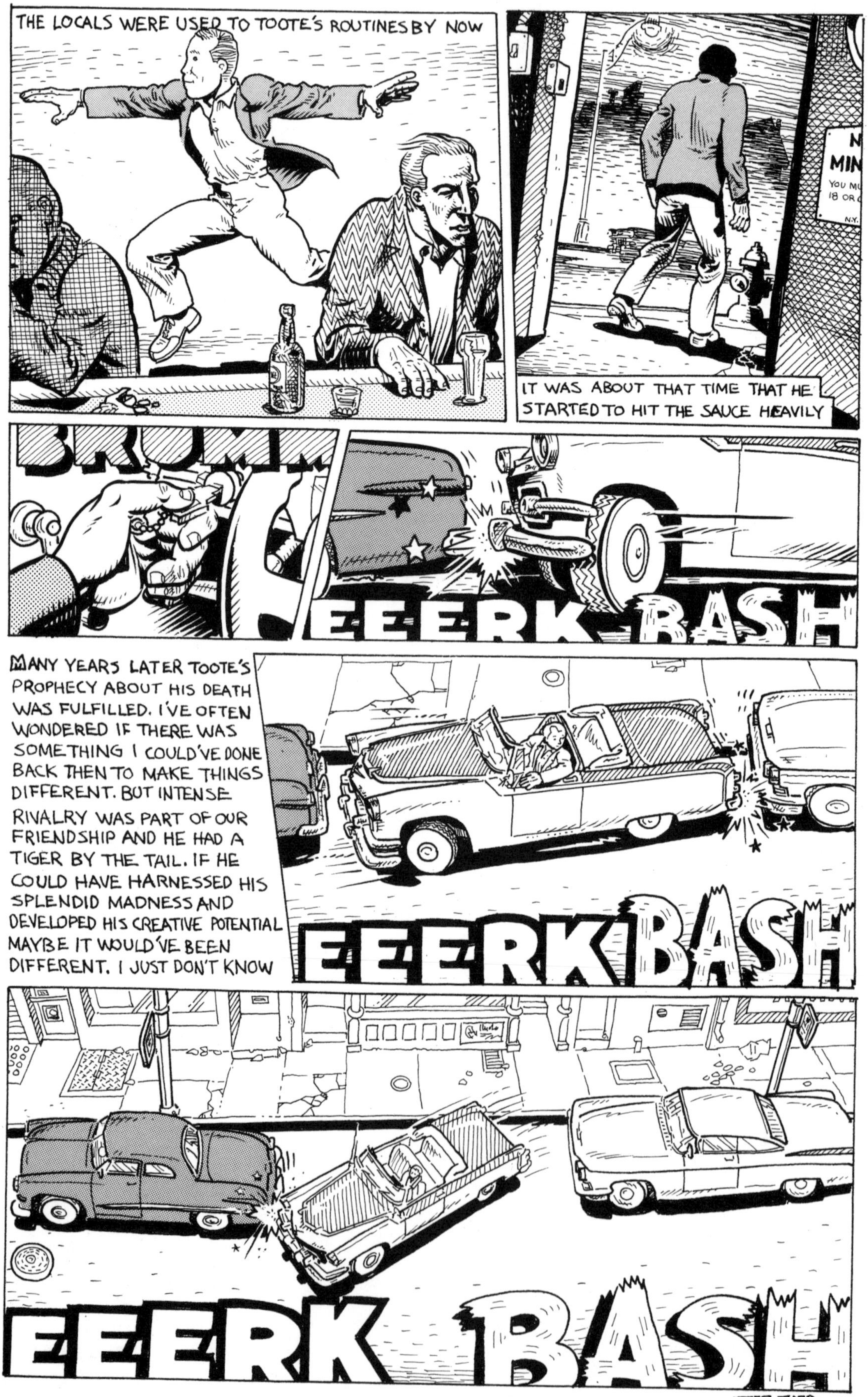
THE LOCALS WERE USED TO TOOTE'S ROUTINES BY NOW
IT WAS ABOUT THAT TIME THAT HE STARTED TO HIT THE SAUCE HEAVILY
BRUMM
EEERK BASH
MANY YEARS LATER TOOTE'S PROPHECY ABOUT HIS DEATH WAS FULFILLED. I'VE OFTEN WONDERED IF THERE WAS SOMETHING I COULD'VE DONE BACK THEN TO MAKE THINGS DIFFERENT. BUT INTENSE RIVALRY WAS PART OF OUR FRIENDSHIP AND HE HAD A TIGER BY THE TAIL. IF HE COULD HAVE HARNESSED HIS SPLENDID MADNESS AND DEVELOPED HIS CREATIVE POTENTIAL MAYBE IT WOULD'VE BEEN DIFFERENT. I JUST DON'T KNOW
EEERK BASH
EEERK BASH
THE END

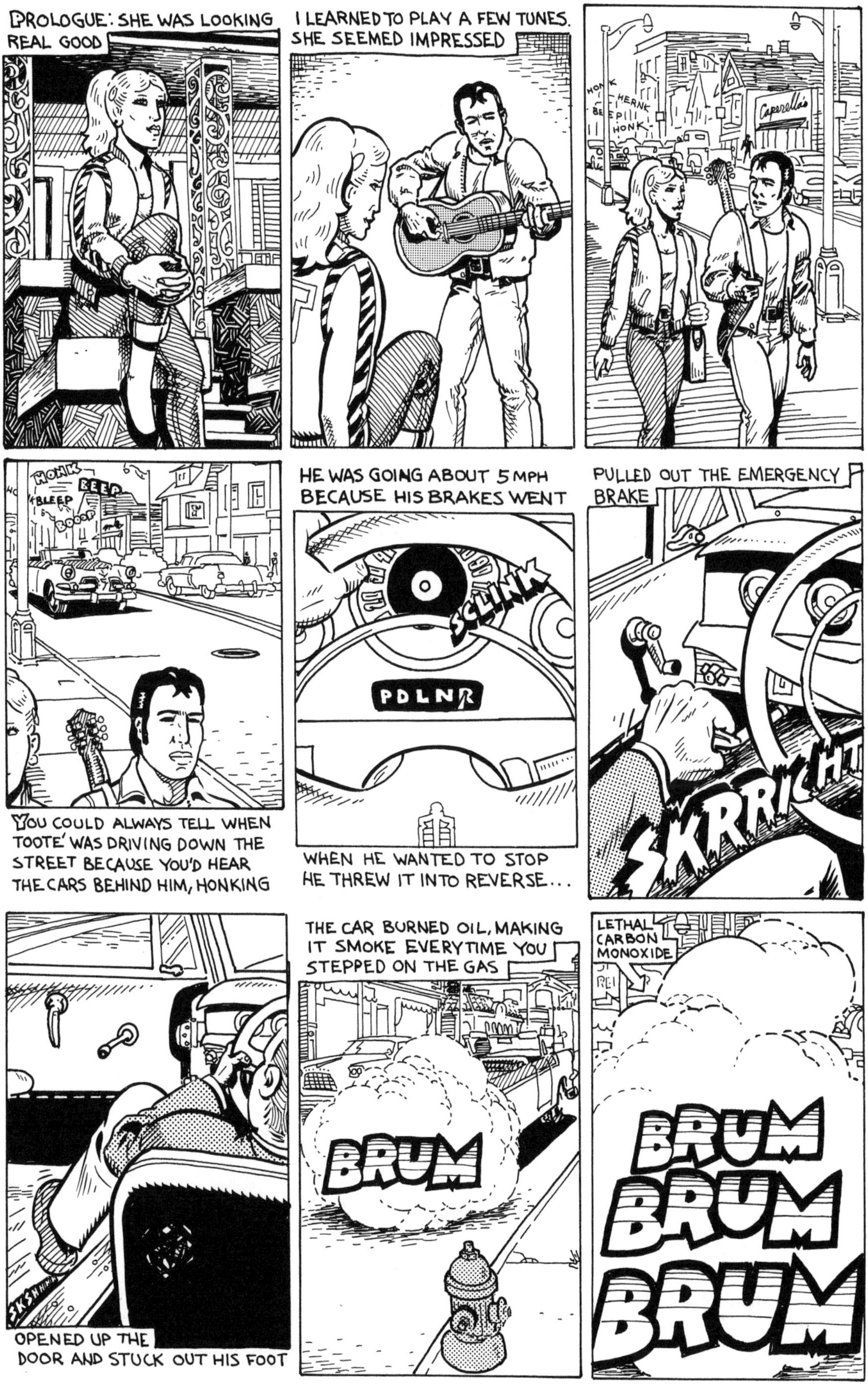
PROLOGUE: SHE WAS LOOKING REAL GOOD
I LEARNED TO PLAY A FEW TUNES. SHE SEEMED IMPRESSED
HONK
HERNK
BEEP
HONK
HONK
BEEP
BLEEP
BOOP
YOU COULD ALWAYS TELL WHEN TOOTE' WAS DRIVING DOWN THE STREET BECAUSE YOU'D HEAR THE CARS BEHIND HIM, HONKING
HE WAS GOING ABOUT 5 MPH BECAUSE HIS BRAKES WENT
SCLINK
PDLNR
WHEN HE WANTED TO STOP HE THREW IT INTO REVERSE...
PULLED OUT THE EMERGENCY BRAKE
SKRRICHT
OPENED UP THE DOOR AND STUCK OUT HIS FOOT
THE CAR BURNED OIL, MAKING IT SMOKE EVERYTIME YOU STEPPED ON THE GAS
BRUM
LETHAL CARBON MONOXIDE
BRUM
BRUM
BRUM

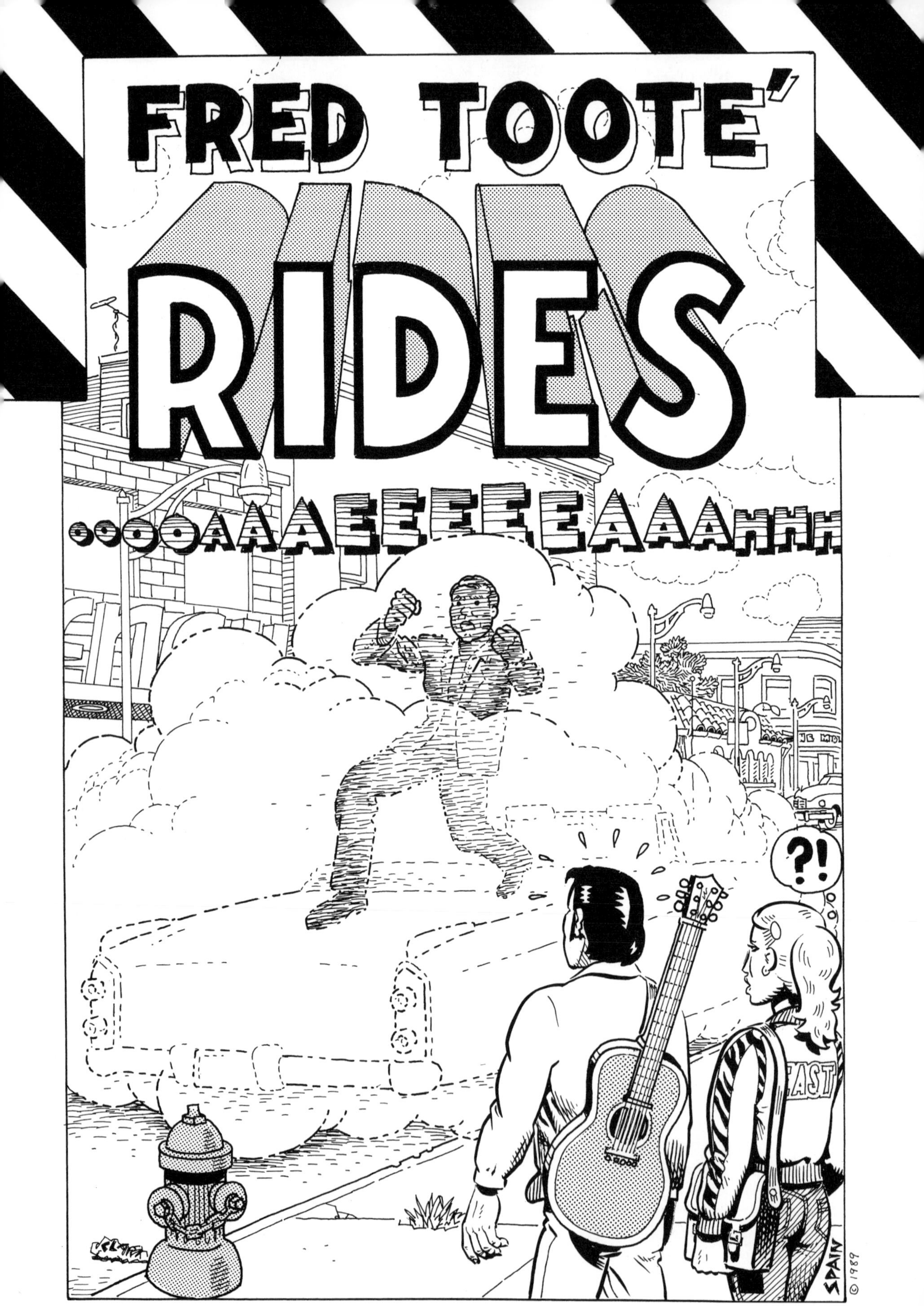
FRED TOOTE'
RIDES
...OOOAAAEEEEEEAAAAHHH
?!
EAST
SPAIN
© 1989

THIS IS FRED TOOTE'

I'M EXALTED TO BE IN YOUR CELESTIAL PRESENCE

"CELESTIAL PRESENCE"? CHRIST

TOOTE' LIKED TO DO THIS EDDIE HASKELL ROUTINE IN FRONT OF OLDER PEOPLE. ONCE HE GOT MY MOTHER MAD

YOUR DAUGHTER CYNTHIA IS QUITE PRECOCIOUS MRS. RODRIGUEZ

I DIDN'T QUITE UNDERSTAND WHY SHE WAS SO UPSET

PRECOCIOUS!?? WHAT ARE YOU TALKING ABOUT? YOU'RE ONLY A FEW YEARS OLDER THAN SHE IS!

ACTUALLY I DIDN'T REALLY KNOW WHAT THE WORD PRECOCIOUS MEANT

IF I TRIED THAT, SPAIN, THERE'D BE A BULL COMING AROUND THE CORNER

TEX, IF I TRIED THAT, I'D FALL ON MY ASS

WHILE HE CULTIVATED AN ULTRA-CONVENTIONAL APPEARANCE, HIS BEHAVIOR WAS QUITE BIZARRE

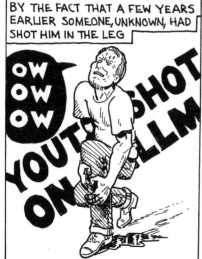

PERHAPS THIS COULD BE EXPLAINED BY THE FACT THAT A FEW YEARS EARLIER SOMEONE, UNKNOWN, HAD SHOT HIM IN THE LEG

OW OW OW OW

YOU'RE SHOT ON ELLM

SAY! THEY'GO OL' FREDDY TOOT

TOOTAY' TOOTAY'

ANYWAY, HE ALWAYS INSISTED THAT PEOPLE PRONOUNCE HIS NAME AS IF IT WERE FRENCH OR SOMETHING

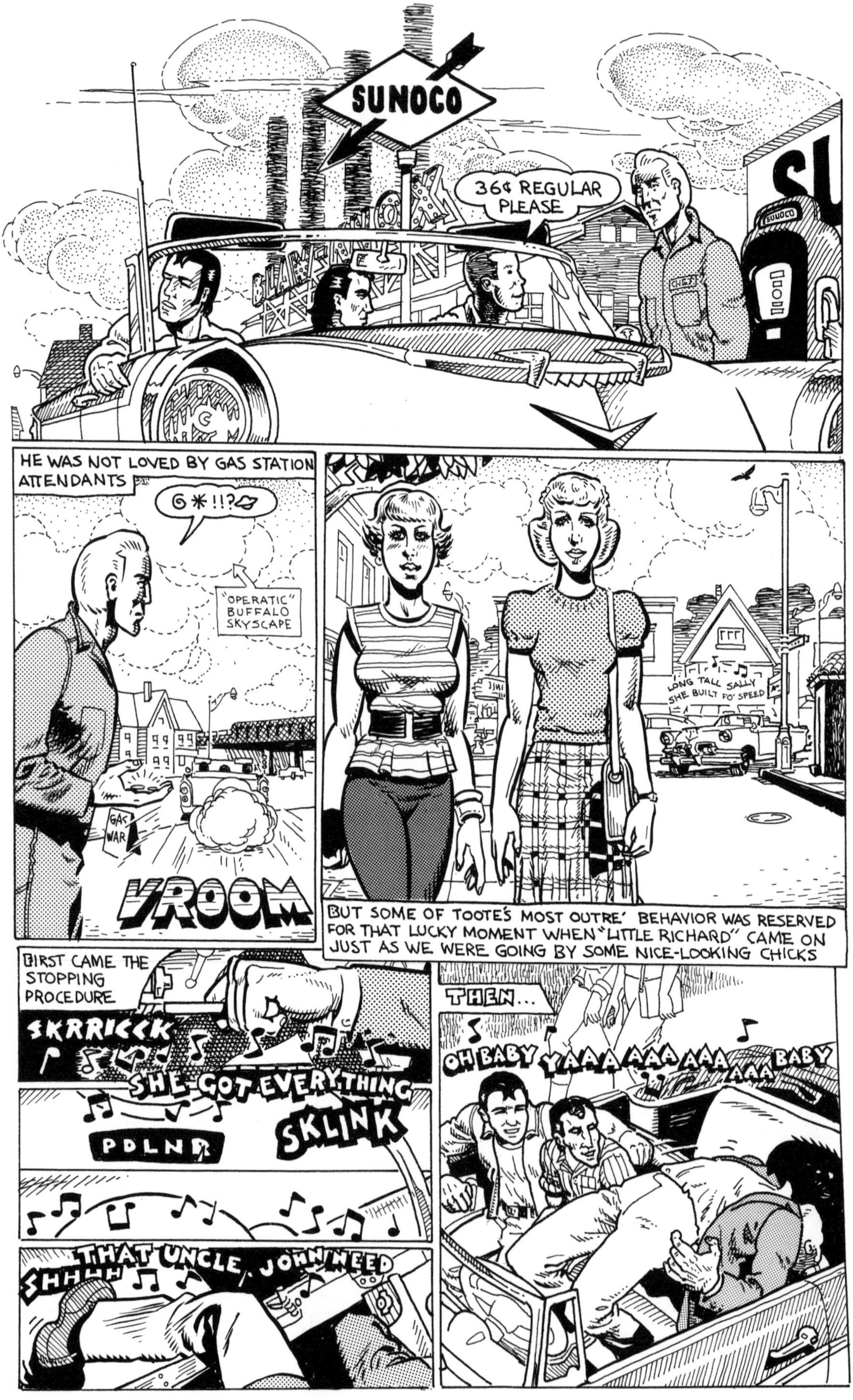
SUNOCO
36¢ REGULAR PLEASE
HE WAS NOT LOVED BY GAS STATION ATTENDANTS
"OPERATIC" BUFFALO SKYSCAPE
GAS WAR
VROOM
LONG TALL SALLY SHE BUILT FO' SPEED
BUT SOME OF TOOTE'S MOST OUTRE' BEHAVIOR WAS RESERVED FOR THAT LUCKY MOMENT WHEN "LITTLE RICHARD" CAME ON JUST AS WE WERE GOING BY SOME NICE-LOOKING CHICKS
FIRST CAME THE STOPPING PROCEDURE
SKRRICCK
SHE GOT EVERYTHING
SKLINK
PDLNR
SHHHH
THAT UNCLE JOHN NEED
THEN...
OH BABY YAAA AAA AAA AAA BABY

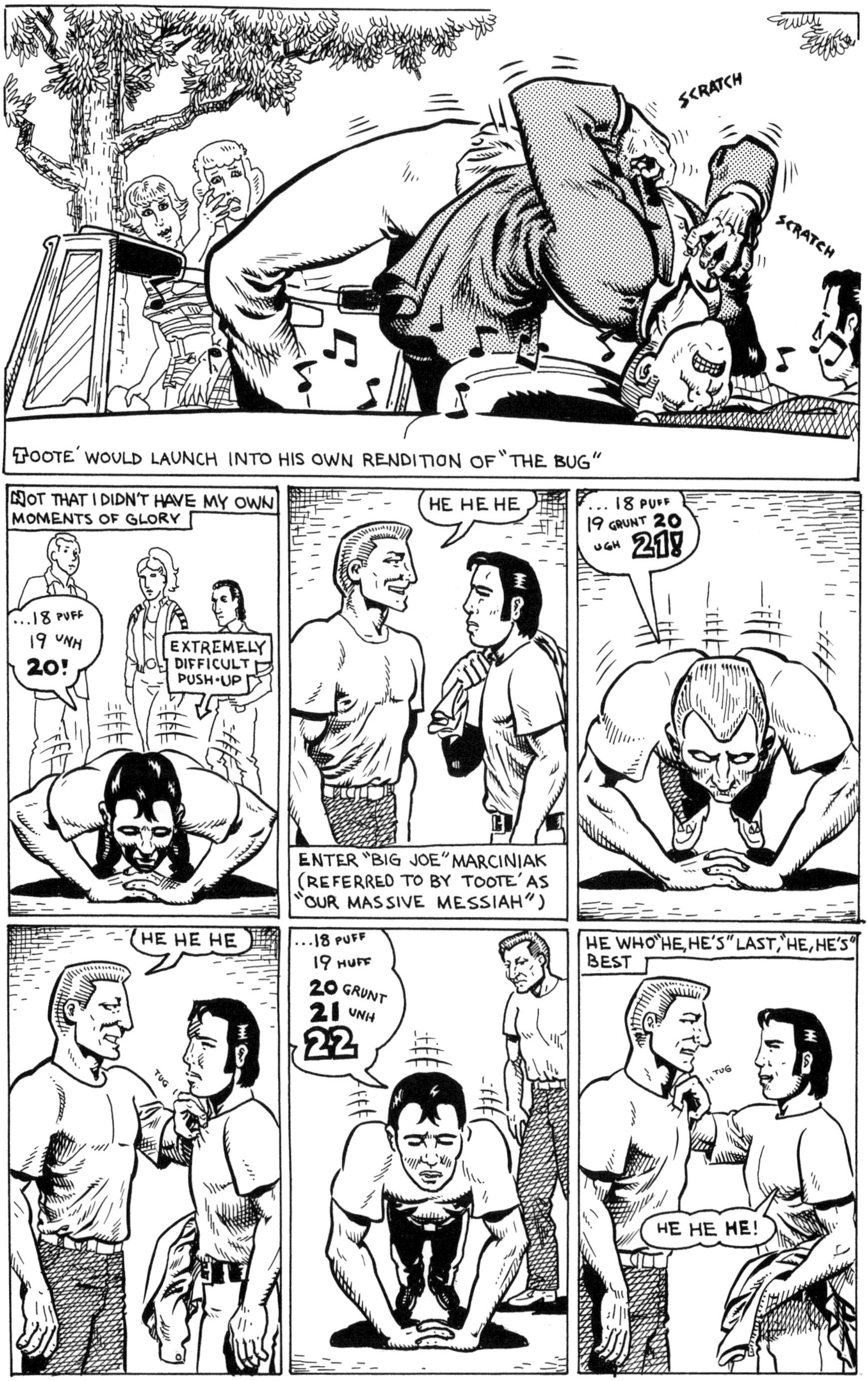
SCRATCH
SCRATCH
TOOTE' WOULD LAUNCH INTO HIS OWN RENDITION OF "THE BUG"
NOT THAT I DIDN'T HAVE MY OWN MOMENTS OF GLORY
...18 PUFF 19 UNH 20!
EXTREMELY DIFFICULT PUSH-UP
HE HE HE
ENTER "BIG JOE" MARCINIAK (REFERRED TO BY TOOTE' AS "OUR MASSIVE MESSIAH")
... 18 PUFF 19 GRUNT 20 UGH 21!
HE HE HE
TUG
...18 PUFF 19 HUFF 20 GRUNT 21 UNH 22
HE WHO "HE, HE'S" LAST, "HE, HE'S" BEST
TUG
HE HE HE!

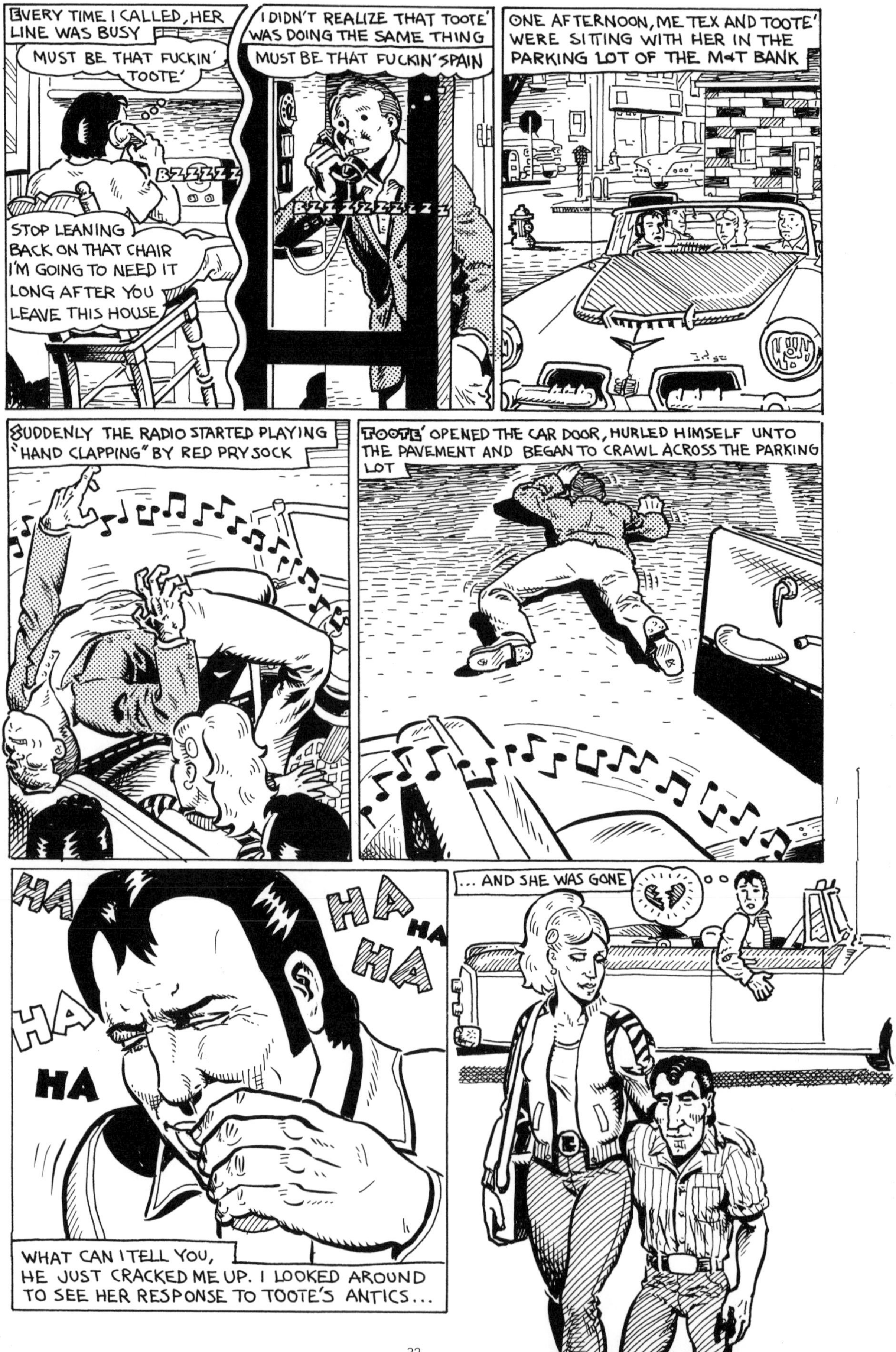
EVERY TIME I CALLED, HER LINE WAS BUSY
MUST BE THAT FUCKIN' TOOTE'
BZZZZZZ
STOP LEANING BACK ON THAT CHAIR I'M GOING TO NEED IT LONG AFTER YOU LEAVE THIS HOUSE
I DIDN'T REALIZE THAT TOOTE' WAS DOING THE SAME THING
MUST BE THAT FUCKIN' SPAIN
BZZZZZZZZZZ
ONE AFTERNOON, ME TEX AND TOOTE' WERE SITTING WITH HER IN THE PARKING LOT OF THE M&T BANK
SUDDENLY THE RADIO STARTED PLAYING "HAND CLAPPING" BY RED PRYSOCK
TOOTE' OPENED THE CAR DOOR, HURLED HIMSELF UNTO THE PAVEMENT AND BEGAN TO CRAWL ACROSS THE PARKING LOT
HA HA HA HA HA HA
WHAT CAN I TELL YOU, HE JUST CRACKED ME UP. I LOOKED AROUND TO SEE HER RESPONSE TO TOOTE'S ANTICS...
... AND SHE WAS GONE

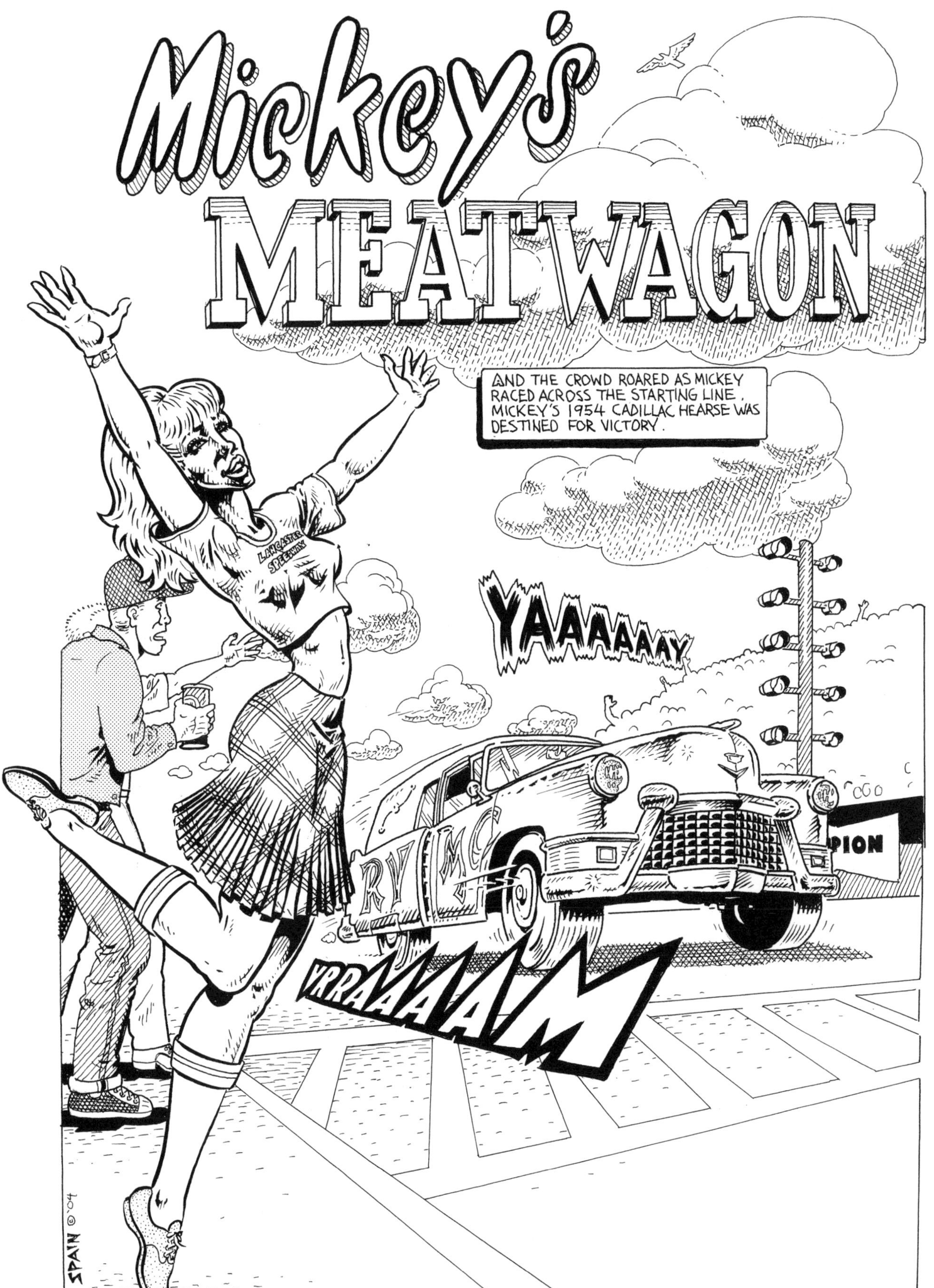
Mickey's
MEATWAGON
AND THE CROWD ROARED AS MICKEY RACED ACROSS THE STARTING LINE. MICKEY'S 1954 CADILLAC HEARSE WAS DESTINED FOR VICTORY.
LANCASTER SPEEDWAY
YAAAAAAY
PION
YRRAAAAAM
SPAIN © '04

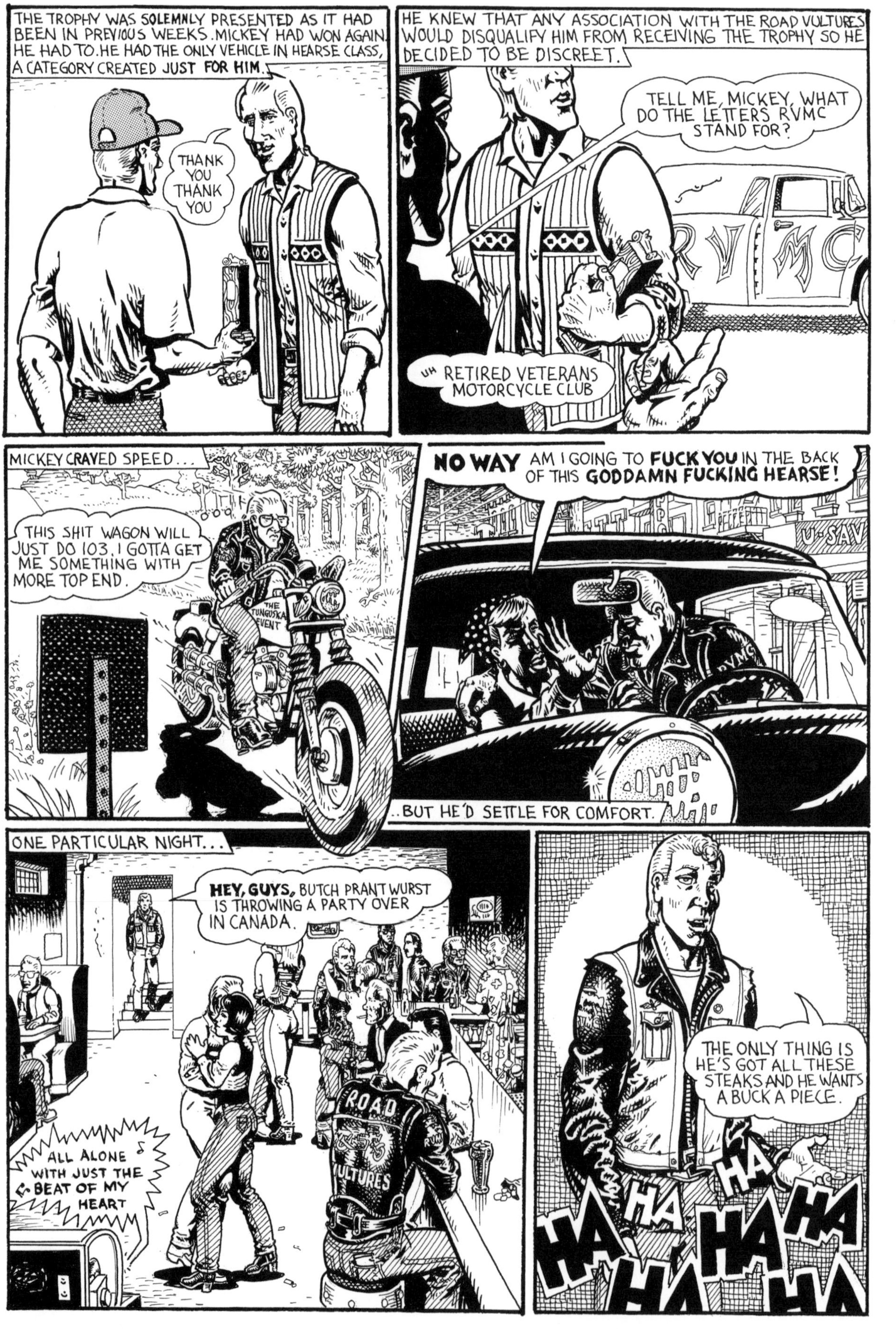
THE TROPHY WAS SOLEMNLY PRESENTED AS IT HAD BEEN IN PREVIOUS WEEKS. MICKEY HAD WON AGAIN. HE HAD TO. HE HAD THE ONLY VEHICLE IN HEARSE CLASS, A CATEGORY CREATED JUST FOR HIM.
THANK YOU THANK YOU
HE KNEW THAT ANY ASSOCIATION WITH THE ROAD VULTURES WOULD DISQUALIFY HIM FROM RECEIVING THE TROPHY SO HE DECIDED TO BE DISCREET.
TELL ME, MICKEY, WHAT DO THE LETTERS RVMC STAND FOR?
RVMC
UH RETIRED VETERANS MOTORCYCLE CLUB
MICKEY CRAVED SPEED...
THIS SHIT WAGON WILL JUST DO 103. I GOTTA GET ME SOMETHING WITH MORE TOP END.
THE TUNGUSKA EVENT
NO WAY AM I GOING TO FUCK YOU IN THE BACK OF THIS GODDAMN FUCKING HEARSE!
U-SAV
..BUT HE'D SETTLE FOR COMFORT.
ONE PARTICULAR NIGHT...
HEY, GUYS, BUTCH PRANTWURST IS THROWING A PARTY OVER IN CANADA.
ALL ALONE WITH JUST THE BEAT OF MY HEART
ROAD VULTURES
THE ONLY THING IS HE'S GOT ALL THESE STEAKS AND HE WANTS A BUCK A PIECE.
HA HA HA HA HA HA HA HA HA HA

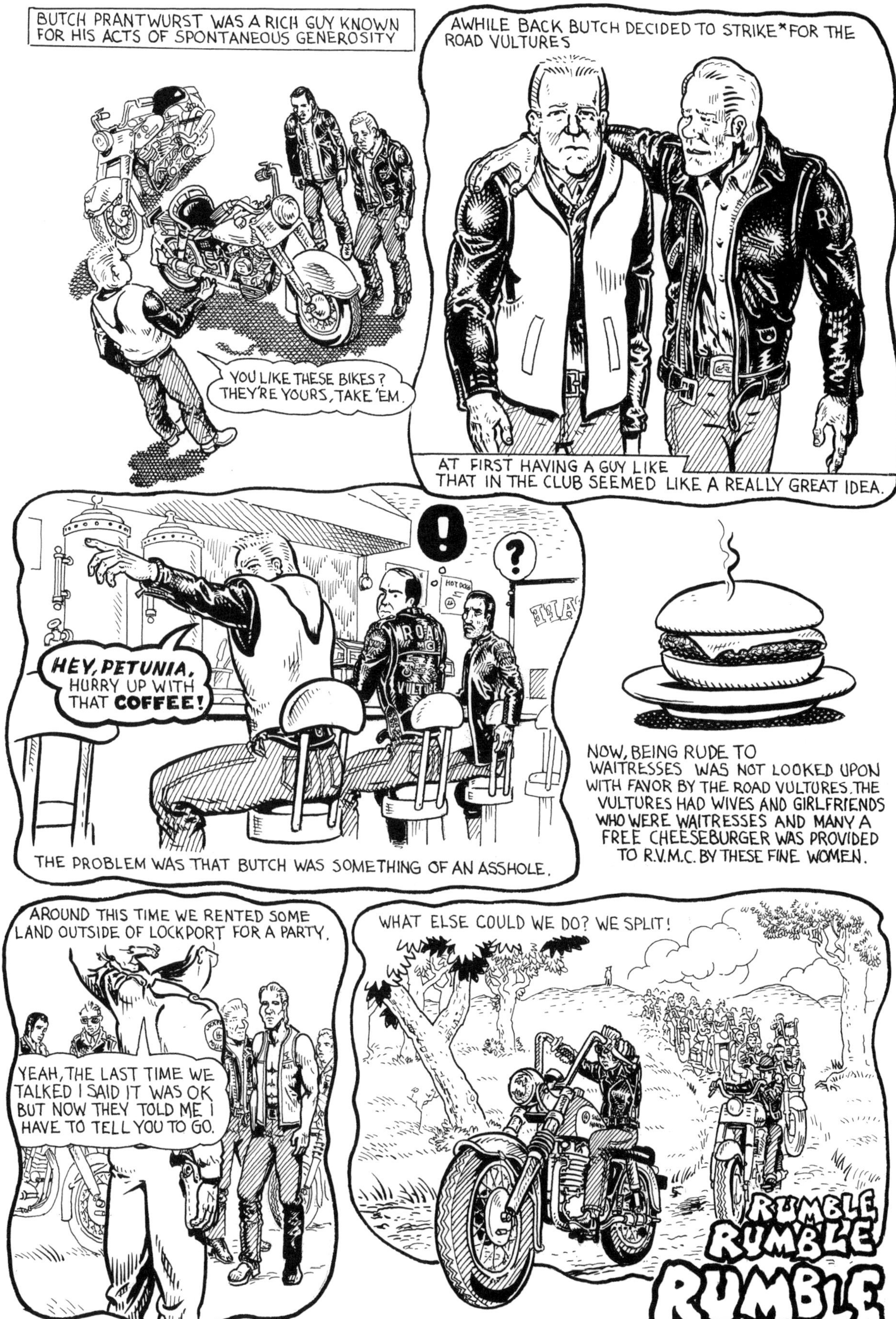
BUTCH PRANTWURST WAS A RICH GUY KNOWN FOR HIS ACTS OF SPONTANEOUS GENEROSITY
YOU LIKE THESE BIKES? THEY'RE YOURS, TAKE 'EM.
AWHILE BACK BUTCH DECIDED TO STRIKE* FOR THE ROAD VULTURES
R
AT FIRST HAVING A GUY LIKE THAT IN THE CLUB SEEMED LIKE A REALLY GREAT IDEA.
!
?
HOT DOG
HEY, PETUNIA, HURRY UP WITH THAT COFFEE!
ROAD
MC
VULTURE
THE PROBLEM WAS THAT BUTCH WAS SOMETHING OF AN ASSHOLE.
NOW, BEING RUDE TO WAITRESSES WAS NOT LOOKED UPON WITH FAVOR BY THE ROAD VULTURES. THE VULTURES HAD WIVES AND GIRLFRIENDS WHO WERE WAITRESSES AND MANY A FREE CHEESEBURGER WAS PROVIDED TO R.V.M.C. BY THESE FINE WOMEN.
AROUND THIS TIME WE RENTED SOME LAND OUTSIDE OF LOCKPORT FOR A PARTY.
YEAH, THE LAST TIME WE TALKED I SAID IT WAS OK BUT NOW THEY TOLD ME I HAVE TO TELL YOU TO GO.
WHAT ELSE COULD WE DO? WE SPLIT!
RUMBLE
RUMBLE
RUMBLE

* A TWO-WEEK TRIAL PERIOD TO SEE IF YOU WERE ROAD VULTURE MATERIAL

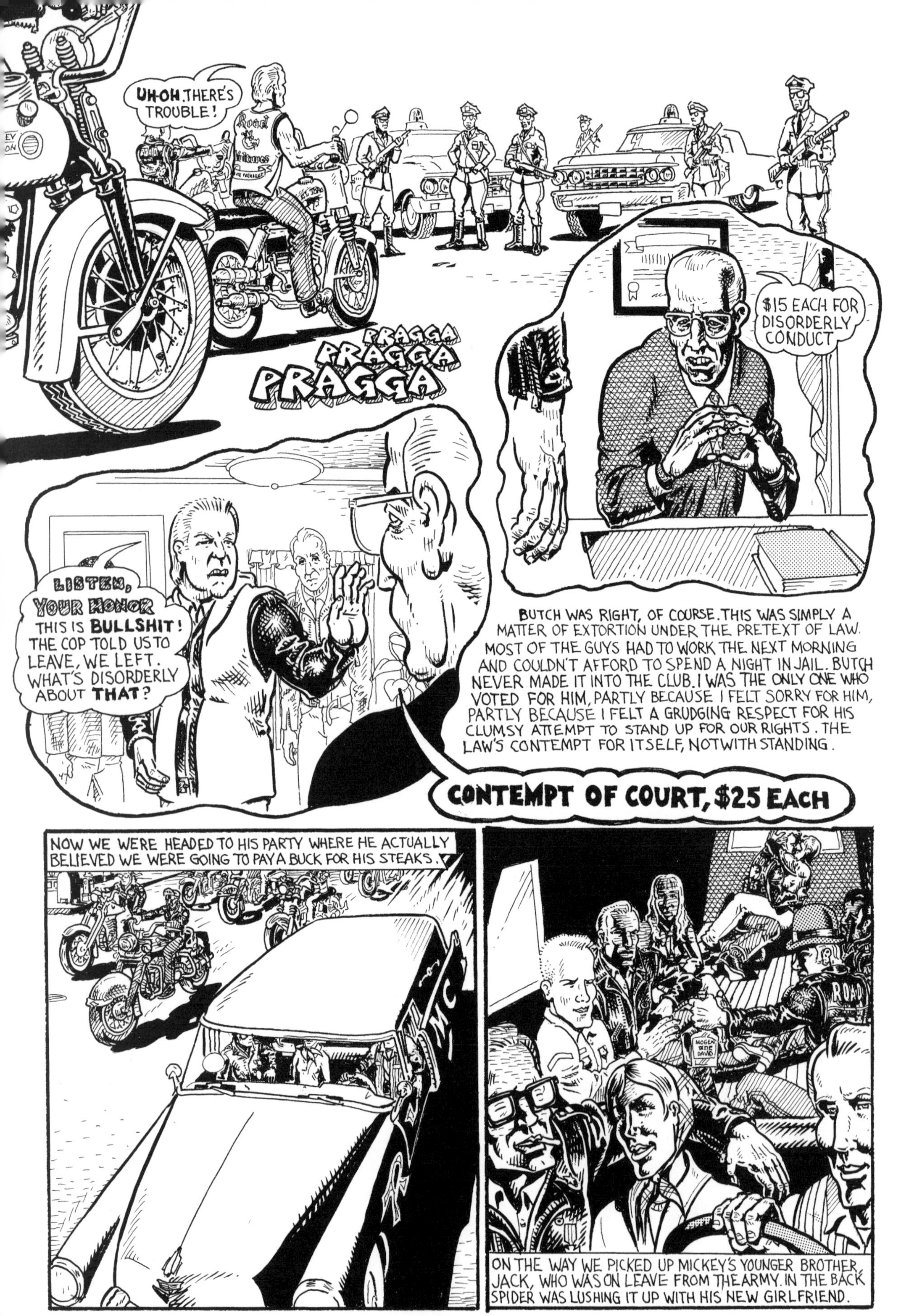
UH-OH. THERE'S TROUBLE!
PRAGGA PRAGGA PRAGGA
$15 EACH FOR DISORDERLY CONDUCT
LISTEN, YOUR HONOR THIS IS BULLSHIT! THE COP TOLD US TO LEAVE, WE LEFT. WHAT'S DISORDERLY ABOUT THAT?
BUTCH WAS RIGHT, OF COURSE. THIS WAS SIMPLY A MATTER OF EXTORTION UNDER THE PRETEXT OF LAW. MOST OF THE GUYS HAD TO WORK THE NEXT MORNING AND COULDN'T AFFORD TO SPEND A NIGHT IN JAIL. BUTCH NEVER MADE IT INTO THE CLUB. I WAS THE ONLY ONE WHO VOTED FOR HIM, PARTLY BECAUSE I FELT SORRY FOR HIM, PARTLY BECAUSE I FELT A GRUDGING RESPECT FOR HIS CLUMSY ATTEMPT TO STAND UP FOR OUR RIGHTS. THE LAW'S CONTEMPT FOR ITSELF, NOTWITHSTANDING.
CONTEMPT OF COURT, $25 EACH
NOW WE WERE HEADED TO HIS PARTY WHERE HE ACTUALLY BELIEVED WE WERE GOING TO PAY A BUCK FOR HIS STEAKS.
MC
ROAD
MOGEN DAVID
ON THE WAY WE PICKED UP MICKEY'S YOUNGER BROTHER, JACK, WHO WAS ON LEAVE FROM THE ARMY. IN THE BACK SPIDER WAS LUSHING IT UP WITH HIS NEW GIRLFRIEND.

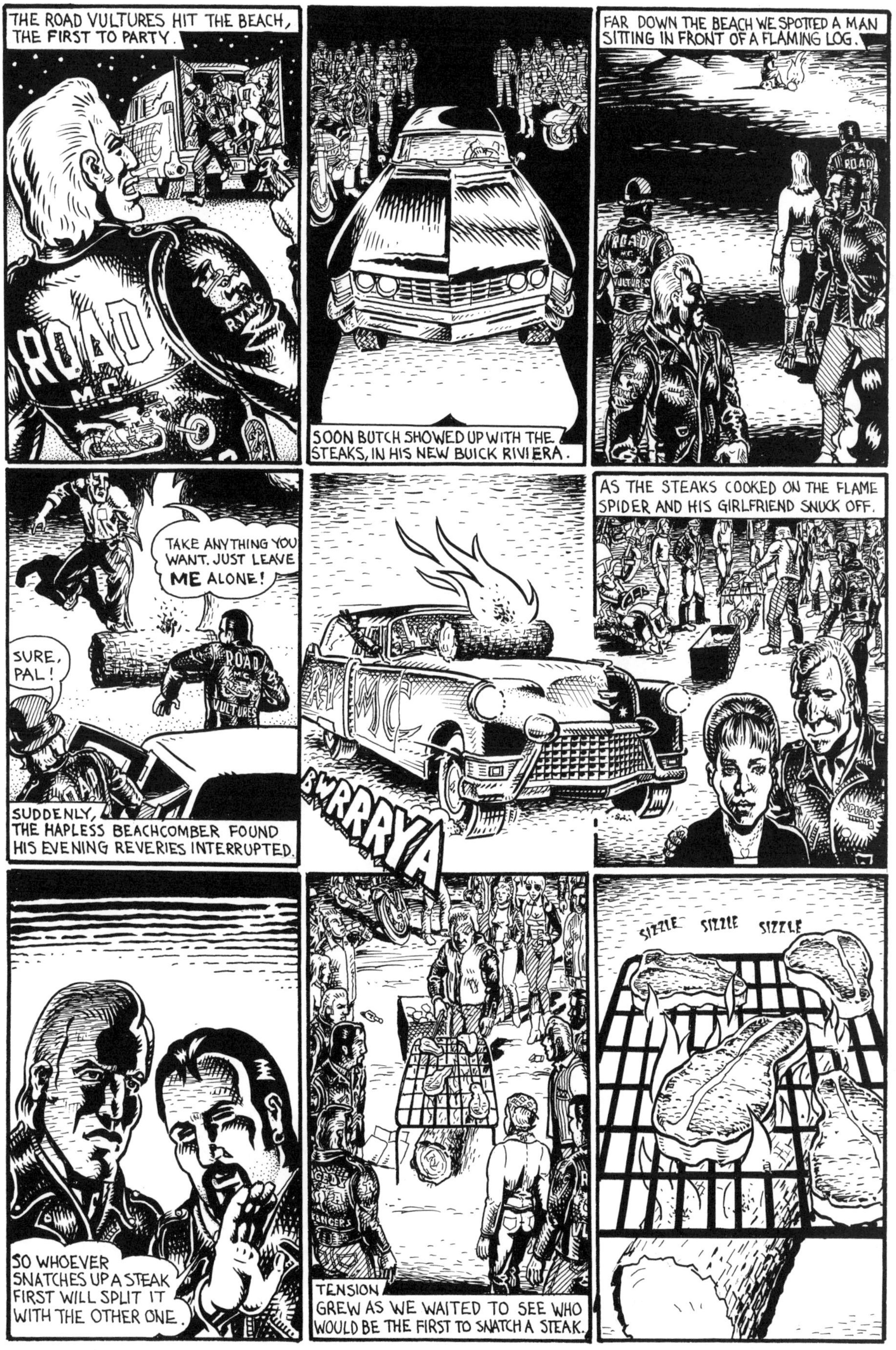
THE ROAD VULTURES HIT THE BEACH, THE FIRST TO PARTY.
SOON BUTCH SHOWED UP WITH THE STEAKS, IN HIS NEW BUICK RIVIERA.
FAR DOWN THE BEACH WE SPOTTED A MAN SITTING IN FRONT OF A FLAMING LOG.
TAKE ANYTHING YOU WANT. JUST LEAVE ME ALONE!
SURE, PAL!
SUDDENLY, THE HAPLESS BEACHCOMBER FOUND HIS EVENING REVERIES INTERRUPTED.
BWRRRYA
AS THE STEAKS COOKED ON THE FLAME SPIDER AND HIS GIRLFRIEND SNUCK OFF.
SO WHOEVER SNATCHES UP A STEAK FIRST WILL SPLIT IT WITH THE OTHER ONE.
TENSION GREW AS WE WAITED TO SEE WHO WOULD BE THE FIRST TO SNATCH A STEAK.
SIZZLE SIZZLE SIZZLE

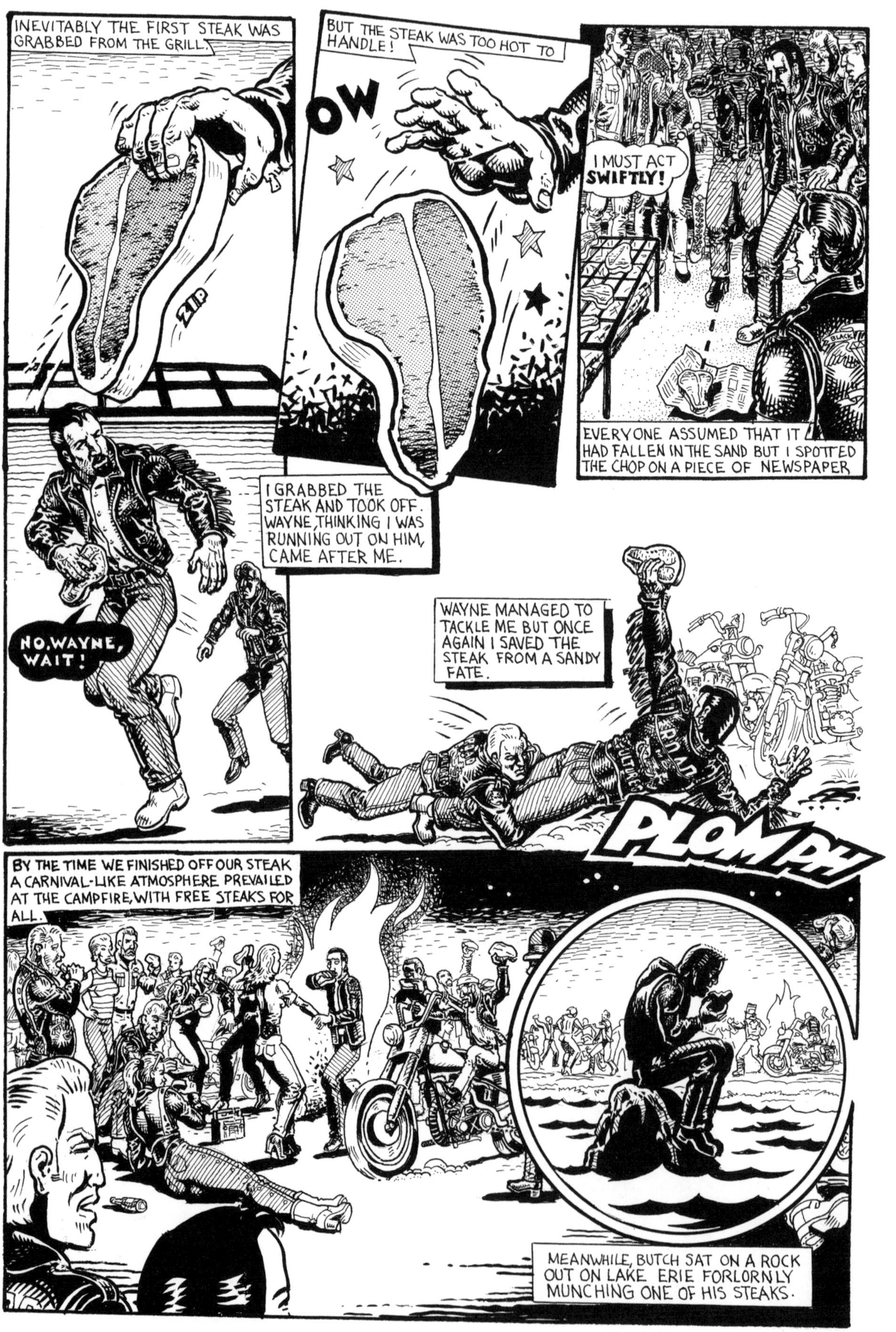
INEVITABLY THE FIRST STEAK WAS GRABBED FROM THE GRILL.
ZIP
BUT THE STEAK WAS TOO HOT TO HANDLE!
OW
I MUST ACT SWIFTLY!
EVERYONE ASSUMED THAT IT HAD FALLEN IN THE SAND BUT I SPOTTED THE CHOP ON A PIECE OF NEWSPAPER
I GRABBED THE STEAK AND TOOK OFF. WAYNE, THINKING I WAS RUNNING OUT ON HIM, CAME AFTER ME.
NO, WAYNE, WAIT!
WAYNE MANAGED TO TACKLE ME BUT ONCE AGAIN I SAVED THE STEAK FROM A SANDY FATE.
PLOMPH
BY THE TIME WE FINISHED OFF OUR STEAK A CARNIVAL-LIKE ATMOSPHERE PREVAILED AT THE CAMPFIRE, WITH FREE STEAKS FOR ALL.
MEANWHILE, BUTCH SAT ON A ROCK OUT ON LAKE ERIE FORLORNLY MUNCHING ONE OF HIS STEAKS.

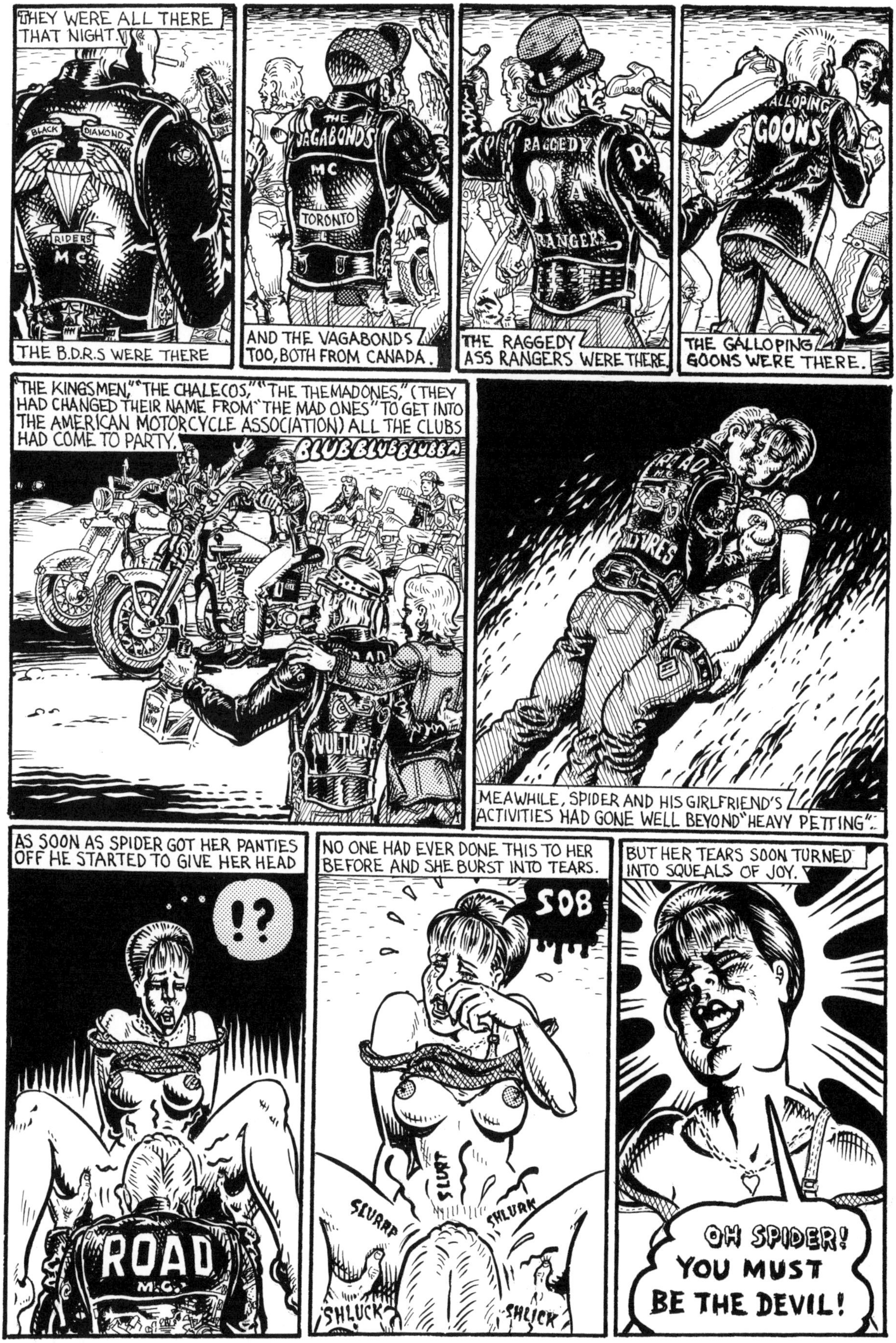
THEY WERE ALL THERE THAT NIGHT.
BLACK DIAMOND RIDERS MC
THE B.D.R.S WERE THERE
THE VAGABONDS MC TORONTO
AND THE VAGABONDS TOO, BOTH FROM CANADA.
RAGGEDY R A RANGERS
THE RAGGEDY ASS RANGERS WERE THERE.
GALLOPING GOONS
THE GALLOPING GOONS WERE THERE.
"THE KINGSMEN," "THE CHALECOS," "THE THEMADONES," (THEY HAD CHANGED THEIR NAME FROM "THE MAD ONES" TO GET INTO THE AMERICAN MOTORCYCLE ASSOCIATION) ALL THE CLUBS HAD COME TO PARTY.
BLUB BLUB BLUBBA
VULTURES
ROAD M.C. VULTURES
MEAWHILE, SPIDER AND HIS GIRLFRIEND'S ACTIVITIES HAD GONE WELL BEYOND "HEAVY PETTING".
AS SOON AS SPIDER GOT HER PANTIES OFF HE STARTED TO GIVE HER HEAD
!?
ROAD M.C.
NO ONE HAD EVER DONE THIS TO HER BEFORE AND SHE BURST INTO TEARS.
SOB
SLURP
SLURRP
SHLURK
SHLUCK
SHLICK
BUT HER TEARS SOON TURNED INTO SQUEALS OF JOY.
OH SPIDER! YOU MUST BE THE DEVIL!

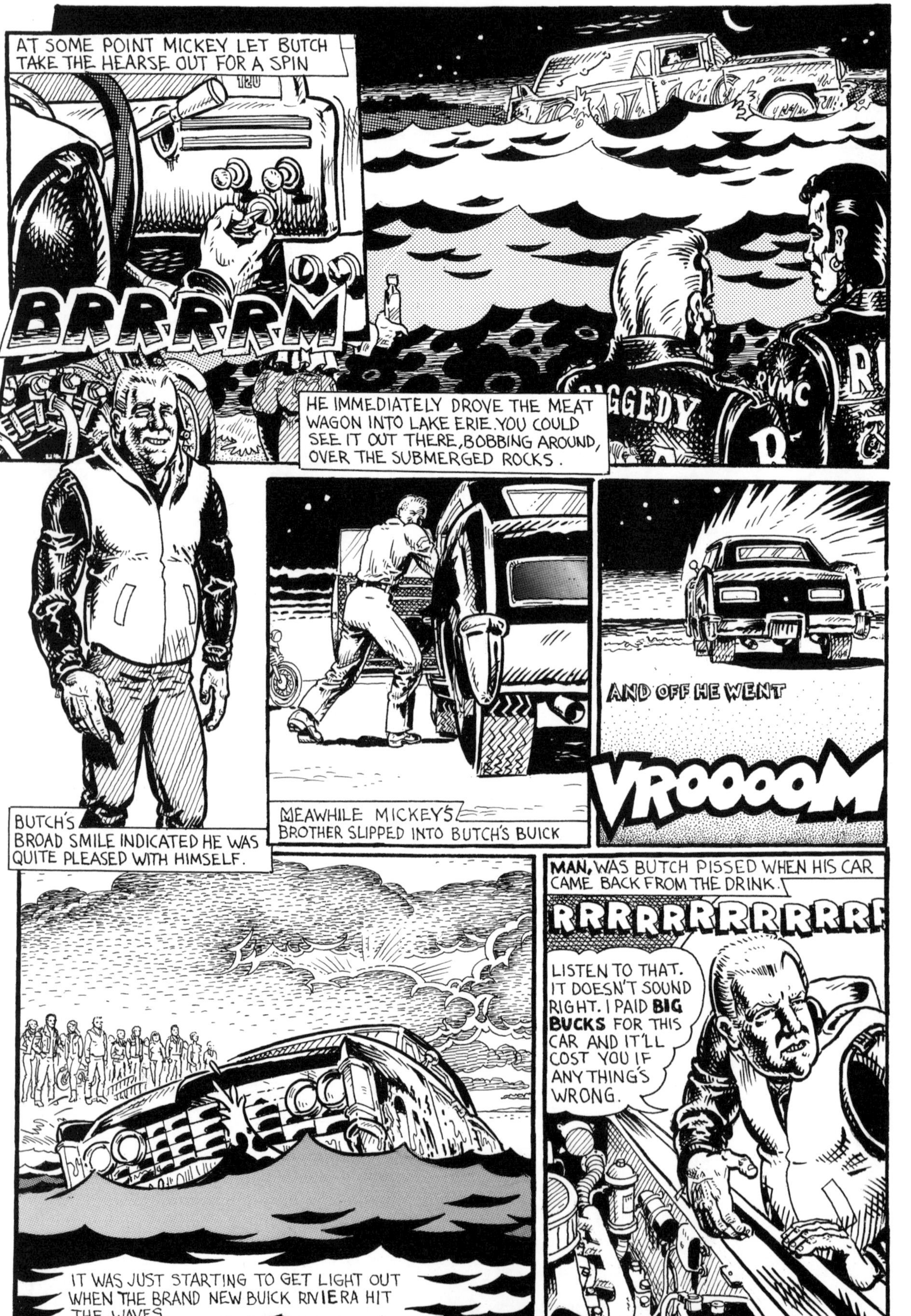
AT SOME POINT MICKEY LET BUTCH TAKE THE HEARSE OUT FOR A SPIN
BRRRRM
HE IMMEDIATELY DROVE THE MEAT WAGON INTO LAKE ERIE. YOU COULD SEE IT OUT THERE, BOBBING AROUND, OVER THE SUBMERGED ROCKS.
BUTCH'S BROAD SMILE INDICATED HE WAS QUITE PLEASED WITH HIMSELF.
MEAWHILE MICKEY'S BROTHER SLIPPED INTO BUTCH'S BUICK
AND OFF HE WENT
VROOOOM
IT WAS JUST STARTING TO GET LIGHT OUT WHEN THE BRAND NEW BUICK RIVIERA HIT THE WAVES.
MAN, WAS BUTCH PISSED WHEN HIS CAR CAME BACK FROM THE DRINK.
RRRRRRRRRRRR
LISTEN TO THAT. IT DOESN'T SOUND RIGHT. I PAID BIG BUCKS FOR THIS CAR AND IT'LL COST YOU IF ANY THING'S WRONG.

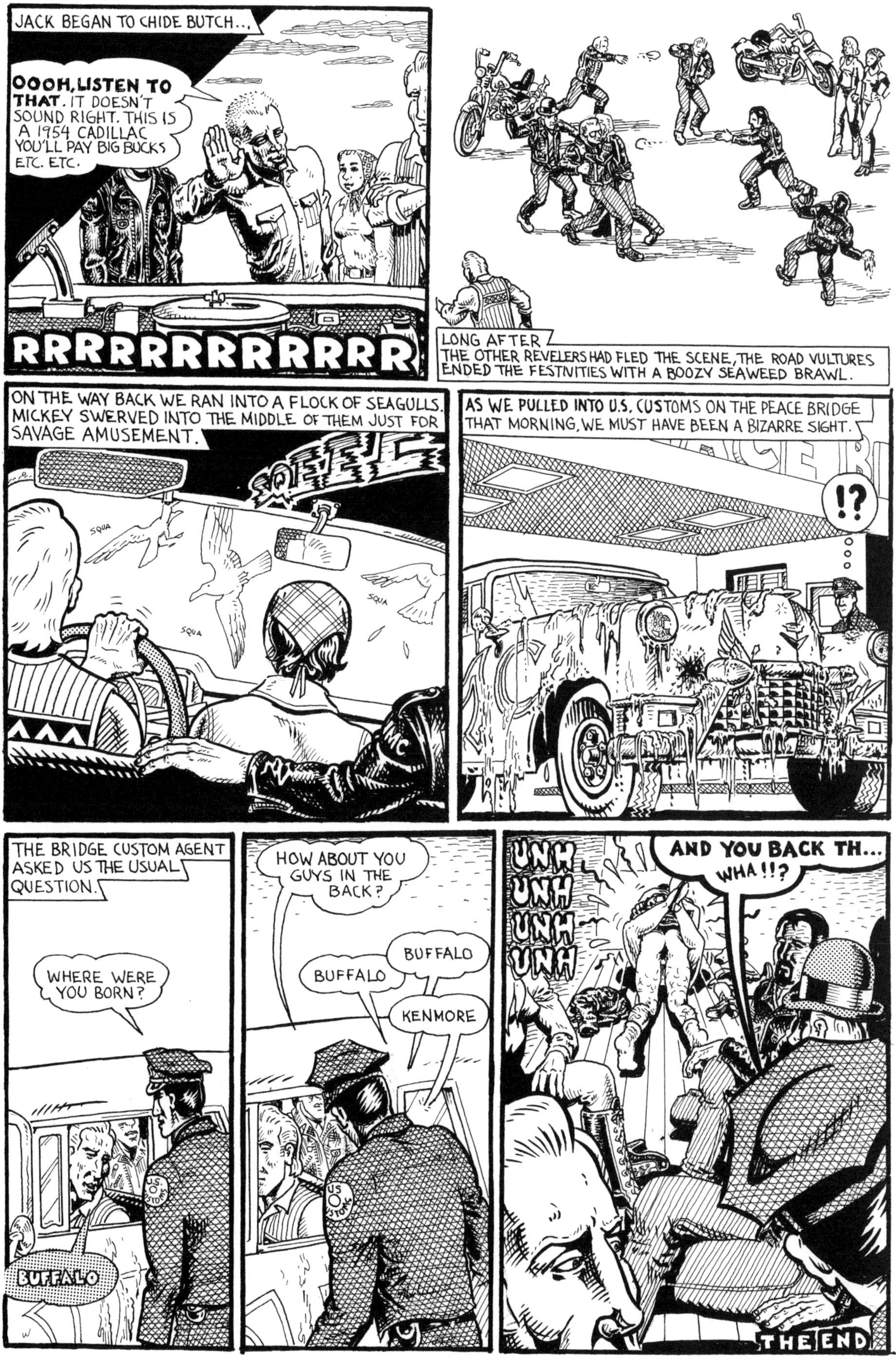
JACK BEGAN TO CHIDE BUTCH...
OOOH, LISTEN TO THAT. IT DOESN'T SOUND RIGHT. THIS IS A 1954 CADILLAC YOU'LL PAY BIG BUCKS ETC. ETC.
RRRRRRRRRRRRR
LONG AFTER
THE OTHER REVELERS HAD FLED THE SCENE, THE ROAD VULTURES ENDED THE FESTIVITIES WITH A BOOZY SEAWEED BRAWL.
ON THE WAY BACK WE RAN INTO A FLOCK OF SEAGULLS. MICKEY SWERVED INTO THE MIDDLE OF THEM JUST FOR SAVAGE AMUSEMENT.
SQUA
SQUA
SQUA
SQUA
AS WE PULLED INTO U.S. CUSTOMS ON THE PEACE BRIDGE THAT MORNING, WE MUST HAVE BEEN A BIZARRE SIGHT.
!?
THE BRIDGE CUSTOM AGENT ASKED US THE USUAL QUESTION.
WHERE WERE YOU BORN?
BUFFALO
HOW ABOUT YOU GUYS IN THE BACK?
BUFFALO
BUFFALO
KENMORE
UNH
UNH
UNH
UNH
AND YOU BACK TH...
WHA!!?
THE END

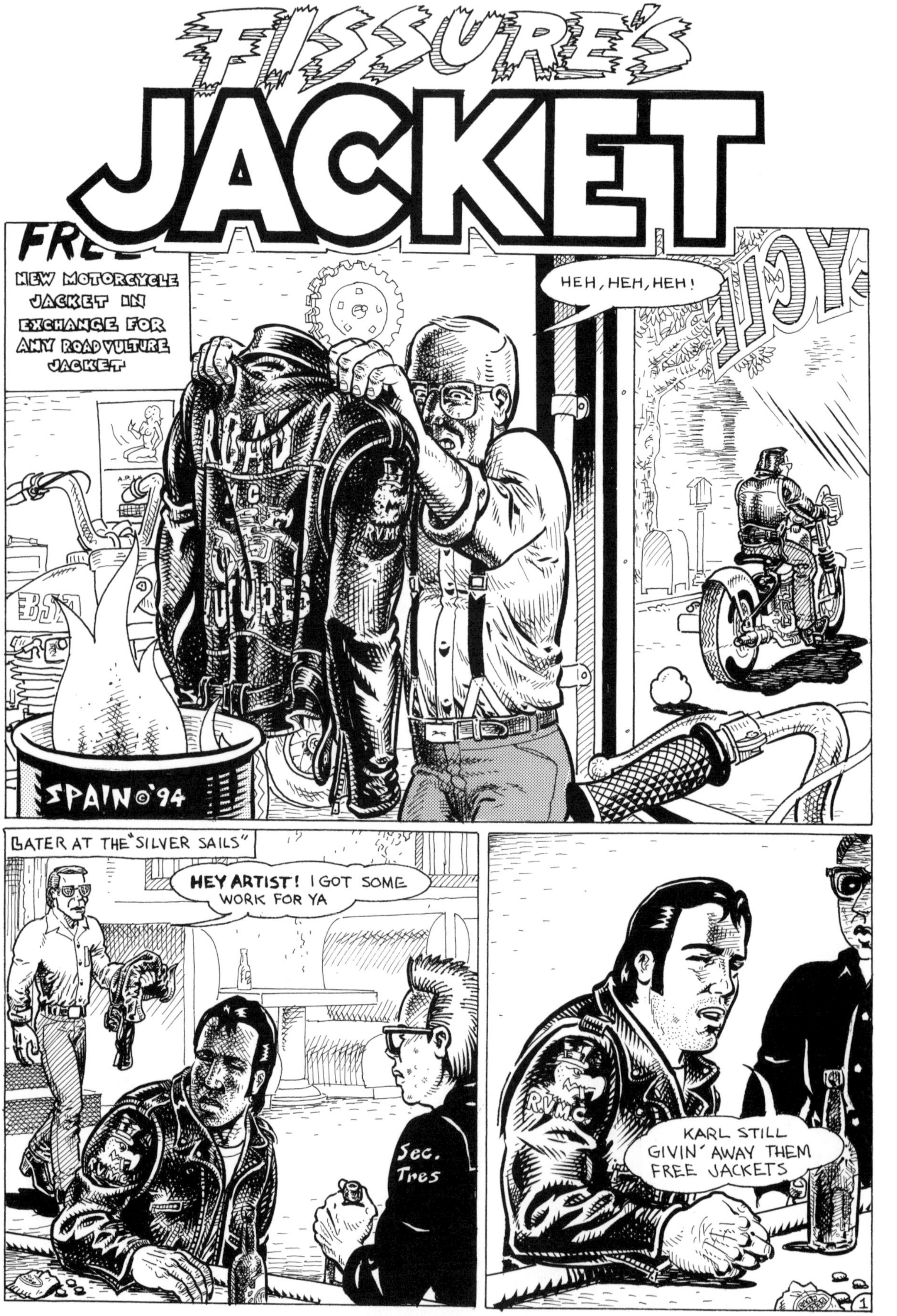
FISSURE'S
JACKET
FREE
NEW MOTORCYCLE
JACKET IN
EXCHANGE FOR
ANY ROAD VULTURE
JACKET
HEH, HEH, HEH!
SPAIN © '94
LATER AT THE "SILVER SAILS"
HEY ARTIST! I GOT SOME WORK FOR YA
Sec. Tres
KARL STILL GIVIN' AWAY THEM FREE JACKETS
1

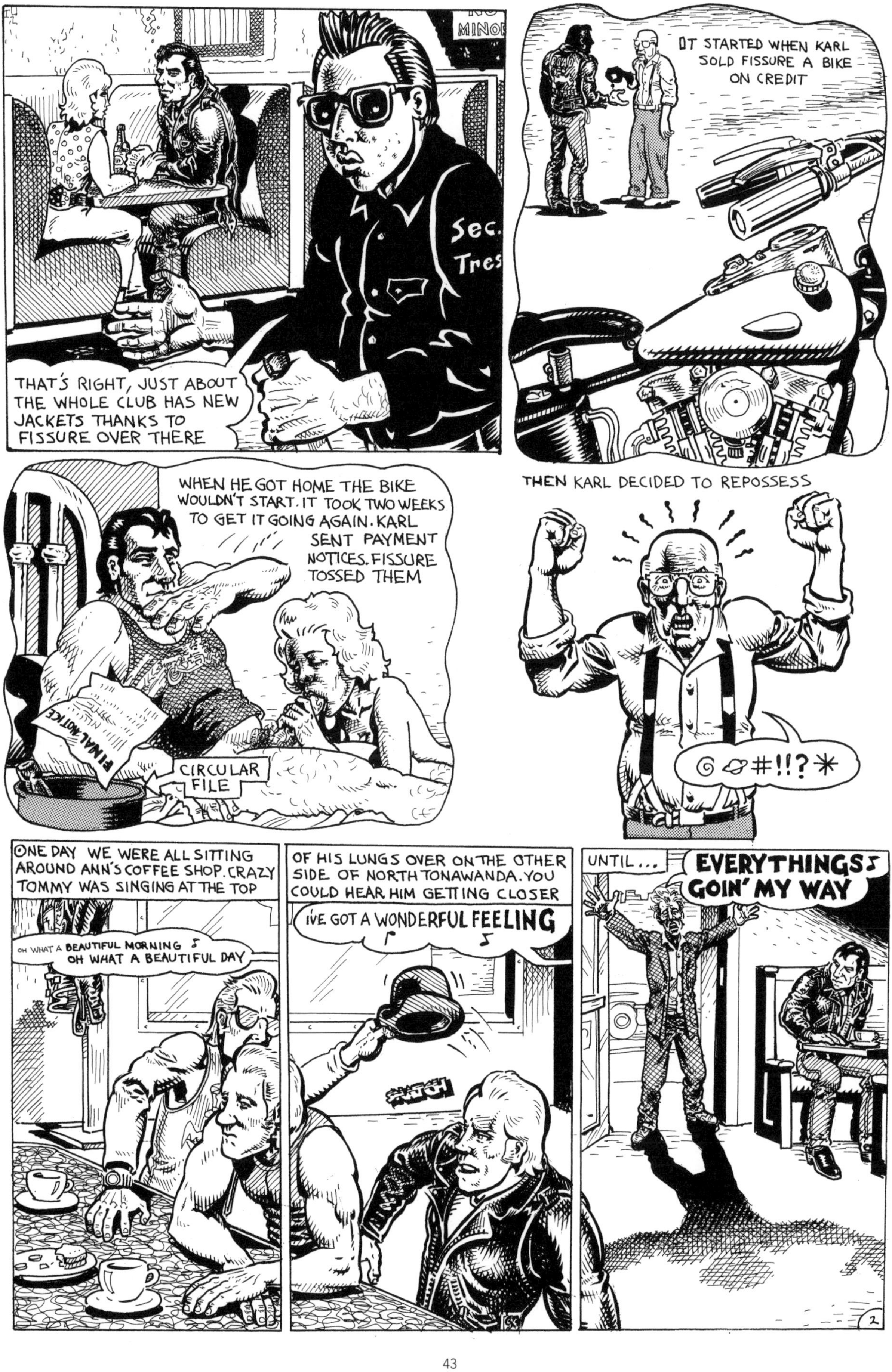
Sec. Tres
THAT'S RIGHT, JUST ABOUT THE WHOLE CLUB HAS NEW JACKETS THANKS TO FISSURE OVER THERE
IT STARTED WHEN KARL SOLD FISSURE A BIKE ON CREDIT
WHEN HE GOT HOME THE BIKE WOULDN'T START. IT TOOK TWO WEEKS TO GET IT GOING AGAIN. KARL SENT PAYMENT NOTICES. FISSURE TOSSED THEM
FINAL NOTICE
CIRCULAR FILE
THEN KARL DECIDED TO REPOSSESS
@#!!?*
ONE DAY WE WERE ALL SITTING AROUND ANN'S COFFEE SHOP. CRAZY TOMMY WAS SINGING AT THE TOP
OH WHAT A BEAUTIFUL MORNING OH WHAT A BEAUTIFUL DAY
OF HIS LUNGS OVER ON THE OTHER SIDE OF NORTH TONAWANDA. YOU COULD HEAR HIM GETTING CLOSER
I'VE GOT A WONDERFUL FEELING
SNATCH
UNTIL...
EVERYTHINGS GOIN' MY WAY
2

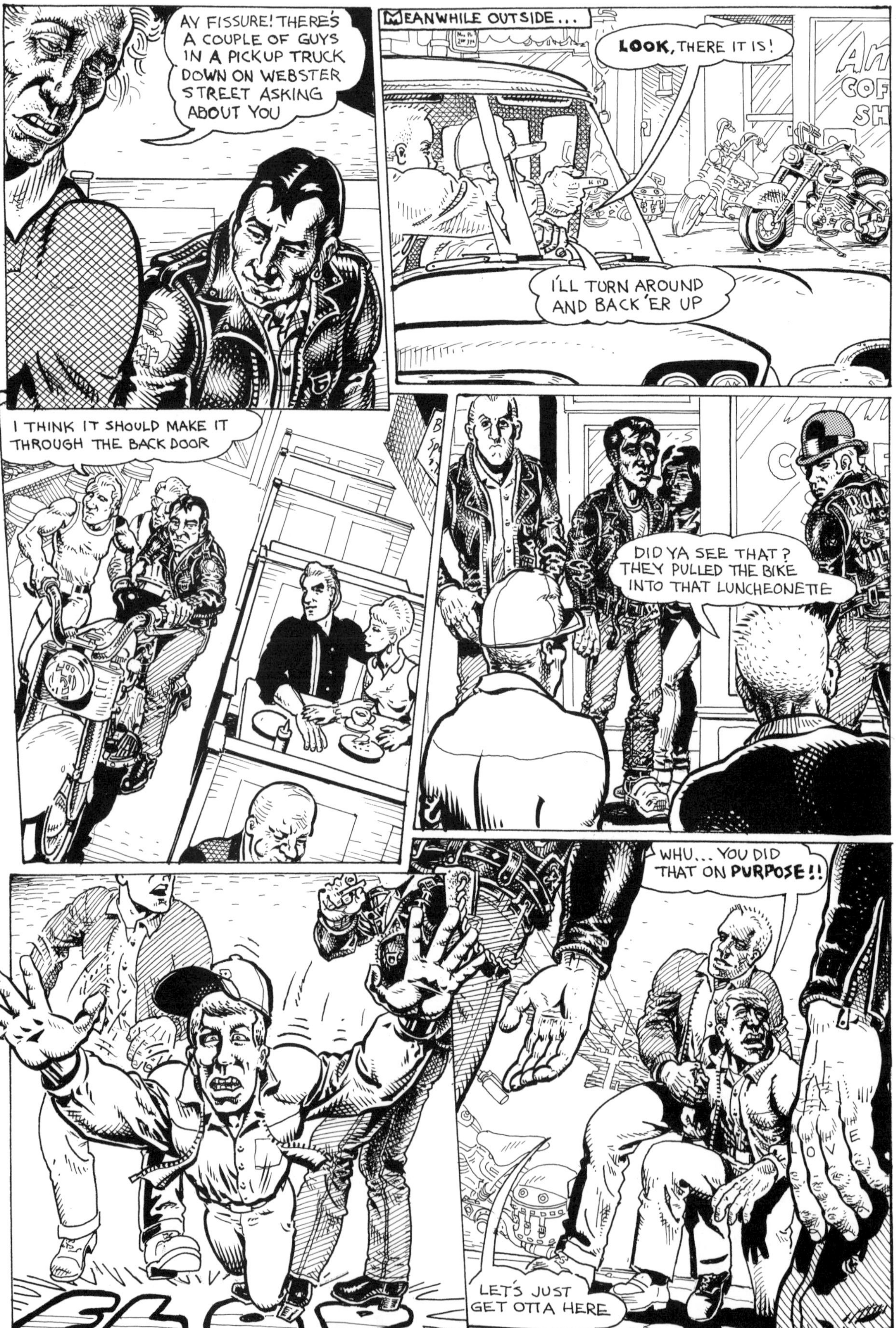
AY FISSURE! THERE'S A COUPLE OF GUYS IN A PICKUP TRUCK DOWN ON WEBSTER STREET ASKING ABOUT YOU
MEANWHILE OUTSIDE...
LOOK, THERE IT IS!
I'LL TURN AROUND AND BACK 'ER UP
I THINK IT SHOULD MAKE IT THROUGH THE BACK DOOR
DID YA SEE THAT? THEY PULLED THE BIKE INTO THAT LUNCHEONETTE
WHU... YOU DID THAT ON PURPOSE!!
LOVE
LET'S JUST GET OTTA HERE

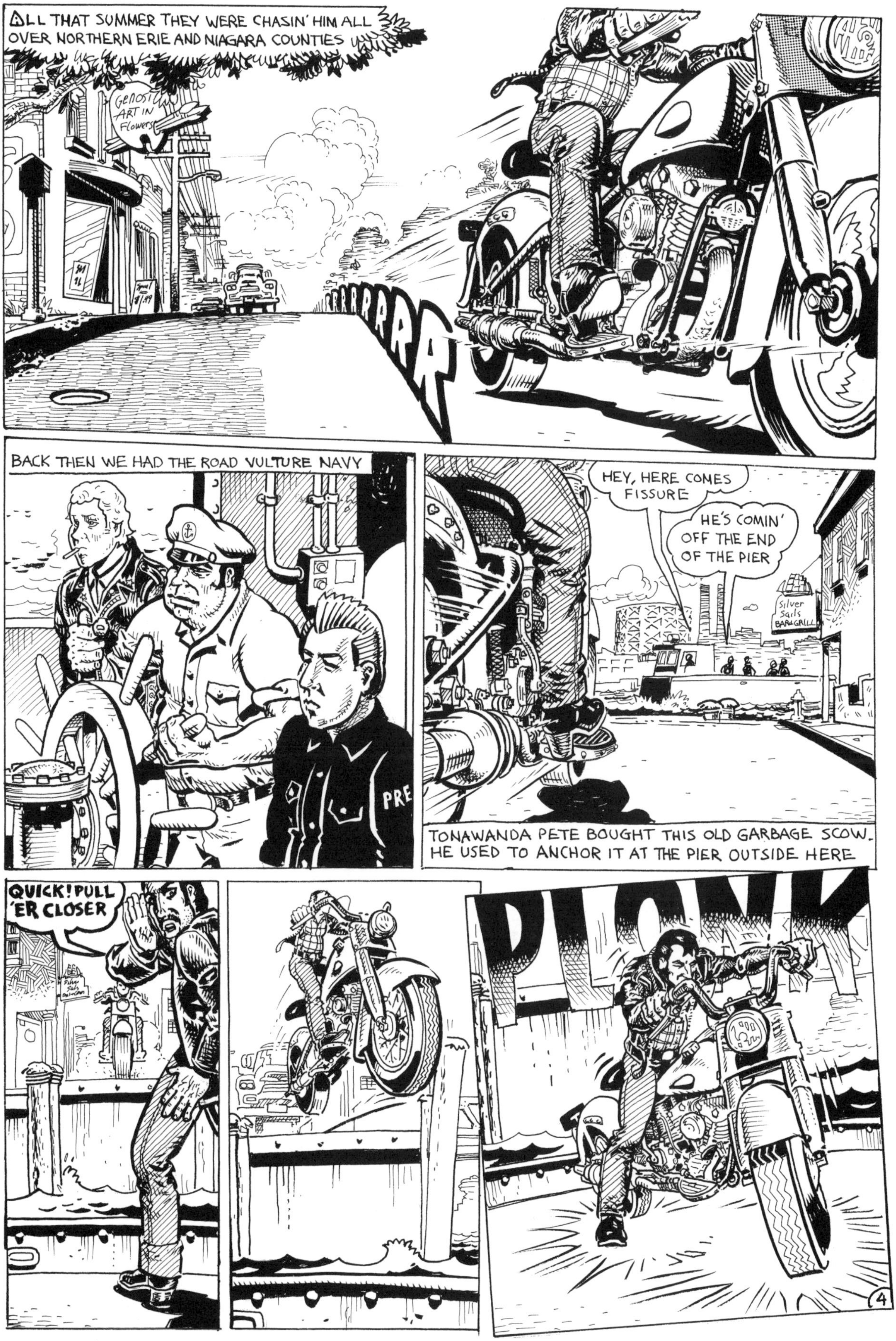
ALL THAT SUMMER THEY WERE CHASIN' HIM ALL OVER NORTHERN ERIE AND NIAGARA COUNTIES
ART IN Flowers
RRRRRRRRR
BACK THEN WE HAD THE ROAD VULTURE NAVY
PRE
HEY, HERE COMES FISSURE
HE'S COMIN' OFF THE END OF THE PIER
Silver Sails BAR&GRILL
TONAWANDA PETE BOUGHT THIS OLD GARBAGE SCOW. HE USED TO ANCHOR IT AT THE PIER OUTSIDE HERE
QUICK! PULL 'ER CLOSER
4

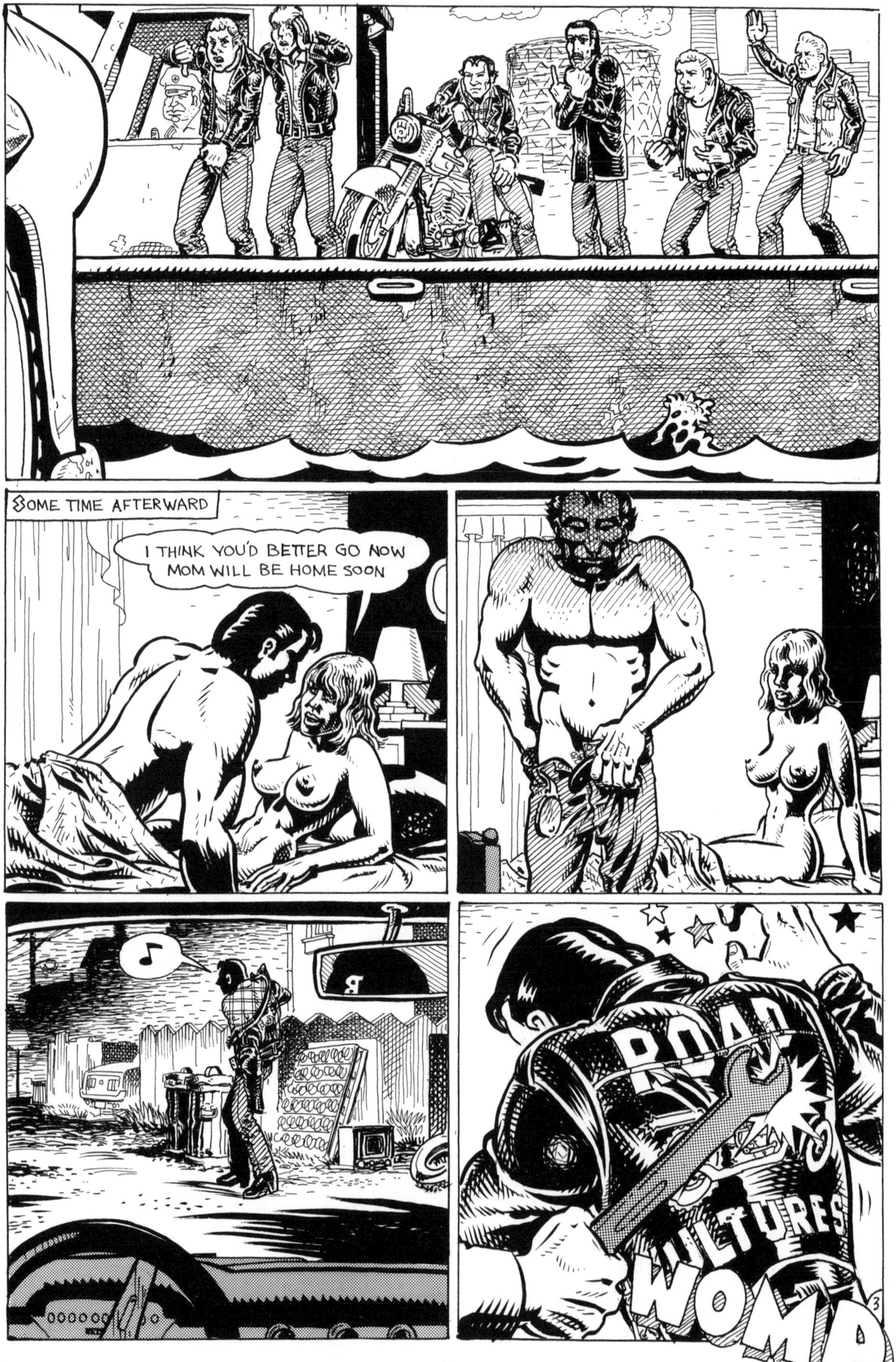
SOME TIME AFTERWARD
I THINK YOU'D BETTER GO NOW MOM WILL BE HOME SOON
♪
ROAD VULTURES
WOMP

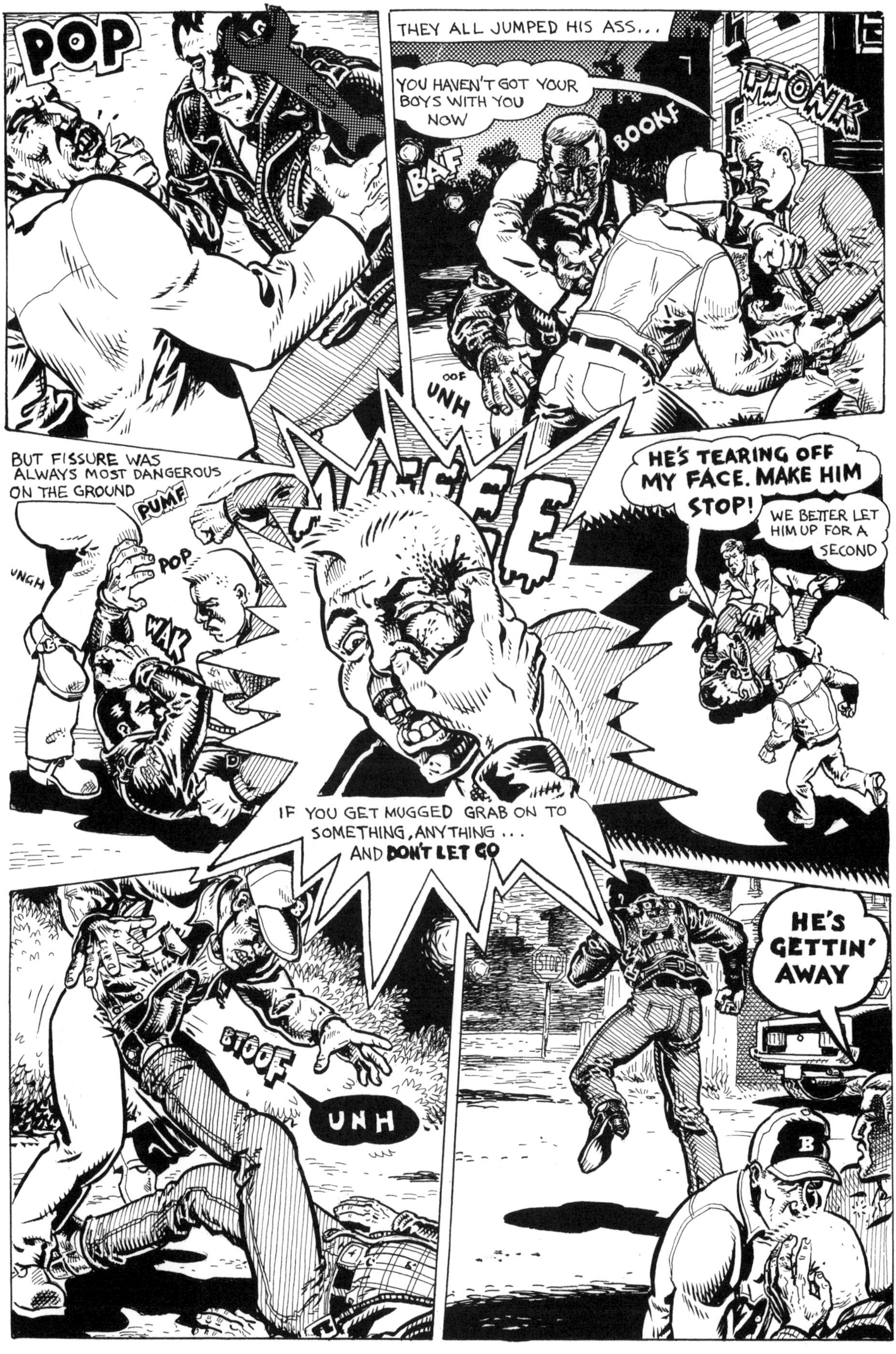
POP
THEY ALL JUMPED HIS ASS...
YOU HAVEN'T GOT YOUR BOYS WITH YOU NOW
BAF
BOOKF
PTONK
OOF
UNH
BUT FISSURE WAS ALWAYS MOST DANGEROUS ON THE GROUND
PUMF
UNGH
POP
WAK
HE'S TEARING OFF MY FACE. MAKE HIM STOP!
WE BETTER LET HIM UP FOR A SECOND
IF YOU GET MUGGED GRAB ON TO SOMETHING, ANYTHING ... AND DON'T LET GO
BTOOF
UNH
HE'S GETTIN' AWAY

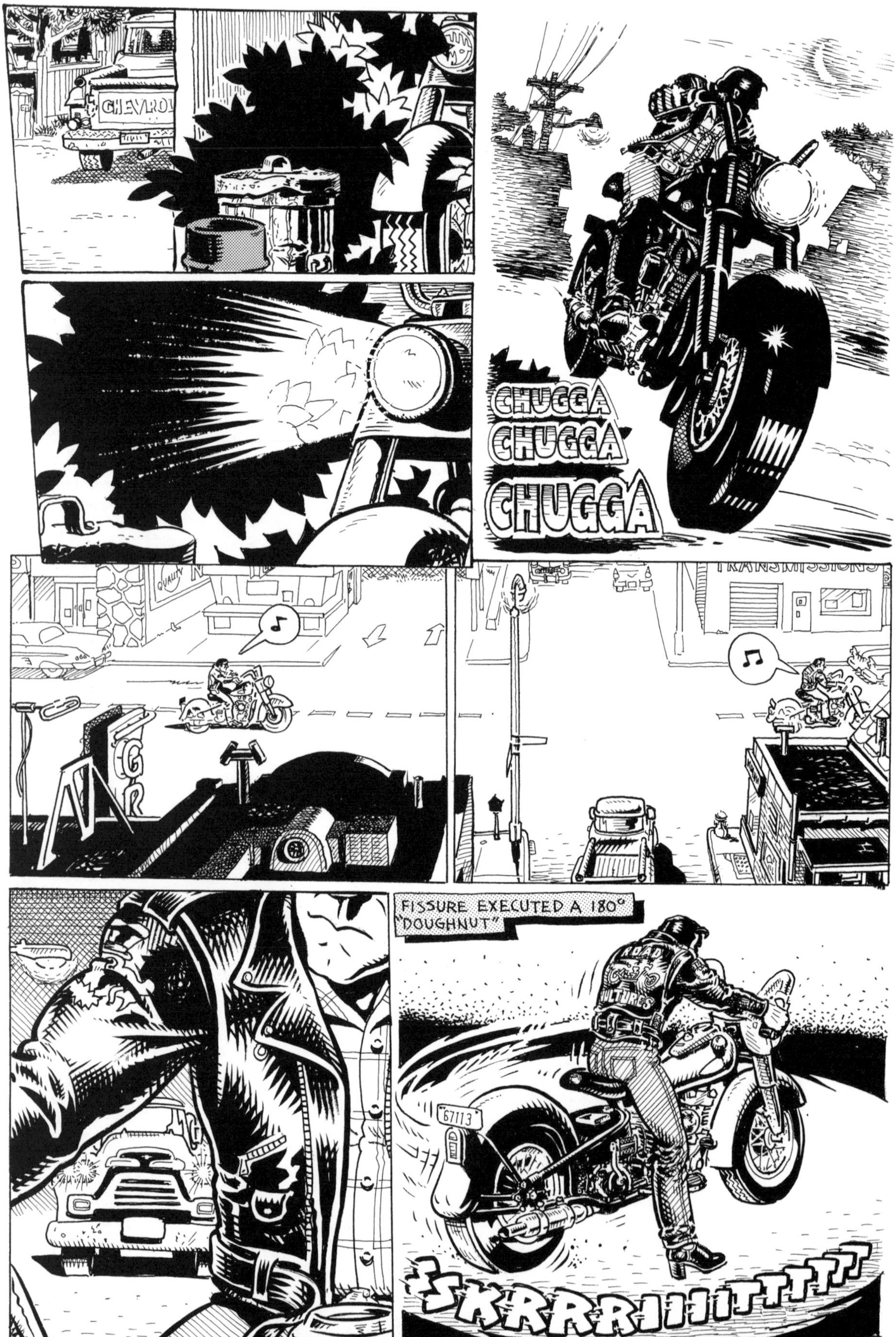
CHEVROL
CHUGGA
CHUGGA
CHUGGA
♪
TRANSMISSIONS
♪
FISSURE EXECUTED A 180° "DOUGHNUT"
ROAD VULTURES
67113
SKRRRIIIITTTTTT
7

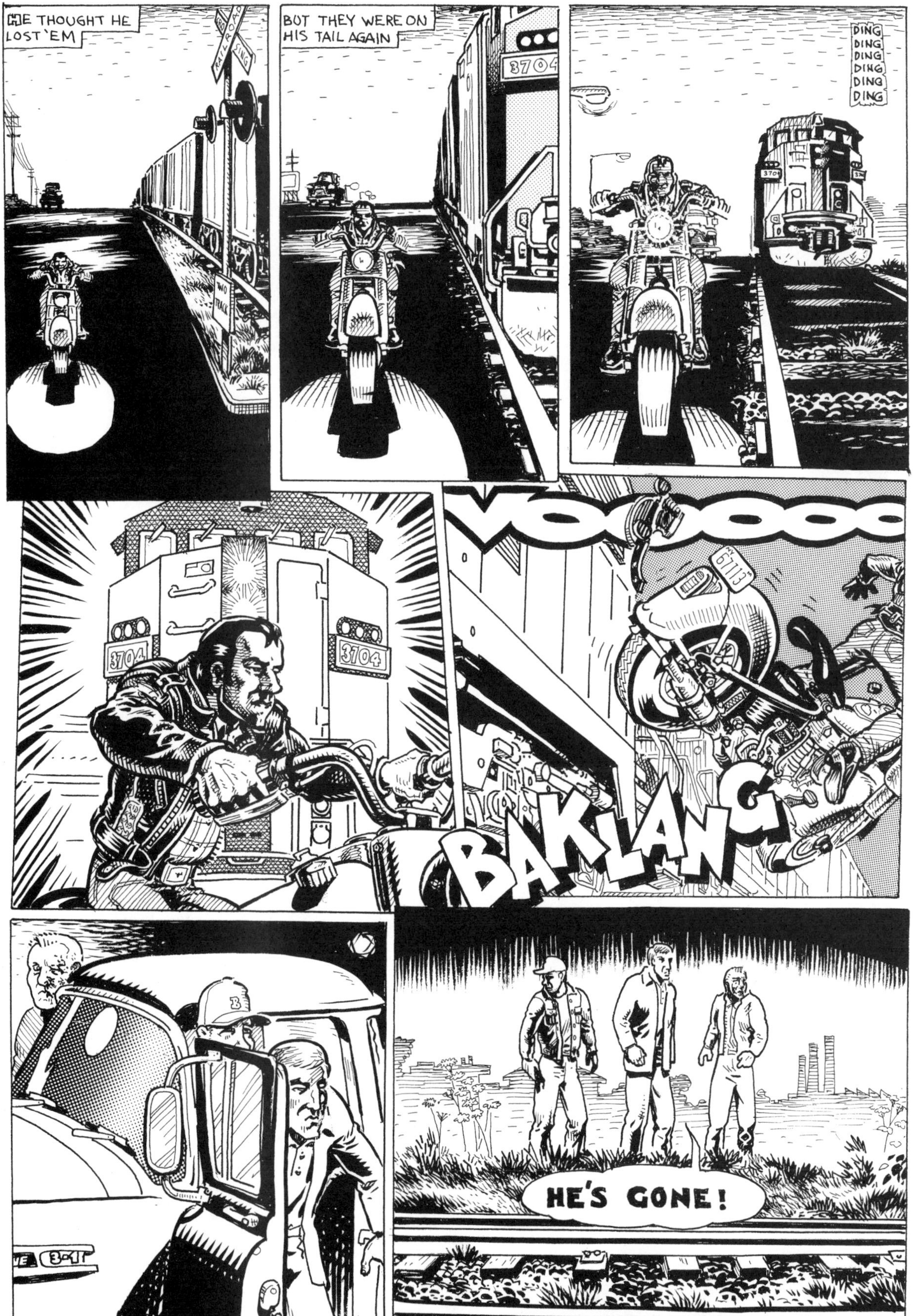
HE THOUGHT HE LOST `EM
BUT THEY WERE ON HIS TAIL AGAIN
3704
DING DING DING DING DING DING
3704
3704
BAKLANG
HE'S GONE!
8

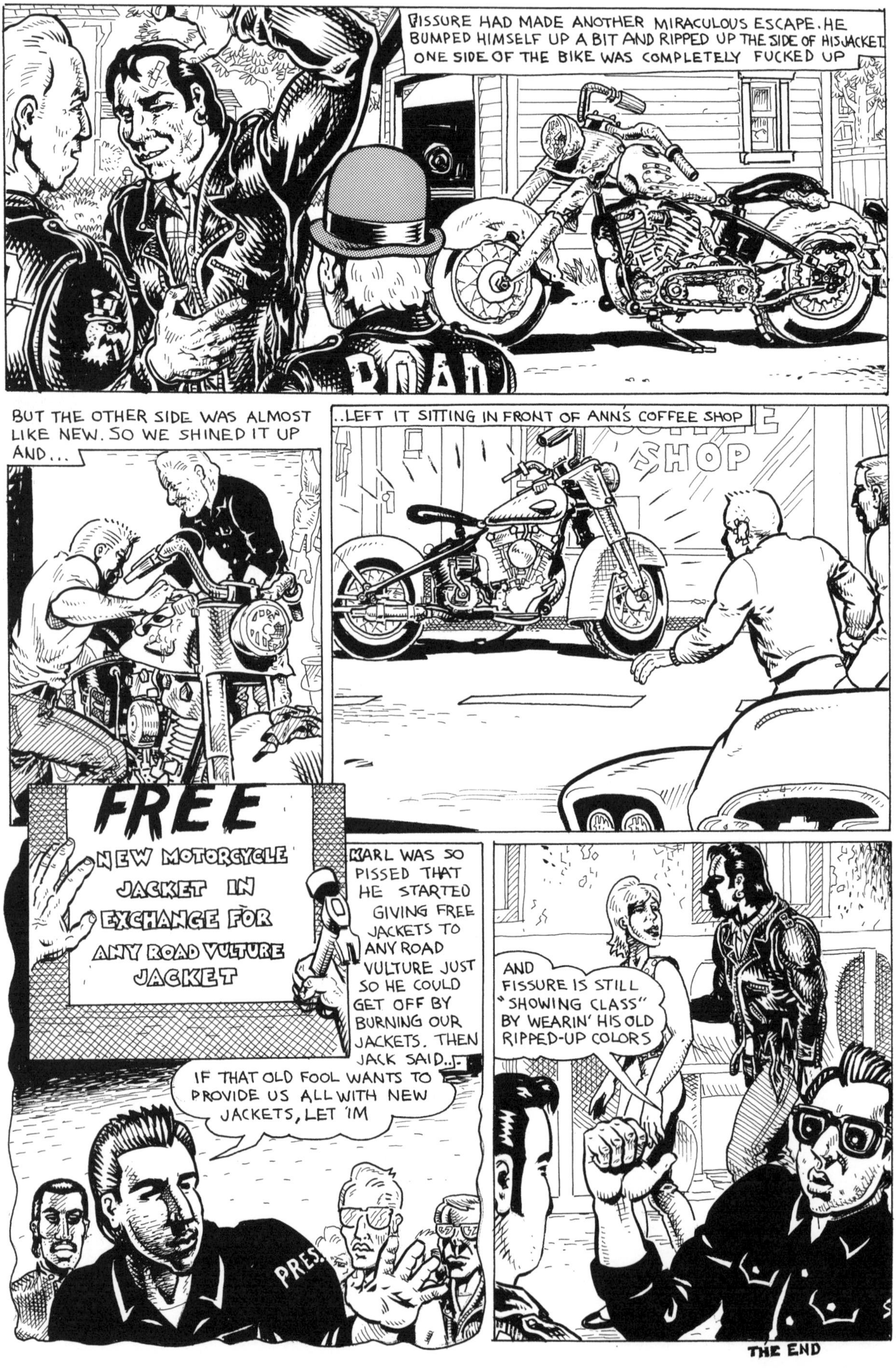
FISSURE HAD MADE ANOTHER MIRACULOUS ESCAPE. HE BUMPED HIMSELF UP A BIT AND RIPPED UP THE SIDE OF HIS JACKET. ONE SIDE OF THE BIKE WAS COMPLETELY FUCKED UP
ROAD
BUT THE OTHER SIDE WAS ALMOST LIKE NEW. SO WE SHINED IT UP AND...
..LEFT IT SITTING IN FRONT OF ANN'S COFFEE SHOP
SHOP
FREE
NEW MOTORCYCLE JACKET IN EXCHANGE FOR ANY ROAD VULTURE JACKET
KARL WAS SO PISSED THAT HE STARTED GIVING FREE JACKETS TO ANY ROAD VULTURE JUST SO HE COULD GET OFF BY BURNING OUR JACKETS. THEN JACK SAID...
IF THAT OLD FOOL WANTS TO PROVIDE US ALL WITH NEW JACKETS, LET 'IM
PRES.
AND FISSURE IS STILL "SHOWING CLASS" BY WEARIN' HIS OLD RIPPED-UP COLORS
THE END

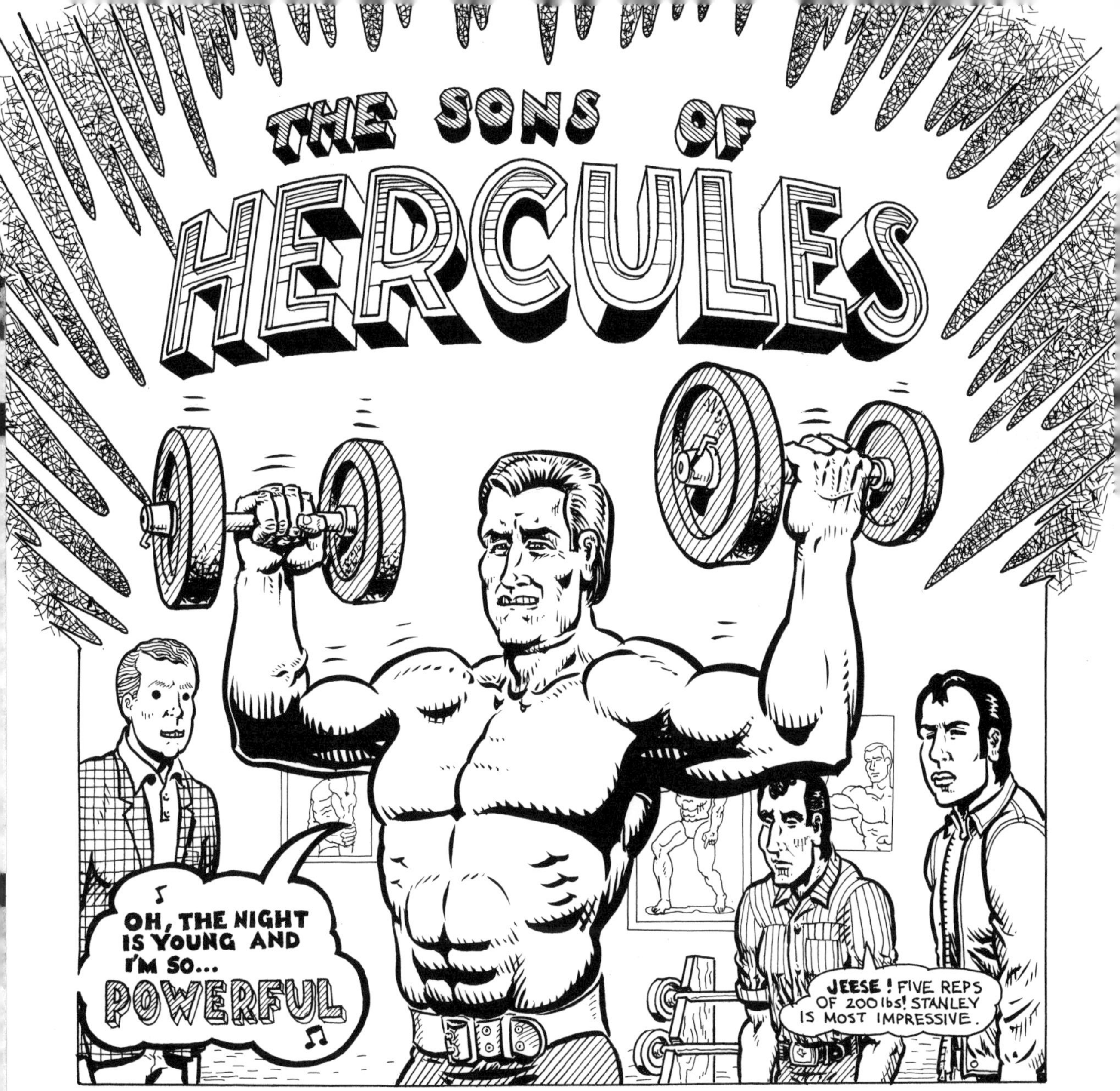
THE SONS OF
HERCULES
OH, THE NIGHT IS YOUNG AND I'M SO... POWERFUL
JEESE! FIVE REPS OF 200 lbs! STANLEY IS MOST IMPRESSIVE.

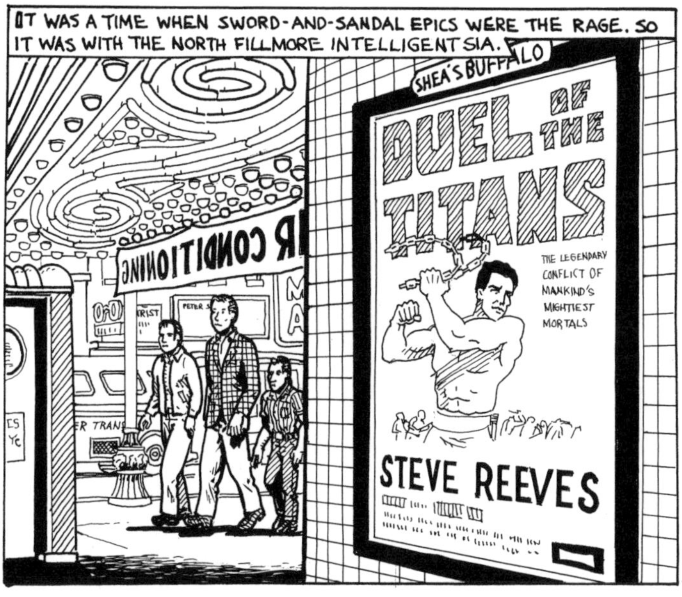
IT WAS A TIME WHEN SWORD-AND-SANDAL EPICS WERE THE RAGE. SO IT WAS WITH THE NORTH FILLMORE INTELLIGENTSIA.
SHEA'S BUFFALO
DUEL OF THE TITANS
THE LEGENDARY CONFLICT OF MANKIND'S MIGHTIEST MORTALS
STEVE REEVES
AIR CONDITIONING

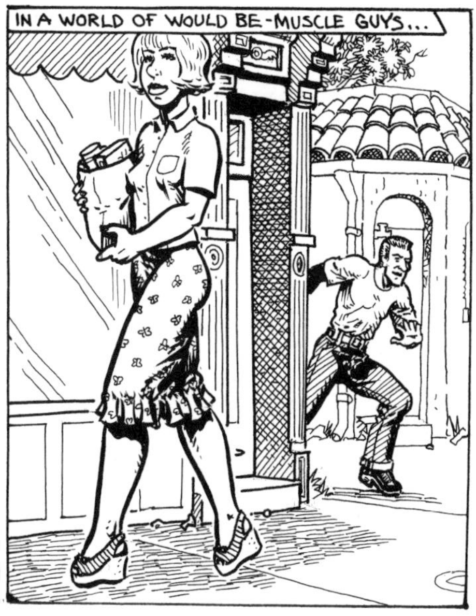
IN A WORLD OF WOULD BE-MUSCLE GUYS...

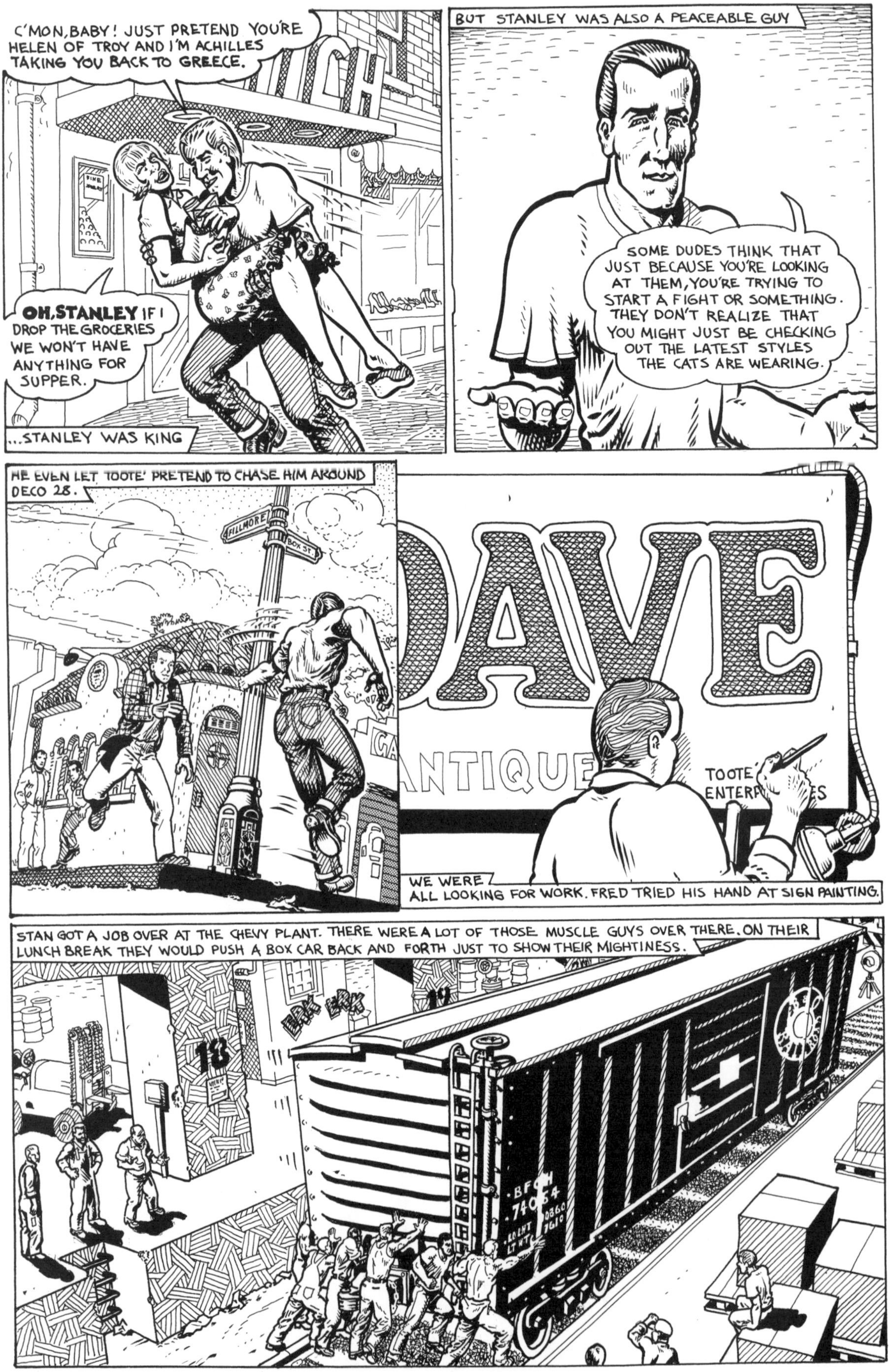
C'MON, BABY! JUST PRETEND YOU'RE HELEN OF TROY AND I'M ACHILLES TAKING YOU BACK TO GREECE.
OH, STANLEY IF I DROP THE GROCERIES WE WON'T HAVE ANYTHING FOR SUPPER.
...STANLEY WAS KING
BUT STANLEY WAS ALSO A PEACEABLE GUY
SOME DUDES THINK THAT JUST BECAUSE YOU'RE LOOKING AT THEM, YOU'RE TRYING TO START A FIGHT OR SOMETHING. THEY DON'T REALIZE THAT YOU MIGHT JUST BE CHECKING OUT THE LATEST STYLES THE CATS ARE WEARING.
HE EVEN LET TOOTE' PRETEND TO CHASE HIM AROUND DECO 28.
FILLMORE
BOX ST.
DAVE
ANTIQUE
WE WERE ALL LOOKING FOR WORK. FRED TRIED HIS HAND AT SIGN PAINTING.
STAN GOT A JOB OVER AT THE CHEVY PLANT. THERE WERE A LOT OF THOSE MUSCLE GUYS OVER THERE. ON THEIR LUNCH BREAK THEY WOULD PUSH A BOX CAR BACK AND FORTH JUST TO SHOW THEIR MIGHTINESS.
ERK ERK
18

JOBS WERE SCARCE THAT SUMMER SO I WENT TO WORK FOR BARGAIN DAVE.

BARGAIN DAVE
WE BUY JUNK
ANTIQUES

HOW THEY HANGIN', BIG BOY?

HANGING THERE JUST FOR YOU, BABY.

KEEP THAT CUNT HOT AND JUICY FOR ME, BABY.

PAT PAT

IT'LL BE ALL FLUFFED UP FOR YOU WHEN YOU GET HOME.

BARGAIN DAVE AND HIS WIFE FRANCESCA HAD A HABIT OF RAUNCHY PUBLIC REPARTEE. HEARING THIS FROM PEOPLE OLDER THAN ME, (WHY, THEY WERE PROBABLY IN THEIR FORTIES) I HAVE TO ADMIT, WAS KIND OF SHOCKING.

I LIKE DEALING WITH YOU, BARGAIN DAVE. AT LEAST YOU'RE NOT LIKE THOSE FUCKING JEWS. THEY REALLY TAKE YOU TO THE CLEANERS.

OH, NO! STAY AWAY FROM THOSE PEOPLE. THEY'LL TAKE YOU FOR EVERY THING YOU GOT.

HEY, DAVE, I THOUGHT YOU WERE JEWISH.

I AM! I SCREW 'EM TOO. JUST NOT AS MUCH AS THOSE OTHER GUYS.

WHEN THE WATERMELONS CAME IN WE STOPPED COLLECTING SCRAP.

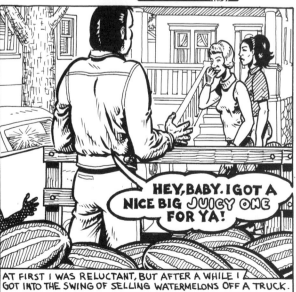

HEY, BABY. I GOT A NICE BIG JUICY ONE FOR YA!

AT FIRST I WAS RELUCTANT, BUT AFTER A WHILE I GOT INTO THE SWING OF SELLING WATERMELONS OFF A TRUCK.

I HAD ONLY VAGUE RECOLLECTIONS OF THE OLD STEREOTYPES, BUT IT WAS HARD NOT TO NOTICE THE ENTHUSIASM THAT GREETED US IN BLACK NEIGHBORHOODS.

MAMA, MAMA, HE GOT **WATERMELON!**

LET THE PEOPLE ENJOY WHAT THEY LIKE. IF SOMEBODY'S GOT A PROBLEM... **FUCK 'EM!**

WORKING FOR BARGAIN DAVE WASN'T EXACTLY THE BIG BUCKS

OK, OK, LET'S MAKE IT SEVEN DOLLARS.

I'M CERTAIN THAT I COULD EVOLVE TO THE POINT WHERE MY BODY WOULD USE EVERYTHING I ATE SO EFFICIENTLY THAT I WOULD NEVER HAVE TO SHIT AGAIN

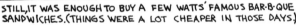

STILL, IT WAS ENOUGH TO BUY A FEW WATTS' FAMOUS BAR-B-QUE SANDWICHES. (THINGS WERE A LOT CHEAPER IN THOSE DAYS.)

YOU KNOW, ALL THOSE E.C. PLOTS WERE BASICALLY REVENGE STORIES. I'LL BET WE COULD COME UP WITH SOME KIND OF PLOT LIKE THAT.

THE TOPIC OF E.C. COMICS WAS NEVER FAR FROM OUR MINDS.

AS USUAL FRED WAS AHEAD OF ME.

THERE'S THIS GUY IN HIGH SCHOOL. HIS CLASSMATES LOVE TO TORMENT HIM BECAUSE OF THE HUMP ON HIS BACK...

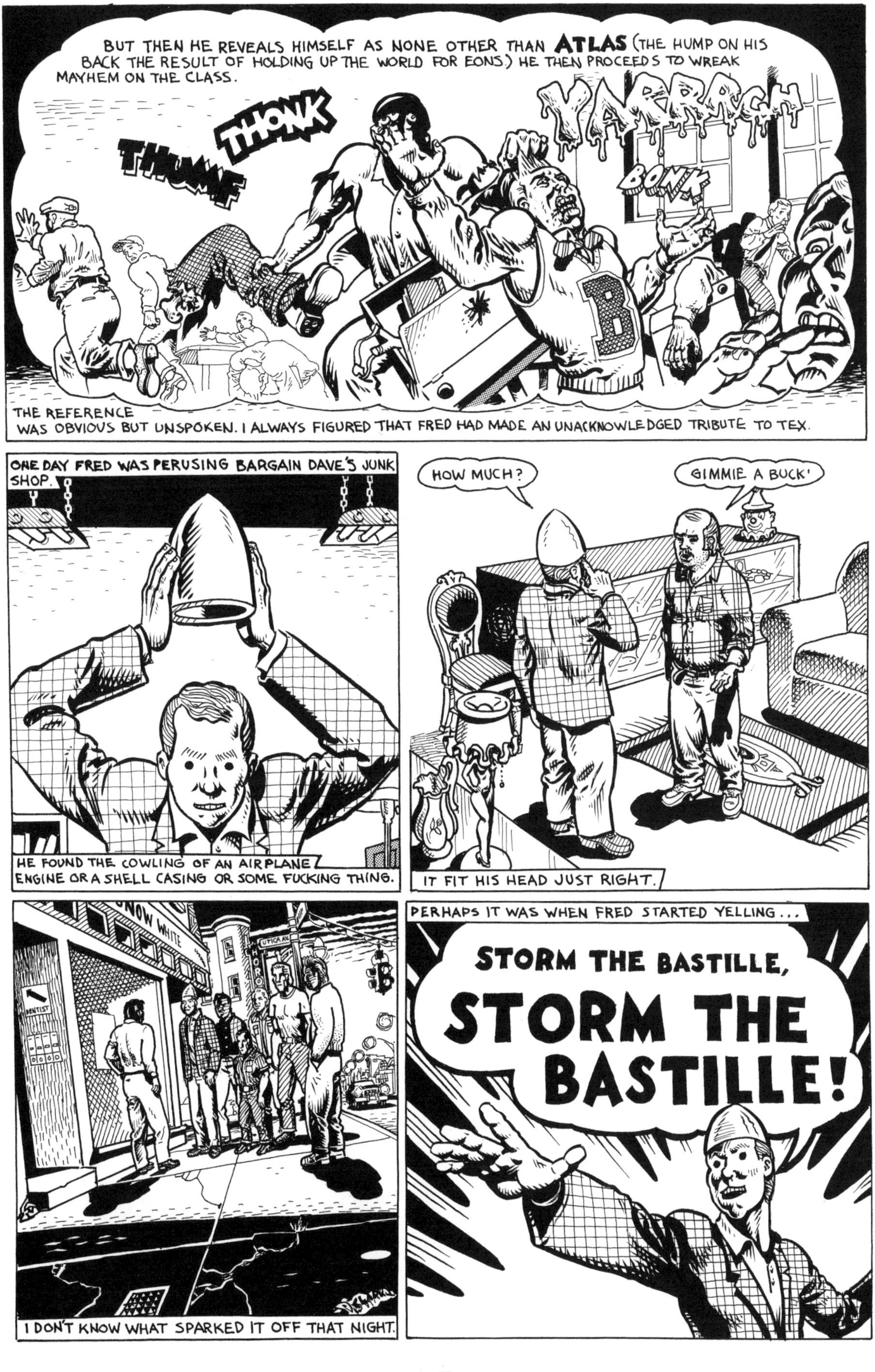
BUT THEN HE REVEALS HIMSELF AS NONE OTHER THAN ATLAS (THE HUMP ON HIS BACK THE RESULT OF HOLDING UP THE WORLD FOR EONS.) HE THEN PROCEEDS TO WREAK MAYHEM ON THE CLASS.
THUMP
THONK
YARRRGH
BONK
THE REFERENCE WAS OBVIOUS BUT UNSPOKEN. I ALWAYS FIGURED THAT FRED HAD MADE AN UNACKNOWLEDGED TRIBUTE TO TEX.
ONE DAY FRED WAS PERUSING BARGAIN DAVE'S JUNK SHOP.
HE FOUND THE COWLING OF AN AIRPLANE ENGINE OR A SHELL CASING OR SOME FUCKING THING.
HOW MUCH?
GIMMIE A BUCK'
IT FIT HIS HEAD JUST RIGHT.
I DON'T KNOW WHAT SPARKED IT OFF THAT NIGHT.
PERHAPS IT WAS WHEN FRED STARTED YELLING...
STORM THE BASTILLE,
STORM THE BASTILLE!

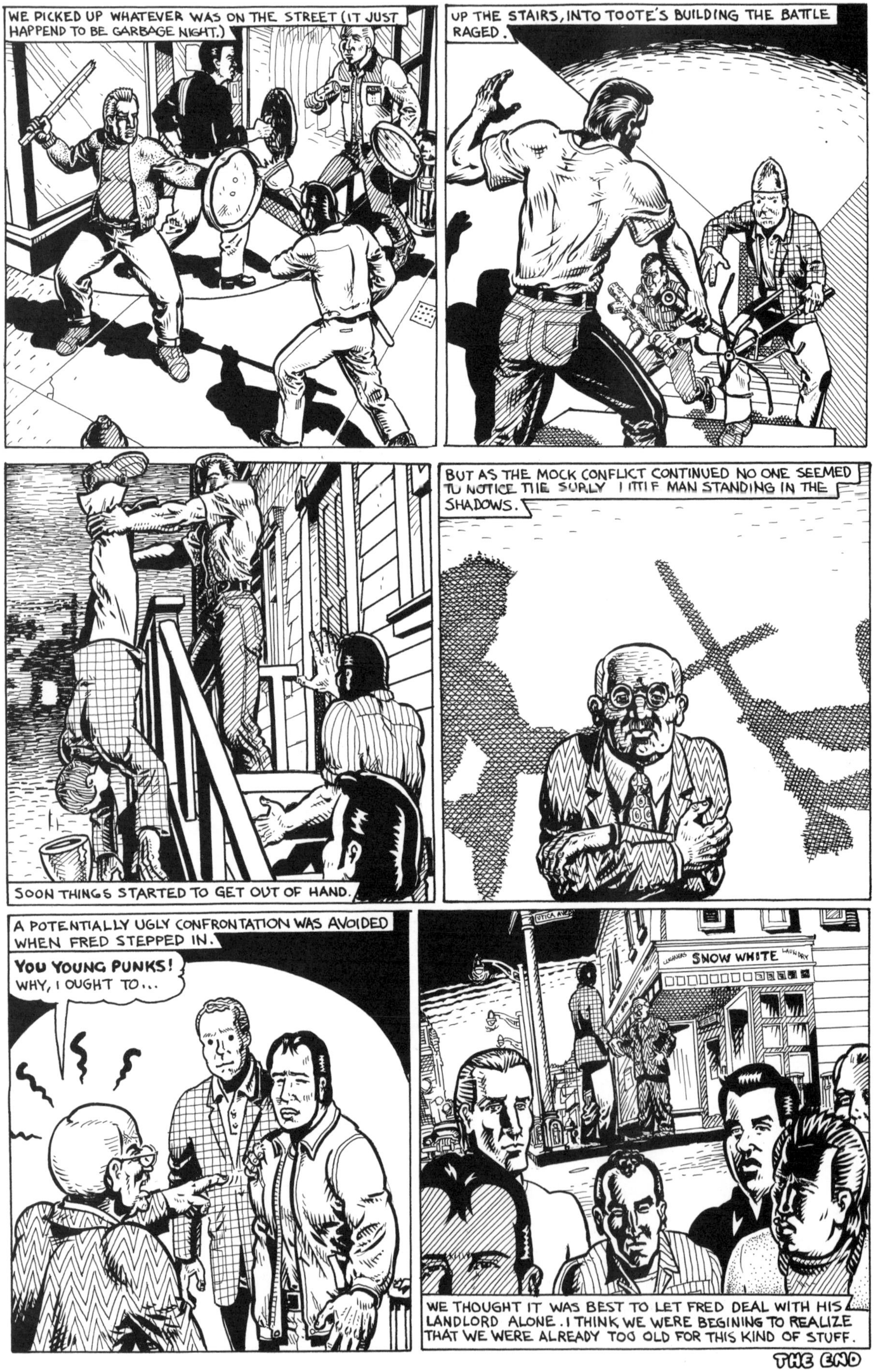
WE PICKED UP WHATEVER WAS ON THE STREET (IT JUST HAPPEND TO BE GARBAGE NIGHT.)
UP THE STAIRS, INTO TOOTE'S BUILDING THE BATTLE RAGED.
SOON THINGS STARTED TO GET OUT OF HAND.
BUT AS THE MOCK CONFLICT CONTINUED NO ONE SEEMED TO NOTICE THE SURLY LITTLE MAN STANDING IN THE SHADOWS.
A POTENTIALLY UGLY CONFRONTATION WAS AVOIDED WHEN FRED STEPPED IN.
YOU YOUNG PUNKS! WHY, I OUGHT TO...
UTICA AVE
SNOW WHITE
WE THOUGHT IT WAS BEST TO LET FRED DEAL WITH HIS LANDLORD ALONE. I THINK WE WERE BEGINING TO REALIZE THAT WE WERE ALREADY TOO OLD FOR THIS KIND OF STUFF.
THE END

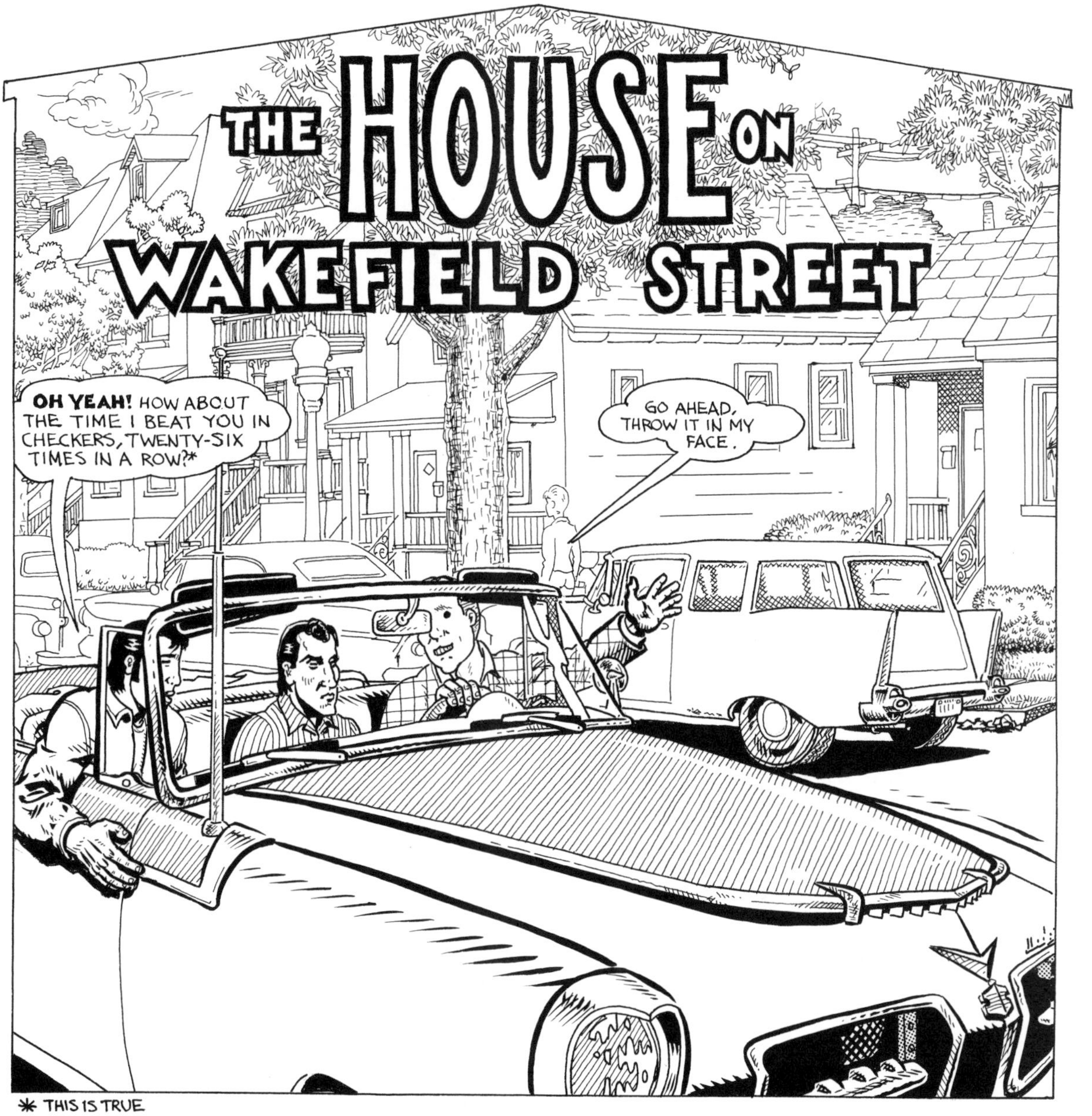
THE HOUSE ON WAKEFIELD STREET
OH YEAH! HOW ABOUT THE TIME I BEAT YOU IN CHECKERS, TWENTY-SIX TIMES IN A ROW?*
GO AHEAD, THROW IT IN MY FACE.

* THIS IS TRUE

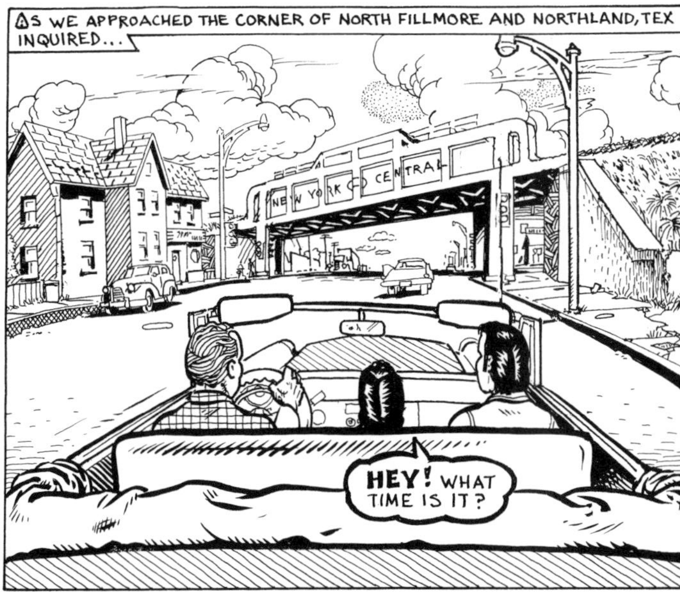
AS WE APPROACHED THE CORNER OF NORTH FILLMORE AND NORTHLAND, TEX INQUIRED...
NEW YORK CENTRAL
HEY! WHAT TIME IS IT?

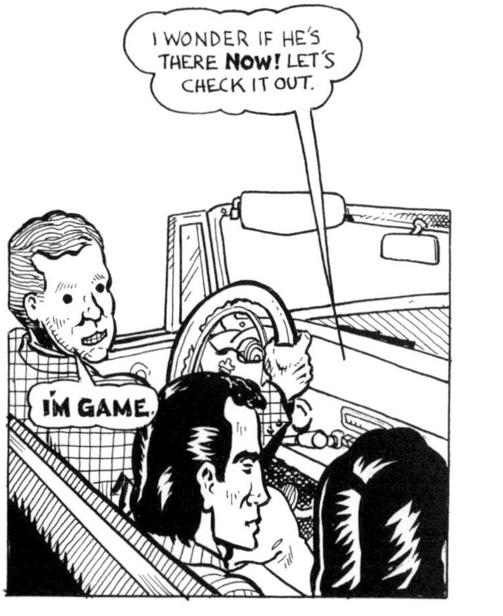
I WONDER IF HE'S THERE NOW! LET'S CHECK IT OUT.
I'M GAME.

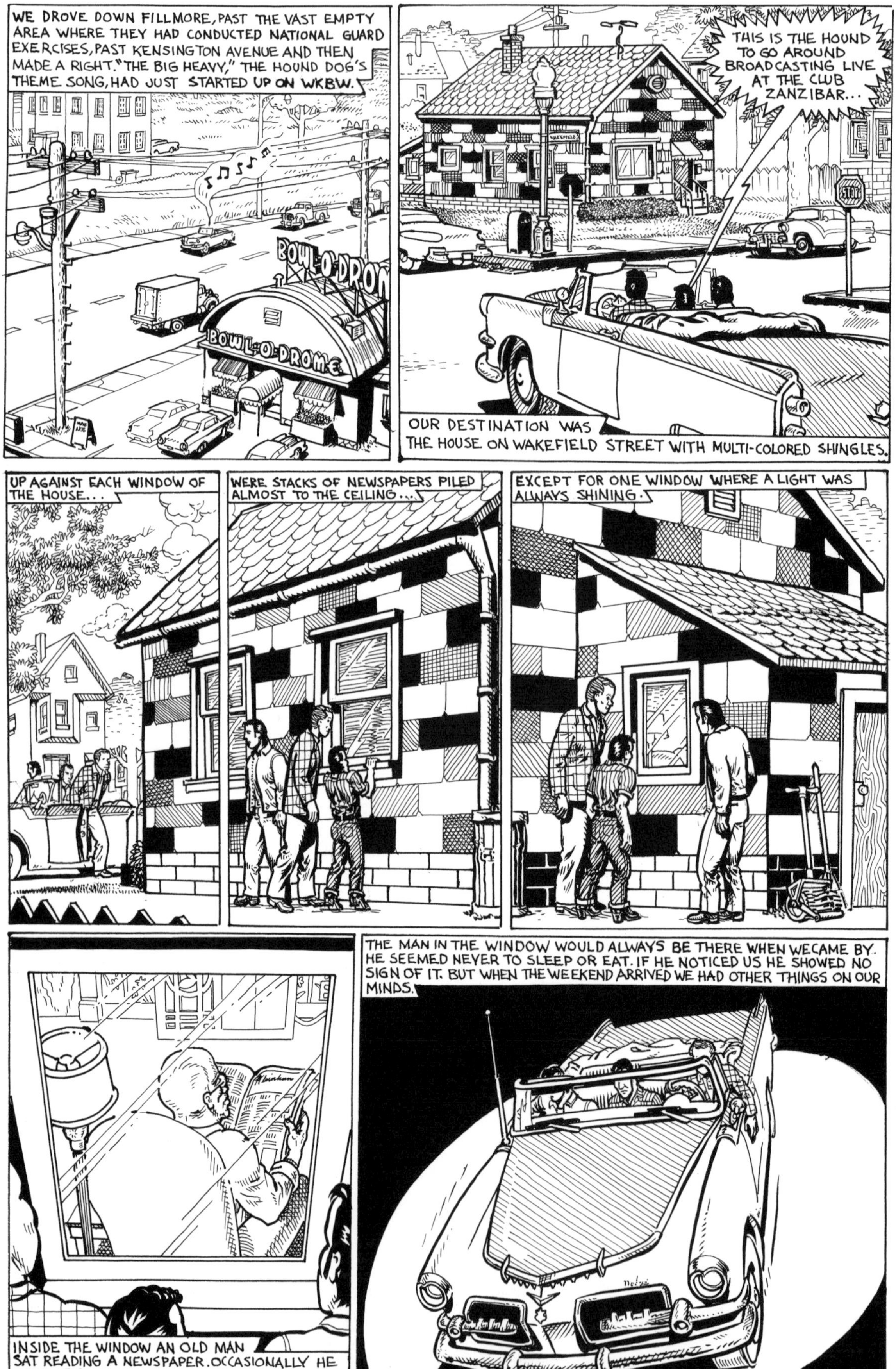

WE DROVE DOWN FILLMORE, PAST THE VAST EMPTY AREA WHERE THEY HAD CONDUCTED NATIONAL GUARD EXERCISES, PAST KENSINGTON AVENUE AND THEN MADE A RIGHT. "THE BIG HEAVY," THE HOUND DOG'S THEME SONG, HAD JUST STARTED UP ON WKBW.
BOWL-O-DROME
BOWL-O-DROME
THIS IS THE HOUND TO GO AROUND BROADCASTING LIVE AT THE CLUB ZANZIBAR...
STOP
OUR DESTINATION WAS THE HOUSE ON WAKEFIELD STREET WITH MULTI-COLORED SHINGLES.
UP AGAINST EACH WINDOW OF THE HOUSE...
WERE STACKS OF NEWSPAPERS PILED ALMOST TO THE CEILING...
EXCEPT FOR ONE WINDOW WHERE A LIGHT WAS ALWAYS SHINING.
INSIDE THE WINDOW AN OLD MAN SAT READING A NEWSPAPER. OCCASIONALLY HE WOULD TURN A PAGE, INDICATING HE WAS ALIVE.
THE MAN IN THE WINDOW WOULD ALWAYS BE THERE WHEN WE CAME BY. HE SEEMED NEVER TO SLEEP OR EAT. IF HE NOTICED US HE SHOWED NO SIGN OF IT. BUT WHEN THE WEEKEND ARRIVED WE HAD OTHER THINGS ON OUR MINDS.

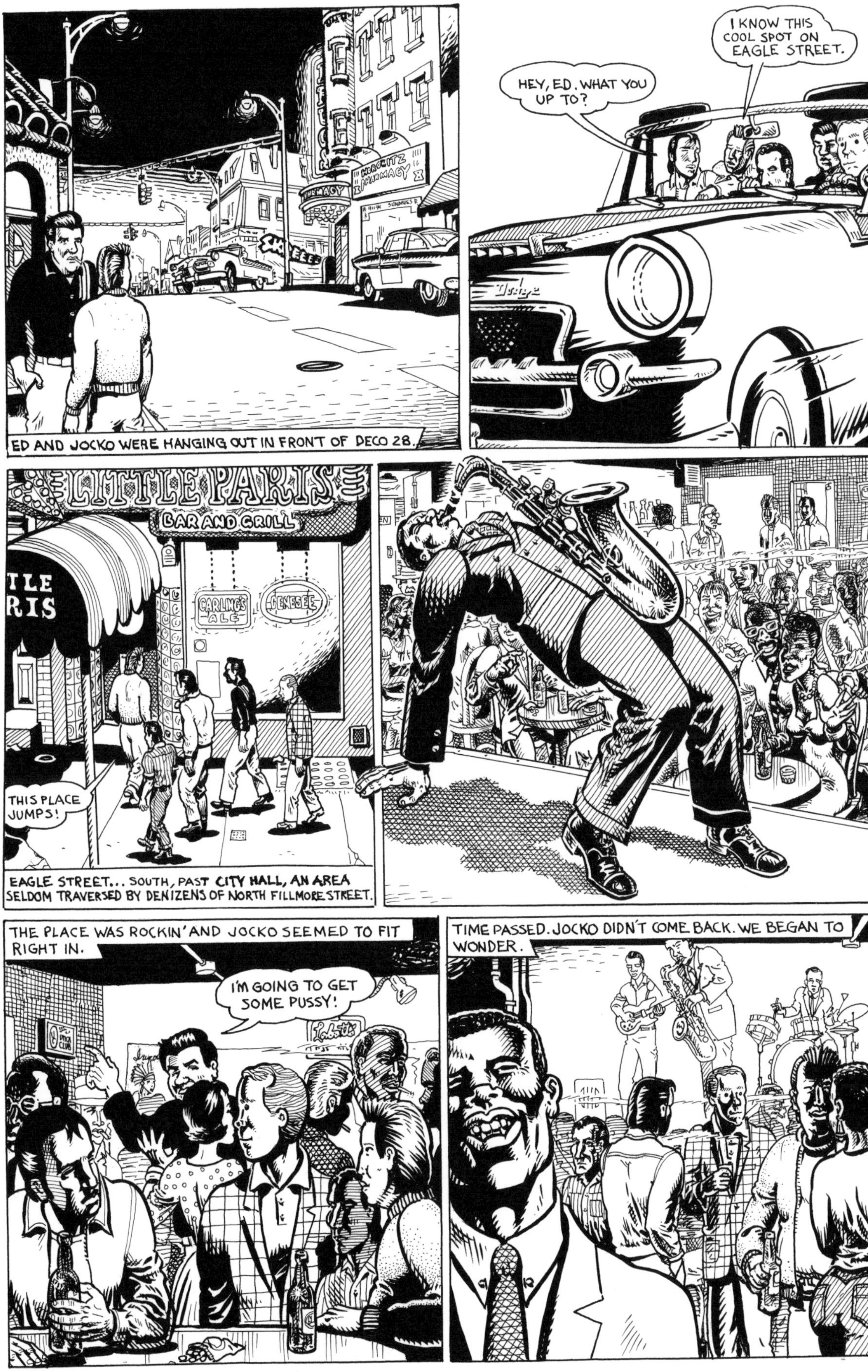
ED AND JOCKO WERE HANGING OUT IN FRONT OF DECO 28.
HEY, ED. WHAT YOU UP TO?
I KNOW THIS COOL SPOT ON EAGLE STREET.
LITTLE PARIS
BAR AND GRILL
CARLING'S ALE
GENESEE
THIS PLACE JUMPS!
EAGLE STREET... SOUTH, PAST CITY HALL, AN AREA SELDOM TRAVERSED BY DENIZENS OF NORTH FILLMORE STREET.
THE PLACE WAS ROCKIN' AND JOCKO SEEMED TO FIT RIGHT IN.
I'M GOING TO GET SOME PUSSY!
TIME PASSED. JOCKO DIDN'T COME BACK. WE BEGAN TO WONDER.

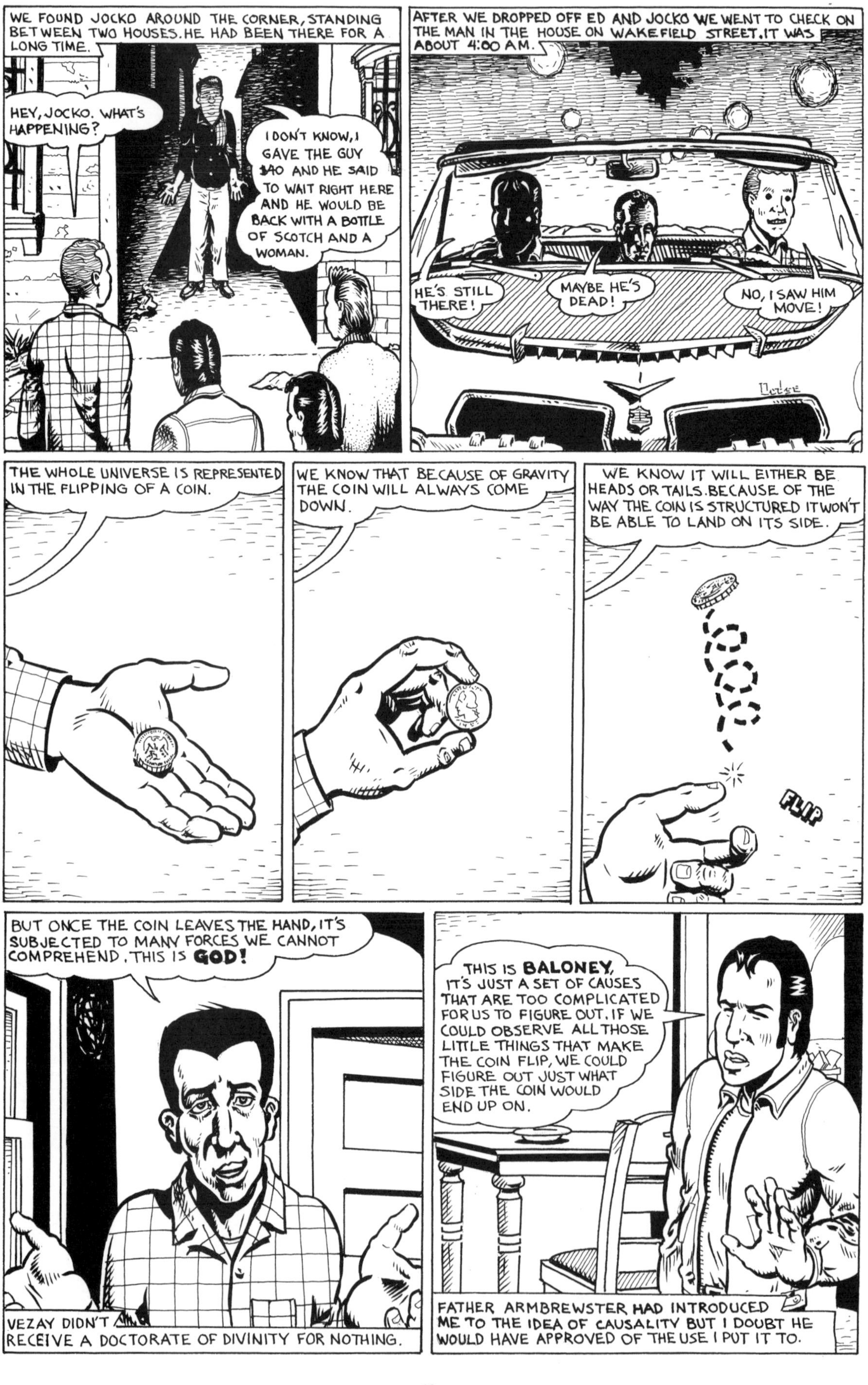
WE FOUND JOCKO AROUND THE CORNER, STANDING BETWEEN TWO HOUSES. HE HAD BEEN THERE FOR A LONG TIME.
HEY, JOCKO. WHAT'S HAPPENING?
I DON'T KNOW, I GAVE THE GUY $40 AND HE SAID TO WAIT RIGHT HERE AND HE WOULD BE BACK WITH A BOTTLE OF SCOTCH AND A WOMAN.
AFTER WE DROPPED OFF ED AND JOCKO WE WENT TO CHECK ON THE MAN IN THE HOUSE ON WAKEFIELD STREET. IT WAS ABOUT 4:00 AM.
HE'S STILL THERE!
MAYBE HE'S DEAD!
NO, I SAW HIM MOVE!
THE WHOLE UNIVERSE IS REPRESENTED IN THE FLIPPING OF A COIN.
WE KNOW THAT BECAUSE OF GRAVITY THE COIN WILL ALWAYS COME DOWN.
WE KNOW IT WILL EITHER BE HEADS OR TAILS. BECAUSE OF THE WAY THE COIN IS STRUCTURED IT WON'T BE ABLE TO LAND ON ITS SIDE.
FLIP
BUT ONCE THE COIN LEAVES THE HAND, IT'S SUBJECTED TO MANY FORCES WE CANNOT COMPREHEND. THIS IS GOD!
VEZAY DIDN'T RECEIVE A DOCTORATE OF DIVINITY FOR NOTHING.
THIS IS BALONEY, IT'S JUST A SET OF CAUSES THAT ARE TOO COMPLICATED FOR US TO FIGURE OUT. IF WE COULD OBSERVE ALL THOSE LITTLE THINGS THAT MAKE THE COIN FLIP, WE COULD FIGURE OUT JUST WHAT SIDE THE COIN WOULD END UP ON.
FATHER ARMBREWSTER HAD INTRODUCED ME TO THE IDEA OF CAUSALITY BUT I DOUBT HE WOULD HAVE APPROVED OF THE USE I PUT IT TO.

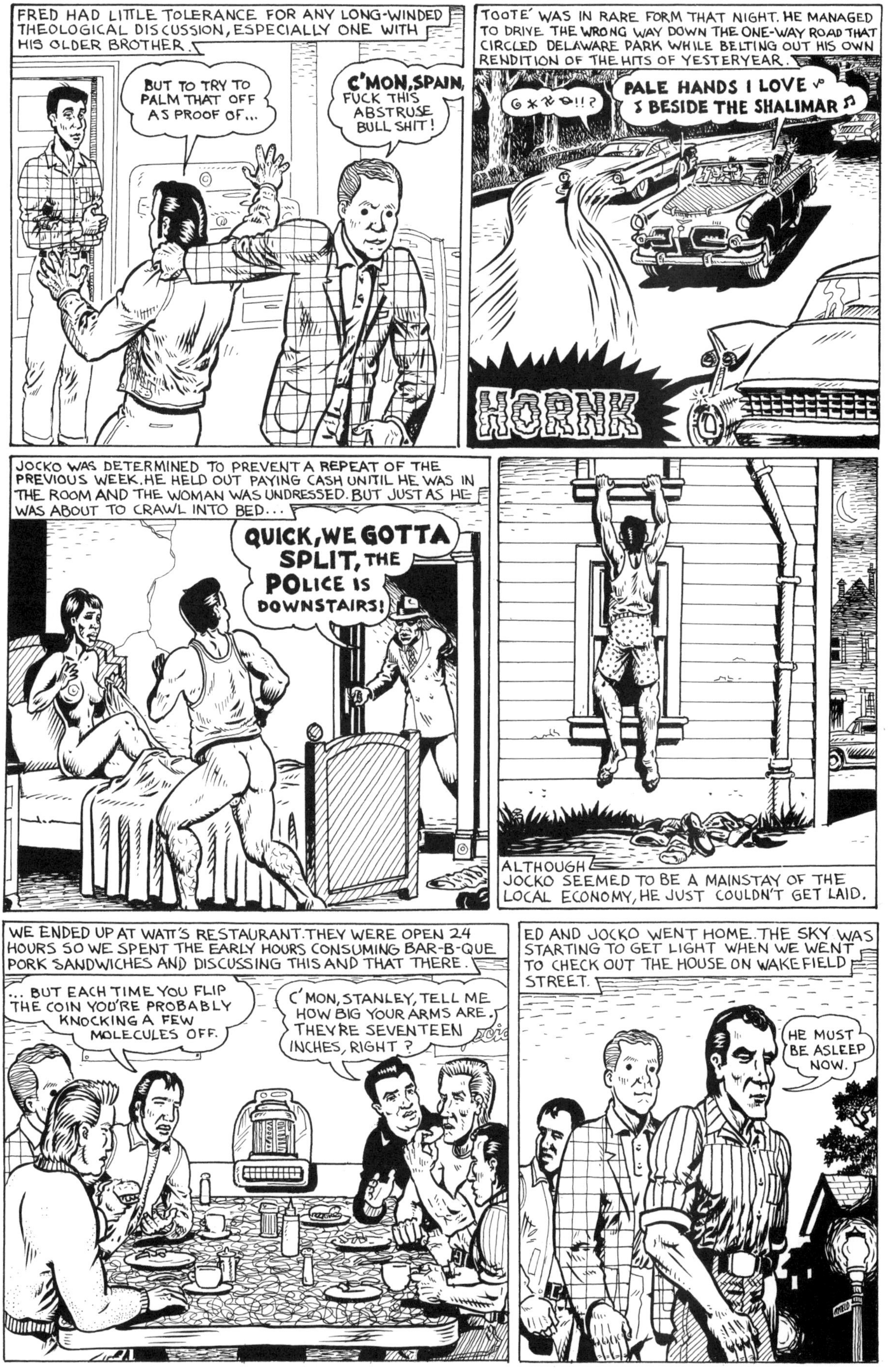
FRED HAD LITTLE TOLERANCE FOR ANY LONG-WINDED THEOLOGICAL DISCUSSION, ESPECIALLY ONE WITH HIS OLDER BROTHER.
BUT TO TRY TO PALM THAT OFF AS PROOF OF...
C'MON, SPAIN, FUCK THIS ABSTRUSE BULL SHIT!
TOOTE' WAS IN RARE FORM THAT NIGHT. HE MANAGED TO DRIVE THE WRONG WAY DOWN THE ONE-WAY ROAD THAT CIRCLED DELAWARE PARK WHILE BELTING OUT HIS OWN RENDITION OF THE HITS OF YESTERYEAR.
PALE HANDS I LOVE BESIDE THE SHALIMAR
HORNK
JOCKO WAS DETERMINED TO PREVENT A REPEAT OF THE PREVIOUS WEEK. HE HELD OUT PAYING CASH UNTIL HE WAS IN THE ROOM AND THE WOMAN WAS UNDRESSED. BUT JUST AS HE WAS ABOUT TO CRAWL INTO BED...
QUICK, WE GOTTA SPLIT, THE POLICE IS DOWNSTAIRS!
ALTHOUGH JOCKO SEEMED TO BE A MAINSTAY OF THE LOCAL ECONOMY, HE JUST COULDN'T GET LAID.
WE ENDED UP AT WATT'S RESTAURANT. THEY WERE OPEN 24 HOURS SO WE SPENT THE EARLY HOURS CONSUMING BAR-B-QUE PORK SANDWICHES AND DISCUSSING THIS AND THAT THERE.
... BUT EACH TIME YOU FLIP THE COIN YOU'RE PROBABLY KNOCKING A FEW MOLECULES OFF.
C'MON, STANLEY, TELL ME HOW BIG YOUR ARMS ARE. THEY'RE SEVENTEEN INCHES, RIGHT?
ED AND JOCKO WENT HOME. THE SKY WAS STARTING TO GET LIGHT WHEN WE WENT TO CHECK OUT THE HOUSE ON WAKEFIELD STREET.
HE MUST BE ASLEEP NOW.

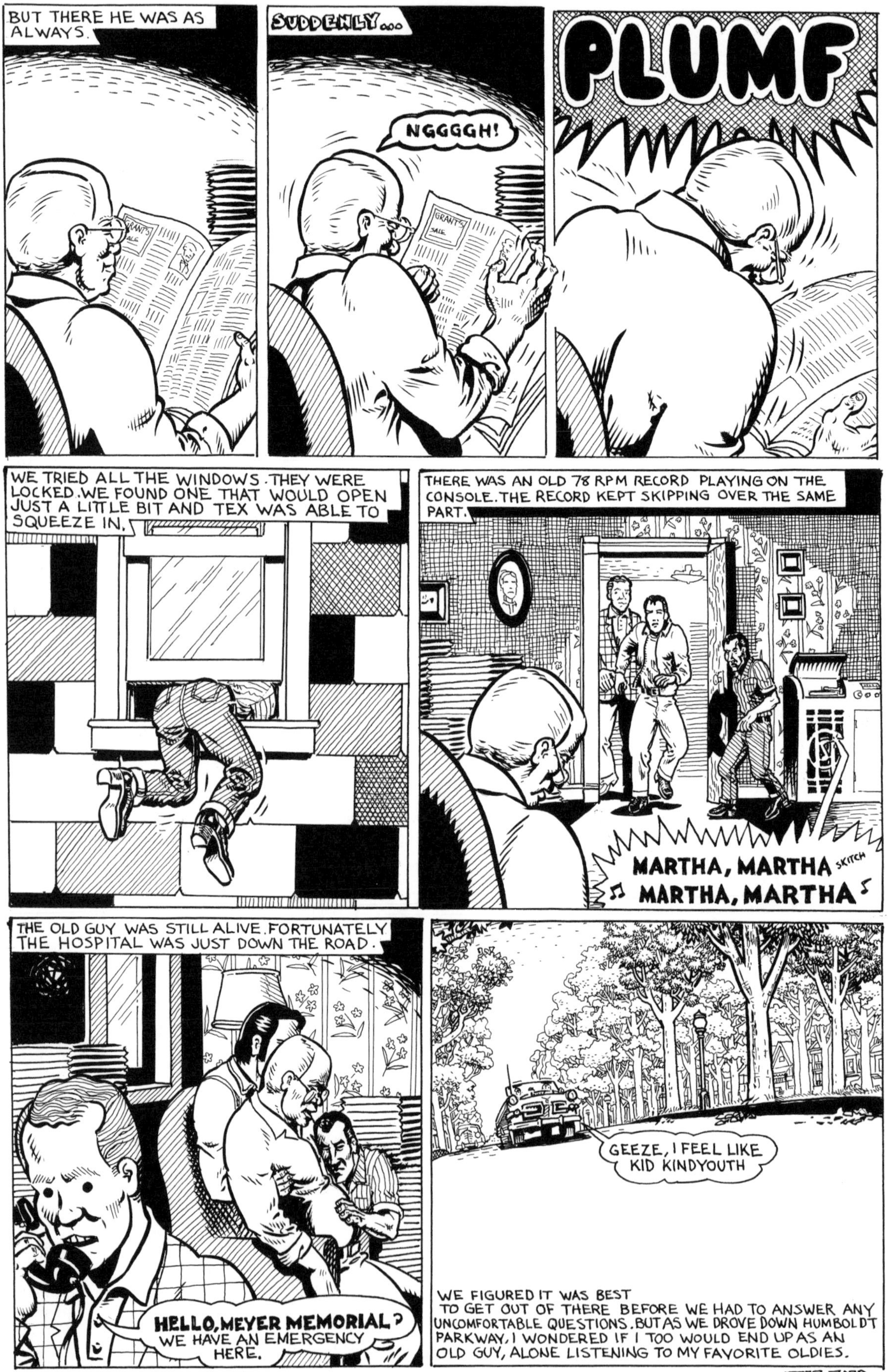
BUT THERE HE WAS AS ALWAYS.
SUDDENLY...
NGGGGH!
PLUMF
WE TRIED ALL THE WINDOWS. THEY WERE LOCKED. WE FOUND ONE THAT WOULD OPEN JUST A LITTLE BIT AND TEX WAS ABLE TO SQUEEZE IN.
THERE WAS AN OLD 78 RPM RECORD PLAYING ON THE CONSOLE. THE RECORD KEPT SKIPPING OVER THE SAME PART.
MARTHA, MARTHA
SKITCH
MARTHA, MARTHA
THE OLD GUY WAS STILL ALIVE. FORTUNATELY THE HOSPITAL WAS JUST DOWN THE ROAD.
HELLO, MEYER MEMORIAL? WE HAVE AN EMERGENCY HERE.
GEEZE, I FEEL LIKE KID KINDYOUTH
WE FIGURED IT WAS BEST TO GET OUT OF THERE BEFORE WE HAD TO ANSWER ANY UNCOMFORTABLE QUESTIONS. BUT AS WE DROVE DOWN HUMBOLDT PARKWAY, I WONDERED IF I TOO WOULD END UP AS AN OLD GUY, ALONE LISTENING TO MY FAVORITE OLDIES.

THE END

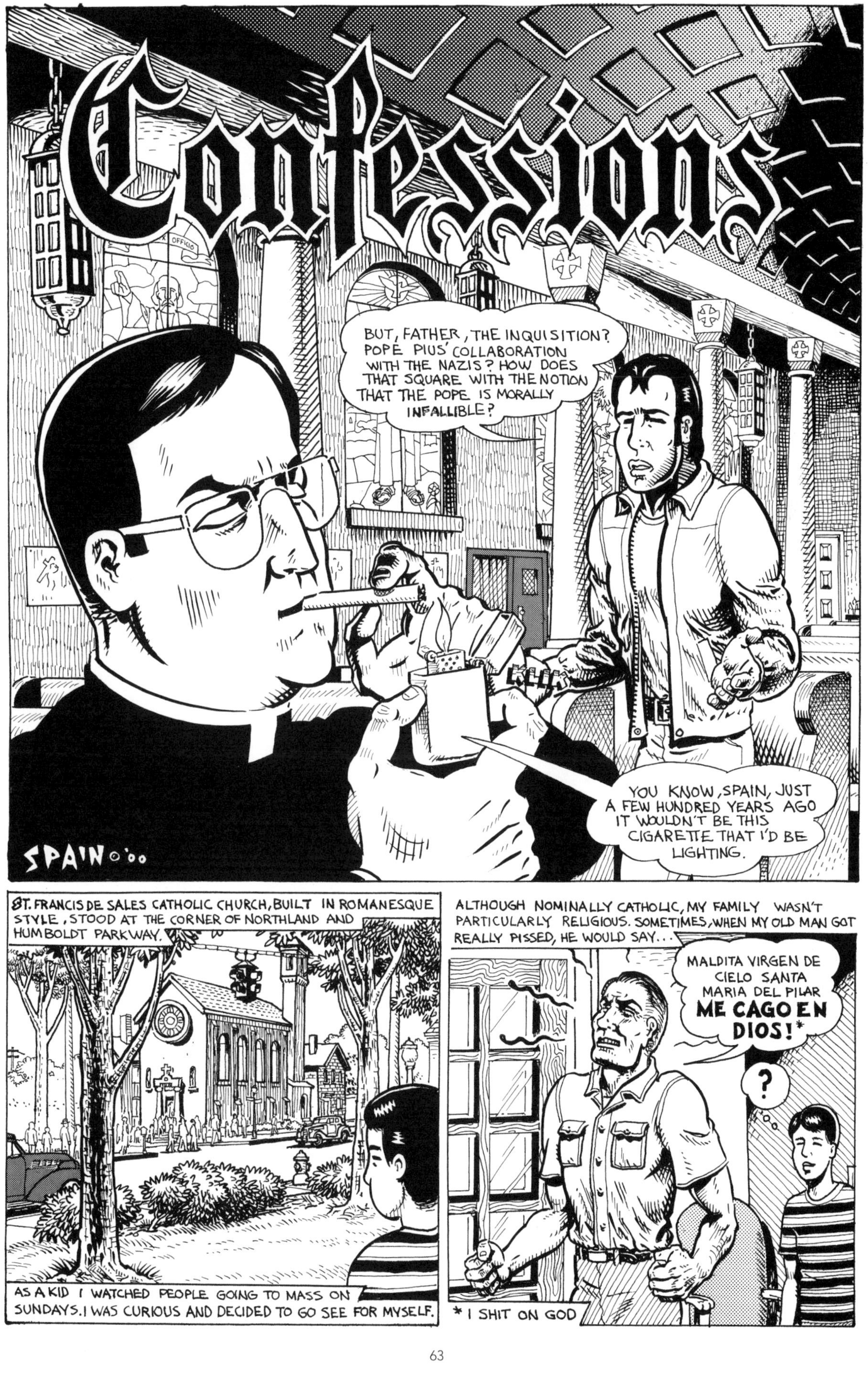
Confessions
BUT, FATHER, THE INQUISITION? POPE PIUS' COLLABORATION WITH THE NAZIS? HOW DOES THAT SQUARE WITH THE NOTION THAT THE POPE IS MORALLY INFALLIBLE?
KLIK
SPAIN ©'00
YOU KNOW, SPAIN, JUST A FEW HUNDRED YEARS AGO IT WOULDN'T BE THIS CIGARETTE THAT I'D BE LIGHTING.
ST. FRANCIS DE SALES CATHOLIC CHURCH, BUILT IN ROMANESQUE STYLE, STOOD AT THE CORNER OF NORTHLAND AND HUMBOLDT PARKWAY.
AS A KID I WATCHED PEOPLE GOING TO MASS ON SUNDAYS. I WAS CURIOUS AND DECIDED TO GO SEE FOR MYSELF.
ALTHOUGH NOMINALLY CATHOLIC, MY FAMILY WASN'T PARTICULARLY RELIGIOUS. SOMETIMES, WHEN MY OLD MAN GOT REALLY PISSED, HE WOULD SAY...
MALDITA VIRGEN DE CIELO SANTA MARIA DEL PILAR ME CAGO EN DIOS!*
?
* I SHIT ON GOD

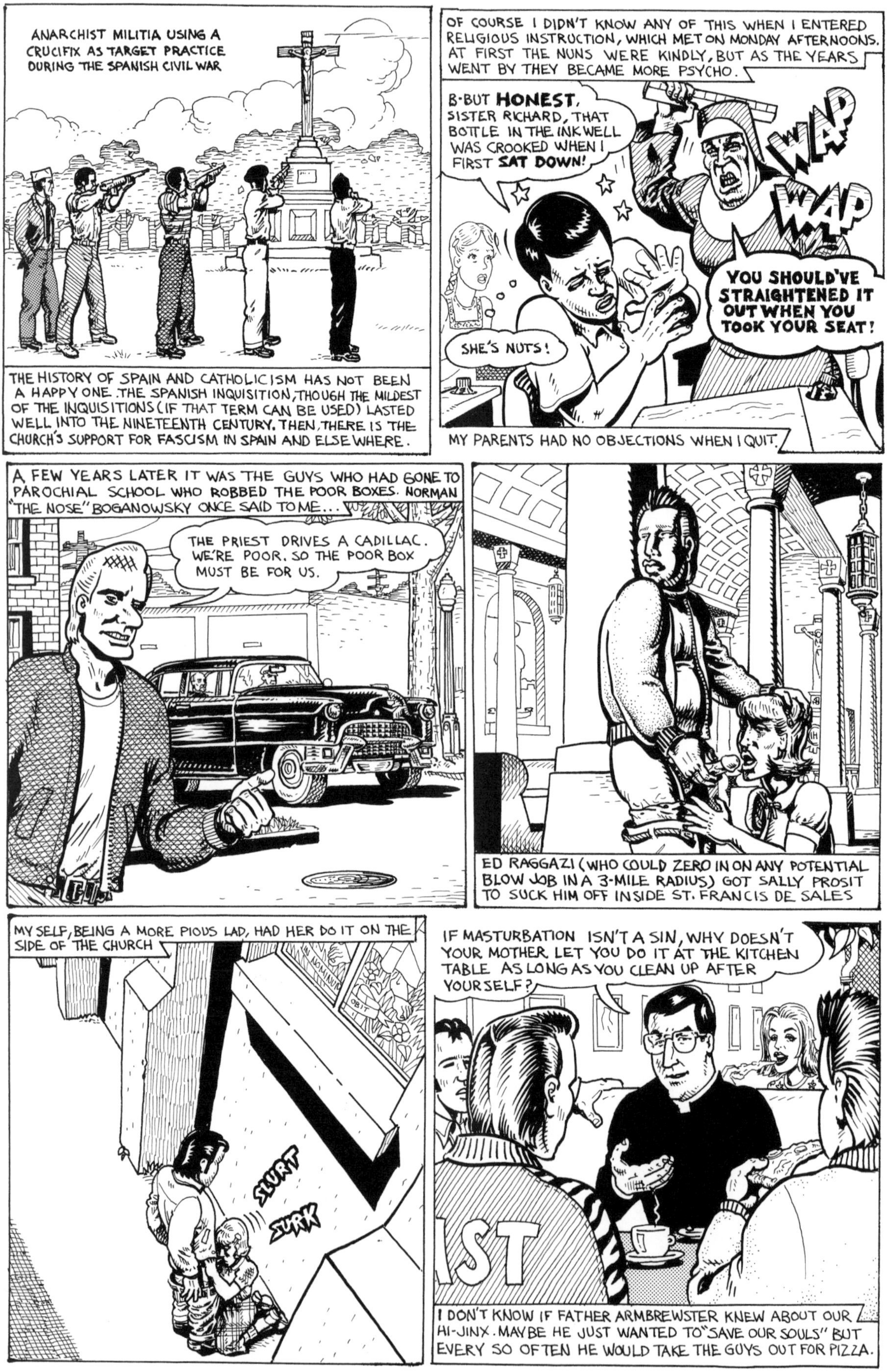
ANARCHIST MILITIA USING A CRUCIFIX AS TARGET PRACTICE DURING THE SPANISH CIVIL WAR
THE HISTORY OF SPAIN AND CATHOLICISM HAS NOT BEEN A HAPPY ONE. THE SPANISH INQUISITION, THOUGH THE MILDEST OF THE INQUISITIONS (IF THAT TERM CAN BE USED) LASTED WELL INTO THE NINETEENTH CENTURY. THEN, THERE IS THE CHURCH'S SUPPORT FOR FASCISM IN SPAIN AND ELSEWHERE.
OF COURSE I DIDN'T KNOW ANY OF THIS WHEN I ENTERED RELIGIOUS INSTRUCTION, WHICH MET ON MONDAY AFTERNOONS. AT FIRST THE NUNS WERE KINDLY, BUT AS THE YEARS WENT BY THEY BECAME MORE PSYCHO.
B-BUT **HONEST**, SISTER RICHARD, THAT BOTTLE IN THE INKWELL WAS CROOKED WHEN I FIRST **SAT DOWN**!
WAP
WAP
YOU SHOULD'VE STRAIGHTENED IT OUT WHEN YOU TOOK YOUR SEAT!
SHE'S NUTS!
MY PARENTS HAD NO OBJECTIONS WHEN I QUIT.
A FEW YEARS LATER IT WAS THE GUYS WHO HAD GONE TO PAROCHIAL SCHOOL WHO ROBBED THE POOR BOXES. NORMAN "THE NOSE" BOGANOWSKY ONCE SAID TO ME...
THE PRIEST DRIVES A CADILLAC. WE'RE POOR. SO THE POOR BOX MUST BE FOR US.
ED RAGGAZI (WHO COULD ZERO IN ON ANY POTENTIAL BLOW JOB IN A 3-MILE RADIUS) GOT SALLY PROSIT TO SUCK HIM OFF INSIDE ST. FRANCIS DE SALES
MYSELF, BEING A MORE PIOUS LAD, HAD HER DO IT ON THE SIDE OF THE CHURCH
IN NOMINUM
OBIT
SLURT
SURK
IF MASTURBATION ISN'T A SIN, WHY DOESN'T YOUR MOTHER LET YOU DO IT AT THE KITCHEN TABLE AS LONG AS YOU CLEAN UP AFTER YOURSELF?
ST
I DON'T KNOW IF FATHER ARMBREWSTER KNEW ABOUT OUR HI-JINX. MAYBE HE JUST WANTED TO "SAVE OUR SOULS" BUT EVERY SO OFTEN HE WOULD TAKE THE GUYS OUT FOR PIZZA.

BUT FATHER ARMBREWSTER'S BEST EFFORTS HAD LITTLE EFFECT. THE ROURKE FAMILY WAS KNOWN FOR BOOSTING BIG-TICKET ITEMS FROM SEARS.

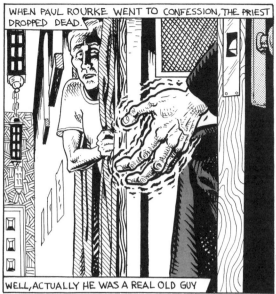

WHEN PAUL ROURKE WENT TO CONFESSION, THE PRIEST DROPPED DEAD.

WELL, ACTUALLY HE WAS A REAL OLD GUY

FATHER ARMBREWSTER WAS A GOOD MAN AND HE TRIED VALIANTLY TO ANSWER MY GROWING SCEPTICISM ABOUT CATHOLICISM.

MAYBE CHRIST WAS JUST SOME **GUY** WHO WAS REALLY CONCERNED ABOUT HUMAN SUFFERING.

IF THAT WERE THE CASE, CHRIST WOULD HAVE BEEN JUST PLAIN CRAZY.* BESIDES, JUST WHAT DO YOU BASE YOUR OPINION ON? REMEMBER...

ONE THING HE SAID REALLY GOT ME THINKING. IT REFUTED ALL RELIGIOUS MYTHOLOGY.

...WHAT IS FREELY ASSERTED CAN BE FREELY DENIED.

HMMMM!

IT'S NOT THAT EVERY DISCUSSION IN THE OLD NEIGHBORHOOD WAS ALL THAT ELEVATED.

HERE COMES FRANK MUTINANI. I KNOW I GOT HIM THIS TIME.

FRANK MUTINANI WAS THE RESIDENT SPORTS SAVANT AND ED HAD BEEN TRYING TO STUMP HIM FOR YEARS.

OK., FRANK, WHO MADE THE WINNING HIT IN THE '48 WORLD SERIES?

IT WAS A GUY NAMED HOLMES WHO WON THE PENNANT FOR THE INDIANS.

* I NEVER QUITE UNDERSTOOD THIS ONE.

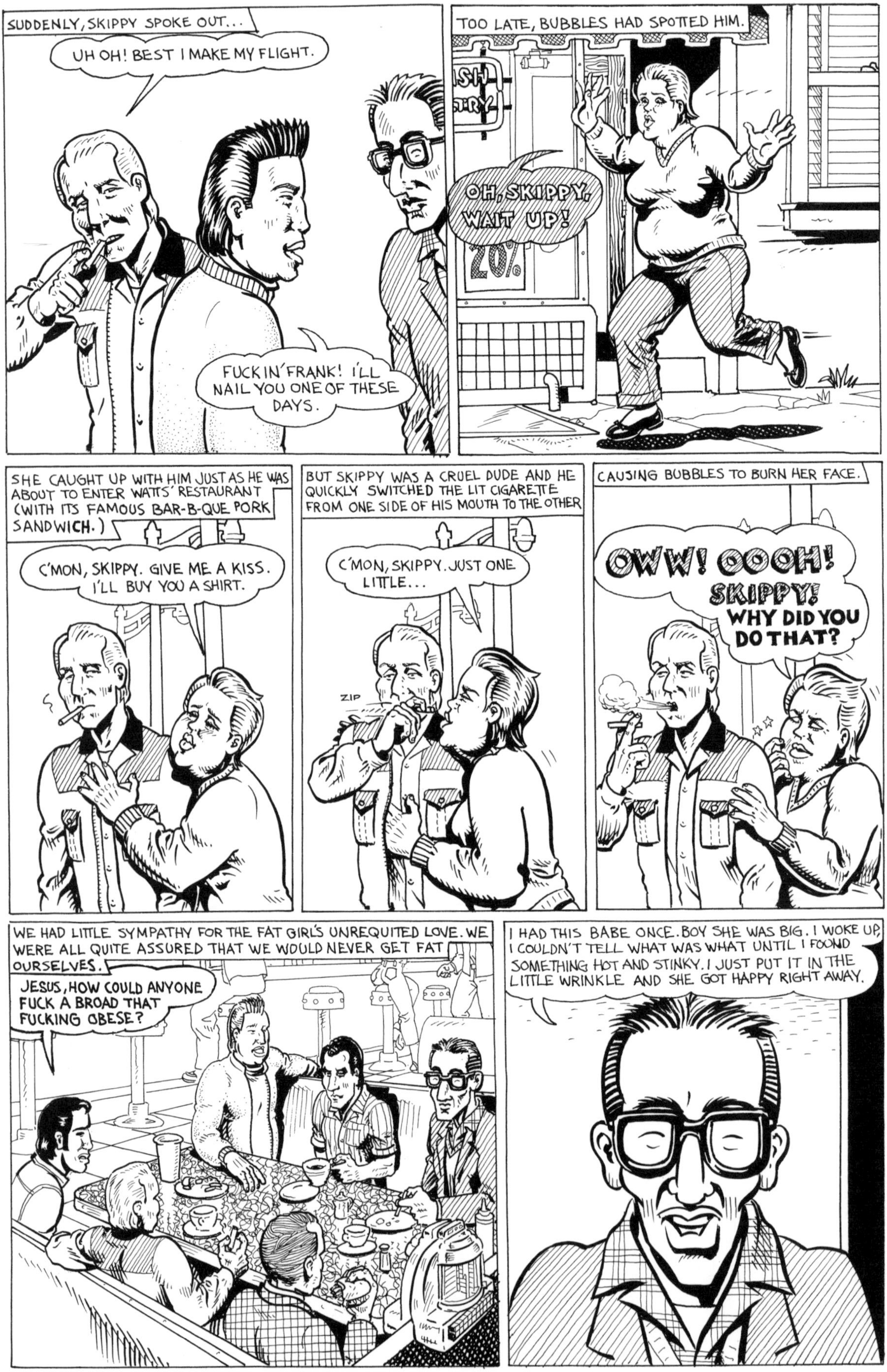
SUDDENLY, SKIPPY SPOKE OUT...
UH OH! BEST I MAKE MY FLIGHT.
FUCKIN' FRANK! I'LL NAIL YOU ONE OF THESE DAYS.
TOO LATE, BUBBLES HAD SPOTTED HIM.
OH, SKIPPY, WAIT UP!
20%
SHE CAUGHT UP WITH HIM JUST AS HE WAS ABOUT TO ENTER WATTS' RESTAURANT (WITH ITS FAMOUS BAR-B-QUE PORK SANDWICH.)
C'MON, SKIPPY. GIVE ME A KISS. I'LL BUY YOU A SHIRT.
BUT SKIPPY WAS A CRUEL DUDE AND HE QUICKLY SWITCHED THE LIT CIGARETTE FROM ONE SIDE OF HIS MOUTH TO THE OTHER
C'MON, SKIPPY. JUST ONE LITTLE...
ZIP
CAUSING BUBBLES TO BURN HER FACE.
OWW! OOOH! SKIPPY! WHY DID YOU DO THAT?
WE HAD LITTLE SYMPATHY FOR THE FAT GIRL'S UNREQUITED LOVE. WE WERE ALL QUITE ASSURED THAT WE WOULD NEVER GET FAT OURSELVES.
JESUS, HOW COULD ANYONE FUCK A BROAD THAT FUCKING OBESE?
I HAD THIS BABE ONCE. BOY SHE WAS BIG. I WOKE UP, I COULDN'T TELL WHAT WAS WHAT UNTIL I FOOND SOMETHING HOT AND STINKY. I JUST PUT IT IN THE LITTLE WRINKLE AND SHE GOT HAPPY RIGHT AWAY.

SOON THE CONVERSATION VEERED OFF INTO OTHER TOPICS, LIKE THE URINATION PROCESS OF WOMEN.

I'M TELLING YOU GUYS, BROADS PISS OUT OF THEIR ASS. THAT'S JUST THE WAY THEY'RE BUILT!

I, MYSELF, WASN'T QUITE SURE. BUT FRED WASN'T BUYING IT.

YOU BUNCH OF YOKELS. WOMEN PEE THROUGH A TUBE IN THEIR PUSSY.

BOX ST.

I GOTTA ADMIT, ED CRACKED ME UP WITH THAT STORY ABOUT WHEN HE WAS A KID, SEEING THE WOMAN PISSING IN THE PARK AND HIS MOM TELLS HIM, "EDWARD, TURN YOUR HEAD."

WE ALL WENT UP TO FRED'S PLACE (HE HAD TO GET SOME BREAD OR SOMETHING). HE WENT INTO ANOTHER ROOM AND AFTER A FEW MINUTES CALLED US IN.

AY, GUYS!

DAH ♪ DAAH

IT'S FAKE. VEZAY FORGOT TO LOCK HIS TRUNK.

FRED'S BROTHER VEZAY HAD A DOCTORATE OF DIVINITY AND A TRUNK FULL OF GOODIES LIKE A REALISTICALLY COLORED 15-INCH DILDO

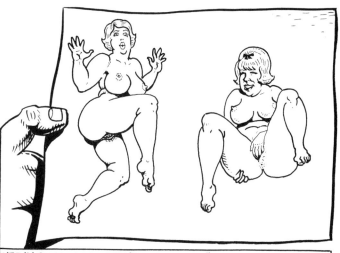

VEZAY, SOMETIMES REFERRED TO BY FRED AS "THE DALAI LAMA OF NORTH FILLMORE," ALSO DID BEAUTIFULLY RENDERED DRAWINGS OF FAT WOMEN. BUBBLES HAD TRULY FOCUSED HER ATTENTION ON THE WRONG GUY.

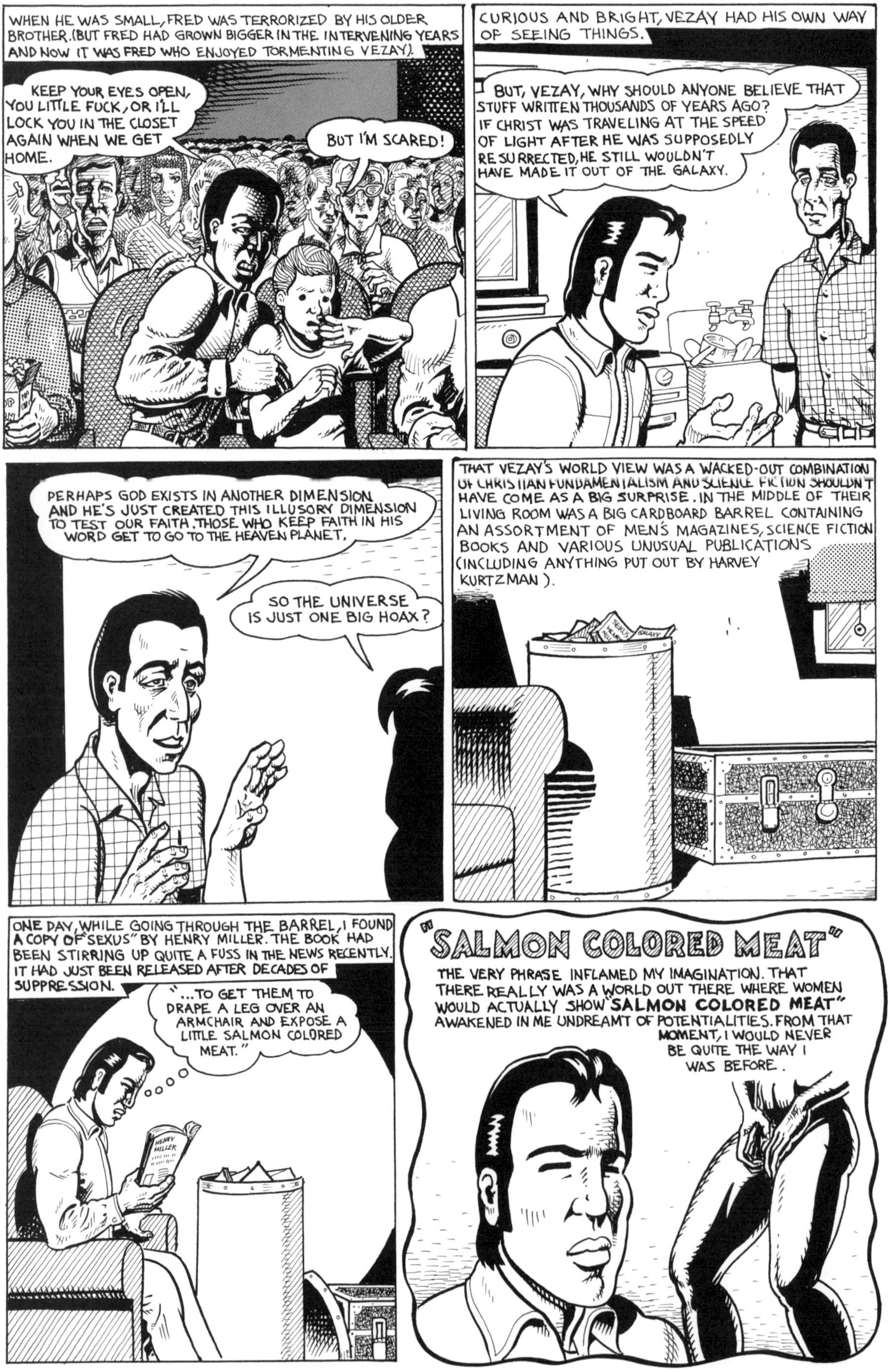
WHEN HE WAS SMALL, FRED WAS TERRORIZED BY HIS OLDER BROTHER. (BUT FRED HAD GROWN BIGGER IN THE INTERVENING YEARS AND NOW IT WAS FRED WHO ENJOYED TORMENTING VEZAY).
KEEP YOUR EYES OPEN, YOU LITTLE FUCK, OR I'LL LOCK YOU IN THE CLOSET AGAIN WHEN WE GET HOME.
BUT I'M SCARED!
CURIOUS AND BRIGHT, VEZAY HAD HIS OWN WAY OF SEEING THINGS.
BUT, VEZAY, WHY SHOULD ANYONE BELIEVE THAT STUFF WRITTEN THOUSANDS OF YEARS AGO? IF CHRIST WAS TRAVELING AT THE SPEED OF LIGHT AFTER HE WAS SUPPOSEDLY RESURRECTED, HE STILL WOULDN'T HAVE MADE IT OUT OF THE GALAXY.
PERHAPS GOD EXISTS IN ANOTHER DIMENSION AND HE'S JUST CREATED THIS ILLUSORY DIMENSION TO TEST OUR FAITH. THOSE WHO KEEP FAITH IN HIS WORD GET TO GO TO THE HEAVEN PLANET.
SO THE UNIVERSE IS JUST ONE BIG HOAX?
THAT VEZAY'S WORLD VIEW WAS A WACKED-OUT COMBINATION OF CHRISTIAN FUNDAMENTALISM AND SCIENCE FICTION SHOULDN'T HAVE COME AS A BIG SURPRISE. IN THE MIDDLE OF THEIR LIVING ROOM WAS A BIG CARDBOARD BARREL CONTAINING AN ASSORTMENT OF MEN'S MAGAZINES, SCIENCE FICTION BOOKS AND VARIOUS UNUSUAL PUBLICATIONS (INCLUDING ANYTHING PUT OUT BY HARVEY KURTZMAN).
SEXUS
GALAXY
ONE DAY, WHILE GOING THROUGH THE BARREL, I FOUND A COPY OF "SEXUS" BY HENRY MILLER. THE BOOK HAD BEEN STIRRING UP QUITE A FUSS IN THE NEWS RECENTLY. IT HAD JUST BEEN RELEASED AFTER DECADES OF SUPPRESSION.
"...TO GET THEM TO DRAPE A LEG OVER AN ARMCHAIR AND EXPOSE A LITTLE SALMON COLORED MEAT."
HENRY MILLER
"SALMON COLORED MEAT"
THE VERY PHRASE INFLAMED MY IMAGINATION. THAT THERE REALLY WAS A WORLD OUT THERE WHERE WOMEN WOULD ACTUALLY SHOW "SALMON COLORED MEAT" AWAKENED IN ME UNDREAMT OF POTENTIALITIES. FROM THAT MOMENT, I WOULD NEVER BE QUITE THE WAY I WAS BEFORE.

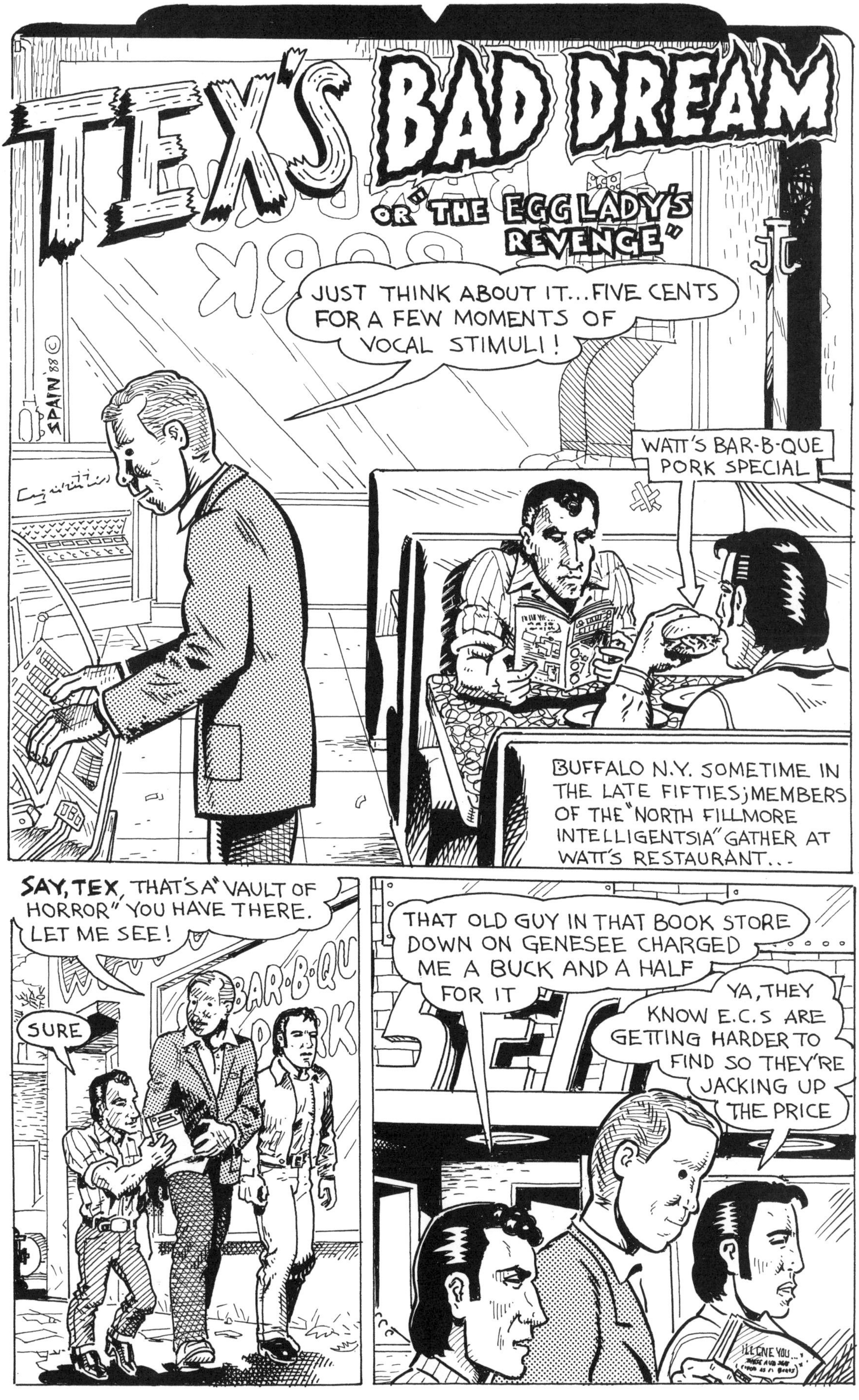
TEX'S BAD DREAM
OR "THE EGG LADY'S REVENGE"
SPAIN '88 ©
JUST THINK ABOUT IT... FIVE CENTS FOR A FEW MOMENTS OF VOCAL STIMULI!
WATT'S BAR-B-QUE PORK SPECIAL
BUFFALO N.Y. SOMETIME IN THE LATE FIFTIES; MEMBERS OF THE "NORTH FILLMORE INTELLIGENTSIA" GATHER AT WATT'S RESTAURANT...
SAY, TEX, THAT'S A "VAULT OF HORROR" YOU HAVE THERE. LET ME SEE!
SURE
THAT OLD GUY IN THAT BOOK STORE DOWN ON GENESEE CHARGED ME A BUCK AND A HALF FOR IT
YA, THEY KNOW E.C.S ARE GETTING HARDER TO FIND SO THEY'RE JACKING UP THE PRICE

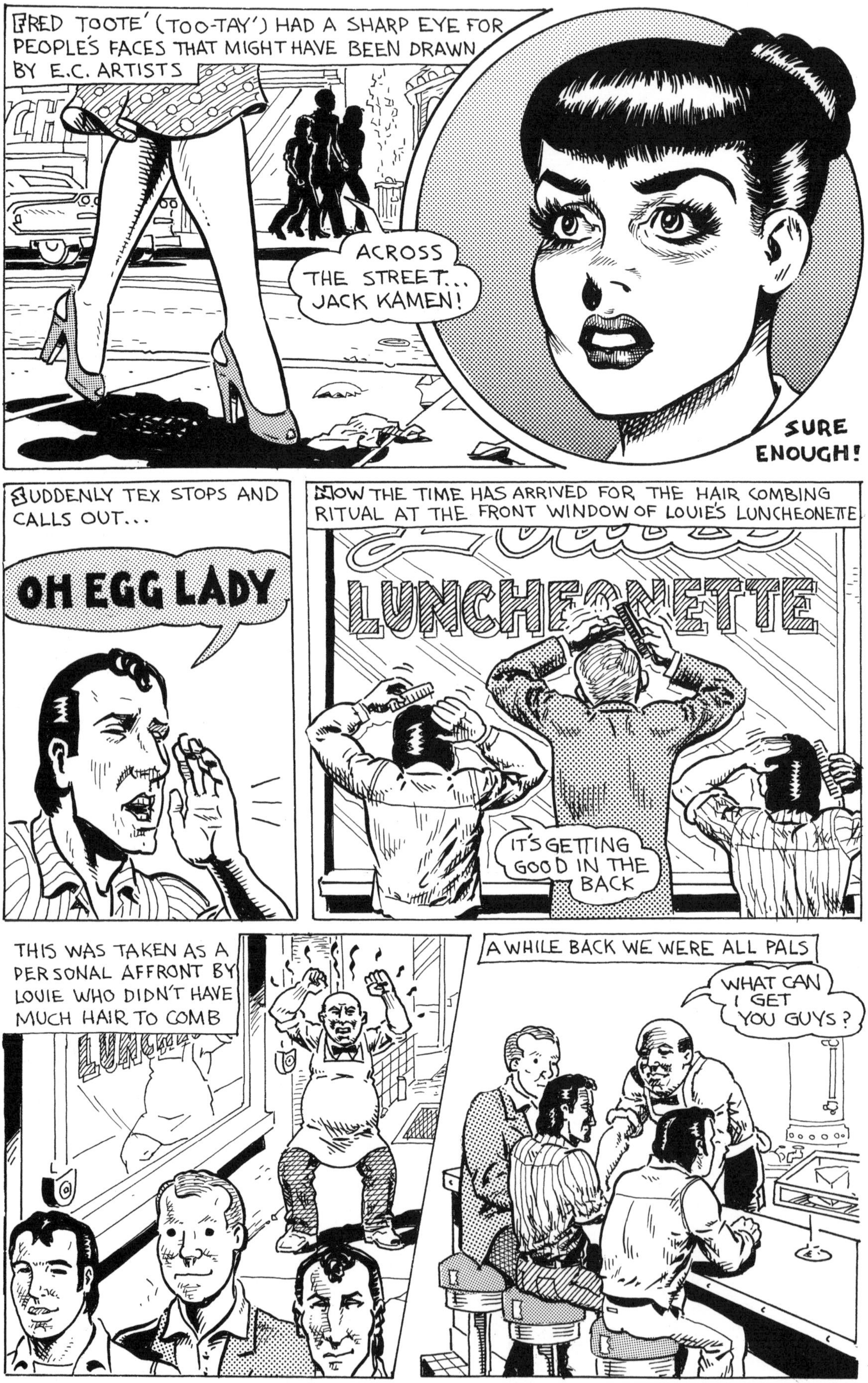
FRED TOOTE' (TOO-TAY') HAD A SHARP EYE FOR PEOPLE'S FACES THAT MIGHT HAVE BEEN DRAWN BY E.C. ARTISTS
ACROSS THE STREET... JACK KAMEN!
SURE ENOUGH!
SUDDENLY TEX STOPS AND CALLS OUT...
OH EGG LADY
NOW THE TIME HAS ARRIVED FOR THE HAIR COMBING RITUAL AT THE FRONT WINDOW OF LOUIE'S LUNCHEONETTE
LUNCHEONETTE
IT'S GETTING GOOD IN THE BACK
THIS WAS TAKEN AS A PERSONAL AFFRONT BY LOUIE WHO DIDN'T HAVE MUCH HAIR TO COMB
A WHILE BACK WE WERE ALL PALS
WHAT CAN I GET YOU GUYS?

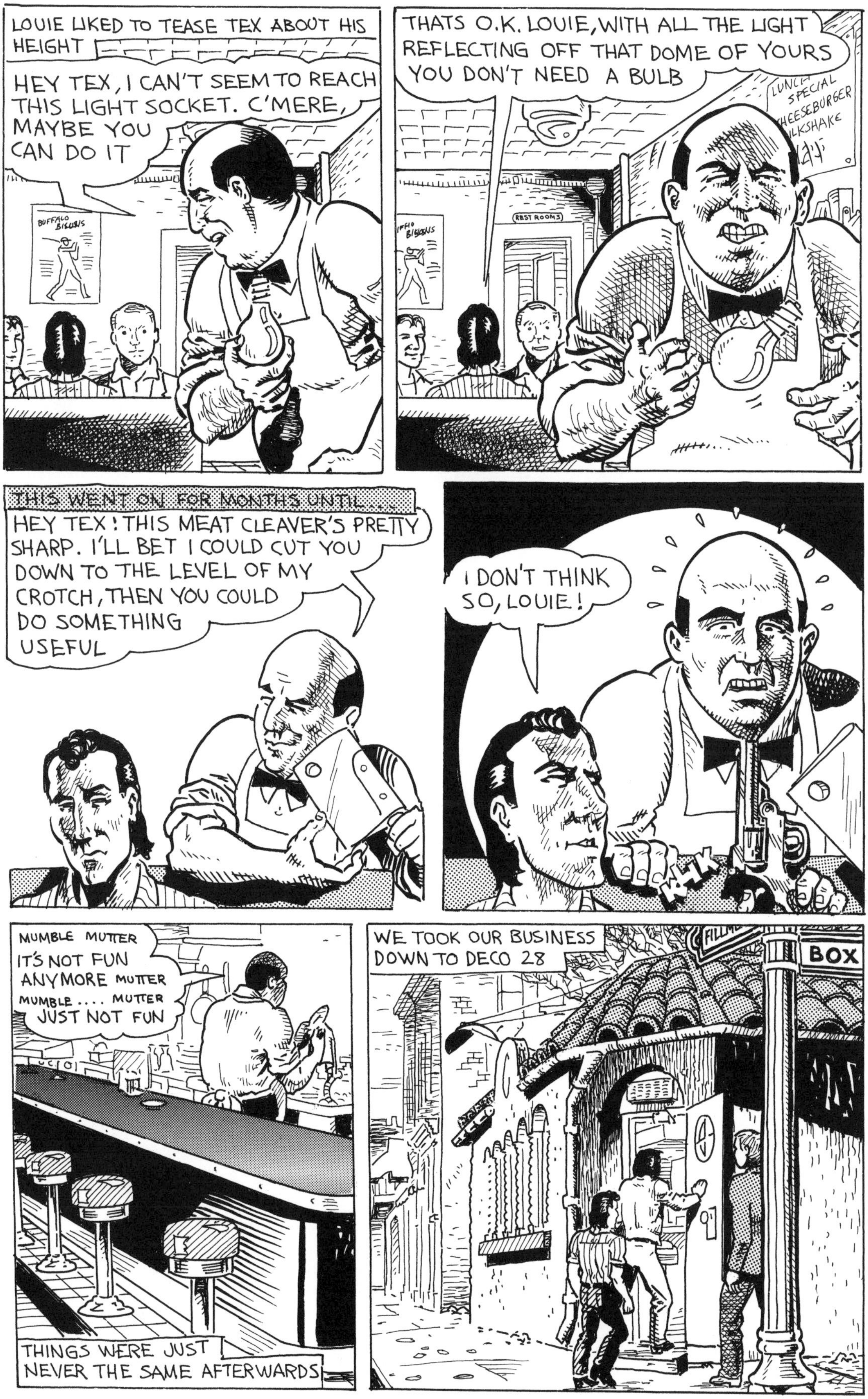
LOUIE LIKED TO TEASE TEX ABOUT HIS HEIGHT
HEY TEX, I CAN'T SEEM TO REACH THIS LIGHT SOCKET. C'MERE, MAYBE YOU CAN DO IT
BUFFALO BISONS
THATS O.K. LOUIE, WITH ALL THE LIGHT REFLECTING OFF THAT DOME OF YOURS YOU DON'T NEED A BULB
LUNCH SPECIAL CHEESEBURGER MILKSHAKE
REST ROOMS
THIS WENT ON FOR MONTHS UNTIL...
HEY TEX! THIS MEAT CLEAVER'S PRETTY SHARP. I'LL BET I COULD CUT YOU DOWN TO THE LEVEL OF MY CROTCH, THEN YOU COULD DO SOMETHING USEFUL
I DON'T THINK SO, LOUIE!
KLIK
MUMBLE MUTTER IT'S NOT FUN ANYMORE MUTTER MUMBLE.... MUTTER JUST NOT FUN
THINGS WERE JUST NEVER THE SAME AFTERWARDS
WE TOOK OUR BUSINESS DOWN TO DECO 28
BOX

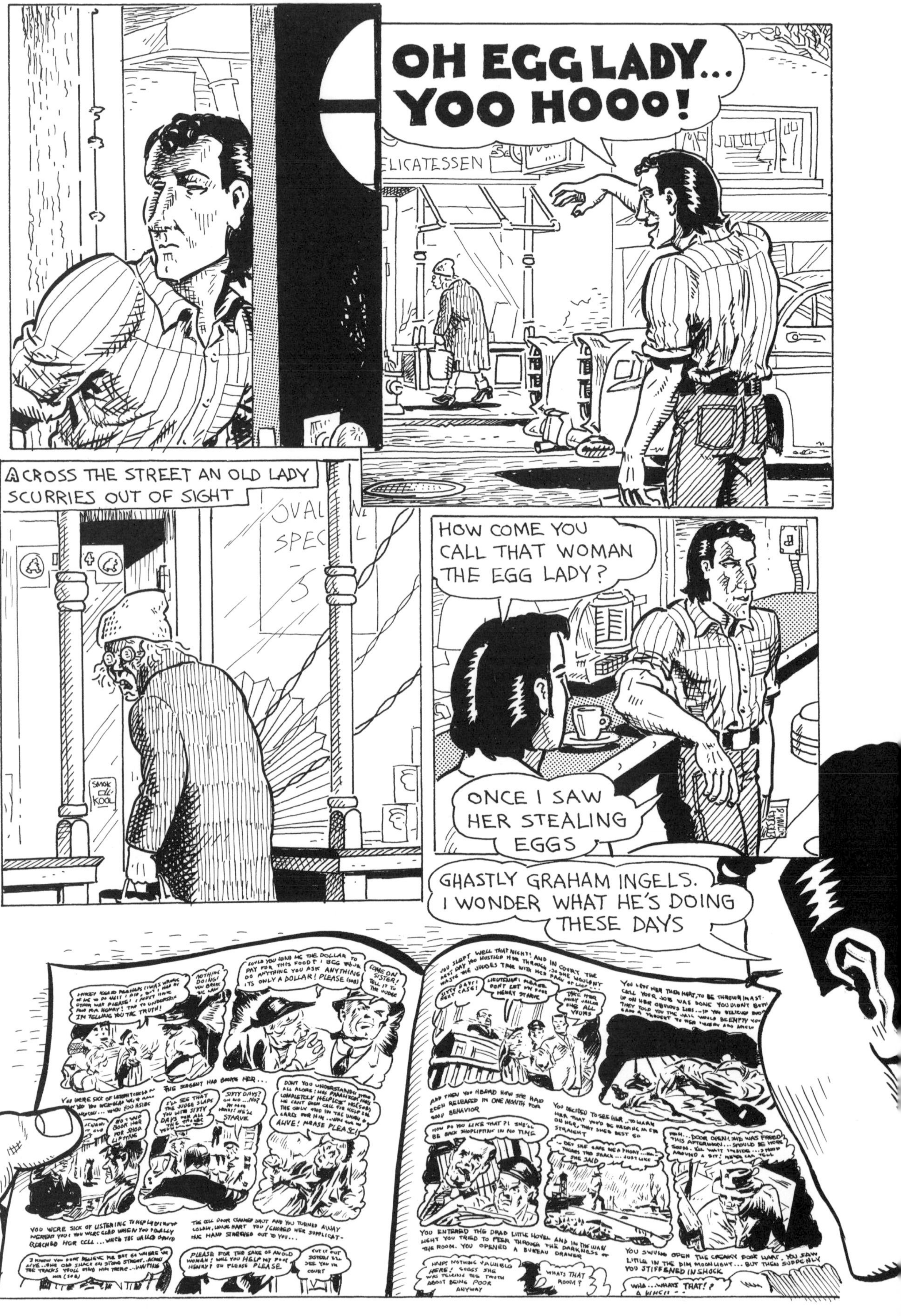
OH EGG LADY... YOO HOOO!
ELICATESSEN
ACROSS THE STREET AN OLD LADY SCURRIES OUT OF SIGHT
HOW COME YOU CALL THAT WOMAN THE EGG LADY?
ONCE I SAW HER STEALING EGGS
GHASTLY GRAHAM INGELS. I WONDER WHAT HE'S DOING THESE DAYS

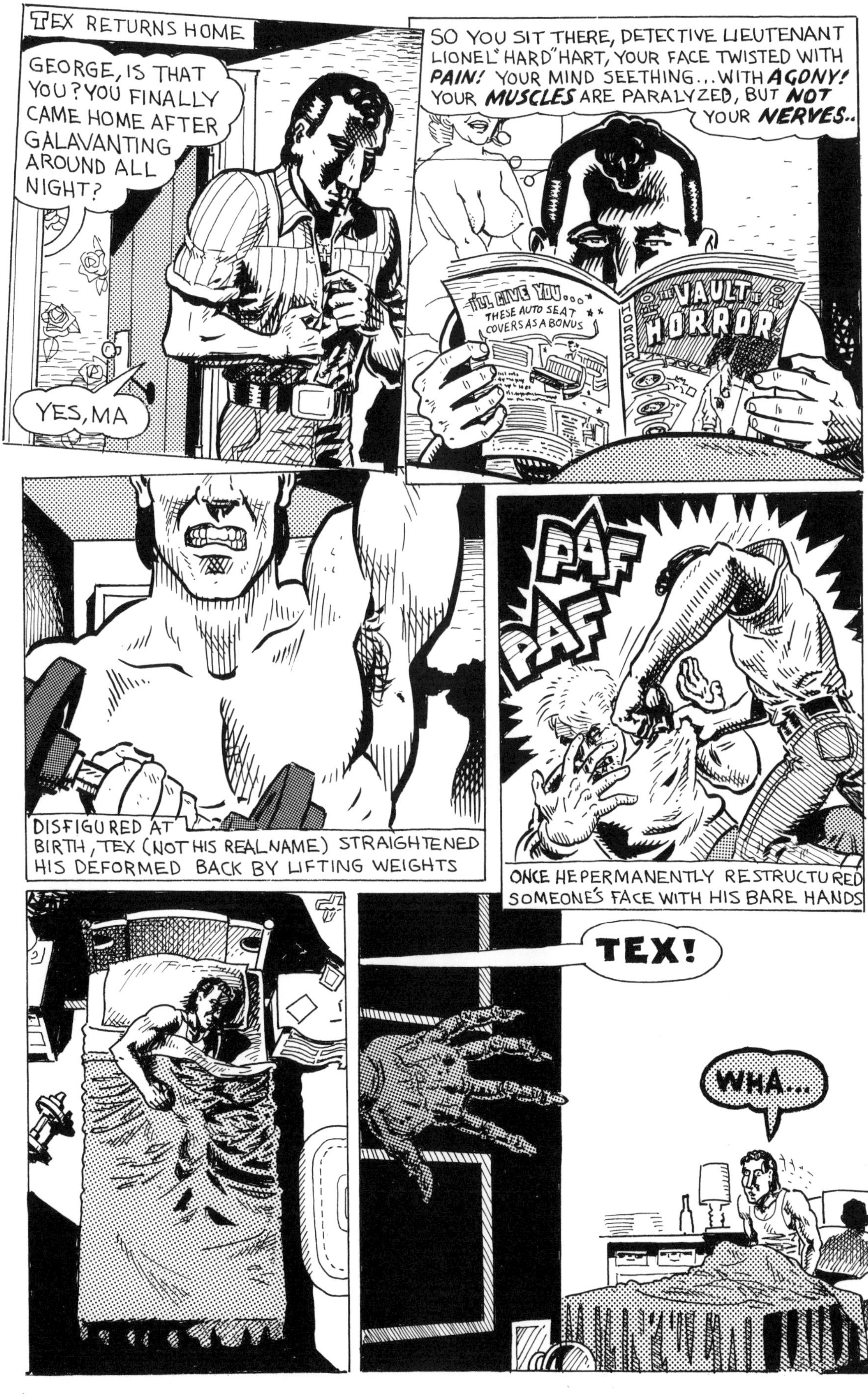
TEX RETURNS HOME
GEORGE, IS THAT YOU? YOU FINALLY CAME HOME AFTER GALAVANTING AROUND ALL NIGHT?
YES, MA
SO YOU SIT THERE, DETECTIVE LIEUTENANT LIONEL "HARD" HART, YOUR FACE TWISTED WITH PAIN! YOUR MIND SEETHING... WITH AGONY! YOUR MUSCLES ARE PARALYZED, BUT NOT YOUR NERVES..
I'LL GIVE YOU...
THESE AUTO SEAT COVERS AS A BONUS
THE VAULT OF HORROR
HORROR
DISFIGURED AT BIRTH, TEX (NOT HIS REAL NAME) STRAIGHTENED HIS DEFORMED BACK BY LIFTING WEIGHTS
PAF
PAF
ONCE HE PERMANENTLY RESTRUCTURED SOMEONE'S FACE WITH HIS BARE HANDS
TEX!
WHA...

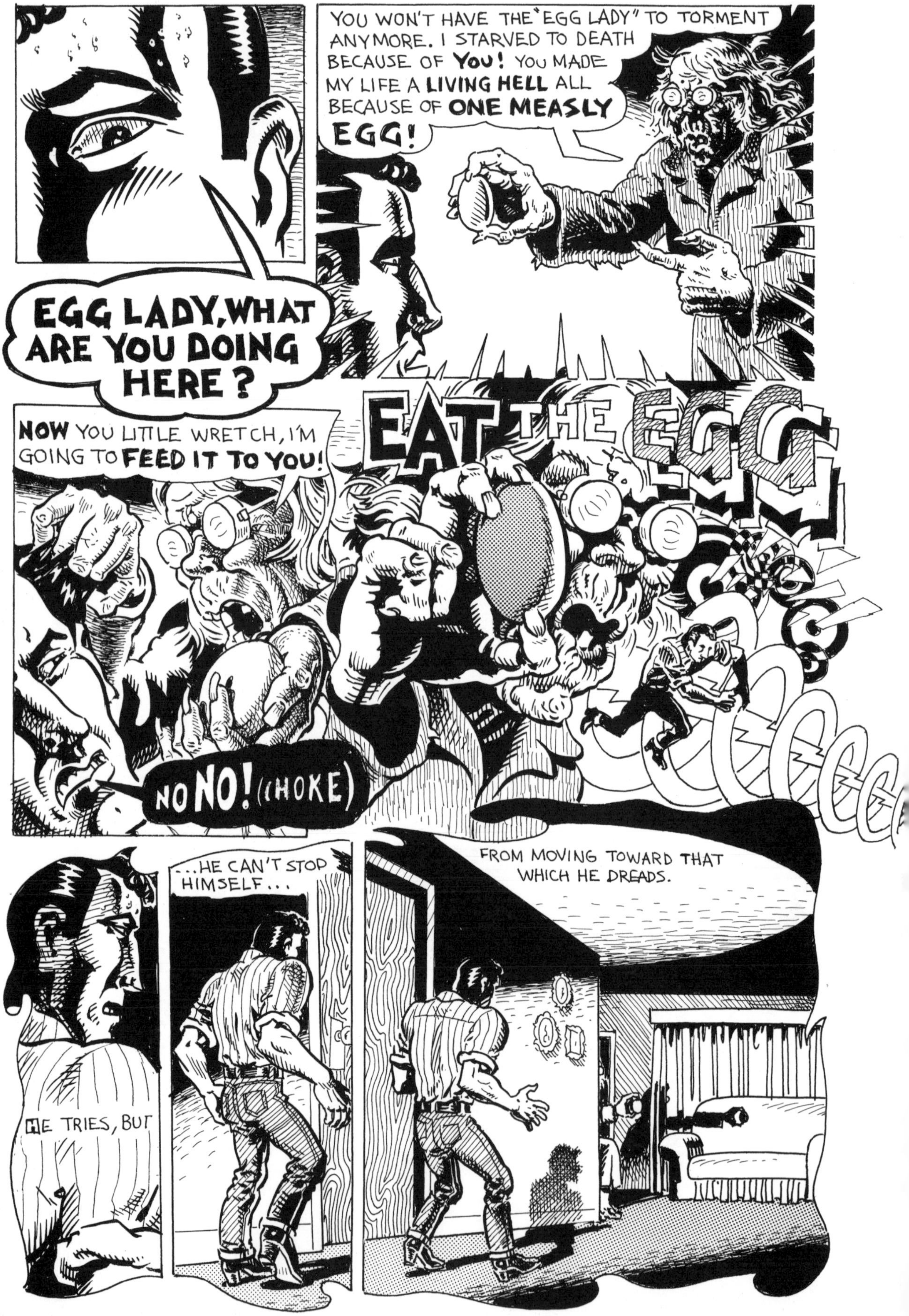
EGG LADY, WHAT ARE YOU DOING HERE?
YOU WON'T HAVE THE "EGG LADY" TO TORMENT ANYMORE. I STARVED TO DEATH BECAUSE OF YOU! YOU MADE MY LIFE A LIVING HELL ALL BECAUSE OF ONE MEASLY EGG!
NOW YOU LITTLE WRETCH, I'M GOING TO FEED IT TO YOU!
EAT THE EGG
NO NO! (CHOKE)
HE TRIES, BUT
...HE CAN'T STOP HIMSELF...
FROM MOVING TOWARD THAT WHICH HE DREADS.

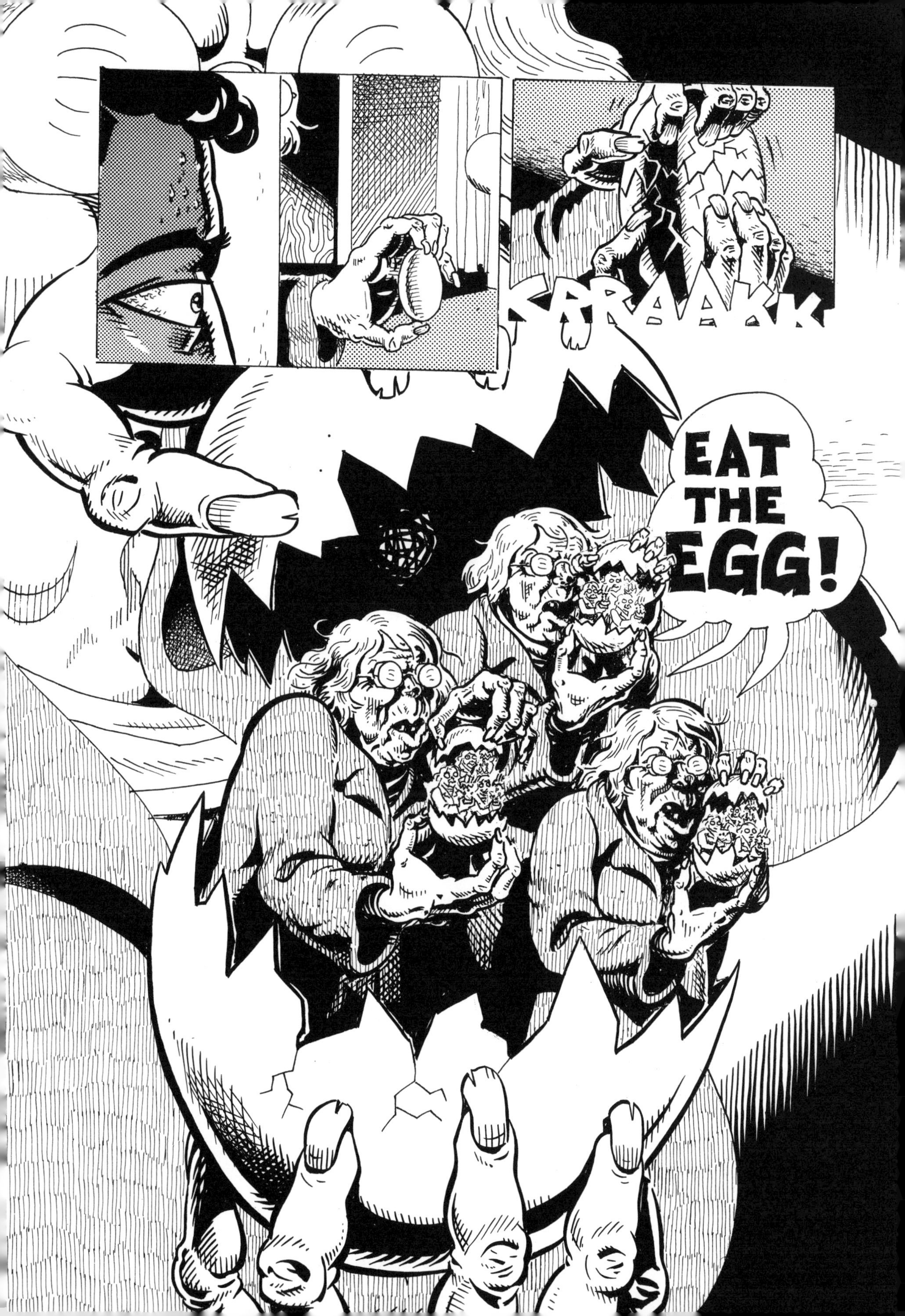
KRAAKK
EAT THE EGG!

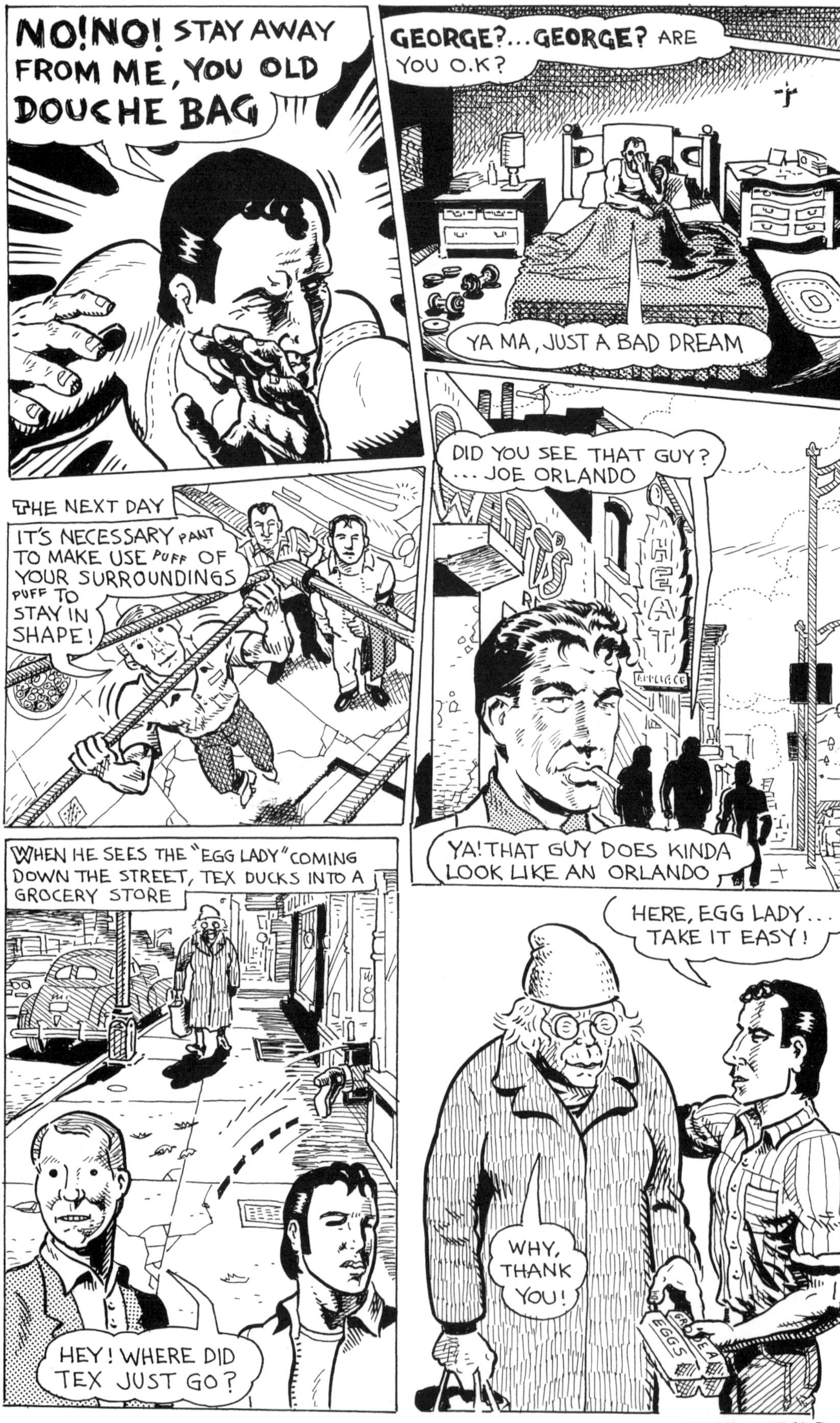
NO!NO! STAY AWAY FROM ME, YOU OLD DOUCHE BAG
GEORGE?...GEORGE? ARE YOU O.K?
YA MA, JUST A BAD DREAM
THE NEXT DAY
IT'S NECESSARY PANT TO MAKE USE PUFF OF YOUR SURROUNDINGS PUFF TO STAY IN SHAPE!
DID YOU SEE THAT GUY? ... JOE ORLANDO
HEAT
YA! THAT GUY DOES KINDA LOOK LIKE AN ORLANDO
WHEN HE SEES THE "EGG LADY" COMING DOWN THE STREET, TEX DUCKS INTO A GROCERY STORE
HEY! WHERE DID TEX JUST GO?
HERE, EGG LADY... TAKE IT EASY!
WHY, THANK YOU!
EGGS
THE END

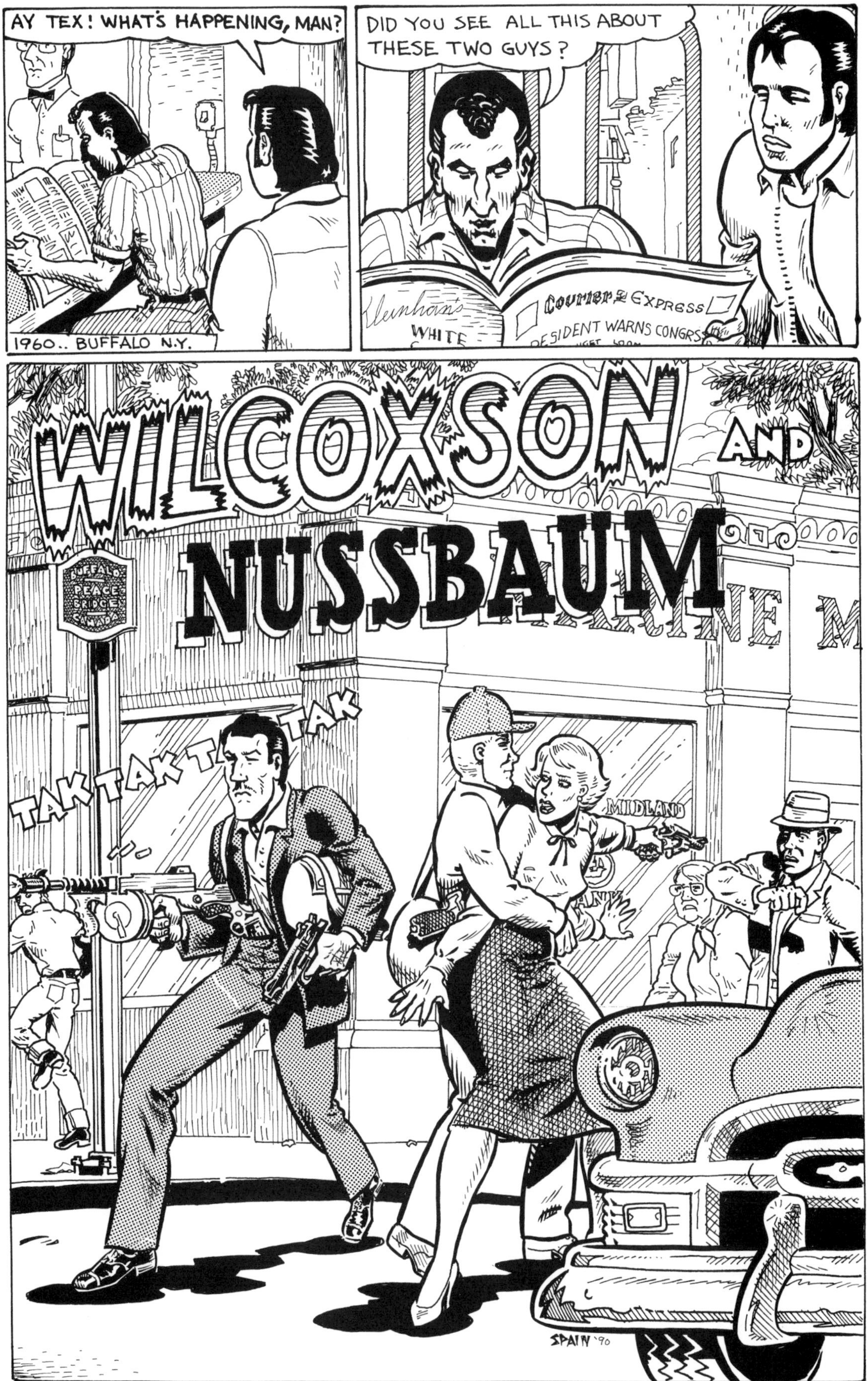
AY TEX! WHAT'S HAPPENING, MAN?
1960.. BUFFALO N.Y.
DID YOU SEE ALL THIS ABOUT THESE TWO GUYS?
Courier Express
WILCOXSON AND NUSSBAUM
BUFFALO PEACE BRIDGE CANADA
TAK TAK TAK TAK
MIDLAND
SPAIN '90

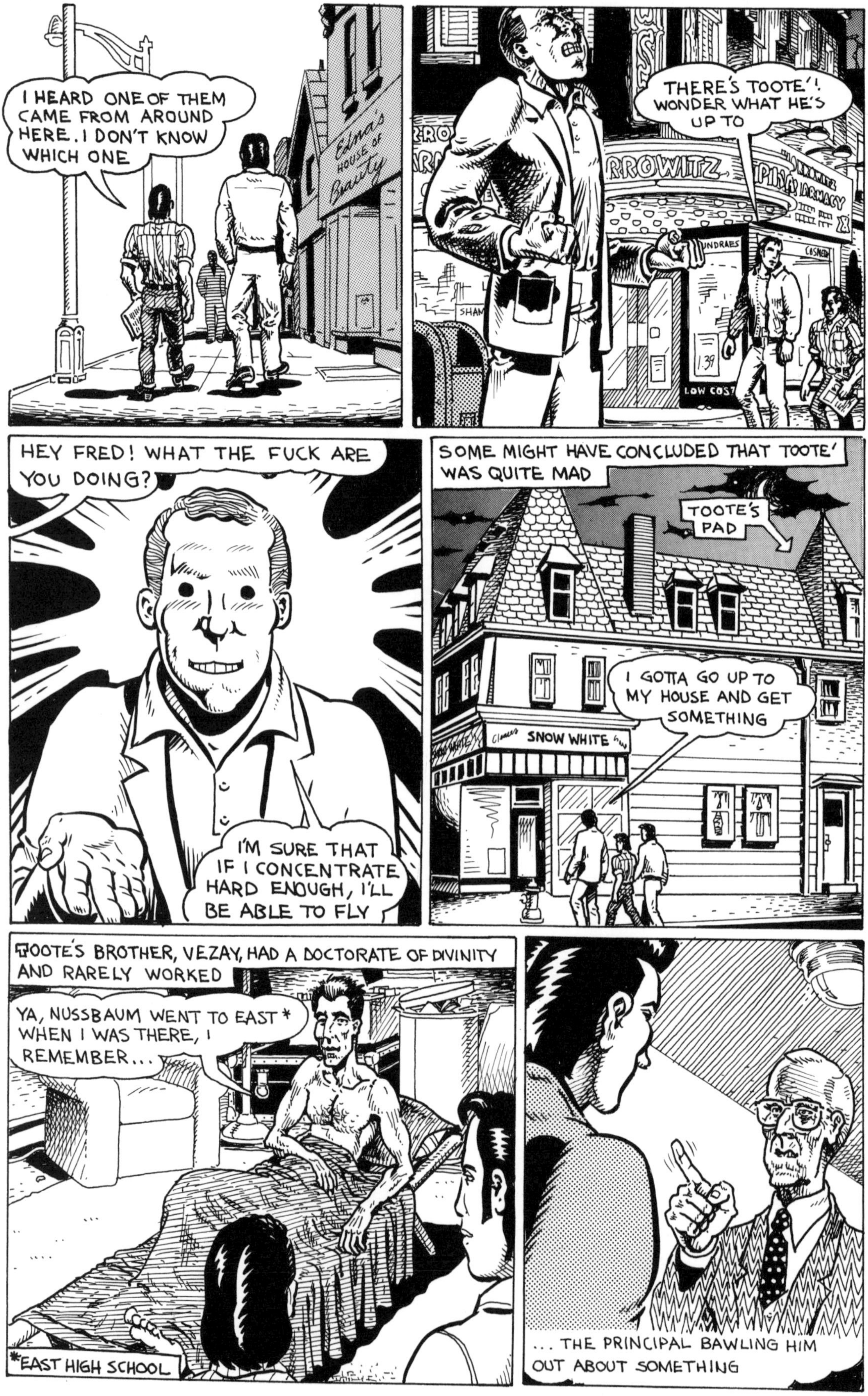
I HEARD ONE OF THEM CAME FROM AROUND HERE. I DON'T KNOW WHICH ONE
Edna's House of Beauty
THERE'S TOOTE'! WONDER WHAT HE'S UP TO
HEY FRED! WHAT THE FUCK ARE YOU DOING?
I'M SURE THAT IF I CONCENTRATE HARD ENOUGH, I'LL BE ABLE TO FLY
SOME MIGHT HAVE CONCLUDED THAT TOOTE' WAS QUITE MAD
TOOTE'S PAD
I GOTTA GO UP TO MY HOUSE AND GET SOMETHING
SNOW WHITE
TOOTE'S BROTHER, VEZAY, HAD A DOCTORATE OF DIVINITY AND RARELY WORKED
YA, NUSSBAUM WENT TO EAST* WHEN I WAS THERE, I REMEMBER...
*EAST HIGH SCHOOL
... THE PRINCIPAL BAWLING HIM OUT ABOUT SOMETHING

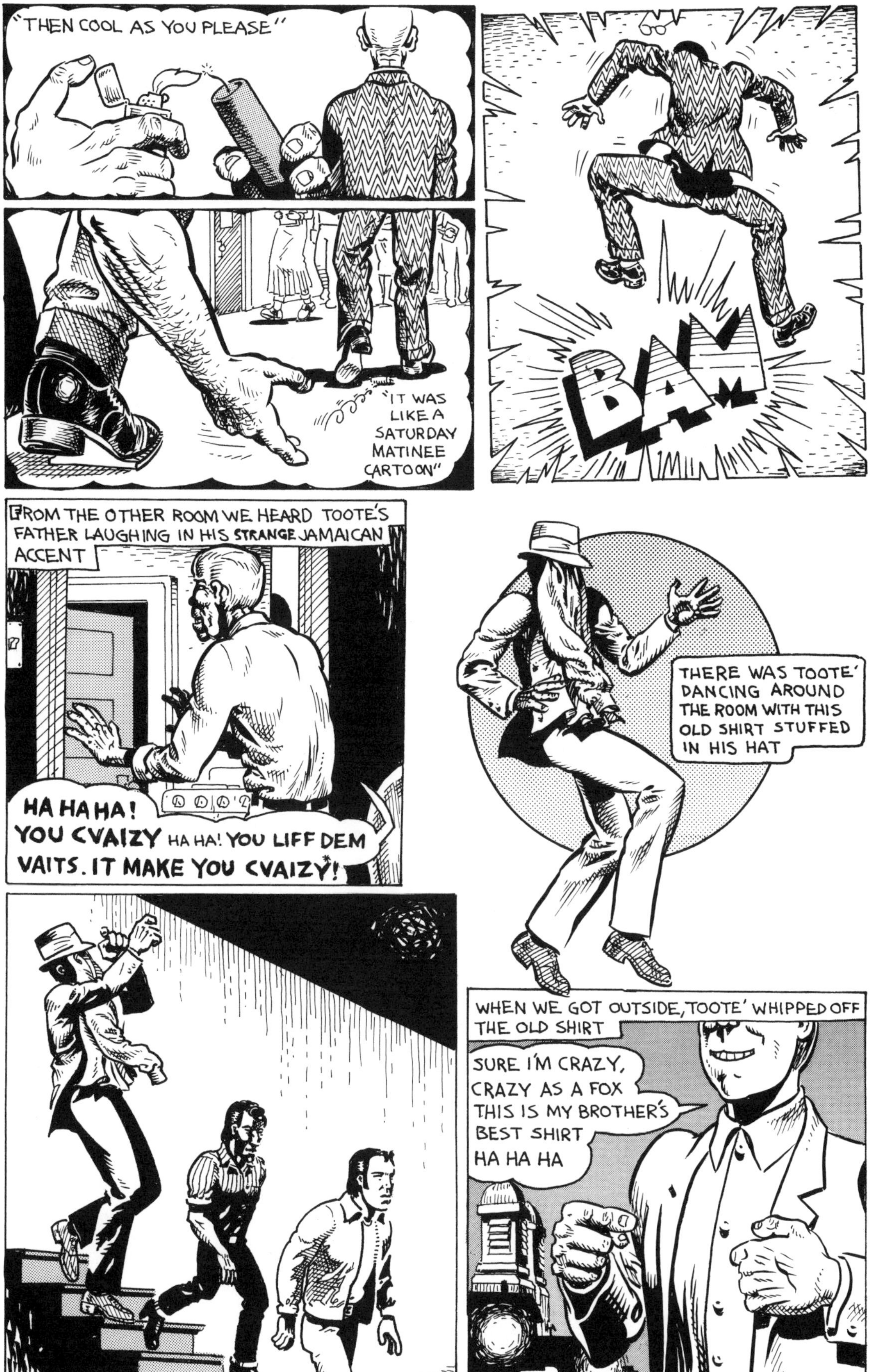
"THEN COOL AS YOU PLEASE"
"IT WAS LIKE A SATURDAY MATINEE CARTOON"
BAM
FROM THE OTHER ROOM WE HEARD TOOTE'S FATHER LAUGHING IN HIS STRANGE JAMAICAN ACCENT
HA HA HA! YOU CVAIZY HA HA! YOU LIFF DEM VAITS. IT MAKE YOU CVAIZY*!
THERE WAS TOOTE' DANCING AROUND THE ROOM WITH THIS OLD SHIRT STUFFED IN HIS HAT
WHEN WE GOT OUTSIDE, TOOTE' WHIPPED OFF THE OLD SHIRT
SURE I'M CRAZY, CRAZY AS A FOX THIS IS MY BROTHER'S BEST SHIRT HA HA HA

* YOU'RE CRAZY, YOU LIFT THEM WEIGHTS IT MAKE YOU CRAZY

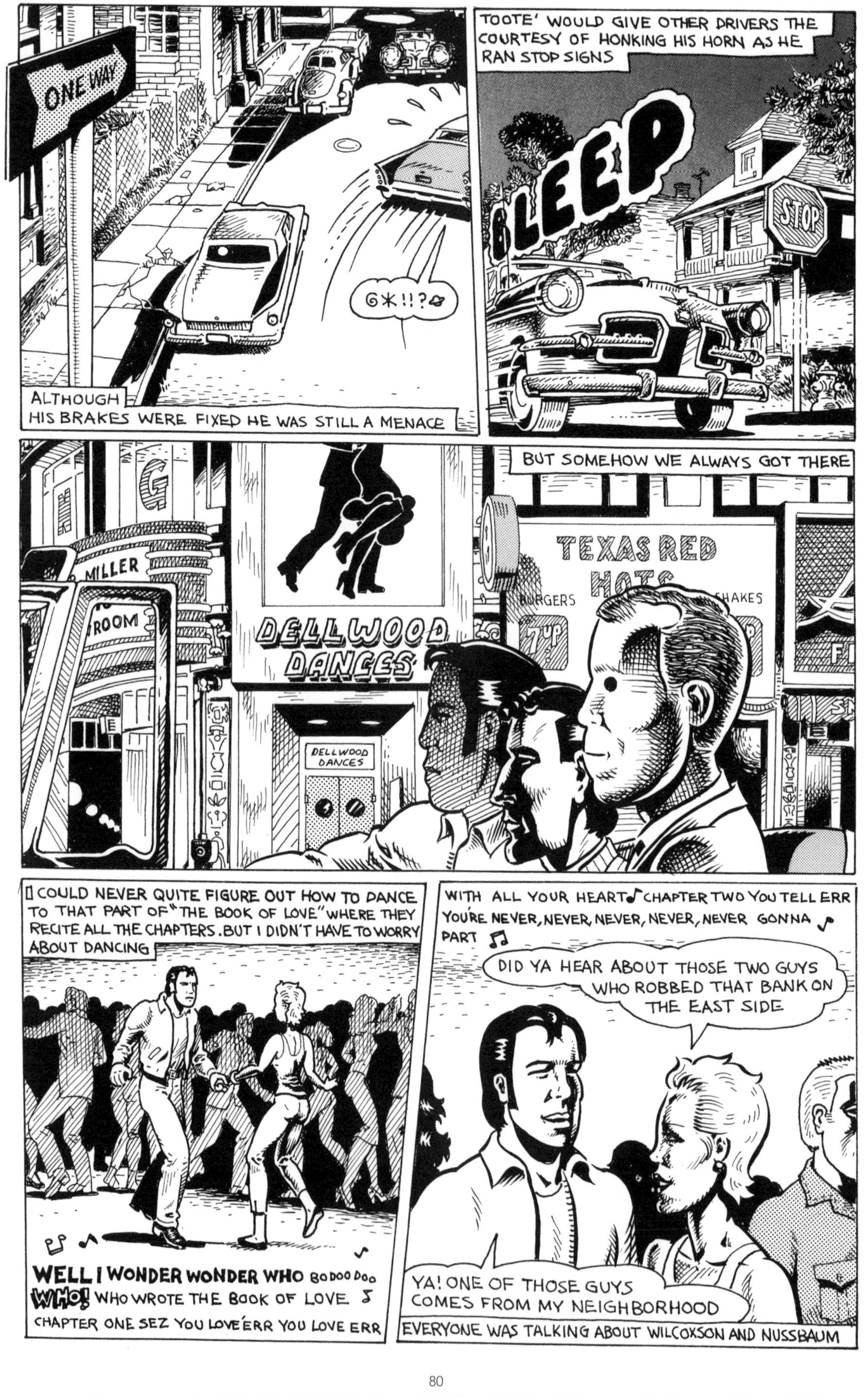
ONE WAY
ALTHOUGH HIS BRAKES WERE FIXED HE WAS STILL A MENACE
TOOTE' WOULD GIVE OTHER DRIVERS THE COURTESY OF HONKING HIS HORN AS HE RAN STOP SIGNS
BLEEP
STOP
BUT SOMEHOW WE ALWAYS GOT THERE
MILLER
ROOM
DELLWOOD DANCES
TEXAS RED HOTS
BURGERS
SHAKES
7up
DELLWOOD DANCES
I COULD NEVER QUITE FIGURE OUT HOW TO DANCE TO THAT PART OF "THE BOOK OF LOVE" WHERE THEY RECITE ALL THE CHAPTERS. BUT I DIDN'T HAVE TO WORRY ABOUT DANCING
WELL I WONDER WONDER WHO BO DOO DOO WHO! WHO WROTE THE BOOK OF LOVE
CHAPTER ONE SEZ YOU LOVE'ERR YOU LOVE ERR
WITH ALL YOUR HEART CHAPTER TWO YOU TELL ERR YOU'RE NEVER, NEVER, NEVER, NEVER, NEVER GONNA PART
DID YA HEAR ABOUT THOSE TWO GUYS WHO ROBBED THAT BANK ON THE EAST SIDE
YA! ONE OF THOSE GUYS COMES FROM MY NEIGHBORHOOD
EVERYONE WAS TALKING ABOUT WILCOXSON AND NUSSBAUM

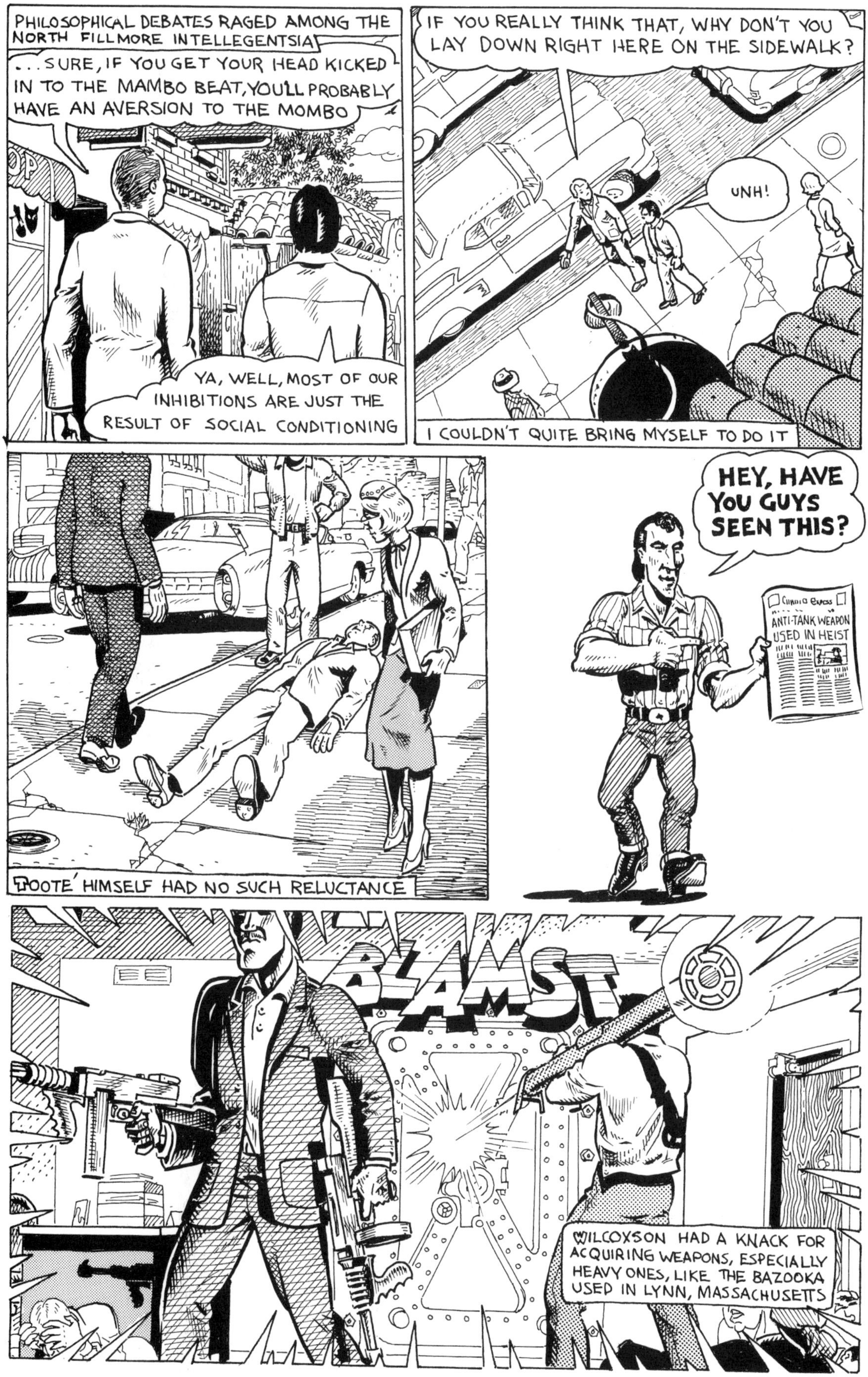
PHILOSOPHICAL DEBATES RAGED AMONG THE NORTH FILLMORE INTELLEGENTSIA
...SURE, IF YOU GET YOUR HEAD KICKED IN TO THE MAMBO BEAT, YOU'LL PROBABLY HAVE AN AVERSION TO THE MOMBO
YA, WELL, MOST OF OUR INHIBITIONS ARE JUST THE RESULT OF SOCIAL CONDITIONING
IF YOU REALLY THINK THAT, WHY DON'T YOU LAY DOWN RIGHT HERE ON THE SIDEWALK?
UNH!
I COULDN'T QUITE BRING MYSELF TO DO IT
FOOTE' HIMSELF HAD NO SUCH RELUCTANCE
HEY, HAVE YOU GUYS SEEN THIS?
ANTI-TANK WEAPON USED IN HEIST
BLAMST
WILCOXSON HAD A KNACK FOR ACQUIRING WEAPONS, ESPECIALLY HEAVY ONES, LIKE THE BAZOOKA USED IN LYNN, MASSACHUSETTS

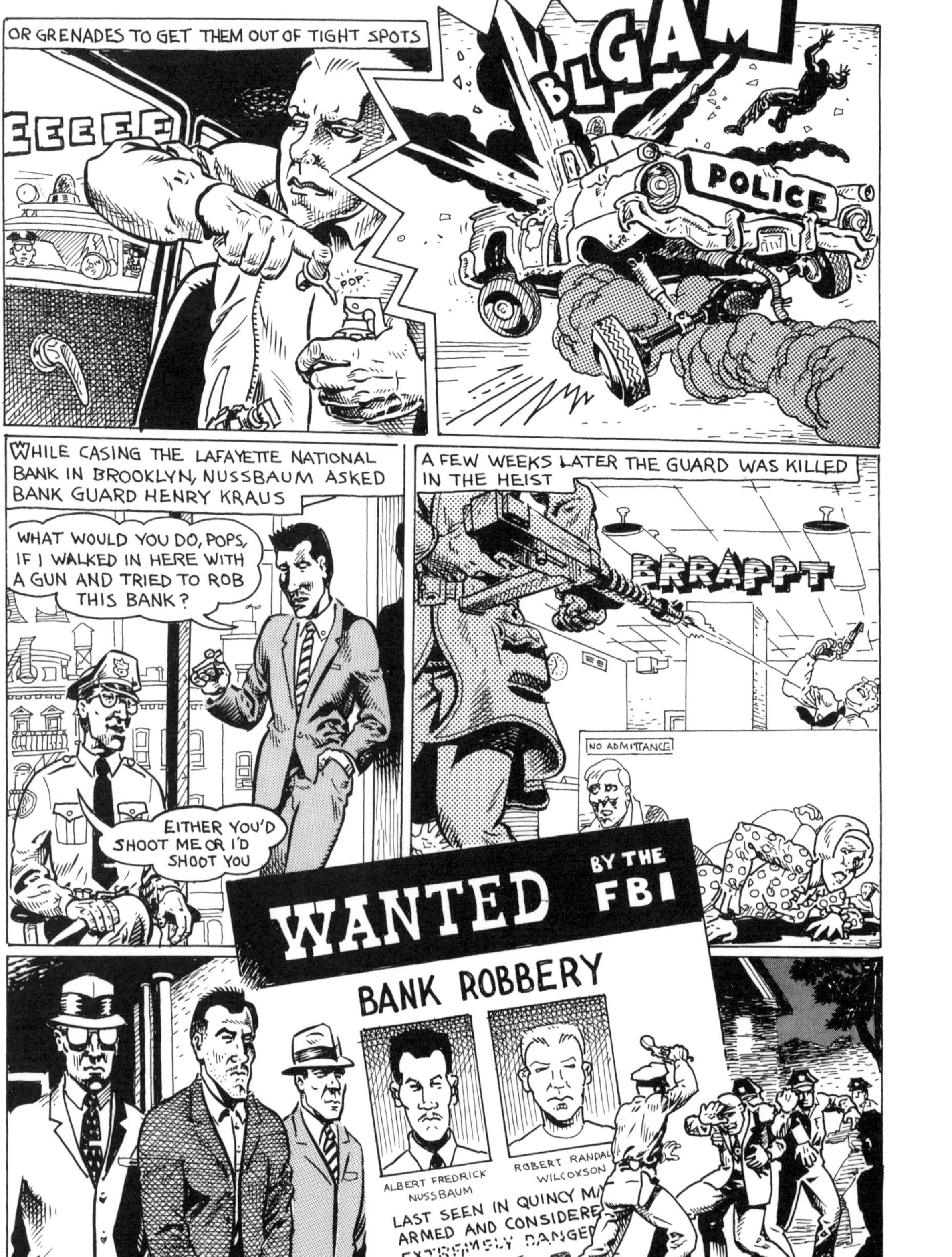
OR GRENADES TO GET THEM OUT OF TIGHT SPOTS
EEEEE
POP
BLGAM
POLICE
WHILE CASING THE LAFAYETTE NATIONAL BANK IN BROOKLYN, NUSSBAUM ASKED BANK GUARD HENRY KRAUS
WHAT WOULD YOU DO, POPS, IF I WALKED IN HERE WITH A GUN AND TRIED TO ROB THIS BANK?
EITHER YOU'D SHOOT ME OR I'D SHOOT YOU
A FEW WEEKS LATER THE GUARD WAS KILLED IN THE HEIST
BRRAPPT
NO ADMITTANCE
WANTED BY THE FBI
BANK ROBBERY
ALBERT FREDRICK NUSSBAUM
ROBERT RANDALL WILCOXSON
LAST SEEN IN QUINCY MA
ARMED AND CONSIDERE
AFTER A NATIONWIDE MANHUNT NUSSBAUM WAS TURNED IN BY HIS MOTHER-IN-LAW
THEY GOT WILCOXSON THE NEXT WEEK

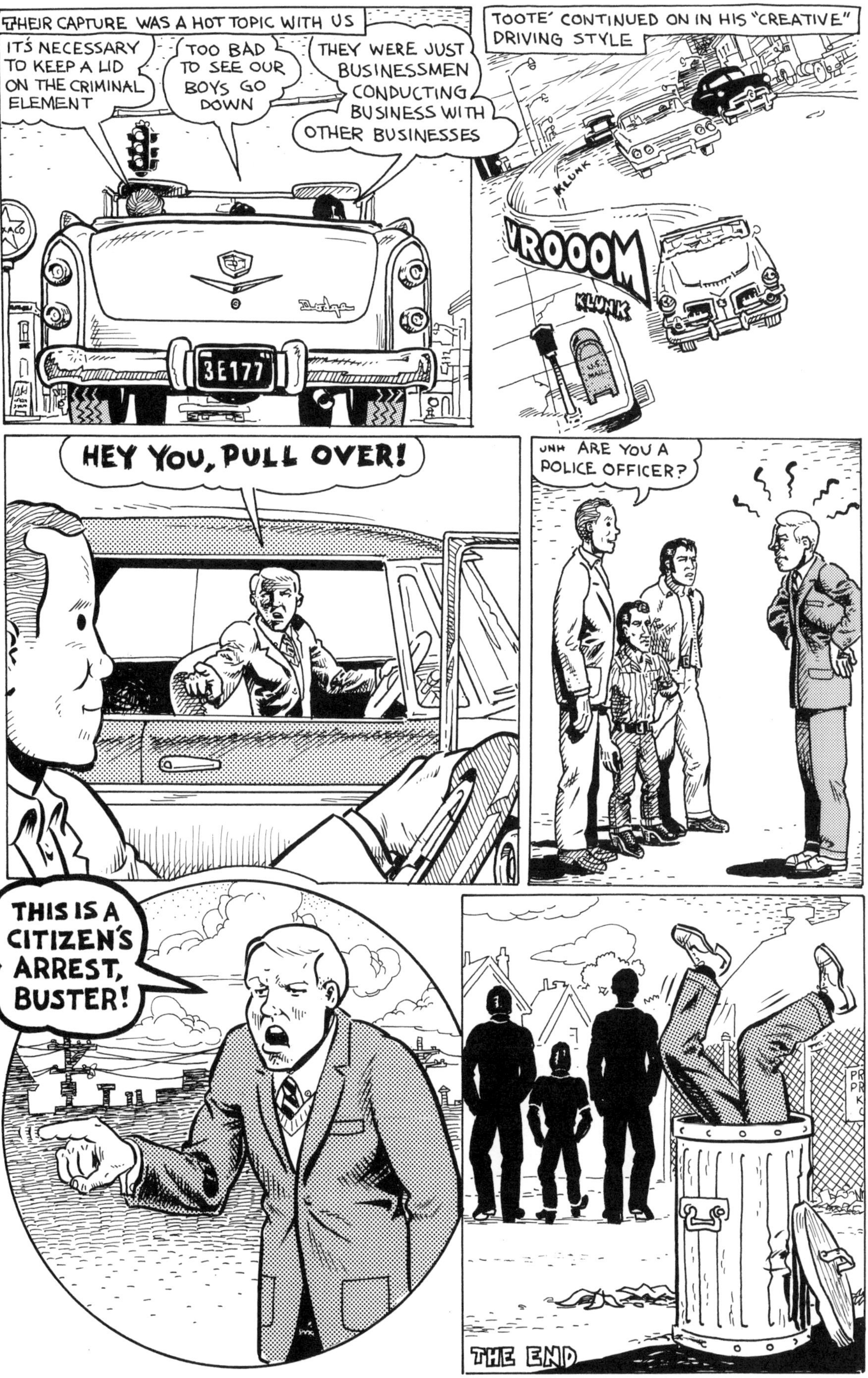
THEIR CAPTURE WAS A HOT TOPIC WITH US
IT'S NECESSARY TO KEEP A LID ON THE CRIMINAL ELEMENT
TOO BAD TO SEE OUR BOYS GO DOWN
THEY WERE JUST BUSINESSMEN CONDUCTING BUSINESS WITH OTHER BUSINESSES
Dodge
3E177
TOOTE' CONTINUED ON IN HIS "CREATIVE" DRIVING STYLE
KLUNK
VROOOM
KLUNK
HEY YOU, PULL OVER!
UNH ARE YOU A POLICE OFFICER?
THIS IS A CITIZEN'S ARREST, BUSTER!
THE END

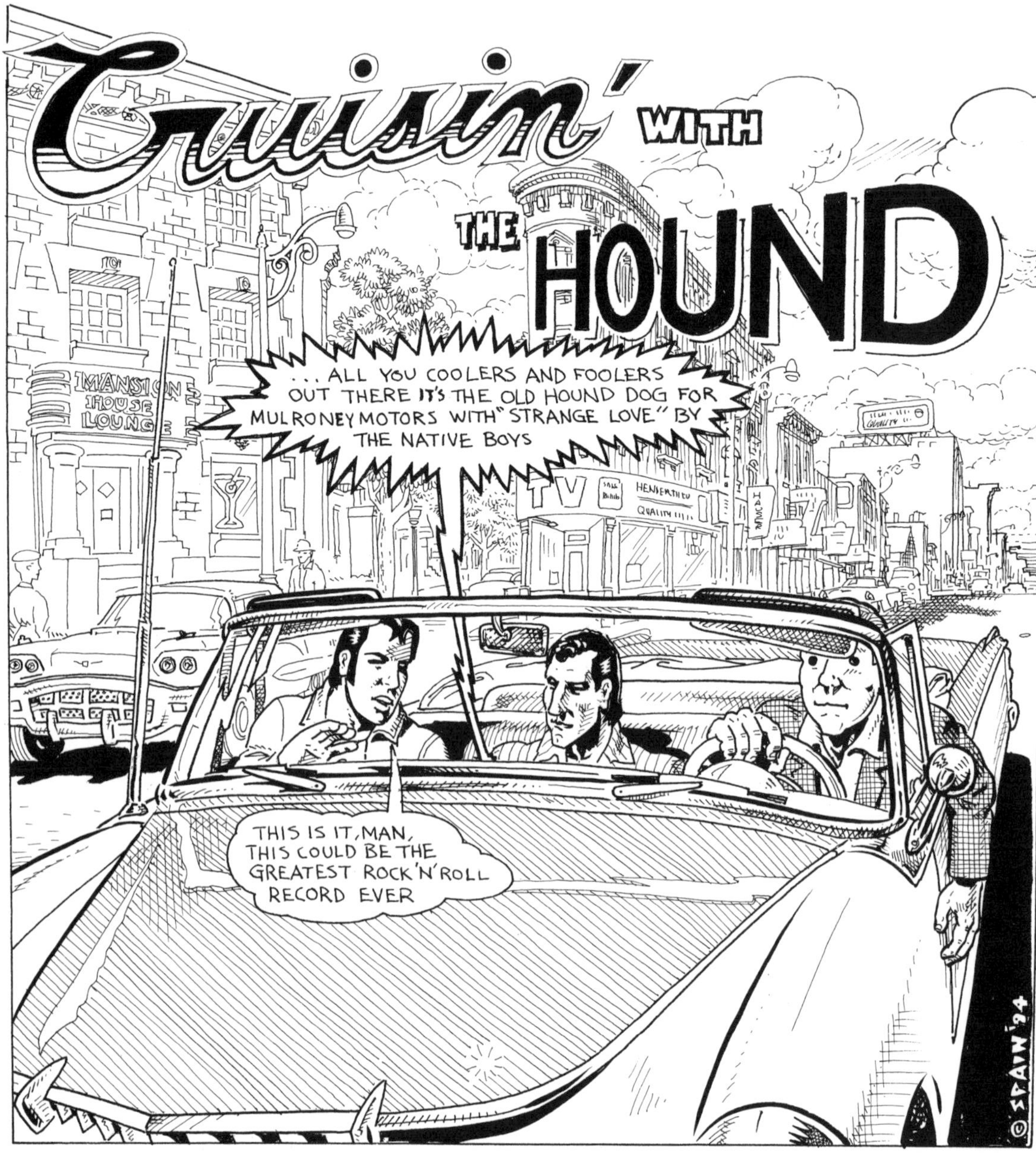
Cruisin' WITH THE HOUND
MANSION HOUSE LOUNGE
...ALL YOU COOLERS AND FOOLERS OUT THERE IT'S THE OLD HOUND DOG FOR MULRONEY MOTORS WITH "STRANGE LOVE" BY THE NATIVE BOYS
TV
THIS IS IT, MAN, THIS COULD BE THE GREATEST ROCK 'N' ROLL RECORD EVER
© SPAIN '94

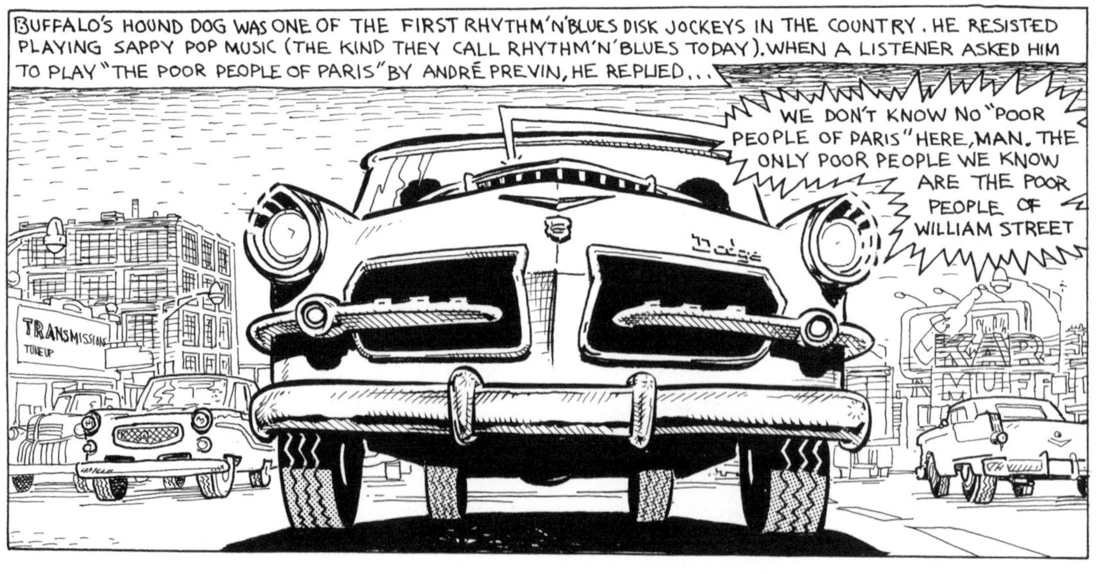
BUFFALO'S HOUND DOG WAS ONE OF THE FIRST RHYTHM 'N' BLUES DISK JOCKEYS IN THE COUNTRY. HE RESISTED PLAYING SAPPY POP MUSIC (THE KIND THEY CALL RHYTHM 'N' BLUES TODAY). WHEN A LISTENER ASKED HIM TO PLAY "THE POOR PEOPLE OF PARIS" BY ANDRÉ PREVIN, HE REPLIED...
WE DON'T KNOW NO "POOR PEOPLE OF PARIS" HERE, MAN. THE ONLY POOR PEOPLE WE KNOW ARE THE POOR PEOPLE OF WILLIAM STREET
TRANSMISSION
TUNEUP
KAR
MUFF

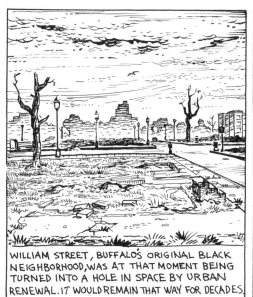

WILLIAM STREET, BUFFALO'S ORIGINAL BLACK NEIGHBORHOOD, WAS AT THAT MOMENT BEING TURNED INTO A HOLE IN SPACE BY URBAN RENEWAL. IT WOULD REMAIN THAT WAY FOR DECADES.

I COULD CARRY A TUNE PRETTY GOOD

PUTIN'N'TAIN, PUTIN'N'TAIN
ASK ME AGAIN AND I'LL TELL YOU THE SAME

NOW WE'RE GOIN' STEADY AND I FOUND OUT HER REAL NAME IS BETTY

BUT THE GUY WHO REALLY HAD IT DOWN WAS JOCKO REESE

HEY, MAN, DO "IN THE CHAPEL OF DREAMS"

"IN THE CHAPEL OF DREAMS"? YOU MUST BE OUT OF YOUR TOILET!

IT NEVER TOOK MUCH TO TALK HIM INTO IT

IN THE CHAPEL OF...

DRE-EEE-EE-EEMS

EVERY DREAM WILL COME TRUE

HIS VOICE HAD AMAZING RANGE. HE WOULD HIT EACH NOTE, INCLUDING THE INSTRUMENTAL, PERFECTLY

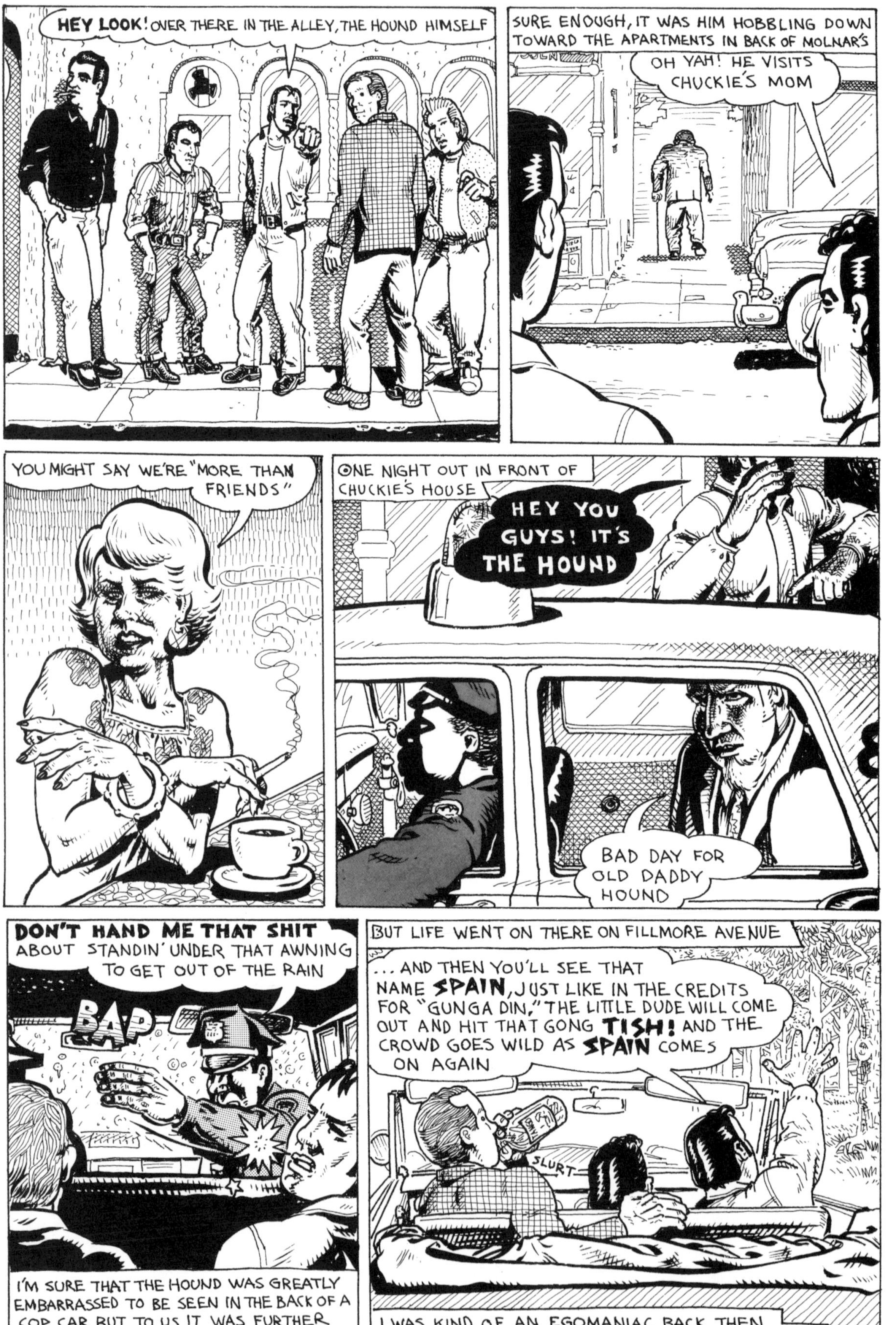
HEY LOOK! OVER THERE IN THE ALLEY, THE HOUND HIMSELF
SURE ENOUGH, IT WAS HIM HOBBLING DOWN TOWARD THE APARTMENTS IN BACK OF MOLNAR'S
OH YAH! HE VISITS CHUCKIE'S MOM
YOU MIGHT SAY WE'RE "MORE THAN FRIENDS"
ONE NIGHT OUT IN FRONT OF CHUCKIE'S HOUSE
HEY YOU GUYS! IT'S THE HOUND
BAD DAY FOR OLD DADDY HOUND
DON'T HAND ME THAT SHIT ABOUT STANDIN' UNDER THAT AWNING TO GET OUT OF THE RAIN
BAP
I'M SURE THAT THE HOUND WAS GREATLY EMBARRASSED TO BE SEEN IN THE BACK OF A COP CAR BUT TO US IT WAS FURTHER EVIDENCE OF COMMON EXPERIENCE
BUT LIFE WENT ON THERE ON FILLMORE AVENUE
...AND THEN YOU'LL SEE THAT NAME SPAIN, JUST LIKE IN THE CREDITS FOR "GUNGA DIN," THE LITTLE DUDE WILL COME OUT AND HIT THAT GONG TISH! AND THE CROWD GOES WILD AS SPAIN COMES ON AGAIN
SLURT
I WAS KIND OF AN EGOMANIAC BACK THEN (I'VE GOTTEN MORE HUMBLE IN RECENT YEARS)

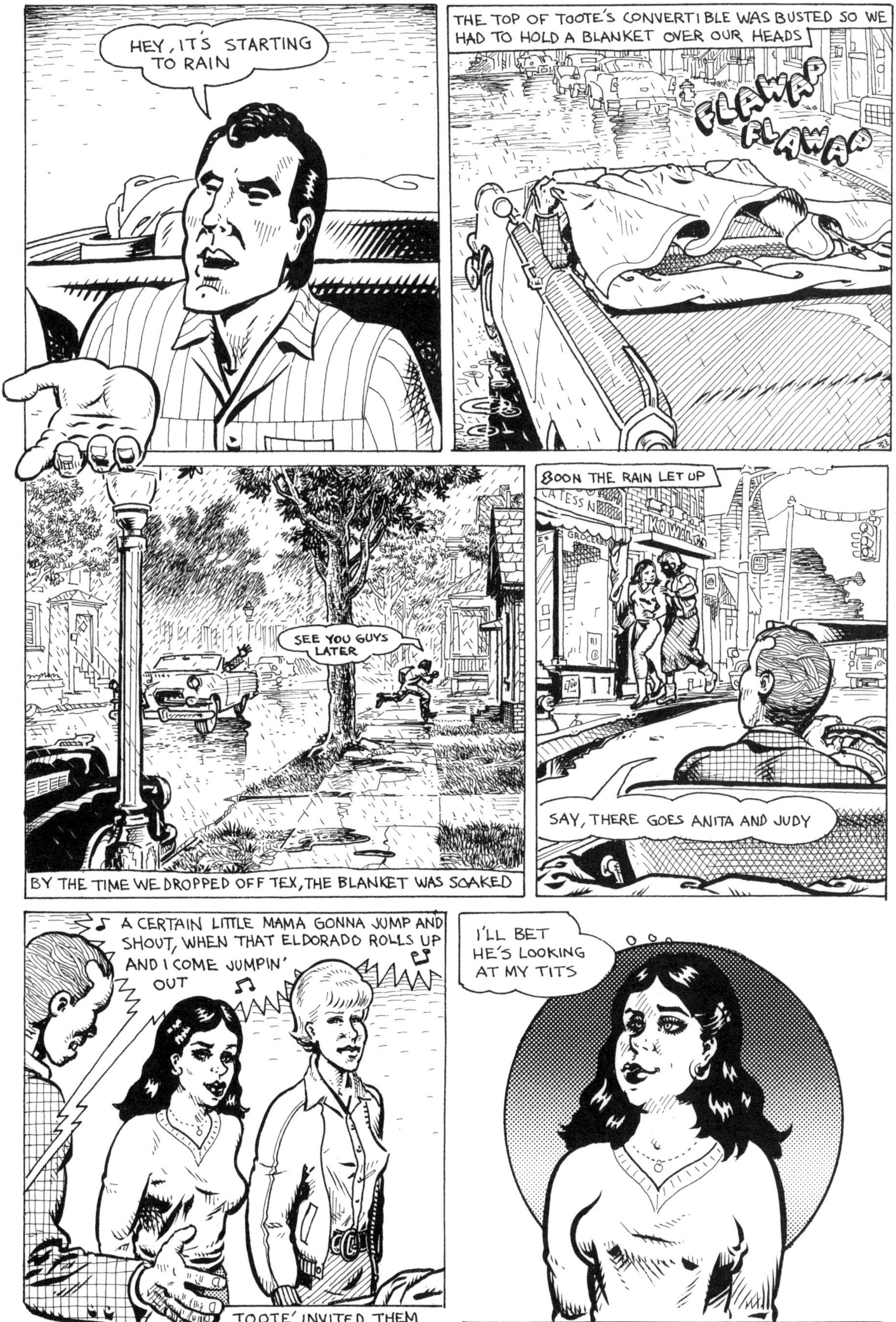
HEY, IT'S STARTING TO RAIN
THE TOP OF TOOTE'S CONVERTIBLE WAS BUSTED SO WE HAD TO HOLD A BLANKET OVER OUR HEADS
FLAWAP FLAWAP
SEE YOU GUYS LATER
BY THE TIME WE DROPPED OFF TEX, THE BLANKET WAS SOAKED
SOON THE RAIN LET UP
GROCERIES
KOWAL
SAY, THERE GOES ANITA AND JUDY
A CERTAIN LITTLE MAMA GONNA JUMP AND SHOUT, WHEN THAT ELDORADO ROLLS UP AND I COME JUMPIN' OUT
TOOTE' INVITED THEM TO JOIN US. THEY WERE GAME
I'LL BET HE'S LOOKING AT MY TITS
ANITA WAS A BIT PLUMP BUT STILL NOT TOO BAD

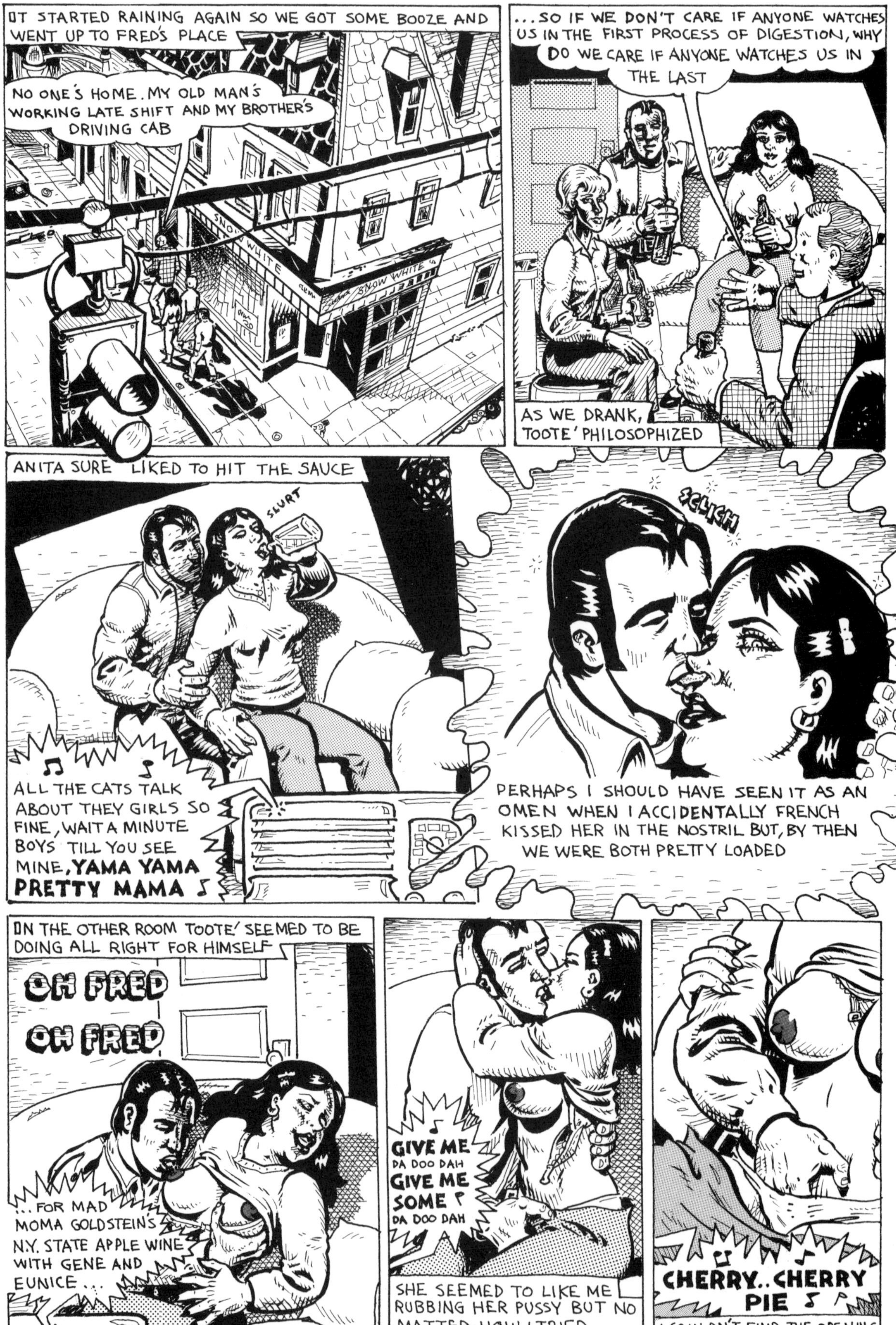
IT STARTED RAINING AGAIN SO WE GOT SOME BOOZE AND WENT UP TO FRED'S PLACE
NO ONE'S HOME. MY OLD MAN'S WORKING LATE SHIFT AND MY BROTHER'S DRIVING CAB
SNOW WHITE
SNOW WHITE
...SO IF WE DON'T CARE IF ANYONE WATCHES US IN THE FIRST PROCESS OF DIGESTION, WHY DO WE CARE IF ANYONE WATCHES US IN THE LAST
AS WE DRANK, TOOTE' PHILOSOPHIZED
ANITA SURE LIKED TO HIT THE SAUCE
SLURT
ALL THE CATS TALK ABOUT THEY GIRLS SO FINE, WAIT A MINUTE BOYS TILL YOU SEE MINE, YAMA YAMA PRETTY MAMA
SCLICH
PERHAPS I SHOULD HAVE SEEN IT AS AN OMEN WHEN I ACCIDENTALLY FRENCH KISSED HER IN THE NOSTRIL BUT, BY THEN WE WERE BOTH PRETTY LOADED
IN THE OTHER ROOM TOOTE' SEEMED TO BE DOING ALL RIGHT FOR HIMSELF
OH FRED
OH FRED
...FOR MAD MOMA GOLDSTEIN'S N.Y. STATE APPLE WINE WITH GENE AND EUNICE...
GIVE ME DA DOO DAH GIVE ME SOME DA DOO DAH
SHE SEEMED TO LIKE ME RUBBING HER PUSSY BUT NO MATTER HOW I TRIED...
CHERRY.. CHERRY PIE
I COULDN'T FIND THE OPENING

AS I ATTEMPTED VAINLY TO GET HER PANTS OFF ONLY THE HOUND UNDERSTOOD MY PLIGHT

MOMA SAID THERE'D BE DAYS LIKE THIS THERE'D BE DAY'S LIKE THIS MAH MAMA SAID MAMA SAID MAMA SAID

N-NO

THEN SUDDENLY SHE GOT UP

I'M A BAD GIRL HIC... I'M A BAD GIRL

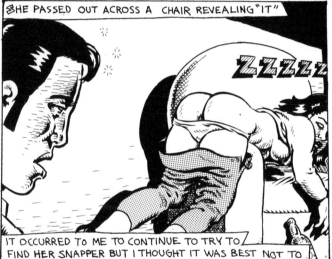

SHE PASSED OUT ACROSS A CHAIR REVEALING "IT"

ZZZZZ

IT OCCURRED TO ME TO CONTINUE TO TRY TO FIND HER SNAPPER BUT I THOUGHT IT WAS BEST NOT TO

I SAW HER ONCE MORE. WE WENT BOWLING. SHE BEAT ME 146 TO 63

IT WAS REAL SQUARE BACK THEN. ONCE WHEN THE HOUND DROPPED IN AT DECO 28, AN OLD TIMER, SEEING HIS GOATEE AND SIDEBURNS, ASKED...

HEY, MISTER! IS THERE A CENTENNIAL GOING ON AROUND HERE SOMEWHERE

HAMBURG SPECIAL 50¢

THE HOUND WAS HEARD TO SAY

THEY'LL NEVER UNDERSTAND, WILL THEY, MAN?

THE END

DOWN AT THE KITTY KAT

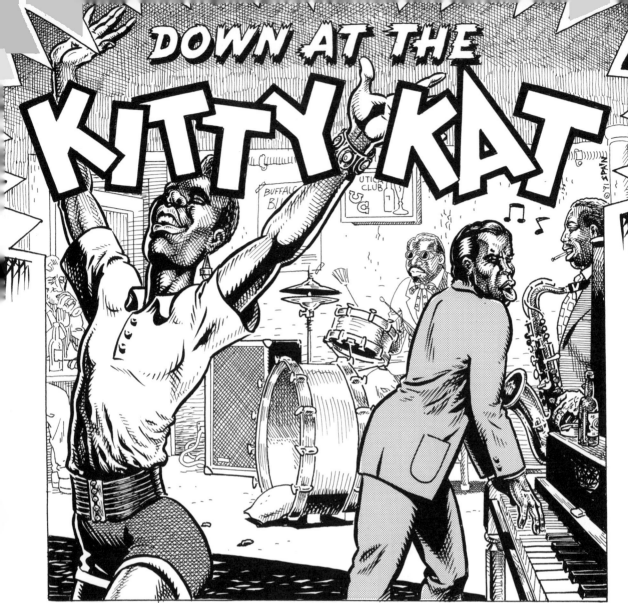

©'91 SPAIN

THEY WERE ALL THERE, THE PIMPS, THE FAGS, THE WHORES, THE CURIOUS, THE ALCOHOLIC, THE WEIRD OF THE LATE '50S

BLUES LOVERS, CANADIAN BIKERS, THRILL SEEKERS, JUNKIES, INSOMNIACS, HEPCATS

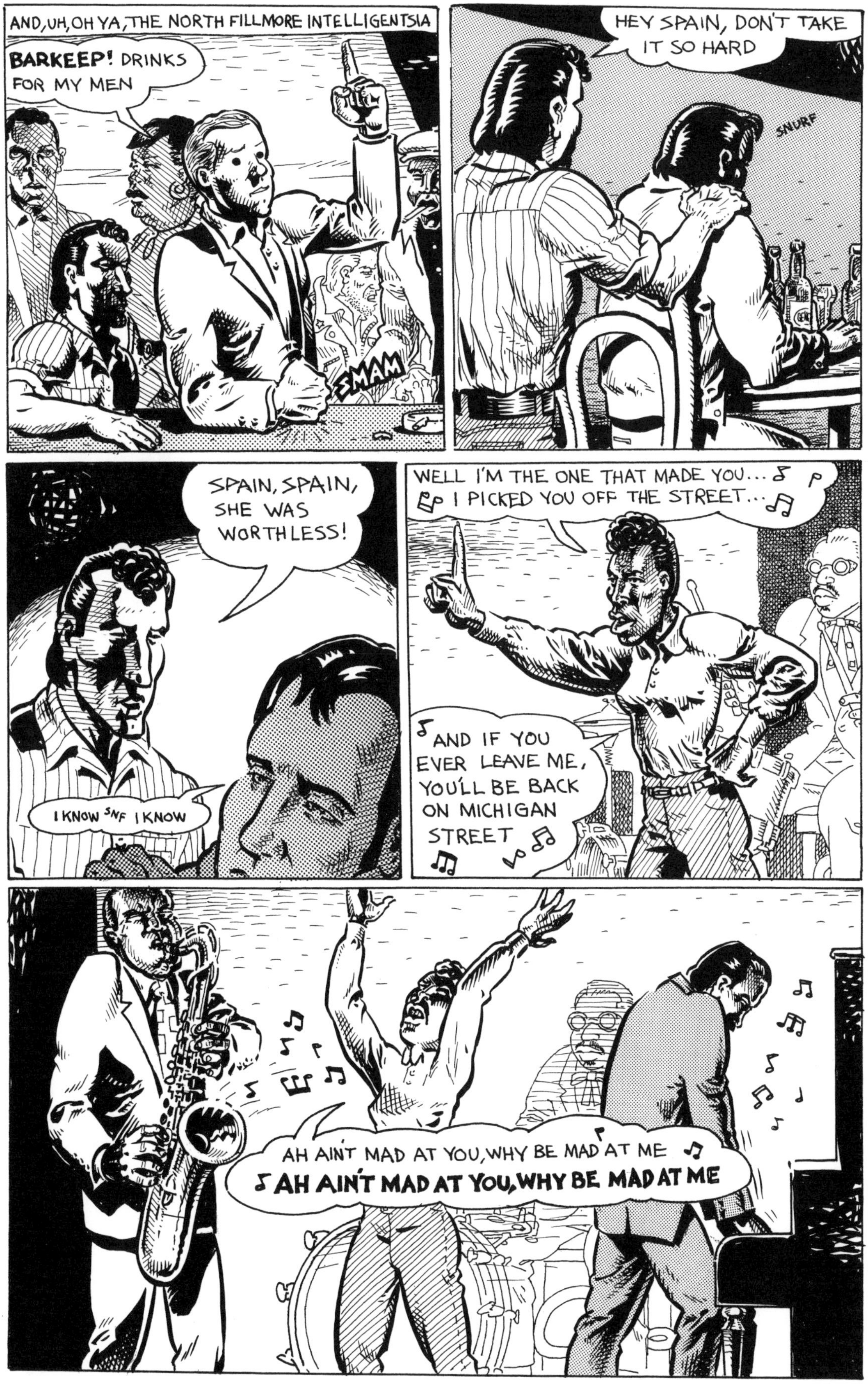
AND, UH, OH YA, THE NORTH FILLMORE INTELLIGENTSIA
BARKEEP! DRINKS FOR MY MEN
EMAM
HEY SPAIN, DON'T TAKE IT SO HARD
SNURF
SPAIN, SPAIN, SHE WAS WORTHLESS!
I KNOW SNF I KNOW
WELL I'M THE ONE THAT MADE YOU...
I PICKED YOU OFF THE STREET...
AND IF YOU EVER LEAVE ME, YOU'LL BE BACK ON MICHIGAN STREET
AH AIN'T MAD AT YOU, WHY BE MAD AT ME
AH AIN'T MAD AT YOU, WHY BE MAD AT ME

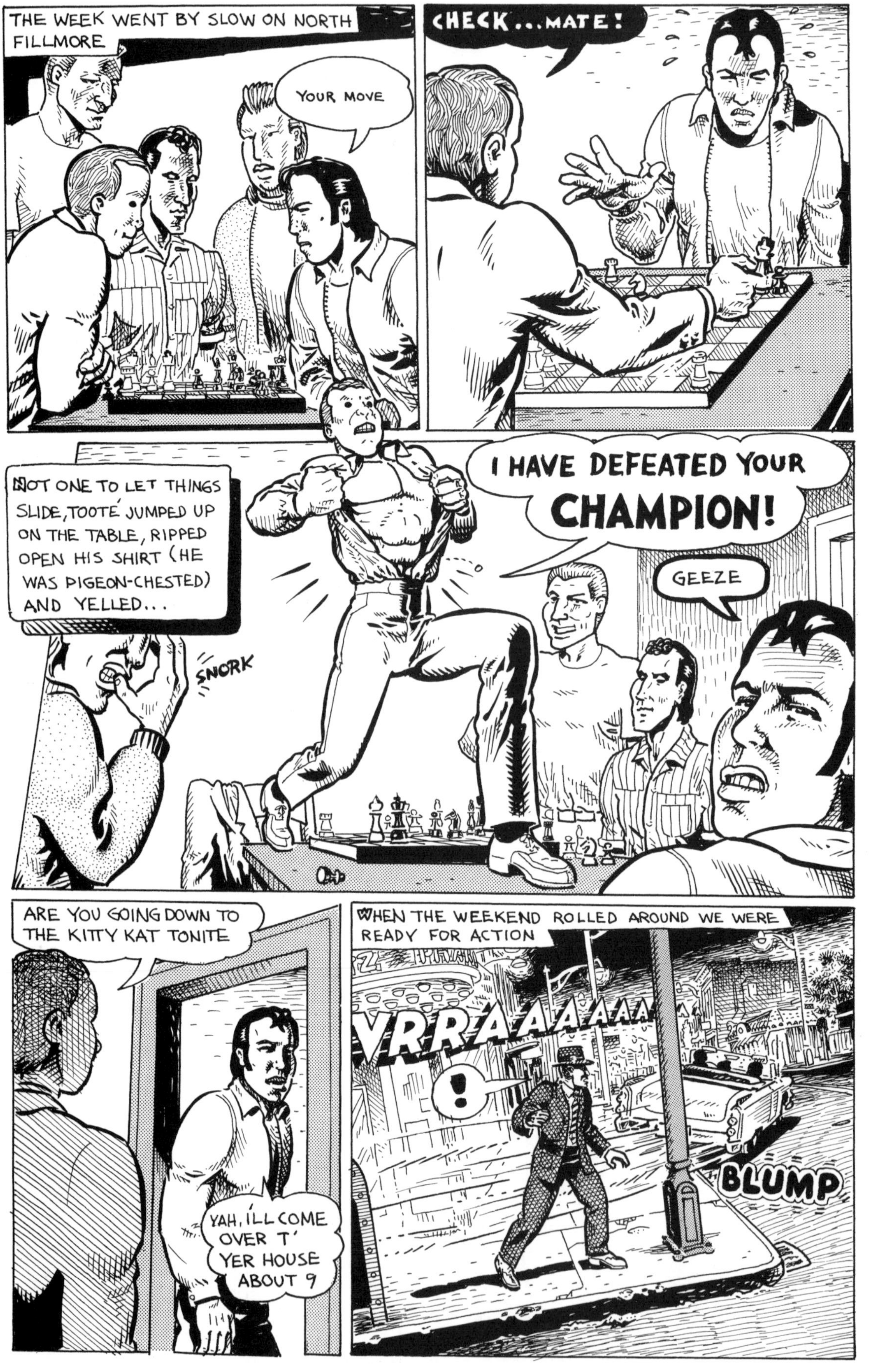
THE WEEK WENT BY SLOW ON NORTH FILLMORE
YOUR MOVE
CHECK...MATE!
NOT ONE TO LET THINGS SLIDE, TOOTÉ JUMPED UP ON THE TABLE, RIPPED OPEN HIS SHIRT (HE WAS PIGEON-CHESTED) AND YELLED...
I HAVE DEFEATED YOUR CHAMPION!
GEEZE
SNORK
ARE YOU GOING DOWN TO THE KITTY KAT TONITE
YAH, I'LL COME OVER T' YER HOUSE ABOUT 9
WHEN THE WEEKEND ROLLED AROUND WE WERE READY FOR ACTION
VRRAAAAAAA
!
BLUMP

YOURR... LIPS ARE TOUCHING MINE A RHAPSODY DIVINE ♫

DIT DIDIT DIT D'DIT D'DIT

DIT DIDIT DIT D'DIT D'DIT

THE KITTY KAT HAD ITS OWN VOCAL GROUP, THE VIBRAHARPS. (THEY EVEN CUT A FEW RECORDS)
DONALD DUCK (LEAD)   TIMMY CHARLES (TENOR)   HARGROVES (BASS)   LESTER PHIPPS (BARITONE)

YOU LOOK LAK YOU GOT THE WORRIES OF THE WORLD ON YO' SHOULDER

HOW LONG IS YO' TONGUE

HOW LONG IS YOURS?

YOU SHOUN' BE AXIN' ME THAT. YOU SHOULD BE AXIN' ME HOW DEEP MAH THROAT IS

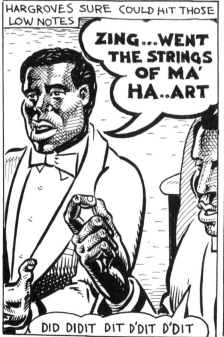

HARGROVES SURE COULD HIT THOSE LOW NOTES

ZING...WENT THE STRINGS OF MA' HA..ART

DID DIDIT DIT D'DIT D'DIT

SO uh WHAT DO YA DO FOR A LIVING?

I DAHNCE

DID DIDIT DID D'DIT D'DIT

TEE HEE

DID DIDIT DIT D'DIT D'DIT

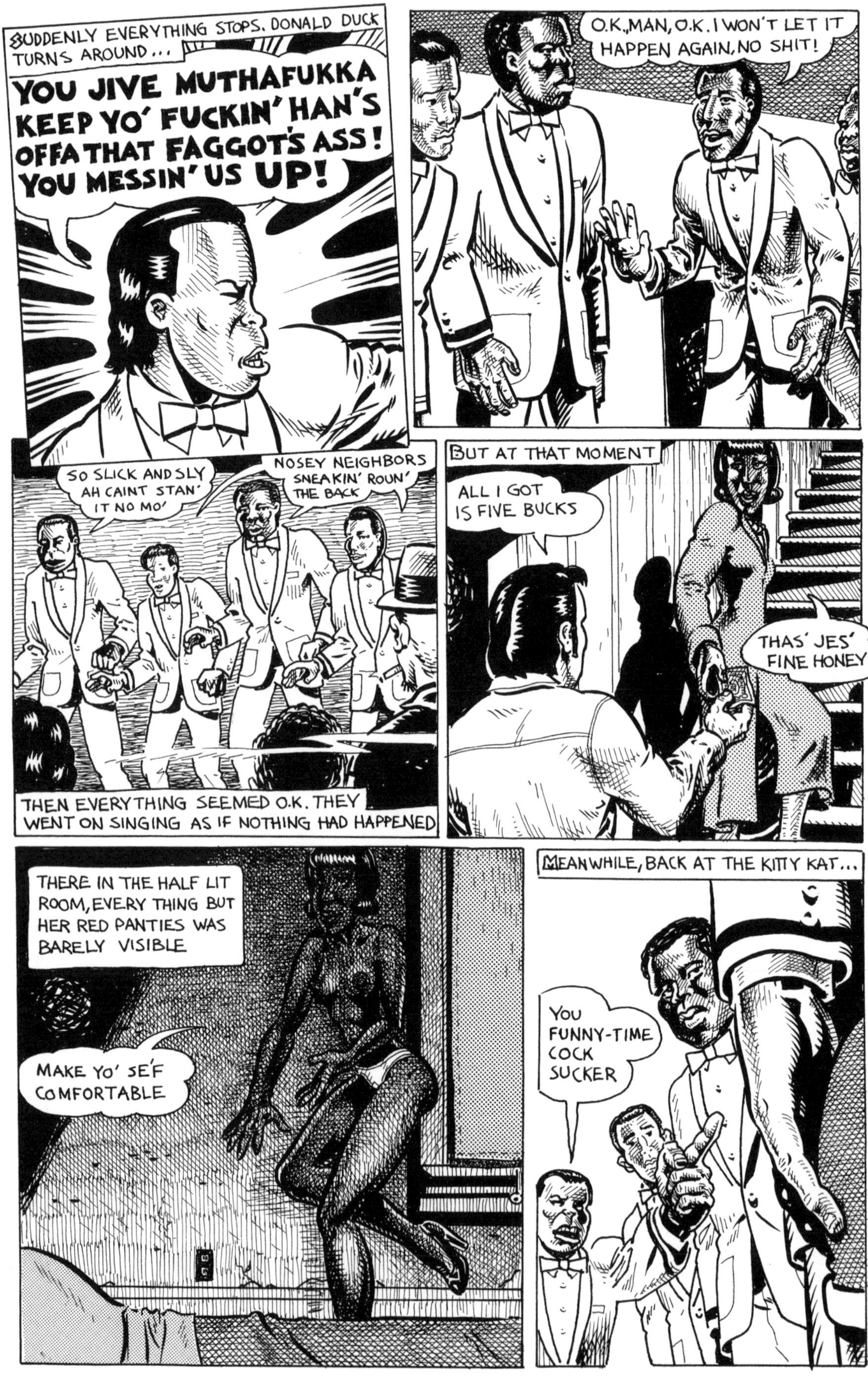
SUDDENLY EVERYTHING STOPS. DONALD DUCK TURNS AROUND...
YOU JIVE MUTHAFUKKA KEEP YO' FUCKIN' HAN'S OFFA THAT FAGGOT'S ASS! YOU MESSIN' US UP!
O.K., MAN, O.K. I WON'T LET IT HAPPEN AGAIN, NO SHIT!
SO SLICK AND SLY AH CAINT STAN' IT NO MO'
NOSEY NEIGHBORS SNEAKIN' ROUN' THE BACK
THEN EVERYTHING SEEMED O.K. THEY WENT ON SINGING AS IF NOTHING HAD HAPPENED
BUT AT THAT MOMENT
ALL I GOT IS FIVE BUCKS
THAS' JES' FINE HONEY
THERE IN THE HALF LIT ROOM, EVERY THING BUT HER RED PANTIES WAS BARELY VISIBLE
MAKE YO' SE'F COMFORTABLE
MEANWHILE, BACK AT THE KITTY KAT...
YOU FUNNY-TIME COCK SUCKER

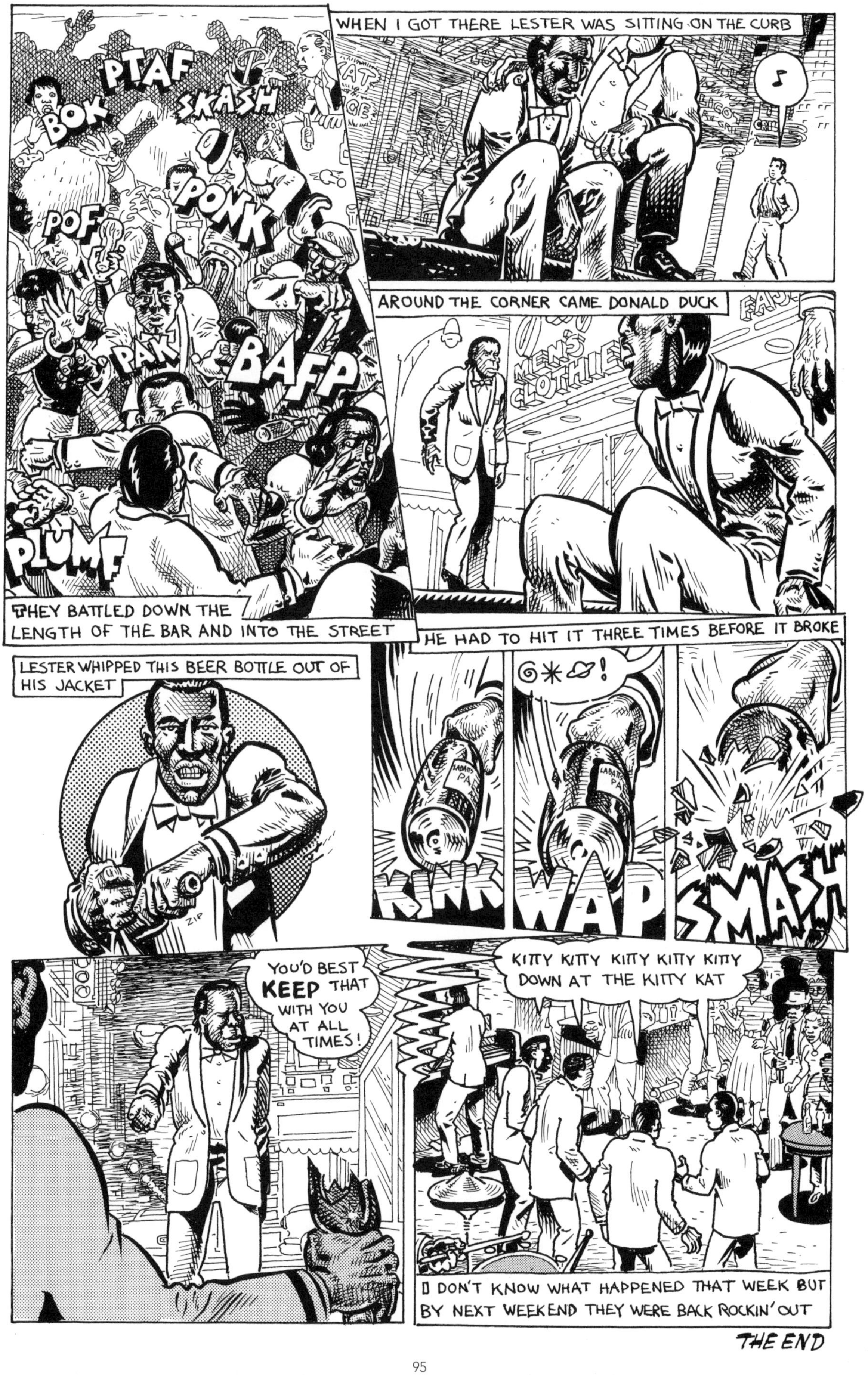
BOK
PTAF
SKASH
PONK
POF
PAK
BAFF
PLUMF
THEY BATTLED DOWN THE LENGTH OF THE BAR AND INTO THE STREET
WHEN I GOT THERE LESTER WAS SITTING ON THE CURB
AROUND THE CORNER CAME DONALD DUCK
MEN'S CLOTHIER
LESTER WHIPPED THIS BEER BOTTLE OUT OF HIS JACKET
ZIP
HE HAD TO HIT IT THREE TIMES BEFORE IT BROKE
KINK
WAP
SMASH
YOU'D BEST KEEP THAT WITH YOU AT ALL TIMES!
KITTY KITTY KITTY KITTY KITTY DOWN AT THE KITTY KAT
I DON'T KNOW WHAT HAPPENED THAT WEEK BUT BY NEXT WEEKEND THEY WERE BACK ROCKIN' OUT
THE END

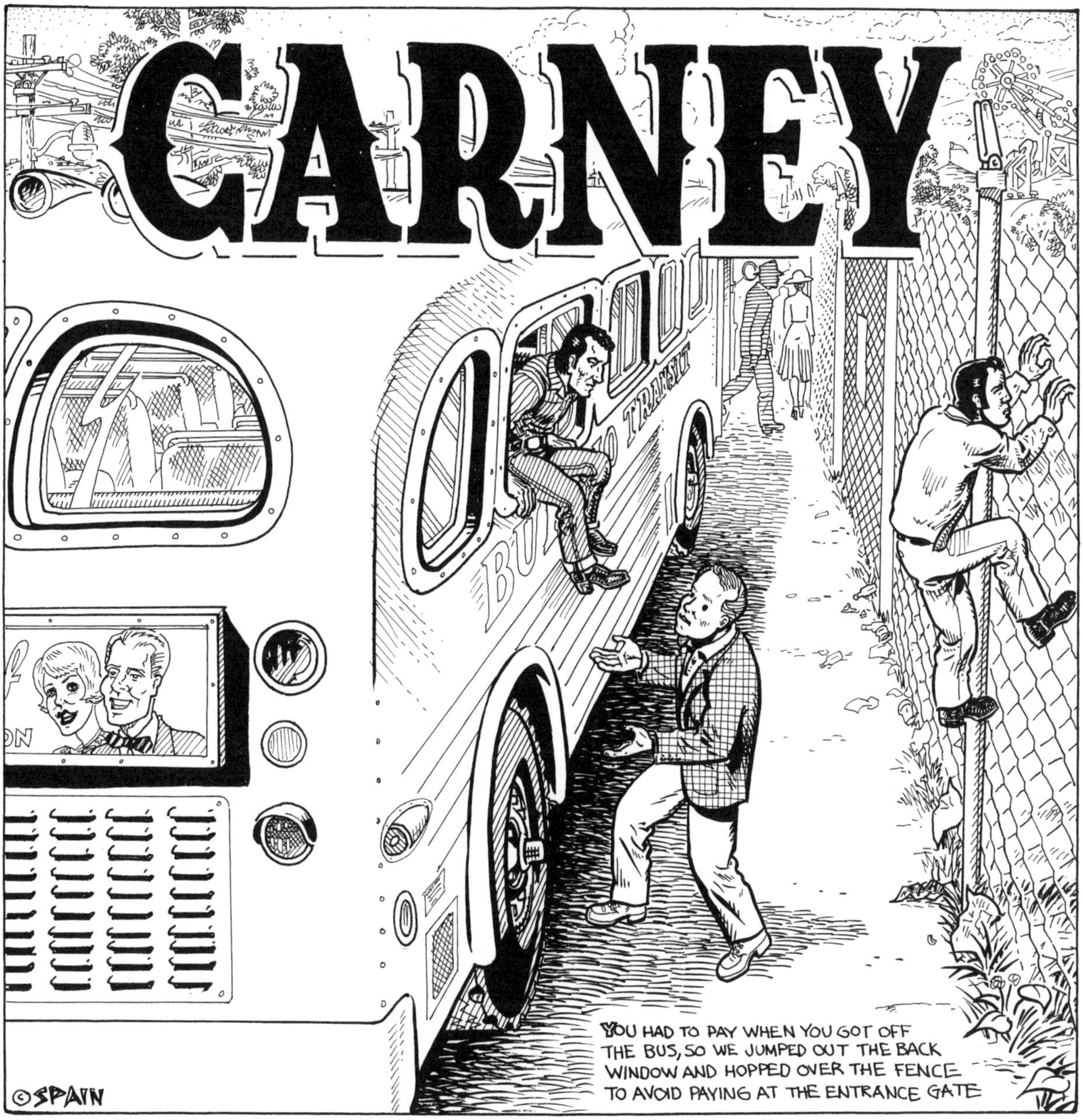

CARNEY
BUFFALO TRANSIT
YOU HAD TO PAY WHEN YOU GOT OFF THE BUS, SO WE JUMPED OUT THE BACK WINDOW AND HOPPED OVER THE FENCE TO AVOID PAYING AT THE ENTRANCE GATE
©SPAIN

DEBAUCHERY & DELINQUENCY IN BUFFALO:

An Interview with Spain Rodriguez

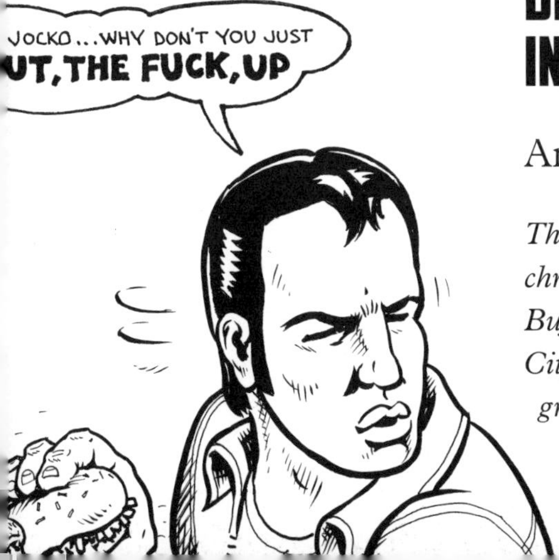

JOCKO...WHY DON'T YOU JUST
UT, THE FUCK, UP

The autobiographical short stories in Cruisin' With the Hound *chronicle the author's rowdy days growing up and living in Buffalo, New York in the '50s and '60s. Before moving to New York City (and ultimately San Francisco) and becoming an underground cartoonist, he spent much of the '50s and '60s straddling biker and working-class culture in Buffalo and living a life of*

WE QUICKLY GOT LOST IN THE CROWD. THE IDEA WAS TO SEE HOW LITTLE WE COULD GET AWAY WITH SPENDING, SO WE IMMEDIATELY HEADED FOR THE FREE STUFF

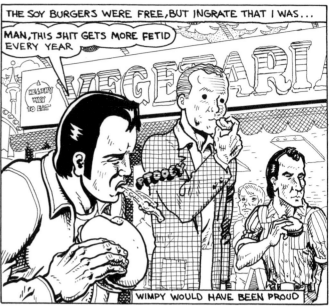

THE SOY BURGERS WERE FREE, BUT INGRATE THAT I WAS...

MAN, THIS SHIT GETS MORE FETID EVERY YEAR

A HEALTHY WAY TO EAT

WIMPY WOULD HAVE BEEN PROUD

OVER AT THE HOG EXHIBIT, SOME FARMER WAS LASCIVIOUSLY STROKING THE PIG'S UNDERSIDE WITH A CHROME-TIPPED POLE

SQORNK

THE PIG SEEMED TO BE GOING FOR IT.

I NOTICED YOU WERE GETTING A LITTLE HOT WHEN THEY WERE STROKING THAT PIG'S BALLS, SPAIN

NO, THAT'S JUST MY DICK IN ITS NORMAL STATE. PERHAPS YOU'D LIKE TO GET DOWN ON YOUR KNEES SO YOU CAN MONITOR MY DONG MORE CLOSELY

proto-juvenile delinqency, and enjoying every minute of it. The following interview with Spain is an excerpt from a 1998 interview I conducted for The Comics Journal *and offers the artist's reflections and recollections of the period in his life that he recounts in this book. Most of the stories we discuss were published in* My True Story *(1994, Fantagraphics Books). We hope this sheds some light on the stories appearing in this volume.*

—Gary Groth

THE IMPRESSIONABLE AGE

GARY GROTH: *You were born and raised in Buffalo.*
SPAIN: Right.
I understand that you started drawing in the second grade and that the comics you read when you were a kid included Captain Marvel *and DC comics. You stopped reading comics when the Code was instituted around '53—*
Yeah, '53, '54. You could still get stuff like *Johnny Dynamite* and *One Million BC*; I think those were the

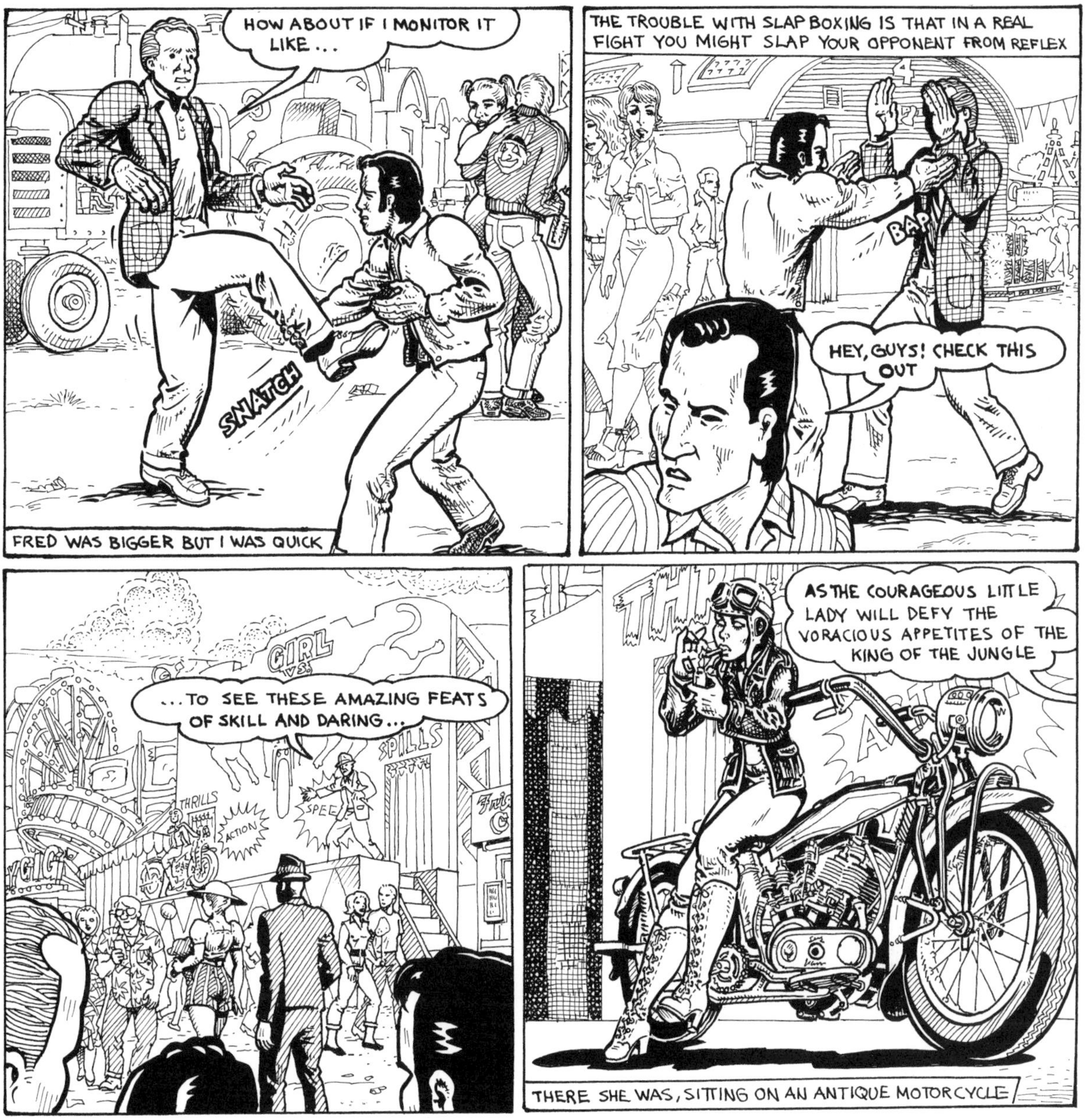
HOW ABOUT IF I MONITOR IT LIKE...
SNATCH
FRED WAS BIGGER BUT I WAS QUICK
THE TROUBLE WITH SLAP BOXING IS THAT IN A REAL FIGHT YOU MIGHT SLAP YOUR OPPONENT FROM REFLEX
BAP
HEY, GUYS! CHECK THIS OUT
GIRL VS.
...TO SEE THESE AMAZING FEATS OF SKILL AND DARING...
SPILLS
THRILLS
ACTION
AS THE COURAGEOUS LITTLE LADY WILL DEFY THE VORACIOUS APPETITES OF THE KING OF THE JUNGLE
THERE SHE WAS, SITTING ON AN ANTIQUE MOTORCYCLE

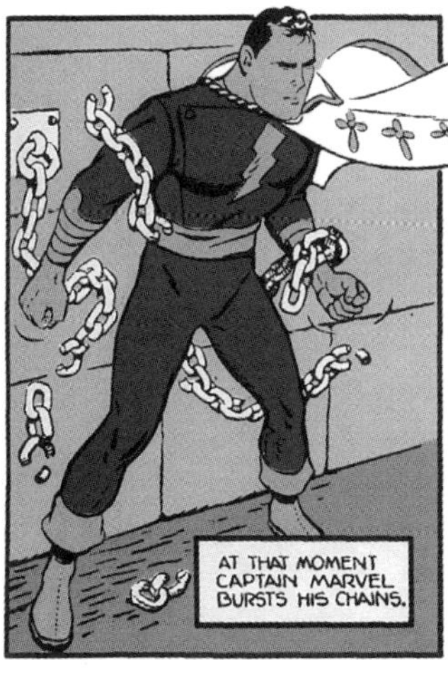
AT THAT MOMENT CAPTAIN MARVEL BURSTS HIS CHAINS.

Panel from "The Return of Sivana" in *Whiz Comics* #3 (March 1940) drawn by C.C. Beck, written by Bill Parker ©1940 DC Comics

last ones to hold out against the Comics Code.

Could you tell me a little bit about what your upbringing was like? Your father was an auto—

My father did collision work, repaired car bodies.

You were born in '40—

I was born in 1940.

So the war was over by the time you were 5. Do you recall the war having an impact on you?

Yeah. I was at an impressionable age, and I remember all that war stuff that was going on, I remember the various phases of the war. Even though I got it through newsreels and movies, and that sort of thing, it had a big impression on me. I had older cousins who were in various branches of the armed services.

I assume your father wasn't involved.

No, my father, and me for that matter, we were just born at a time when we missed wars. It seems that wars come with a certain schedule,

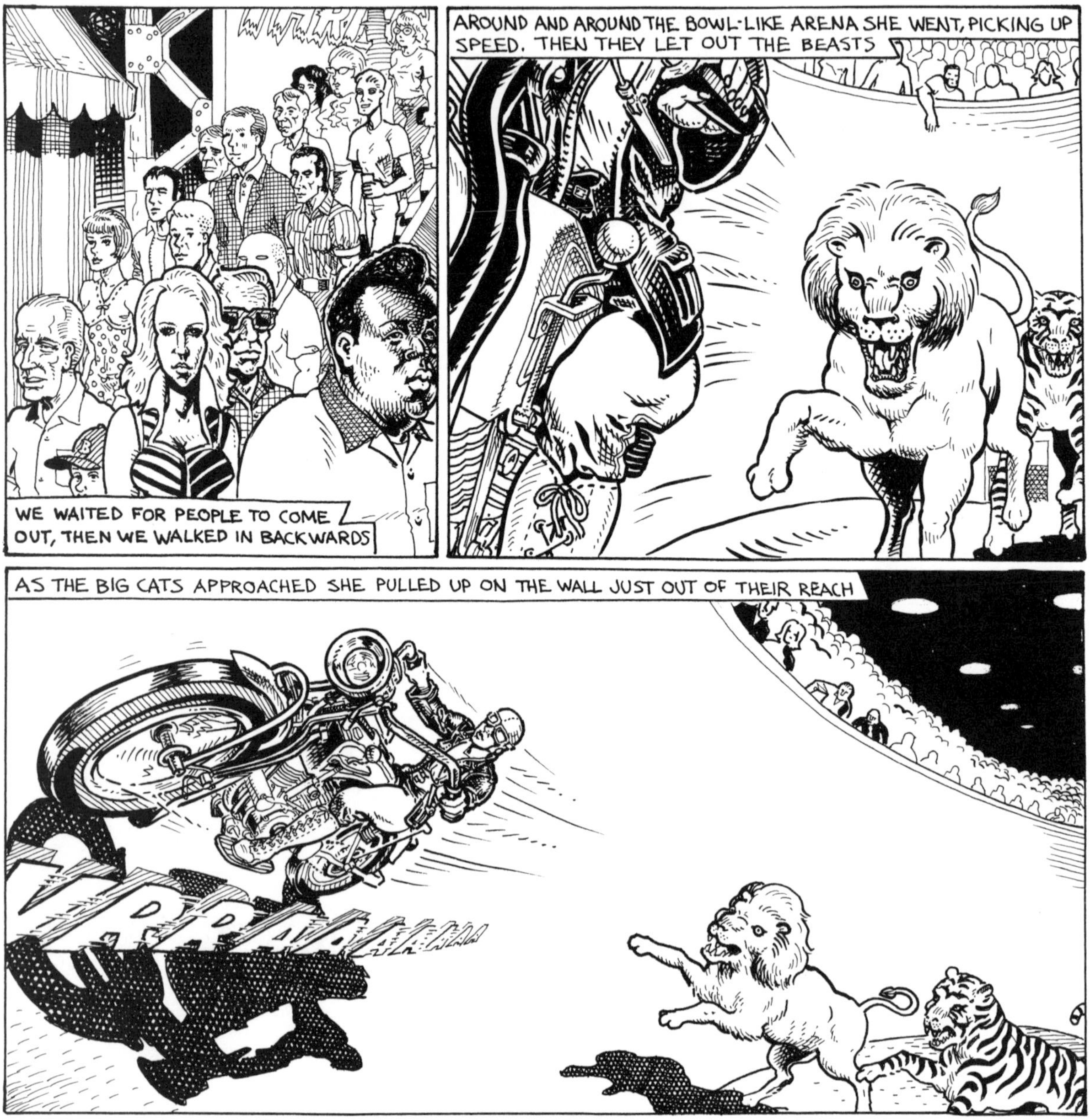
WE WAITED FOR PEOPLE TO COME OUT, THEN WE WALKED IN BACKWARDS
AROUND AND AROUND THE BOWL-LIKE ARENA SHE WENT, PICKING UP SPEED. THEN THEY LET OUT THE BEASTS
AS THE BIG CATS APPROACHED SHE PULLED UP ON THE WALL JUST OUT OF THEIR REACH

and both me and my father were just lucky to miss them—my father was too young for World War I and too old for World War II.

Were you too old for Vietnam?

Yeah, I was too old for Vietnam. I had actually gotten a 4F.

TAKING HIS LUMPS

Would you characterize your dad as working class?

Yeah.

What was your upbringing like, what was your childhood like?

I had a lot of good times. I certainly took my lumps. My neighborhood had various ethnicities, it was an Italian neighborhood, a Jewish neighborhood and a black neighborhood. The block I lived on was mixed, but if you went to the Irish neighborhood you had to worry about getting punched out by the Irish bully, the Jewish neighborhood you had to worry about getting punched out by the Jewish bully, the black bully, or the Polish bully or—

What were your parents' ethnic backgrounds?

My mother was born here, but her family is Italian, and she grew up in Italy. My father's Spanish. In Buffalo there's a Spanish community, but it's spread out, there's no real Spanish neighborhood. Where I grew up there were all kinds of different people—Irish, Polish and Greek—

Did they form cliques, like New York City?

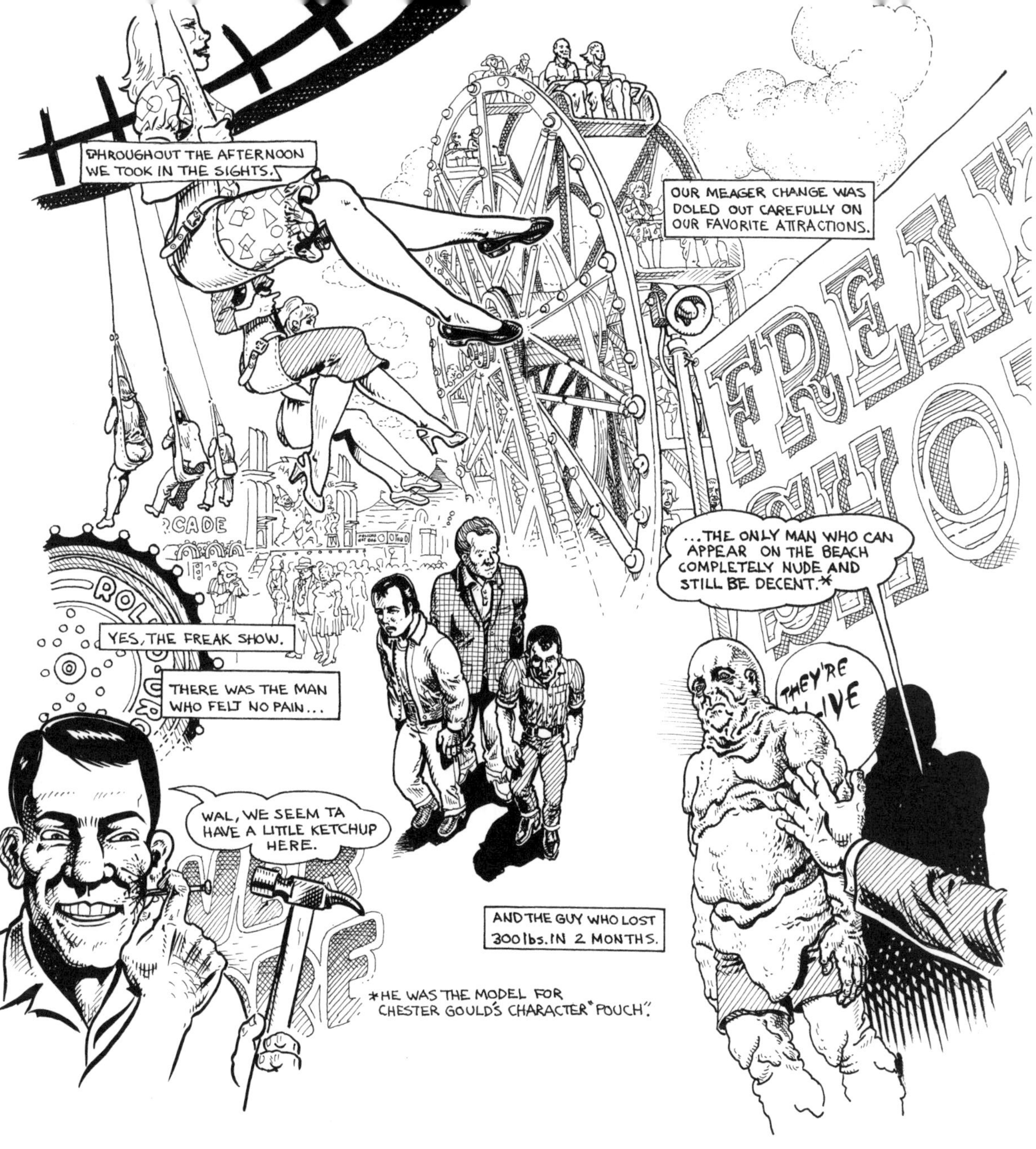
THROUGHOUT THE AFTERNOON WE TOOK IN THE SIGHTS.
OUR MEAGER CHANGE WAS DOLED OUT CAREFULLY ON OUR FAVORITE ATTRACTIONS.
FREAK SHOW
YES, THE FREAK SHOW.
THERE WAS THE MAN WHO FELT NO PAIN...
...THE ONLY MAN WHO CAN APPEAR ON THE BEACH COMPLETELY NUDE AND STILL BE DECENT.*
THEY'RE
WAL, WE SEEM TA HAVE A LITTLE KETCHUP HERE.
AND THE GUY WHO LOST 300 lbs. IN 2 MONTHS.
*HE WAS THE MODEL FOR CHESTER GOULD'S CHARACTER "POUCH".

Not so much in my neighborhood. The guys who grew up together were the real formation point. Even though most of us were from Catholic backgrounds, they wouldn't let us into the Catholic Cub Scouts, but they would let us into the Jewish Cub Scouts. Jews were more liberal. For the Catholics, we were just bad kids. But what happened in the Jewish Cub Scouts was that all the bad Jewish kids ended up being in one den with us, and all the good Catholic kids and Protestant kids were in another den with the nice Jewish kids. And then there was this kid... a Jewish kid, who was a Boy Scout. He was in charge of the bad kids' den; he tried to foment a revolution. I don't know, we were probably 11 or 12 or something like that, we were pretty young, and somebody was talking about having a revolution. We were going to split off from the nice kids' den. We were all very earnest about it, we even wrote up Declarations of Independence. But each time we tried to make the edges brown (so it would look more official), we would burn up our document.

I went to religious instruction. My family was not that religious. My mother was nominally Catholic... but there was a church on the corner, so I just started going, I just got into it.

On your own?

On my own, yeah. And my parents just let me go.

At what age?

Probably from about 7 or 8 to 11

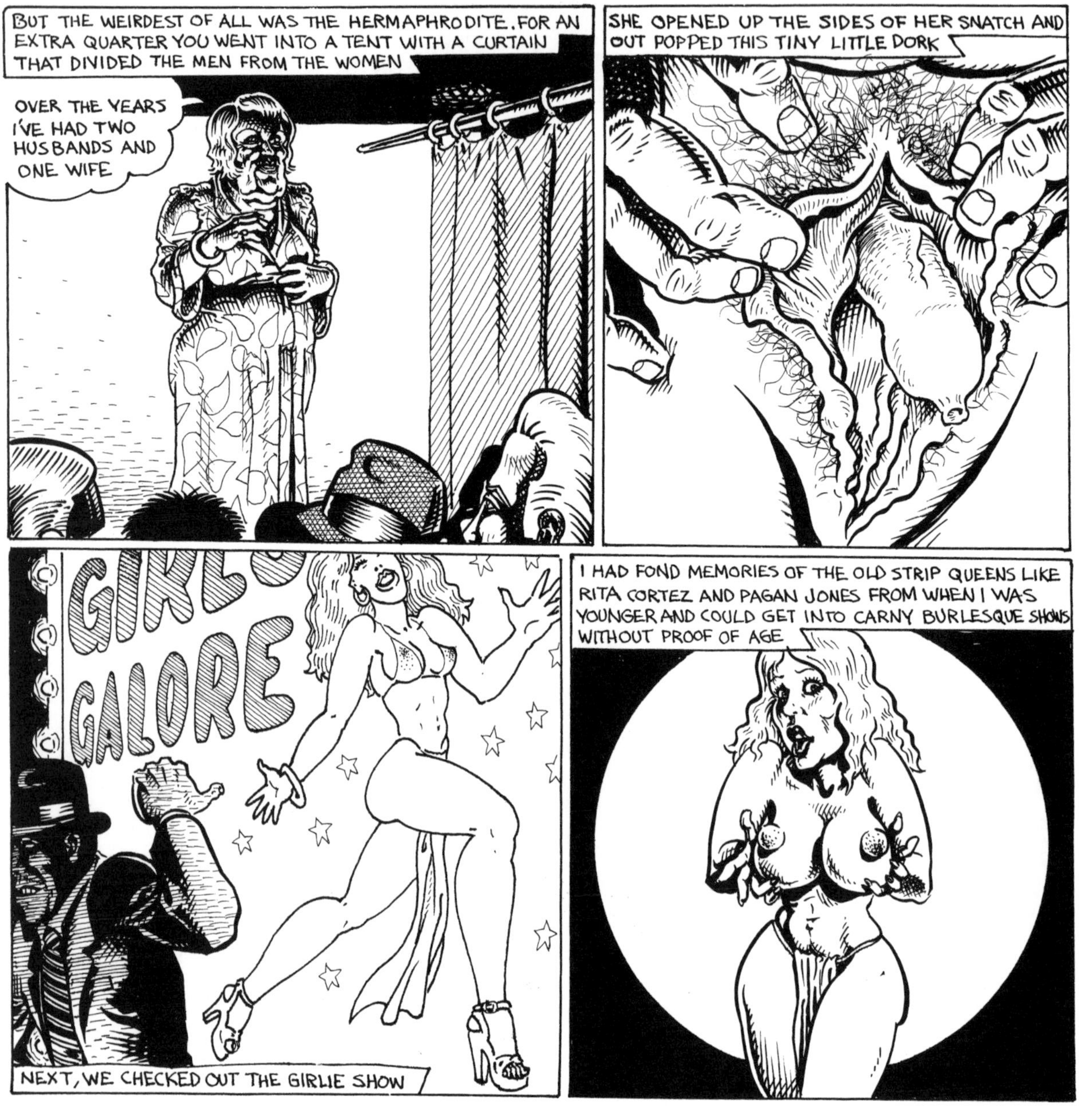
BUT THE WEIRDEST OF ALL WAS THE HERMAPHRODITE. FOR AN EXTRA QUARTER YOU WENT INTO A TENT WITH A CURTAIN THAT DIVIDED THE MEN FROM THE WOMEN
OVER THE YEARS I'VE HAD TWO HUSBANDS AND ONE WIFE
SHE OPENED UP THE SIDES OF HER SNATCH AND OUT POPPED THIS TINY LITTLE DORK
GALORE
NEXT, WE CHECKED OUT THE GIRLIE SHOW
I HAD FOND MEMORIES OF THE OLD STRIP QUEENS LIKE RITA CORTEZ AND PAGAN JONES FROM WHEN I WAS YOUNGER AND COULD GET INTO CARNY BURLESQUE SHOWS WITHOUT PROOF OF AGE

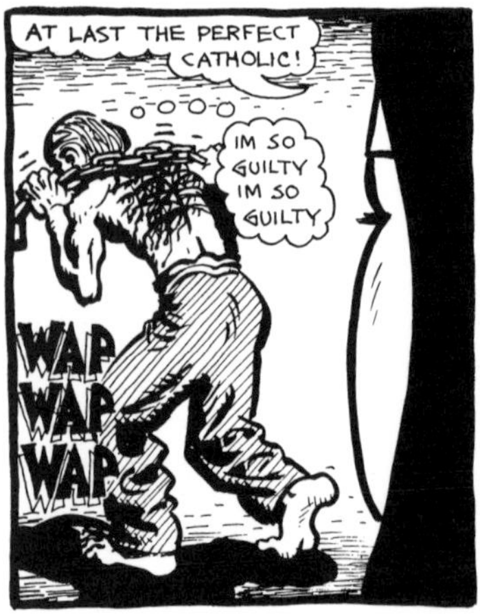
AT LAST THE PERFECT CATHOLIC!
IM SO GUILTY IM SO GUILTY
WAP WAP WAP

Panel from "The Leather Nun Gets Hers" in *Tales From The Leather Nun* by Spain ©1973 Last Gasp

or 12.

What prompted that?

I wonder, but it just seemed—it was an impulse to be "good." Religion lays out a framework—if you want to be "good," do this. As a kid, it seemed to make sense. Obviously, a lot of adults are doing it. You would go to the confessional, and you would have these little sins to confess. You'd have to think them up, because you forgot them. "I disobeyed my parents seven times. I swore nine times."

Right, you just have to guess.

Right. In this half-assed, backward way they prompt you to lie. Who can keep track of all that stuff? And things like… you ate meat on Friday. What are you going to do? This is what your mom cooks. [*Laughs.*] One of the things that turned me around was… I was making my Confirmation, and the nun's instruction was you were supposed to go up to the communion rail

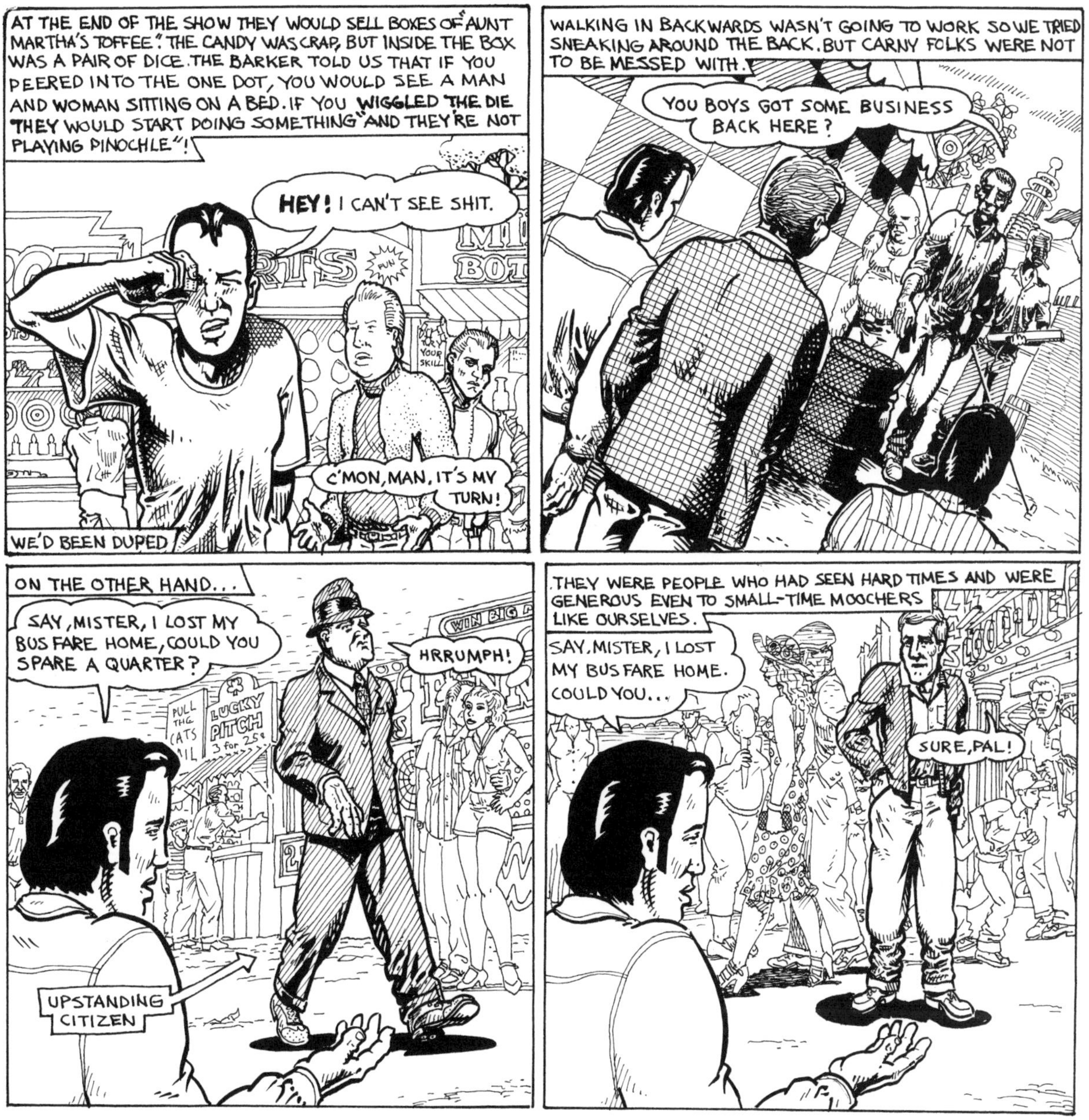
AT THE END OF THE SHOW THEY WOULD SELL BOXES OF "AUNT MARTHA'S TOFFEE." THE CANDY WAS CRAP, BUT INSIDE THE BOX WAS A PAIR OF DICE. THE BARKER TOLD US THAT IF YOU PEERED INTO THE ONE DOT, YOU WOULD SEE A MAN AND WOMAN SITTING ON A BED. IF YOU WIGGLED THE DIE THEY WOULD START DOING SOMETHING "AND THEY'RE NOT PLAYING PINOCHLE"!
HEY! I CAN'T SEE SHIT.
C'MON, MAN, IT'S MY TURN!
WE'D BEEN DUPED
WALKING IN BACKWARDS WASN'T GOING TO WORK SO WE TRIED SNEAKING AROUND THE BACK. BUT CARNY FOLKS WERE NOT TO BE MESSED WITH.
YOU BOYS GOT SOME BUSINESS BACK HERE?
ON THE OTHER HAND...
SAY, MISTER, I LOST MY BUS FARE HOME, COULD YOU SPARE A QUARTER?
HRRUMPH!
PULL THE CATS TAIL
LUCKY PITCH 3 for 25¢
UPSTANDING CITIZEN
THEY WERE PEOPLE WHO HAD SEEN HARD TIMES AND WERE GENEROUS EVEN TO SMALL-TIME MOOCHERS LIKE OURSELVES.
SAY, MISTER, I LOST MY BUS FARE HOME. COULD YOU...
SURE, PAL!

and cut a round corner, but the kid in front of me cut a square corner. I thought maybe I heard it wrong. So I cut a square corner, too. I was temporarily confused. The nun snatched me out and sent me down to Father Bent, who was an ex-wrestler and a drunk. I came into raw contact with God's hierarchy, and I thought, being a good Catholic, he had some special insight from God, and if I sincerely told him the truth, everything would be OK. So I went down there without a sense of trepidation, and I told him what happened, and he just wasn't hearing it. "We know you, you're a wise guy." And as a matter of fact, in religious instruction I was always pretty well behaved. I wasn't going there because I had to, after all. But he just went through this whole Gestapo act and suddenly I realized that this guy didn't have any insight from God. So it was a revelation… the scales being lifted from my eyes, that this guy didn't have any special knowledge, so it just opened the door to questioning… well, if he doesn't have any special knowledge—and, in fact, the guy was a fool—what does this imply about the institution he represents? Even at the time it seemed very comical to me that he was making a big stink over some minor bullshit. I could see that this guy was a whole lot stupider than me, man. This was my first insight into the phoney pretentiousness of official authority. [*Laughs.*]

You were 11 or 12?

WE WAITED IN ANTICIPATION FOR THE WOMEN. BUT FIRST WE HAD TO SIT THROUGH SOME CORNBALL COMEDIAN

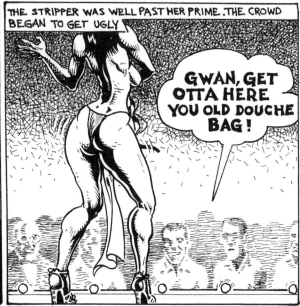

THE STRIPPER WAS WELL PAST HER PRIME. THE CROWD BEGAN TO GET UGLY

GWAN, GET OTTA HERE YOU OLD DOUCHE BAG!

THE AGING STRIP TEASER AND THE COMEDIAN (PROBABLY HER HUSBAND) RAGED BACK AT THE AUDIENCE

YOU WOP BASTARD, YOU PROBABLY NEVER HAD A WOMAN WHO WASN'T YOUR MOTHER!

MY MOTHER'S DEAD BUT I'M SURE SHE LOOKS BETTER THAN YOU!

THE ARGUMENT RAGED BACK AND FORTH FOR A WHILE. THEN THE TWO PERFORMERS LEFT THE STAGE. THERE WOULD BE FEW BOXES OF AUNT MARTHA'S TOFFEE WITH THE RISQUÉ DICE SOLD AFTER THAT PERFORMANCE

I was 11 or 12, yeah.

Did that pretty much end your interest in religious instruction?

Well, I still went to religious instruction 'til the next grade. Sister Richard was the teacher… funny these names that they have. I sat down on the first day of instruction and suddenly she comes over and starts to flail away at me with a ruler. And I said, "What? What did I do?" She says, "That inkwell's crooked." When I told her that it was that way when I took my seat, she was

not appeased. All she had to do was mention it, and I would gladly put it any fucking way she wanted it. Between this and the crazy "Square Corner Incident," it was pretty clear that the Catholic Church was run by a bunch of sadistic loonies (and I hadn't even read any history yet). At that point, I realized, "I'm not going to that crazy place." [*Laughs.*]

You did not go to a parochial school?

No. My parents, especially my old man, were not especially religious.

Were they agnostic? Or were they just

indifferent?

A little of both—my mother was nominally a Catholic, but in terms of my dad, the Spanish experience with Catholicism is not a happy one, you know, they have an especially nasty history. My father just had no identification with the Catholic Church, but he was sufficiently in awe of authority in general that he didn't express any overt hostility; on the other hand, he wasn't about to support it if he didn't have to. As a kid I remember him making anti-

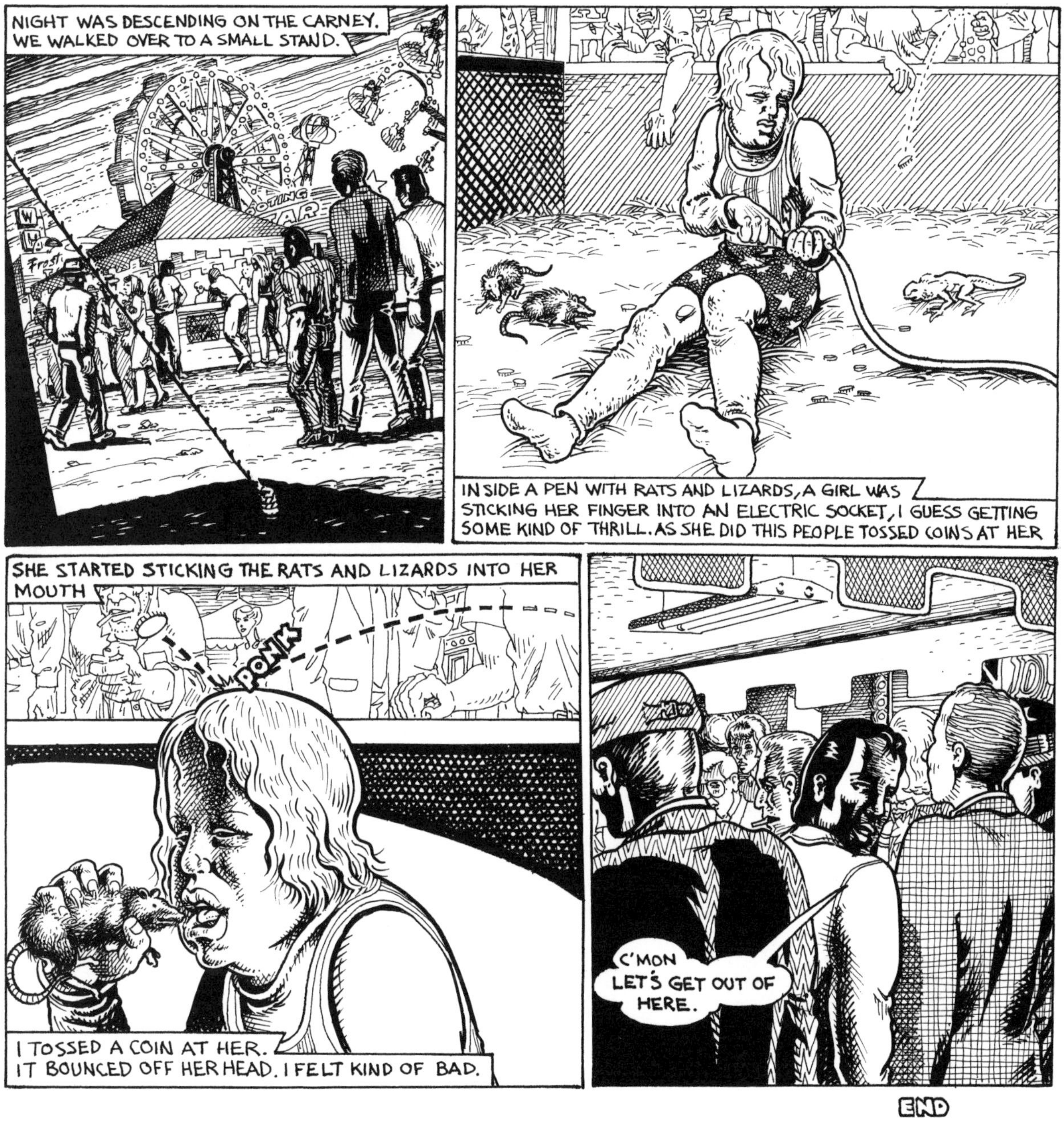
NIGHT WAS DESCENDING ON THE CARNEY. WE WALKED OVER TO A SMALL STAND.
INSIDE A PEN WITH RATS AND LIZARDS, A GIRL WAS STICKING HER FINGER INTO AN ELECTRIC SOCKET, I GUESS GETTING SOME KIND OF THRILL. AS SHE DID THIS PEOPLE TOSSED COINS AT HER
SHE STARTED STICKING THE RATS AND LIZARDS INTO HER MOUTH
PONK
I TOSSED A COIN AT HER. IT BOUNCED OFF HER HEAD. I FELT KIND OF BAD.
C'MON LET'S GET OUT OF HERE.
END

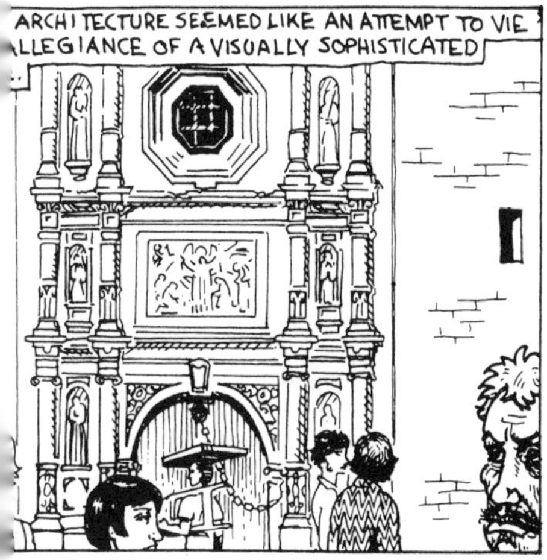
ARCHITECTURE SEEMED LIKE AN ATTEMPT TO VIE
LLEGIANCE OF A VISUALLY SOPHISTICATED

Panel from "Mexico and Me" in *My True Story* ©1992 Spain

religious statements, but it wasn't a big thing in my household. But on the other hand, some kids would have to go; I guess you did.

Yeah. Seven years. But you went through a few years where you did go to church, and you did—

Yeah, I would go to church every Sunday.

What did you get out of that?

Eventually I went through a period where I tried to go to church, but I would tend to fall back to sleep and end up missing mass entirely. When I did manage to make it, I tended to nod out.

During the church ceremony?

Yeah… at some point I had Art Appreciation class in high school, I must have been maybe 13. Going to church became more interesting, because I could check out the architecture and stuff like that. That lessened some of the boredom.

But after I hadn't gone for a long time, I went to "confession," and

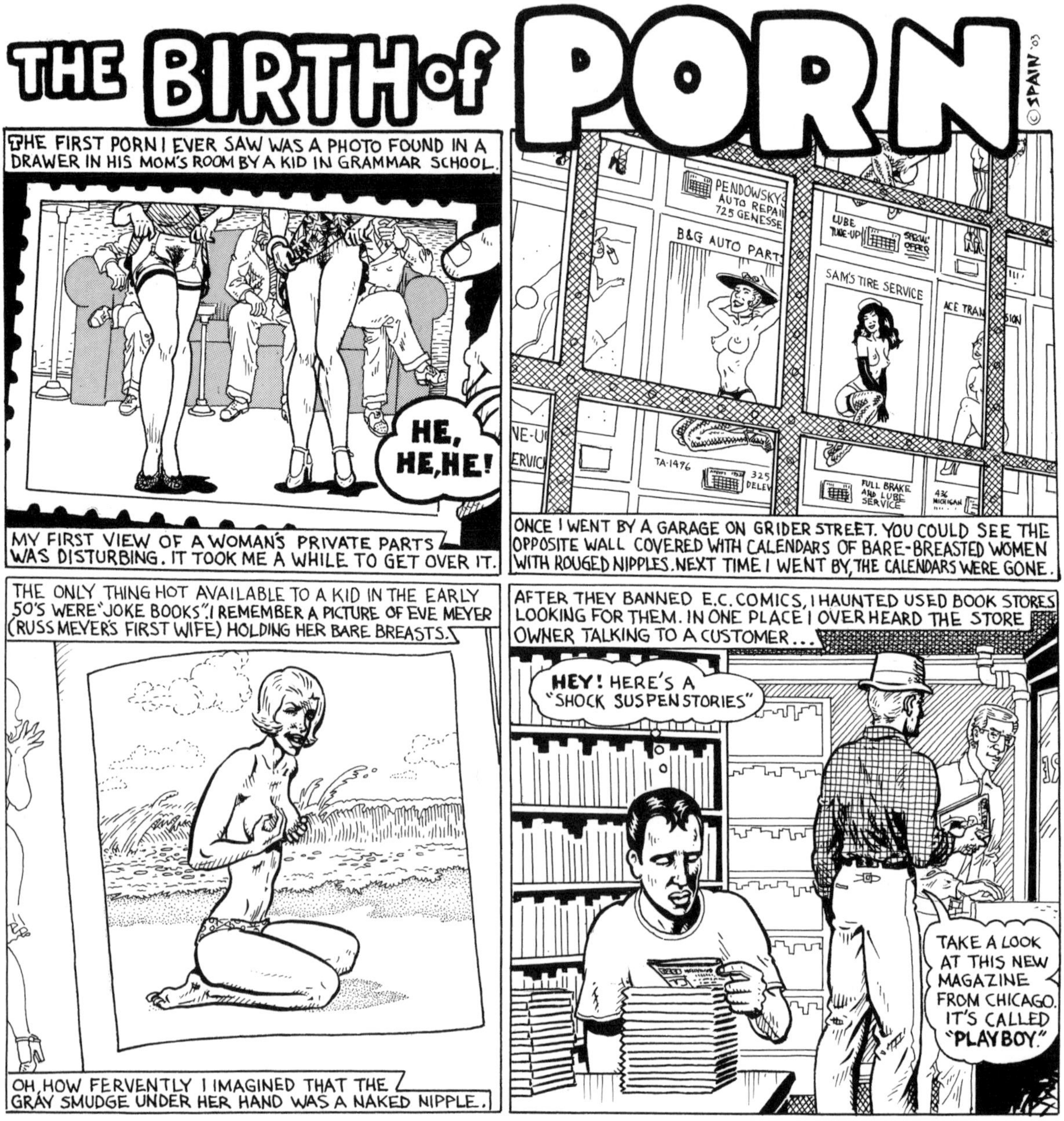
THE BIRTH of PORN
© SPAIN '03
THE FIRST PORN I EVER SAW WAS A PHOTO FOUND IN A DRAWER IN HIS MOM'S ROOM BY A KID IN GRAMMAR SCHOOL.
HE, HE, HE!
MY FIRST VIEW OF A WOMAN'S PRIVATE PARTS WAS DISTURBING. IT TOOK ME A WHILE TO GET OVER IT.
B&G AUTO PARTS
SAM'S TIRE SERVICE
ONCE I WENT BY A GARAGE ON GRIDER STREET. YOU COULD SEE THE OPPOSITE WALL COVERED WITH CALENDARS OF BARE-BREASTED WOMEN WITH ROUGED NIPPLES. NEXT TIME I WENT BY, THE CALENDARS WERE GONE.
THE ONLY THING HOT AVAILABLE TO A KID IN THE EARLY 50'S WERE "JOKE BOOKS". I REMEMBER A PICTURE OF EVE MEYER (RUSS MEYER'S FIRST WIFE) HOLDING HER BARE BREASTS.
OH, HOW FERVENTLY I IMAGINED THAT THE GRAY SMUDGE UNDER HER HAND WAS A NAKED NIPPLE.
AFTER THEY BANNED E.C. COMICS, I HAUNTED USED BOOK STORES LOOKING FOR THEM. IN ONE PLACE I OVERHEARD THE STORE OWNER TALKING TO A CUSTOMER...
HEY! HERE'S A "SHOCK SUSPENSTORIES"
TAKE A LOOK AT THIS NEW MAGAZINE FROM CHICAGO. IT'S CALLED "PLAYBOY."

as a matter of fact it was the selfsame Father Bent who was in the confessional and I told him I had missed mass about 30 times or something like that, and he said, "Why?"

And I said, "I'd try to wake up for the 9 o'clock mass, and I'd fall asleep, same for the 10:30 mass and so on and I always oversleep."

There was a stunned silence. And then he went into some long rant about how God had done all this stuff for me and I couldn't even give him one lousy hour. He gave me—I forgot all this—25 Our Fathers and 25 Hail Marys, but by that time the whole framework was just so obviously fallacious that I didn't even finish them. I was told that when you walk out of confession you always feel better than when you go in. I remember even as a kid, coming out of confession and thinking, "Well now, honestly, do I feel any better?" And I would have to answer, "No, not really, if I'm going to be honest with myself," which is what I understood you should be as a religious person.

So it did not give you the guidance you had hoped for? Were you searching for absolutes? Were you searching for some sort of standard to measure yourself against?

I guess that's what it was: yeah. My case is a little unique, not having been pushed into it, volunteering for it. But it just seemed to me as a kid, not being very sophisticated, I wanted to be good, and I guess as you say it was some sort of

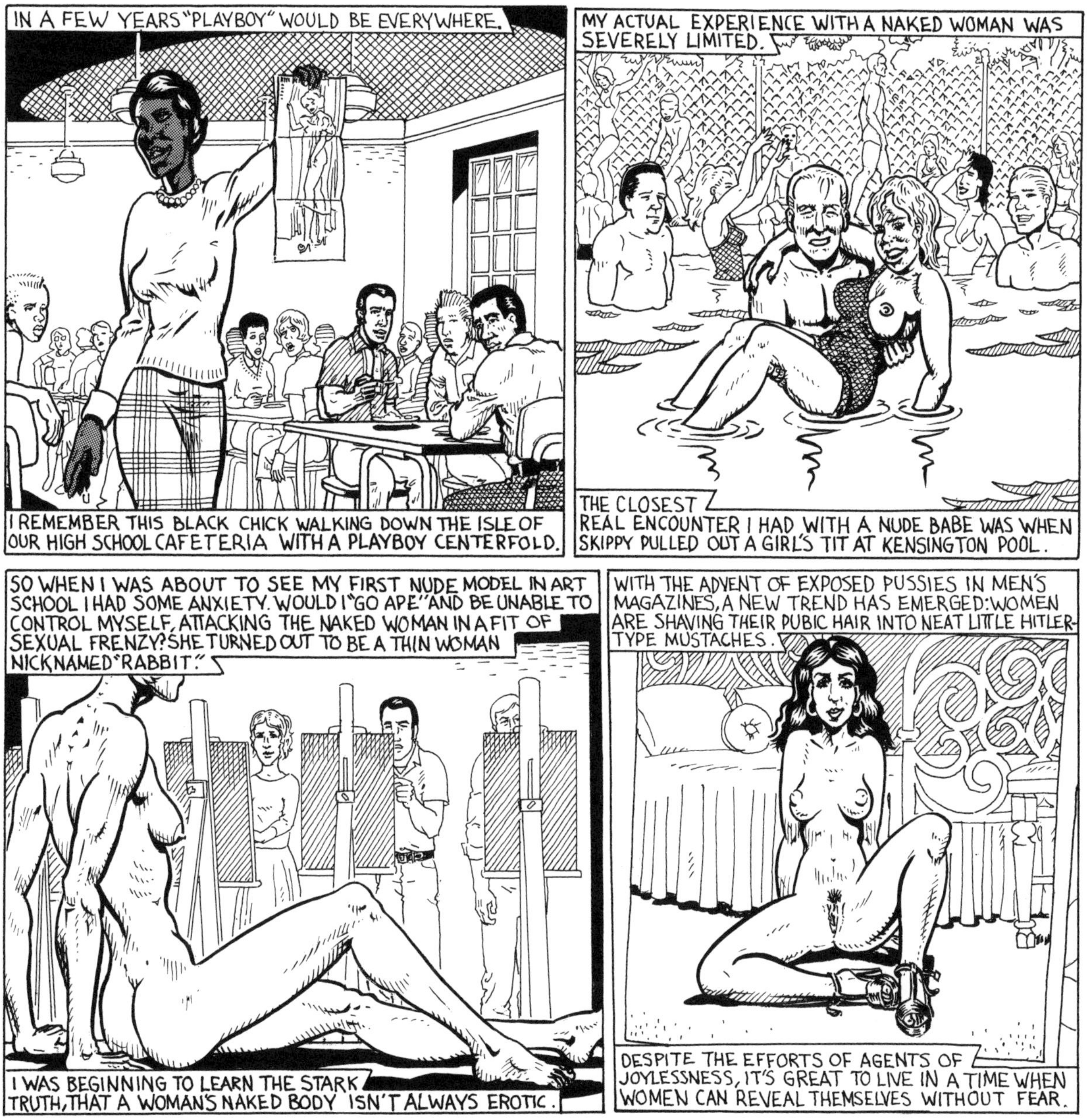
IN A FEW YEARS "PLAYBOY" WOULD BE EVERYWHERE.
I REMEMBER THIS BLACK CHICK WALKING DOWN THE ISLE OF OUR HIGH SCHOOL CAFETERIA WITH A PLAYBOY CENTERFOLD.
MY ACTUAL EXPERIENCE WITH A NAKED WOMAN WAS SEVERELY LIMITED.
THE CLOSEST REAL ENCOUNTER I HAD WITH A NUDE BABE WAS WHEN SKIPPY PULLED OUT A GIRL'S TIT AT KENSINGTON POOL.
SO WHEN I WAS ABOUT TO SEE MY FIRST NUDE MODEL IN ART SCHOOL I HAD SOME ANXIETY. WOULD I "GO APE" AND BE UNABLE TO CONTROL MYSELF, ATTACKING THE NAKED WOMAN IN A FIT OF SEXUAL FRENZY? SHE TURNED OUT TO BE A THIN WOMAN NICKNAMED "RABBIT."
I WAS BEGINNING TO LEARN THE STARK TRUTH, THAT A WOMAN'S NAKED BODY ISN'T ALWAYS EROTIC.
WITH THE ADVENT OF EXPOSED PUSSIES IN MEN'S MAGAZINES, A NEW TREND HAS EMERGED: WOMEN ARE SHAVING THEIR PUBIC HAIR INTO NEAT LITTLE HITLER-TYPE MUSTACHES.
DESPITE THE EFFORTS OF AGENTS OF JOYLESSNESS, IT'S GREAT TO LIVE IN A TIME WHEN WOMEN CAN REVEAL THEMSELVES WITHOUT FEAR.

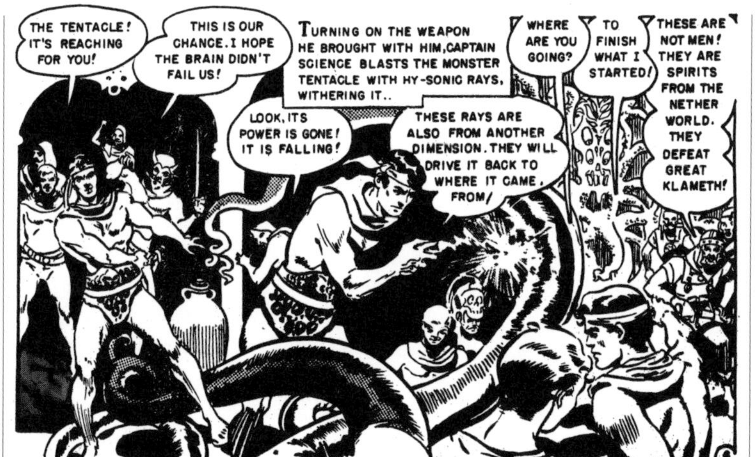
THE TENTACLE! IT'S REACHING FOR YOU!
THIS IS OUR CHANCE. I HOPE THE BRAIN DIDN'T FAIL US!
TURNING ON THE WEAPON HE BROUGHT WITH HIM, CAPTAIN SCIENCE BLASTS THE MONSTER TENTACLE WITH HY-SONIC RAYS, WITHERING IT..
LOOK, ITS POWER IS GONE! IT IS FALLING!
THESE RAYS ARE ALSO FROM ANOTHER DIMENSION. THEY WILL DRIVE IT BACK TO WHERE IT CAME FROM!
WHERE ARE YOU GOING?
TO FINISH WHAT I STARTED!
THESE ARE NOT MEN! THEY ARE SPIRITS FROM THE NETHER WORLD. THEY DEFEAT GREAT KLAMETH!

standard by which you could define yourself as good. As you get older, you increasingly see the evil of the world. This seemed to be a way to attempt to counter that with some personal goodness. The first teacher I had in religious instruction was a very nice nun… you know, she was like some nun out of the movies, a very kind old lady who expounded a very benign religious ideology, so it seemed cool.

Sequence from "The Insidious Doctor Khartoum" from *Captain Science* #4 (June 1951) drawn by Joe Orlando and Wally Wood ©1951 Youthful

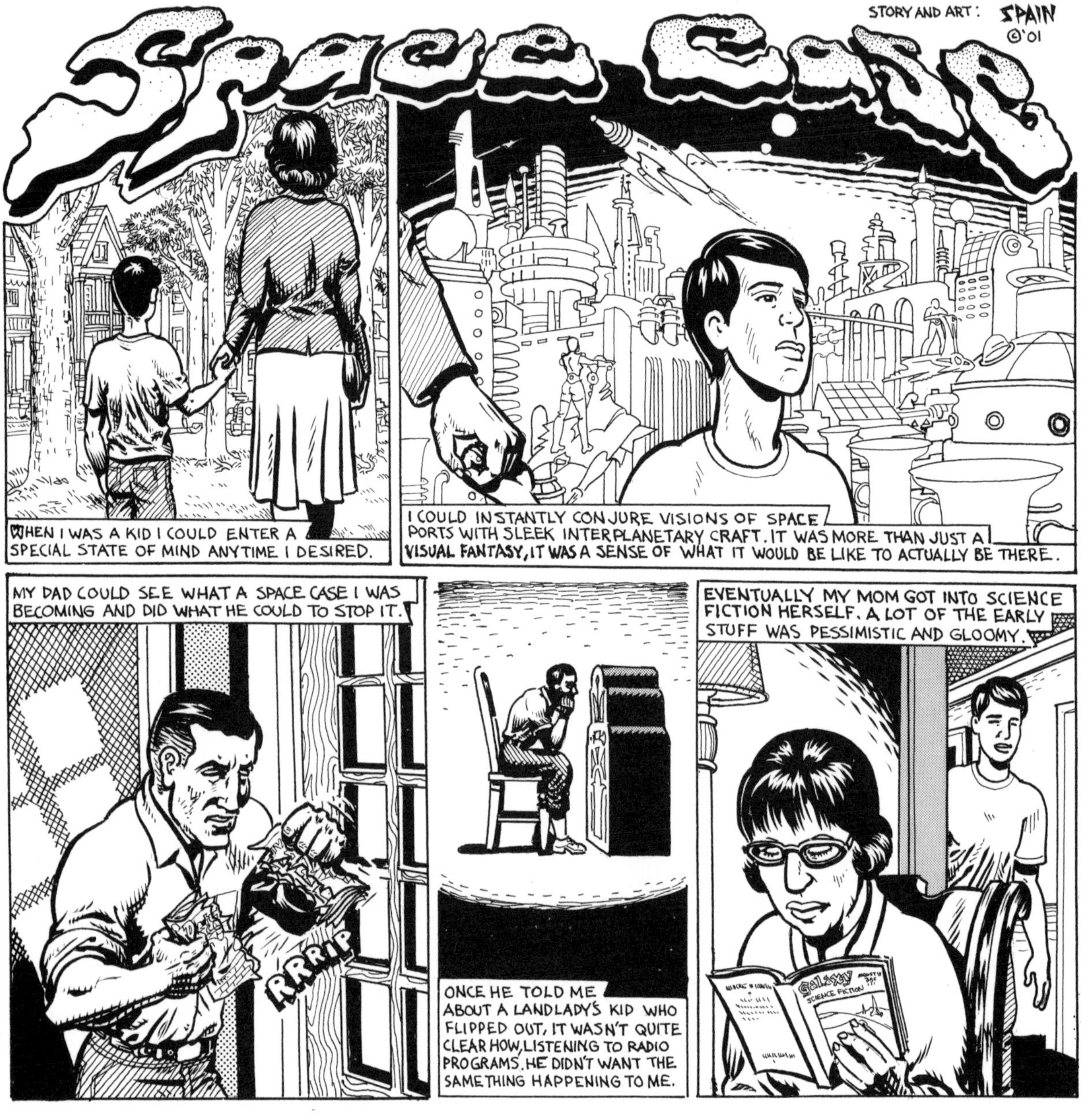
STORY AND ART: SPAIN ©'01
SPACE CASE
WHEN I WAS A KID I COULD ENTER A SPECIAL STATE OF MIND ANYTIME I DESIRED.
I COULD INSTANTLY CONJURE VISIONS OF SPACE PORTS WITH SLEEK INTERPLANETARY CRAFT. IT WAS MORE THAN JUST A VISUAL FANTASY, IT WAS A SENSE OF WHAT IT WOULD BE LIKE TO ACTUALLY BE THERE.
MY DAD COULD SEE WHAT A SPACE CASE I WAS BECOMING AND DID WHAT HE COULD TO STOP IT.
RRRIP
ONCE HE TOLD ME ABOUT A LANDLADY'S KID WHO FLIPPED OUT, IT WASN'T QUITE CLEAR HOW, LISTENING TO RADIO PROGRAMS. HE DIDN'T WANT THE SAME THING HAPPENING TO ME.
EVENTUALLY MY MOM GOT INTO SCIENCE FICTION HERSELF. A LOT OF THE EARLY STUFF WAS PESSIMISTIC AND GLOOMY.
galaxy
SCIENCE FICTION

READING COMICS AS A KID

So what was your interest in comics like when you were growing up? Was it intense, or was it—

Yeah, intense. I'd read *Captain Marvel* religiously, and even joined the Captain Marvel Fan Club.

I was always searching for good stuff. I got that photojournalist's review of comics, and I found the cover in there that scared the shit out of me. There was a store on the corner that would have a big stack of comics, I would go through that stack once a week. That's where I saw that cover that just sent chills down my spine. My dad really didn't like comics.

Did you read Captain Marvel *prior to EC? Did your interest evolve into EC?*

Yeah. Well, I'd seen them around. I mean, it's funny how comics would go through periods where it didn't seem that there were too many good comics around, so you'd be looking around trying to find something that was cool. I got into *Captain Science* for a while. I didn't know who Wallace Wood was, but there was something about his drawing that stood out. My family went to Spain, I must have been about 11 or 12. On the way back, the ship stopped at Halifax, and I went into a used-book store, and they had a *Weird Science* with no cover. I looked at that, man, and I was just knocked on my ass. The story was intriguing, the artwork was better than anything I had seen. After that, I just started buying that stuff, grabbing it up.

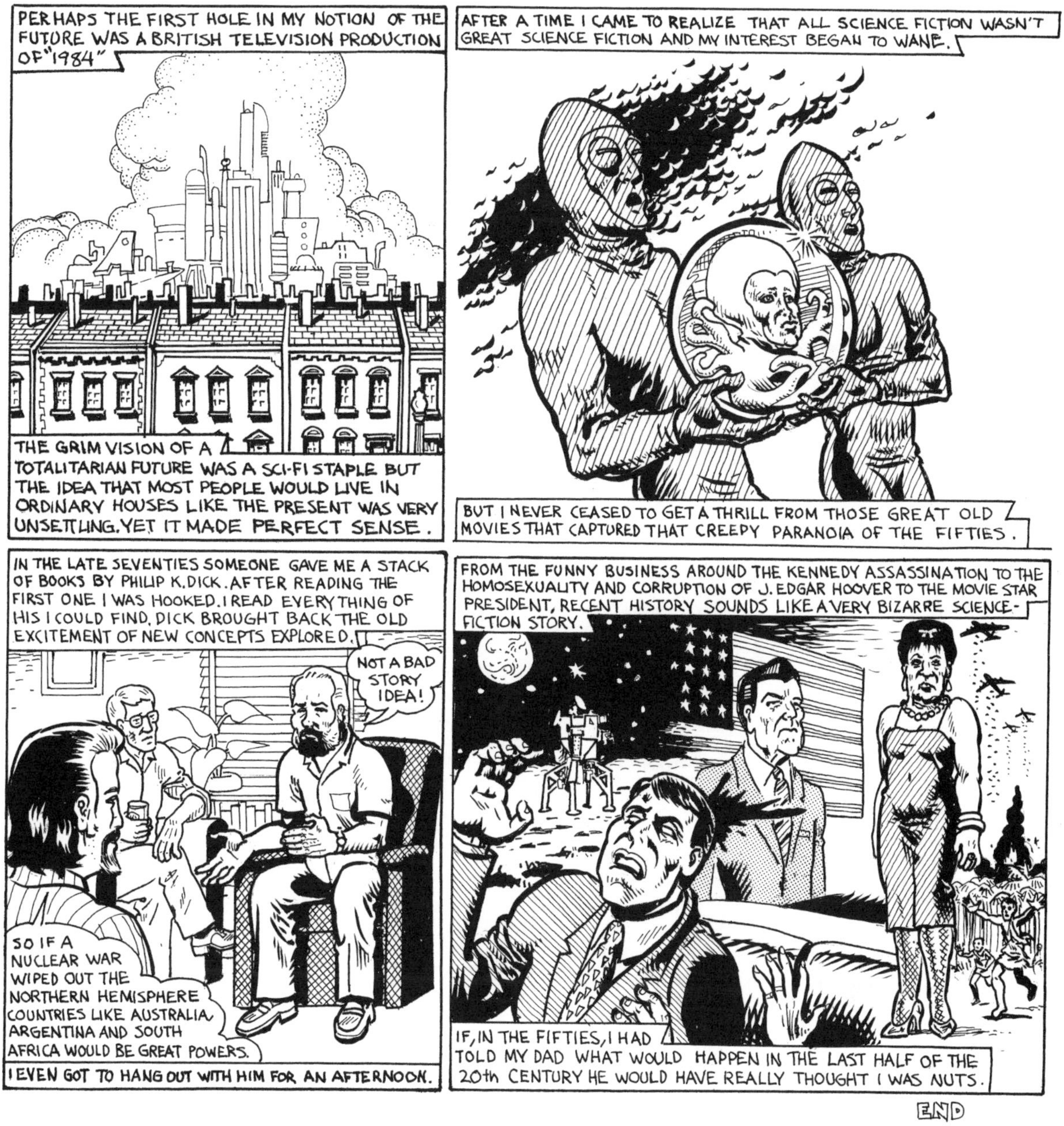
PERHAPS THE FIRST HOLE IN MY NOTION OF THE FUTURE WAS A BRITISH TELEVISION PRODUCTION OF "1984"
THE GRIM VISION OF A TOTALITARIAN FUTURE WAS A SCI-FI STAPLE BUT THE IDEA THAT MOST PEOPLE WOULD LIVE IN ORDINARY HOUSES LIKE THE PRESENT WAS VERY UNSETTLING. YET IT MADE PERFECT SENSE.
AFTER A TIME I CAME TO REALIZE THAT ALL SCIENCE FICTION WASN'T GREAT SCIENCE FICTION AND MY INTEREST BEGAN TO WANE.
BUT I NEVER CEASED TO GET A THRILL FROM THOSE GREAT OLD MOVIES THAT CAPTURED THAT CREEPY PARANOIA OF THE FIFTIES.
IN THE LATE SEVENTIES SOMEONE GAVE ME A STACK OF BOOKS BY PHILIP K. DICK. AFTER READING THE FIRST ONE I WAS HOOKED. I READ EVERYTHING OF HIS I COULD FIND. DICK BROUGHT BACK THE OLD EXCITEMENT OF NEW CONCEPTS EXPLORED.
NOT A BAD STORY IDEA!
SO IF A NUCLEAR WAR WIPED OUT THE NORTHERN HEMISPHERE COUNTRIES LIKE AUSTRALIA, ARGENTINA AND SOUTH AFRICA WOULD BE GREAT POWERS.
I EVEN GOT TO HANG OUT WITH HIM FOR AN AFTERNOON.
FROM THE FUNNY BUSINESS AROUND THE KENNEDY ASSASSINATION TO THE HOMOSEXUALITY AND CORRUPTION OF J. EDGAR HOOVER TO THE MOVIE STAR PRESIDENT, RECENT HISTORY SOUNDS LIKE A VERY BIZARRE SCIENCE-FICTION STORY.
IF, IN THE FIFTIES, I HAD TOLD MY DAD WHAT WOULD HAPPEN IN THE LAST HALF OF THE 20th CENTURY HE WOULD HAVE REALLY THOUGHT I WAS NUTS.
END

LIFE OF CRIME

Now, you would have been 10, 11, 12 when you started reading the EC comics?

Yeah. Right.

So in fact you would have been starting to be interested in history before your juvenile delinquent phase, which would have been, I guess, post-18?

No, no, it was kind of from about 13 to—

To approximately now.

[*Laughs.*] 13 to 16. After they suppressed ECs, they had Picto-Fiction. Around this time I saw a stack of comics behind the counter in a drug store with a Picto-Fiction comic on top. They had that cover by Jack Kamen of the kid in a leather jacket with the switchblade. And I kept waiting for them to put it on the stand; about a week went by and the stack remained unopened behind the counter. I finally asked the clerk when he was going to put

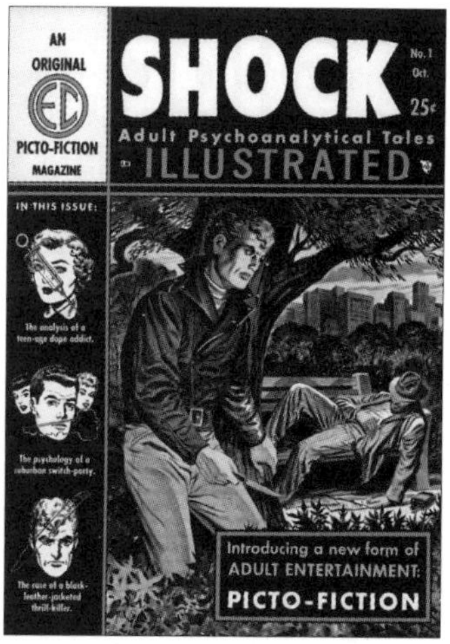
AN ORIGINAL
EC
PICTO-FICTION MAGAZINE
SHOCK
No. 1 Oct.
25¢
Adult Psychoanalytical Tales
ILLUSTRATED
IN THIS ISSUE:
The analysis of a teen-age dope addict.
The psychology of a suburban switch-party.
The case of a black-leather-jacketed thrill-killer.
Introducing a new form of ADULT ENTERTAINMENT: PICTO-FICTION

Cover from *Shock Illustrated* #1 (October 1955) drawn by Jack Kamen ©2012 William M. Gaines Agent, Inc.

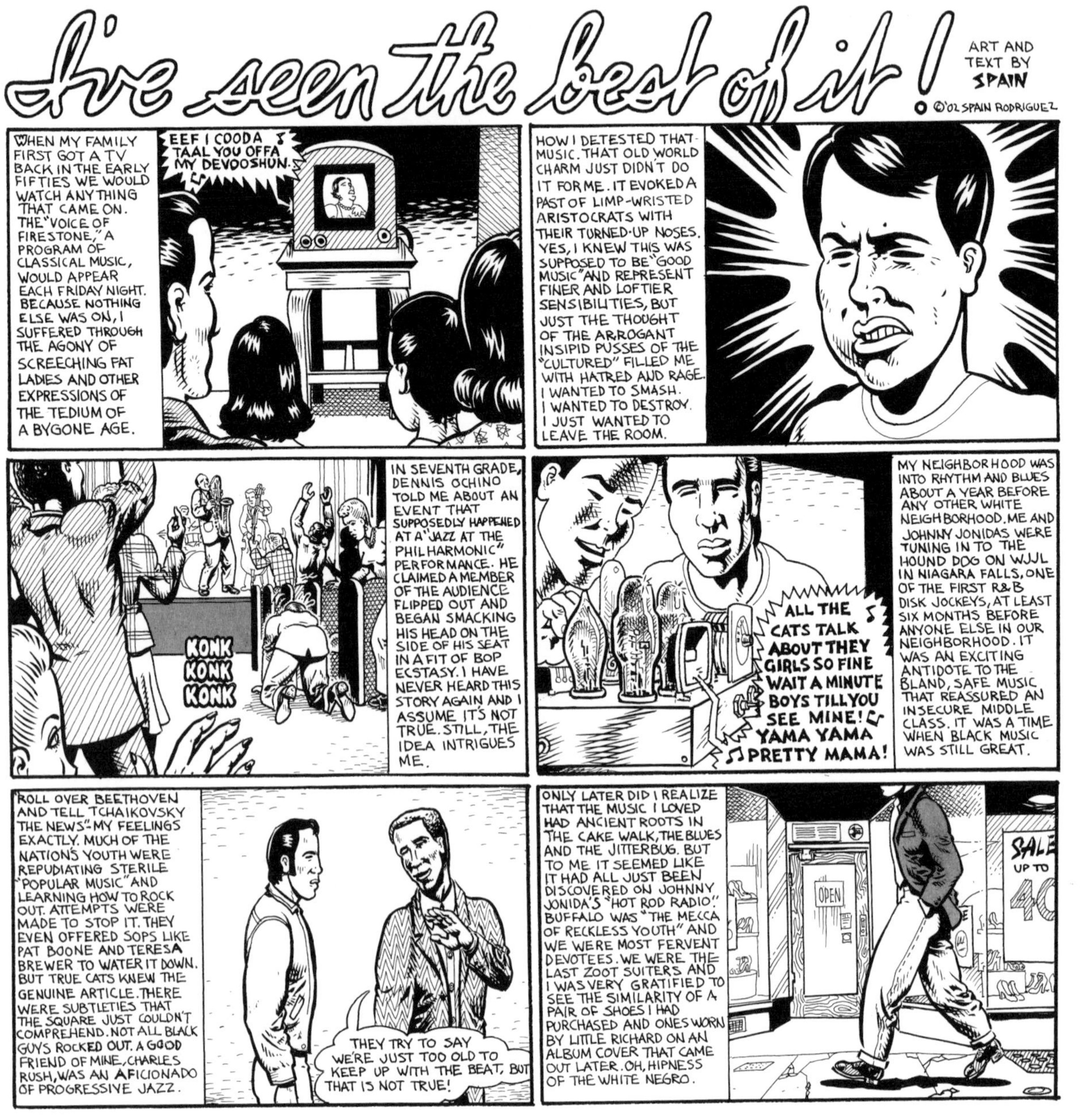
I've seen the best of it!
ART AND TEXT BY SPAIN
©'02 SPAIN RODRIGUEZ
WHEN MY FAMILY FIRST GOT A TV BACK IN THE EARLY FIFTIES WE WOULD WATCH ANYTHING THAT CAME ON. THE "VOICE OF FIRESTONE," A PROGRAM OF CLASSICAL MUSIC, WOULD APPEAR EACH FRIDAY NIGHT. BECAUSE NOTHING ELSE WAS ON, I SUFFERED THROUGH THE AGONY OF SCREECHING FAT LADIES AND OTHER EXPRESSIONS OF THE TEDIUM OF A BYGONE AGE.
EEF I COODA TAAL YOU OFFA MY DEVOOSHUN.
HOW I DETESTED THAT MUSIC. THAT OLD WORLD CHARM JUST DIDN'T DO IT FOR ME. IT EVOKED A PAST OF LIMP-WRISTED ARISTOCRATS WITH THEIR TURNED-UP NOSES. YES, I KNEW THIS WAS SUPPOSED TO BE "GOOD MUSIC" AND REPRESENT FINER AND LOFTIER SENSIBILITIES, BUT JUST THE THOUGHT OF THE ARROGANT INSIPID PUSSES OF THE "CULTURED" FILLED ME WITH HATRED AND RAGE. I WANTED TO SMASH. I WANTED TO DESTROY. I JUST WANTED TO LEAVE THE ROOM.
KONK KONK KONK
IN SEVENTH GRADE, DENNIS OCHINO TOLD ME ABOUT AN EVENT THAT SUPPOSEDLY HAPPENED AT A "JAZZ AT THE PHILHARMONIC" PERFORMANCE. HE CLAIMED A MEMBER OF THE AUDIENCE FLIPPED OUT AND BEGAN SMACKING HIS HEAD ON THE SIDE OF HIS SEAT IN A FIT OF BOP ECSTASY. I HAVE NEVER HEARD THIS STORY AGAIN AND I ASSUME IT'S NOT TRUE. STILL, THE IDEA INTRIGUES ME.
ALL THE CATS TALK ABOUT THEY GIRLS SO FINE WAIT A MINUTE BOYS TILL YOU SEE MINE! YAMA YAMA PRETTY MAMA!
MY NEIGHBORHOOD WAS INTO RHYTHM AND BLUES ABOUT A YEAR BEFORE ANY OTHER WHITE NEIGHBORHOOD. ME AND JOHNNY JONIDAS WERE TUNING IN TO THE HOUND DOG ON WJJL IN NIAGARA FALLS, ONE OF THE FIRST R&B DISK JOCKEYS, AT LEAST SIX MONTHS BEFORE ANYONE ELSE IN OUR NEIGHBORHOOD. IT WAS AN EXCITING ANTIDOTE TO THE BLAND, SAFE MUSIC THAT REASSURED AN INSECURE MIDDLE CLASS. IT WAS A TIME WHEN BLACK MUSIC WAS STILL GREAT.
"ROLL OVER BEETHOVEN AND TELL TCHAIKOVSKY THE NEWS" - MY FEELINGS EXACTLY. MUCH OF THE NATION'S YOUTH WERE REPUDIATING STERILE "POPULAR MUSIC" AND LEARNING HOW TO ROCK OUT. ATTEMPTS WERE MADE TO STOP IT. THEY EVEN OFFERED SOPS LIKE PAT BOONE AND TERESA BREWER TO WATER IT DOWN. BUT TRUE CATS KNEW THE GENUINE ARTICLE. THERE WERE SUBTLETIES THAT THE SQUARE JUST COULDN'T COMPREHEND. NOT ALL BLACK GUYS ROCKED OUT. A GOOD FRIEND OF MINE, CHARLES RUSH, WAS AN AFICIONADO OF PROGRESSIVE JAZZ.
THEY TRY TO SAY WE'RE JUST TOO OLD TO KEEP UP WITH THE BEAT, BUT THAT IS NOT TRUE!
ONLY LATER DID I REALIZE THAT THE MUSIC I LOVED HAD ANCIENT ROOTS IN THE CAKE WALK, THE BLUES AND THE JITTERBUG. BUT TO ME IT SEEMED LIKE IT HAD ALL JUST BEEN DISCOVERED ON JOHNNY JONIDA'S "HOT ROD RADIO." BUFFALO WAS "THE MECCA OF RECKLESS YOUTH" AND WE WERE MOST FERVENT DEVOTEES. WE WERE THE LAST ZOOT SUITERS AND I WAS VERY GRATIFIED TO SEE THE SIMILARITY OF A PAIR OF SHOES I HAD PURCHASED AND ONES WORN BY LITTLE RICHARD ON AN ALBUM COVER THAT CAME OUT LATER. OH, HIPNESS OF THE WHITE NEGRO.
OPEN
SALE UP TO 40

that particular book on the rack. And the guy said, "We're not going to put it on the stand because it makes juvenile delinquents. Are you a juvenile delinquent?" And I said, "Fuckin' A." I guess that was a transforming moment.

You liked that because it was a romanticized image of…

Some sort of recognition of disaffected youth like myself. At that time, my whole neighborhood was getting into that kind of rebellion. The whole neighborhood went on a crime spree that lasted until we were 16, when everybody got busted, and after that… there were guys who became hardcore criminals. One guy, a guy I got busted in a stolen car with, made it to the top of the FBI Wanted list.

Tell me a little bit about your criminal career.

Well, it was just juvenile delinquency; it was us against the world. We'd just go to other neighborhoods and rob the department stores, and then there was a big car-stealing spree that lasted for almost a year.

Tell me how that worked. You'd break into a car?

Yeah, you'd get into a car. Well, things were a lot looser. A lot of cars would be open, there were certain cars that you… well, you'd get under the ignition and put some tinfoil or a church key or something, start them up, and this got to be a big thing.

What would you do with them?

We would joyride, and do damage, run them into walls, run them over

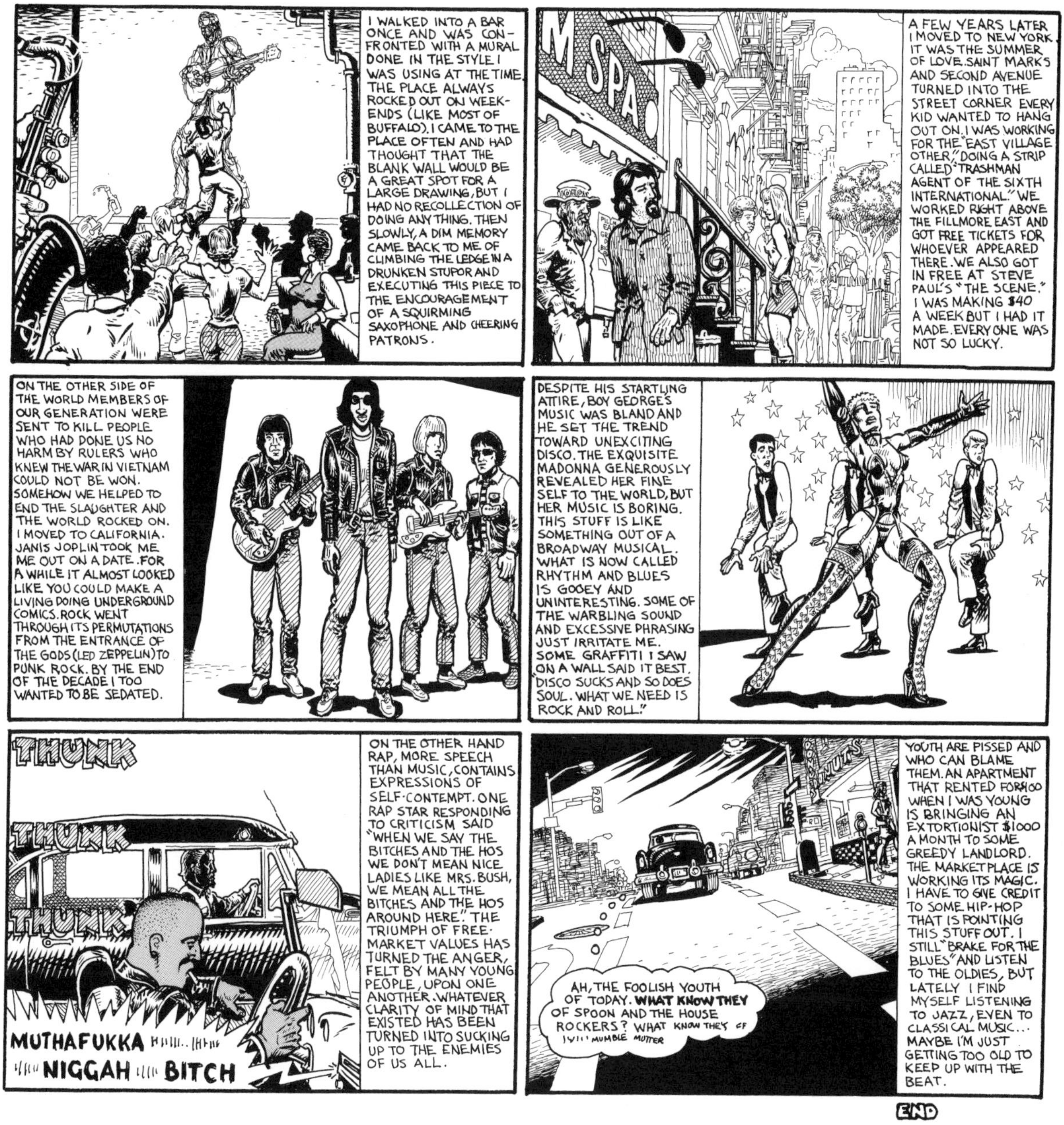
I WALKED INTO A BAR ONCE AND WAS CONFRONTED WITH A MURAL DONE IN THE STYLE I WAS USING AT THE TIME. THE PLACE ALWAYS ROCKED OUT ON WEEKENDS (LIKE MOST OF BUFFALO). I CAME TO THE PLACE OFTEN AND HAD THOUGHT THAT THE BLANK WALL WOULD BE A GREAT SPOT FOR A LARGE DRAWING, BUT I HAD NO RECOLLECTION OF DOING ANYTHING. THEN SLOWLY, A DIM MEMORY CAME BACK TO ME OF CLIMBING THE LEDGE IN A DRUNKEN STUPOR AND EXECUTING THIS PIECE TO THE ENCOURAGEMENT OF A SQUIRMING SAXOPHONE AND CHEERING PATRONS.
A FEW YEARS LATER I MOVED TO NEW YORK. IT WAS THE SUMMER OF LOVE. SAINT MARKS AND SECOND AVENUE TURNED INTO THE STREET CORNER EVERY KID WANTED TO HANG OUT ON. I WAS WORKING FOR THE "EAST VILLAGE OTHER," DOING A STRIP CALLED "TRASHMAN AGENT OF THE SIXTH INTERNATIONAL." WE WORKED RIGHT ABOVE THE FILLMORE EAST AND GOT FREE TICKETS FOR WHOEVER APPEARED THERE. WE ALSO GOT IN FREE AT STEVE PAUL'S "THE SCENE." I WAS MAKING $40 A WEEK BUT I HAD IT MADE. EVERYONE WAS NOT SO LUCKY.
ON THE OTHER SIDE OF THE WORLD MEMBERS OF OUR GENERATION WERE SENT TO KILL PEOPLE WHO HAD DONE US NO HARM BY RULERS WHO KNEW THE WAR IN VIETNAM COULD NOT BE WON. SOMEHOW WE HELPED TO END THE SLAUGHTER AND THE WORLD ROCKED ON. I MOVED TO CALIFORNIA. JANIS JOPLIN TOOK ME ME OUT ON A DATE. FOR A WHILE IT ALMOST LOOKED LIKE YOU COULD MAKE A LIVING DOING UNDERGROUND COMICS. ROCK WENT THROUGH ITS PERMUTATIONS FROM THE ENTRANCE OF THE GODS (LED ZEPPELIN) TO PUNK ROCK. BY THE END OF THE DECADE I TOO WANTED TO BE SEDATED.
DESPITE HIS STARTLING ATTIRE, BOY GEORGE'S MUSIC WAS BLAND AND HE SET THE TREND TOWARD UNEXCITING DISCO. THE EXQUISITE MADONNA GENEROUSLY REVEALED HER FINE SELF TO THE WORLD, BUT HER MUSIC IS BORING. THIS STUFF IS LIKE SOMETHING OUT OF A BROADWAY MUSICAL. WHAT IS NOW CALLED RHYTHM AND BLUES IS GOOEY AND UNINTERESTING. SOME OF THE WARBLING SOUND AND EXCESSIVE PHRASING JUST IRRITATE ME. SOME GRAFFITI I SAW ON A WALL SAID IT BEST. "DISCO SUCKS AND SO DOES SOUL. WHAT WE NEED IS ROCK AND ROLL."
THUNK
THUNK
THUNK
MUTHAFUKKA
NIGGAH
BITCH
ON THE OTHER HAND RAP, MORE SPEECH THAN MUSIC, CONTAINS EXPRESSIONS OF SELF-CONTEMPT. ONE RAP STAR RESPONDING TO CRITICISM SAID "WHEN WE SAY THE BITCHES AND THE HOS WE DON'T MEAN NICE LADIES LIKE MRS. BUSH, WE MEAN ALL THE BITCHES AND THE HOS AROUND HERE." THE TRIUMPH OF FREE-MARKET VALUES HAS TURNED THE ANGER, FELT BY MANY YOUNG PEOPLE, UPON ONE ANOTHER. WHATEVER CLARITY OF MIND THAT EXISTED HAS BEEN TURNED INTO SUCKING UP TO THE ENEMIES OF US ALL.
AH, THE FOOLISH YOUTH OF TODAY. WHAT KNOW THEY OF SPOON AND THE HOUSE ROCKERS? WHAT KNOW THEY OF
MUMBLE MUTTER
YOUTH ARE PISSED AND WHO CAN BLAME THEM. AN APARTMENT THAT RENTED FOR $100 WHEN I WAS YOUNG IS BRINGING AN EXTORTIONIST $1000 A MONTH TO SOME GREEDY LANDLORD. THE MARKETPLACE IS WORKING ITS MAGIC. I HAVE TO GIVE CREDIT TO SOME HIP-HOP THAT IS POINTING THIS STUFF OUT. I STILL "BRAKE FOR THE BLUES" AND LISTEN TO THE OLDIES, BUT LATELY I FIND MYSELF LISTENING TO JAZZ, EVEN TO CLASSICAL MUSIC... MAYBE I'M JUST GETTING TOO OLD TO KEEP UP WITH THE BEAT.
END

cliffs and stuff like that.

And this "career" lasted between the ages of 13 and 16?

No, I was 15. It just lasted a few months. It lasted maybe a half a year. But I got busted… this guy had stolen this car for my birthday. We were driving around the zoo and the back wheel came off, and I tried to help the driver, he had fallen out of the car, and I tried to help him across Delaware Park. They nailed us, and they eventually nailed the other guys a few weeks later. I said I didn't know the car was stolen, and I got off.

Were you ever arrested during that time?

Well, one time the cops took me home for playing chess in this little park area. The cop told me to wipe that look off my face, and I said, "It's my face, I'll have any look I want on it." And the guy dragged me home and told my old man that any time I wanted to step outside with him, he would be glad to oblige me. He was a big guy, and I was about 14 or something. You really saw that things were not at all what was portrayed in the mass media… at least not in our neighborhood. It was just a conclusion that most of the kids of that age came to, that things were extremely corrupt. But of course we didn't really understand how corrupt they were. When you think about that period that conservatives allude to as some sort of a Golden Age, here you had the head of the FBI who was utterly corrupt, who was in bed with the

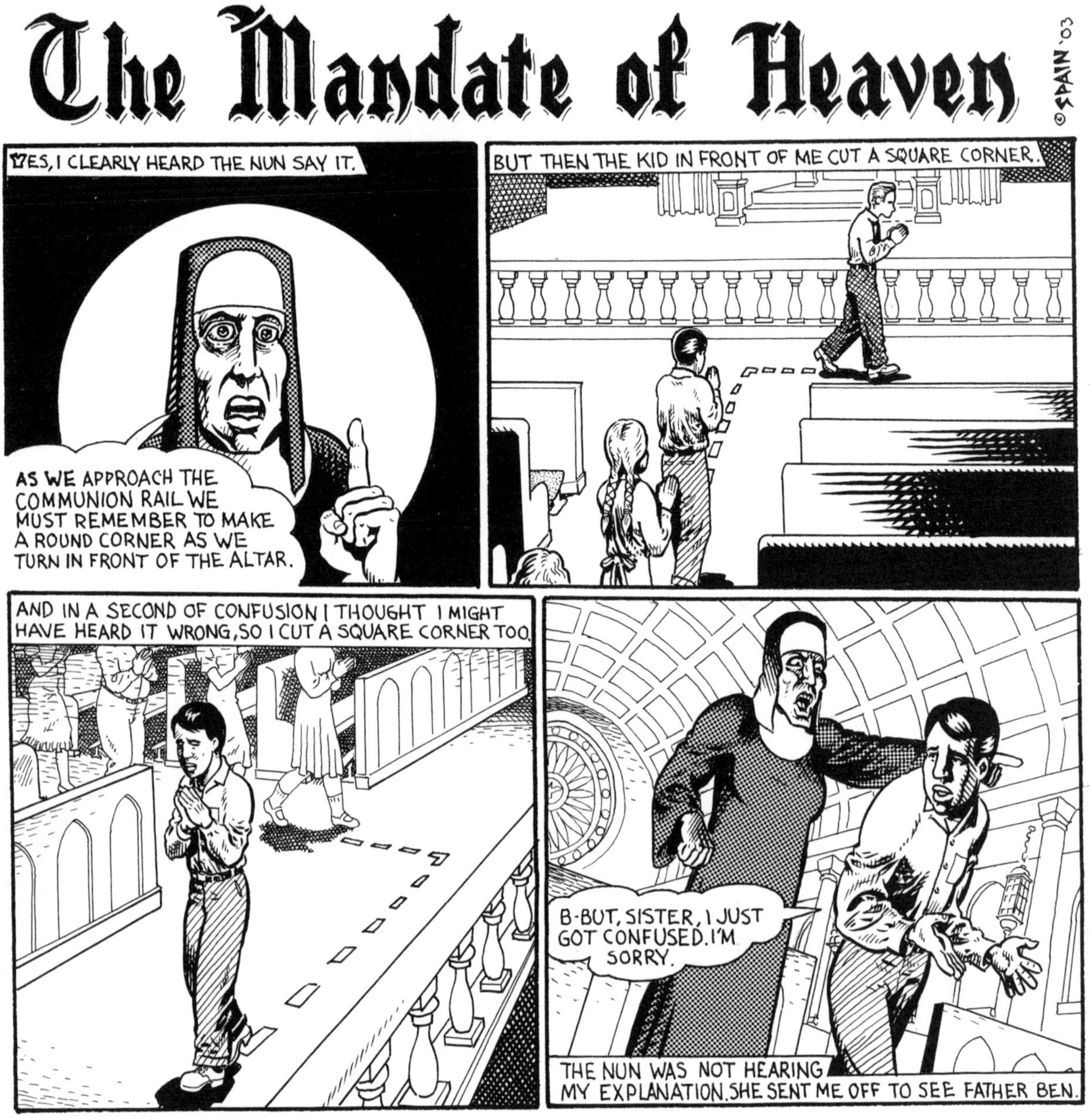
The Mandate of Heaven
©SPAIN '03
YES, I CLEARLY HEARD THE NUN SAY IT.
AS WE APPROACH THE COMMUNION RAIL WE MUST REMEMBER TO MAKE A ROUND CORNER AS WE TURN IN FRONT OF THE ALTAR.
BUT THEN THE KID IN FRONT OF ME CUT A SQUARE CORNER.
AND IN A SECOND OF CONFUSION I THOUGHT I MIGHT HAVE HEARD IT WRONG, SO I CUT A SQUARE CORNER TOO.
B-BUT, SISTER, I JUST GOT CONFUSED. I'M SORRY.
THE NUN WAS NOT HEARING MY EXPLANATION. SHE SENT ME OFF TO SEE FATHER BEN.

mafia, just about literally, who was a homosexual denouncing other homosexuals. Hoover wanted a list of every homosexual in America, he was a rabid racist, and the mob, especially in New York, the mob, the mafia had really made inroads into the political machine. And where I grew up there was a general sense of this. We knew about the guy who was about to testify against the mob who had mysteriously fallen out of a 10-story window in a room guarded by police. How did he fall out? They don't know. I don't know if you catch any of that history of crime on TV. It's fascinating, but this sort of thing was folklore where I grew up. Everything seemed to reinforce a deep-seated cynicism. Frank Costello was the guy who had all the political machinery oiled, so that guys like Lucky Luciano could live a luxurious life. So those were the guys who seemed like role models to us, you know. But for me, when I

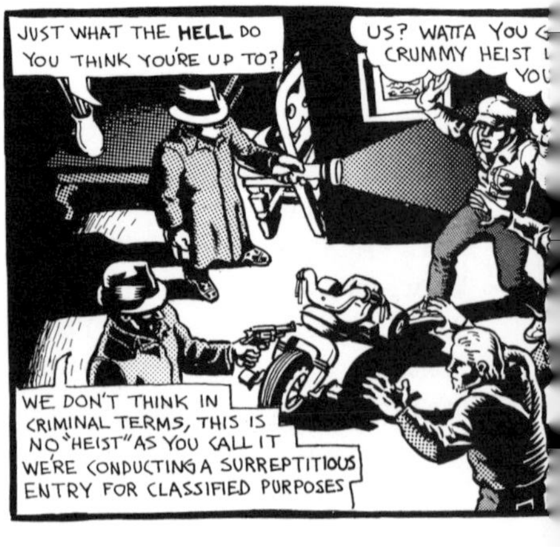
JUST WHAT THE HELL DO YOU THINK YOU'RE UP TO?
US? WATTA YOU
CRUMMY HEIST
WE DON'T THINK IN CRIMINAL TERMS, THIS IS NO "HEIST" AS YOU CALL IT WE'RE CONDUCTING A SURREPTITIOUS ENTRY FOR CLASSIFIED PURPOSES

Panel from "The Breaks" in *Zap* #9 ©1978 Spain

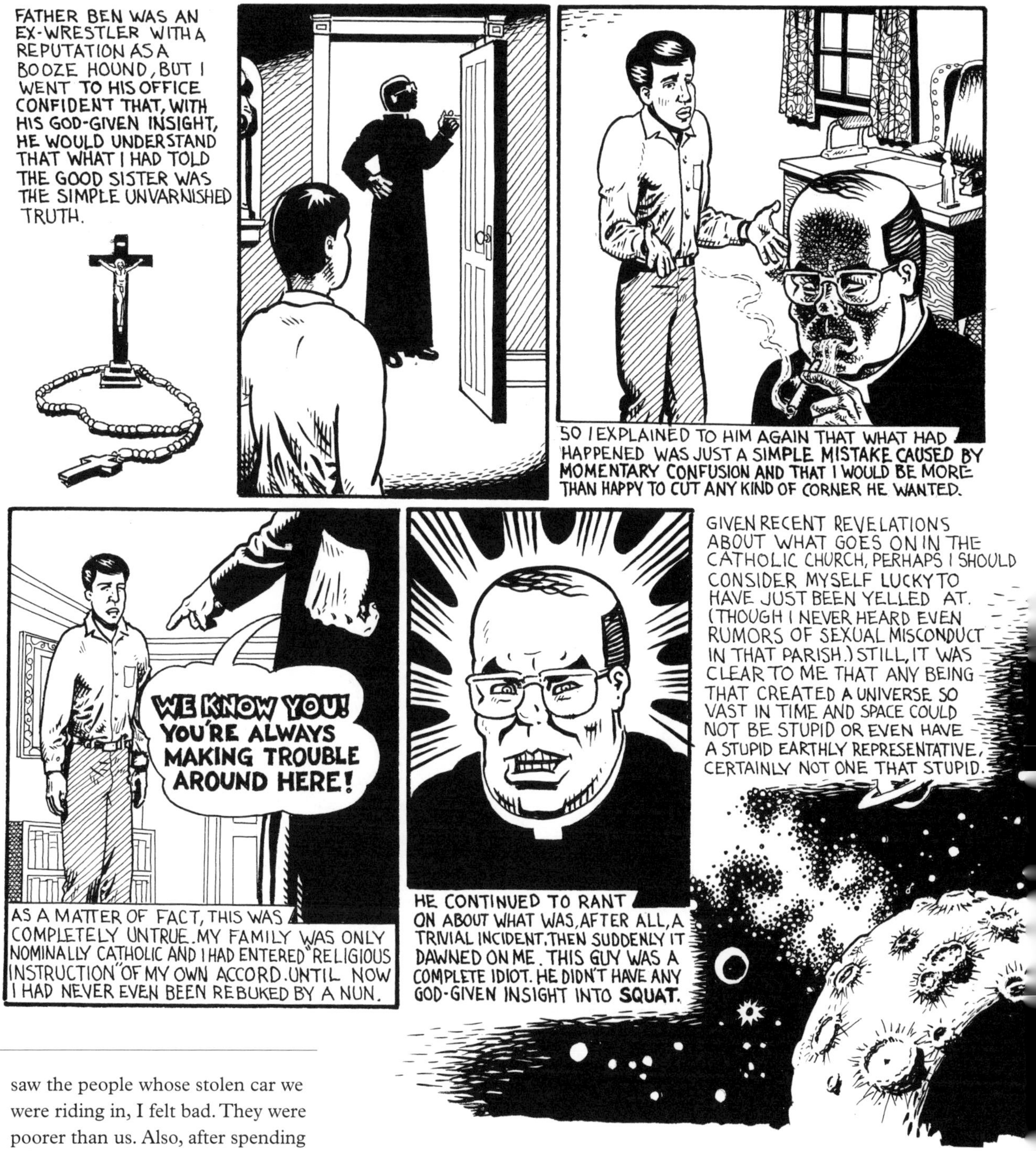
FATHER BEN WAS AN EX-WRESTLER WITH A REPUTATION AS A BOOZE HOUND, BUT I WENT TO HIS OFFICE CONFIDENT THAT, WITH HIS GOD-GIVEN INSIGHT, HE WOULD UNDERSTAND THAT WHAT I HAD TOLD THE GOOD SISTER WAS THE SIMPLE UNVARNISHED TRUTH.
SO I EXPLAINED TO HIM AGAIN THAT WHAT HAD HAPPENED WAS JUST A SIMPLE MISTAKE CAUSED BY MOMENTARY CONFUSION AND THAT I WOULD BE MORE THAN HAPPY TO CUT ANY KIND OF CORNER HE WANTED.
WE KNOW YOU! YOU'RE ALWAYS MAKING TROUBLE AROUND HERE!
AS A MATTER OF FACT, THIS WAS COMPLETELY UNTRUE. MY FAMILY WAS ONLY NOMINALLY CATHOLIC AND I HAD ENTERED "RELIGIOUS INSTRUCTION" OF MY OWN ACCORD. UNTIL NOW I HAD NEVER EVEN BEEN REBUKED BY A NUN.
HE CONTINUED TO RANT ON ABOUT WHAT WAS, AFTER ALL, A TRIVIAL INCIDENT. THEN SUDDENLY IT DAWNED ON ME. THIS GUY WAS A COMPLETE IDIOT. HE DIDN'T HAVE ANY GOD-GIVEN INSIGHT INTO SQUAT.
GIVEN RECENT REVELATIONS ABOUT WHAT GOES ON IN THE CATHOLIC CHURCH, PERHAPS I SHOULD CONSIDER MYSELF LUCKY TO HAVE JUST BEEN YELLED AT. (THOUGH I NEVER HEARD EVEN RUMORS OF SEXUAL MISCONDUCT IN THAT PARISH.) STILL, IT WAS CLEAR TO ME THAT ANY BEING THAT CREATED A UNIVERSE SO VAST IN TIME AND SPACE COULD NOT BE STUPID OR EVEN HAVE A STUPID EARTHLY REPRESENTATIVE, CERTAINLY NOT ONE THAT STUPID.

saw the people whose stolen car we were riding in, I felt bad. They were poorer than us. Also, after spending an afternoon in jail, I decided I didn't want to be a criminal. I had other things to do with myself.

So you actually spent an afternoon in jail—

The other kids were under 16, but because I was 16, I spent an afternoon in jail. And then the other guys in the gang—it was really a despicable thing that they did. They ended up hitting this old guy over the head with a beer bottle, some guy's store that we used to go in and shoplift. And there was no need to do it, because the guy was very old. He probably had Alzheimer's, and one of our guys hit him over the head with a beer bottle; it was really a rotten thing.

What prompted you to engage in that kind of activity?

It was basically hatred for established society. We just saw ourselves in a predatory world and we could trust one another. It was a sense of comradeship among the guys, but anybody else was just a potential victim. That's the way the world was. The world is there to prey on you, and you have an arena where you can prey upon others.

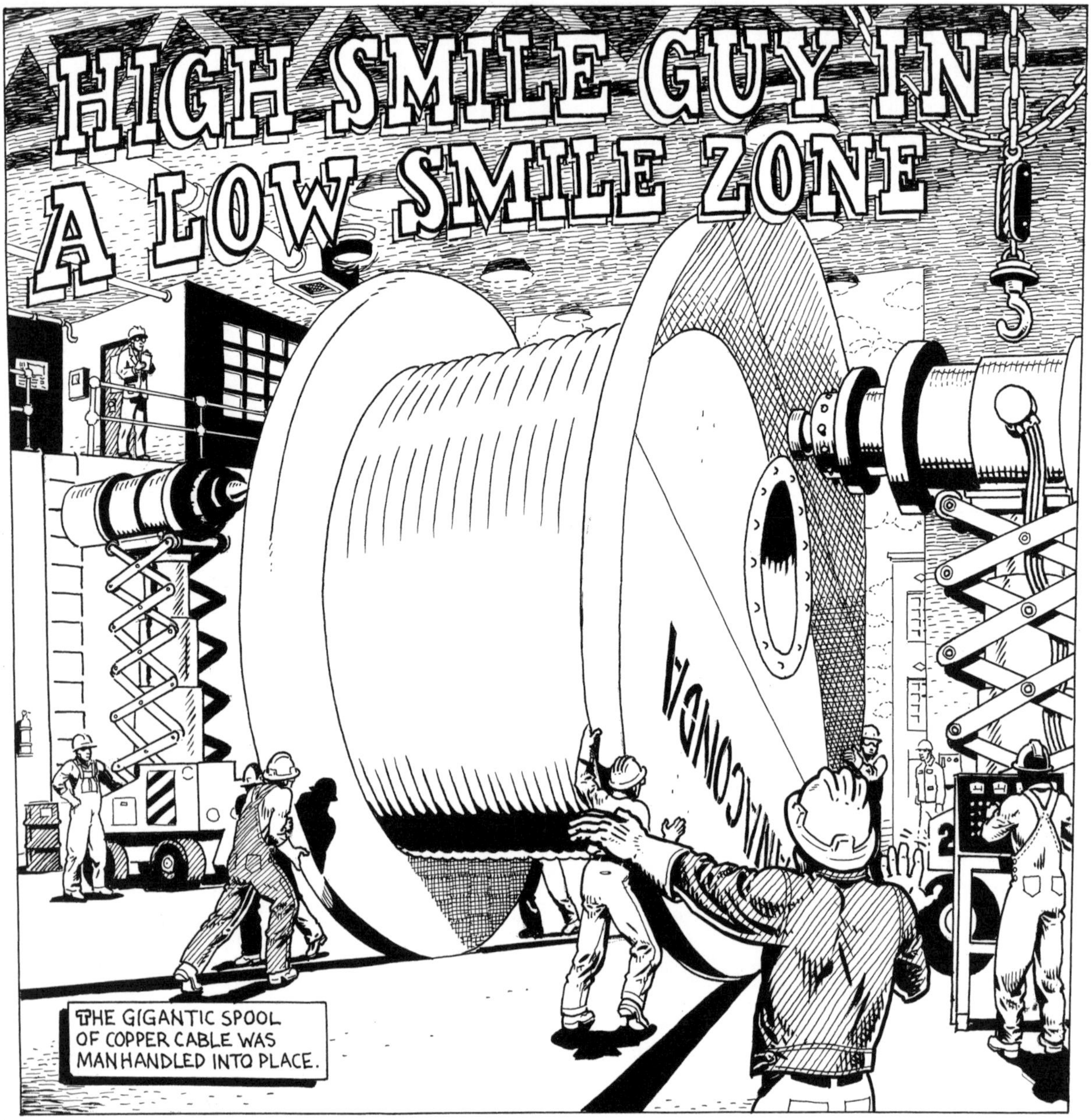
HIGH SMILE GUY IN A LOW SMILE ZONE
THE GIGANTIC SPOOL OF COPPER CABLE WAS MANHANDLED INTO PLACE.

I think that that's the way that all criminals see things, and that's the way society is set up, really. It's just that people on the top put a mantle of respectability upon their predation. But, on the other hand, who are you doing harm to? It's really the bottom of the food chain, doing harm to this old guy. Mr. Blimey, we called him. Just some old guy, man, who had a store and probably was on Social Security, and here we were, victimizing this guy, and victimizing other people who were just like us. It was like there wasn't really a class solidarity as such, just more of a solidarity among us guys. Which was a good experience, in itself.

There was no class consciousness involved?

In a way, but it was more instinctual than conscious. There was antagonism between the squares and the hoods. Squares were mostly middle-class Pat Boone types. A lot of it was played out in the high school I went to, which was mostly middle and upper class… my mother always tried to put me with a better class of people, which never quite had the intended effect. [*Laughs.*]

You actually gravitated towards the criminal element? [Laughter.]

Yeah, right. When I was in art school, these were the only people I could really relate to.

Were your parents really disturbed by your getting arrested?

Oh yeah, they were really, right.

What was your father's—

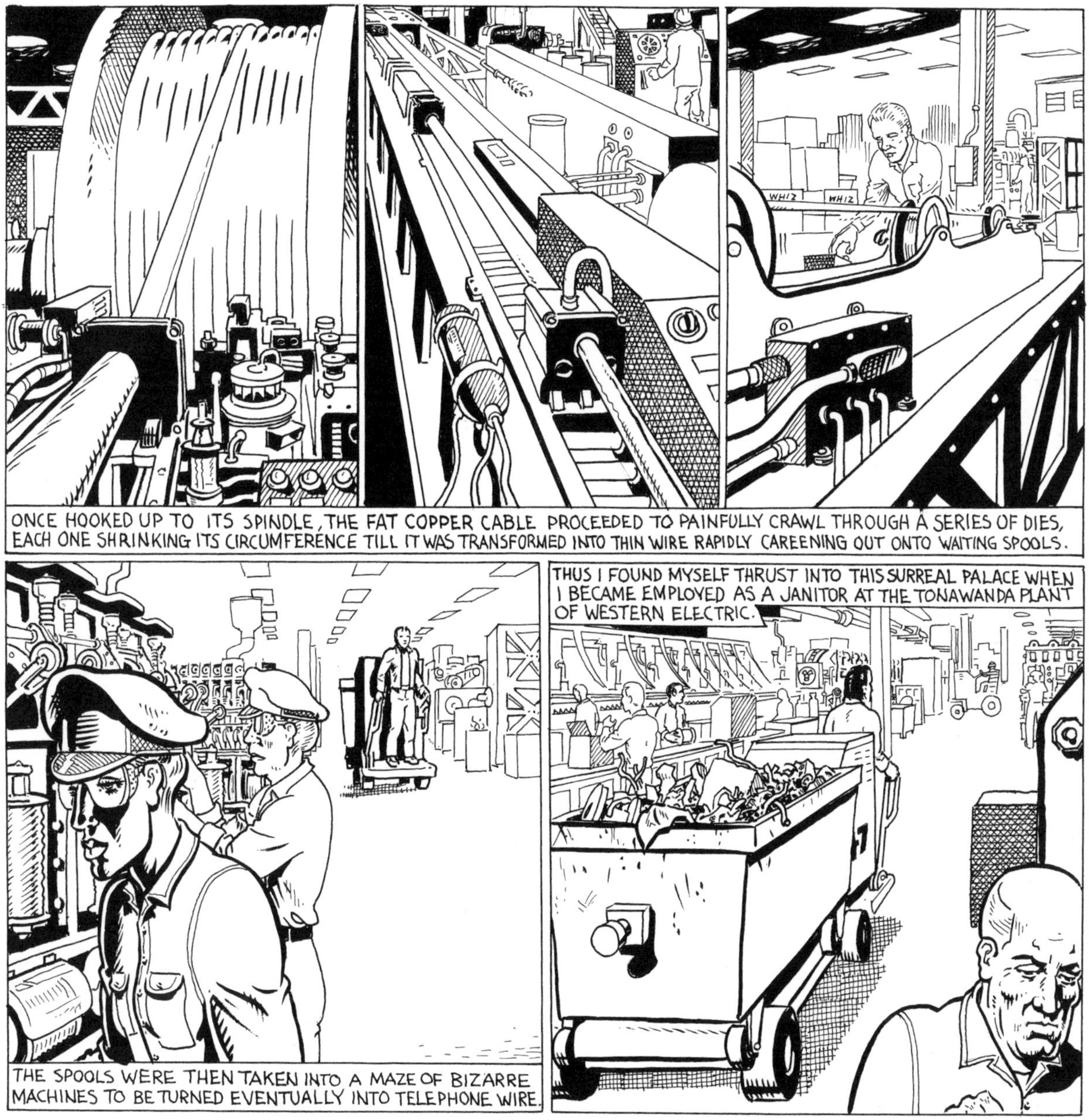
ONCE HOOKED UP TO ITS SPINDLE, THE FAT COPPER CABLE PROCEEDED TO PAINFULLY CRAWL THROUGH A SERIES OF DIES, EACH ONE SHRINKING ITS CIRCUMFERENCE TILL IT WAS TRANSFORMED INTO THIN WIRE RAPIDLY CAREENING OUT ONTO WAITING SPOOLS.
WHIZ
WHIZ
THE SPOOLS WERE THEN TAKEN INTO A MAZE OF BIZARRE MACHINES TO BE TURNED EVENTUALLY INTO TELEPHONE WIRE.
THUS I FOUND MYSELF THRUST INTO THIS SURREAL PALACE WHEN I BECAME EMPLOYED AS A JANITOR AT THE TONAWANDA PLANT OF WESTERN ELECTRIC.

Well, there was some point where he couldn't beat my ass any more. I did get a shot on him, and he understood that the time for me to get my ass kicked by him was over.
When you say that, do you mean you actually had a physical confrontation?
Yeah.
What was the subsequent relationship like?
Well… It was clear that I was no longer a child.
Were you ever close to your father?
Well… In a way, yeah, and in a way, no. I finally came to realize that we really were the product of our respective backgrounds. It was something that took me a long time to realize: my dad just came from Europe, which is more authoritarian. In fact, even here that generation was less inclined to listen to what they regarded as back talk. My dad would have been coming from a more libertarian part of that tradition, but basically you're not expected to question. You just do as you're told, otherwise you get your ass kicked. That's just what it is. But my old man was always trying to do right by me, as he understood it. I was a spaced-out kid and now I'm a spaced-out adult, and to my dad it must have seemed as if he just had to knock some sense in to me. How's this kid going to be able to survive? He couldn't articulate that, and it was something that bothered him.
So after he couldn't physically intimidate you, what was your relationship like? How did he deal with these issues?

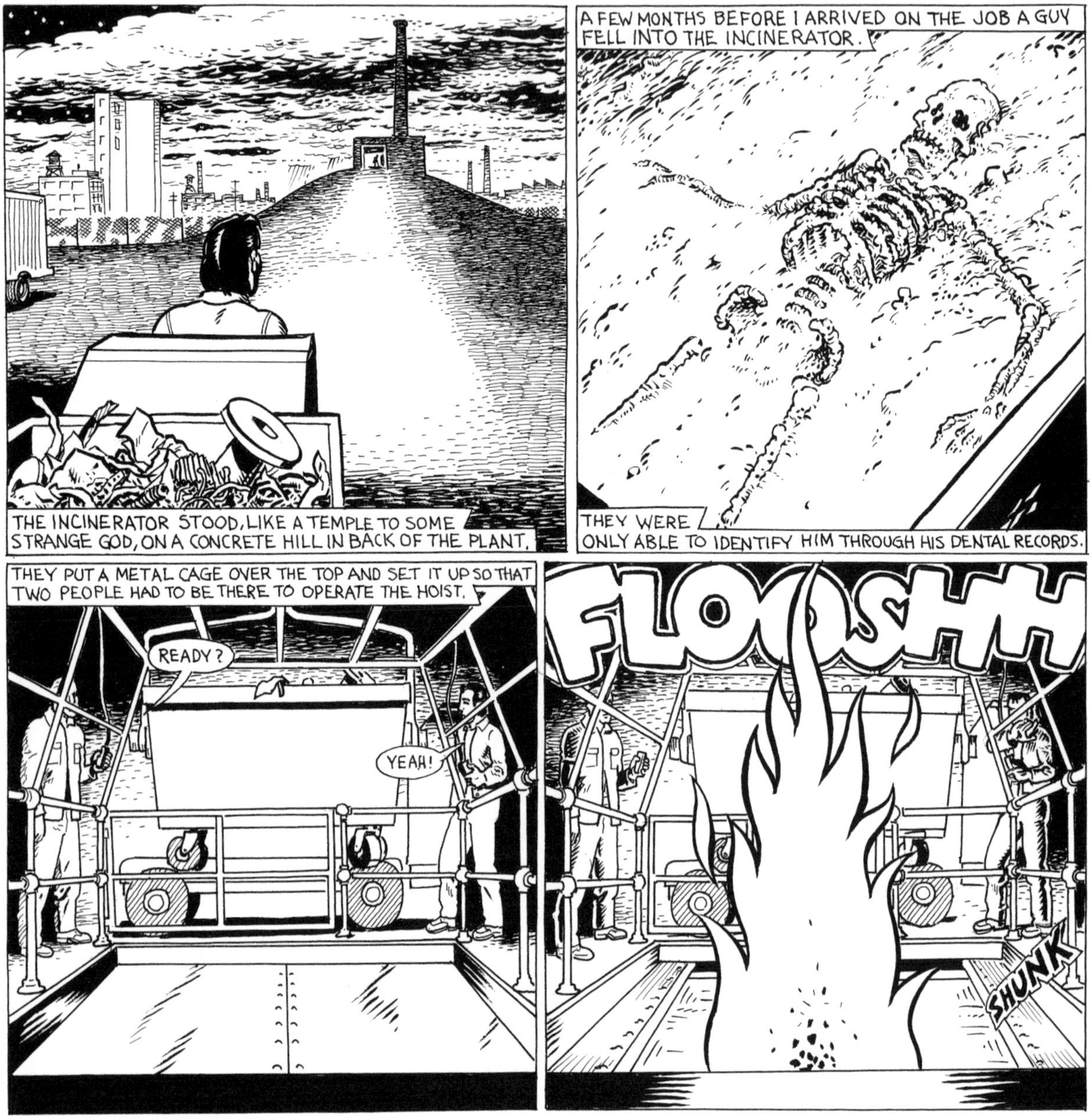
THE INCINERATOR STOOD, LIKE A TEMPLE TO SOME STRANGE GOD, ON A CONCRETE HILL IN BACK OF THE PLANT.
A FEW MONTHS BEFORE I ARRIVED ON THE JOB A GUY FELL INTO THE INCINERATOR.
THEY WERE ONLY ABLE TO IDENTIFY HIM THROUGH HIS DENTAL RECORDS.
THEY PUT A METAL CAGE OVER THE TOP AND SET IT UP SO THAT TWO PEOPLE HAD TO BE THERE TO OPERATE THE HOIST.
READY?
YEAH!
FLOOSHH
SHUNK

We would get into discussions, but at some point he would just get really pissed. We'd be watching television, and I'd say, "I hope that the bad guy shoots the sheriff." Of course he never did, but my dad would get real pissed off at stuff like that. You know, he was a law-and-order, working-class guy, but at that point, I just had a dislike for the established order that I have today. It hasn't changed. And it's funny, my kid goes to school, and I understand that she needs an education, and I try to do my best to foster a respect for learning, and she certainly has a good attitude toward school, but my attitude hasn't changed, man.

CONFORMING

When did your family get a TV?
We must have got a TV around '52.
You were 12, so that means you experienced TV in its infancy?
Yeah, right. And also what I experienced was the anticipation of TV. They used to have those great programs that came on between 5 and 6, the serials. And so just the idea—think of that, man, you can actually see that stuff on TV like a little movie in your own house. When it finally came, I'd watch it intensely, but by the time I was 14, I hardly ever watched it. I would watch a few things, but it just wasn't the completely absorbing thing that it was when it first came. My wife complains about my daughter watching TV all the time, but I think

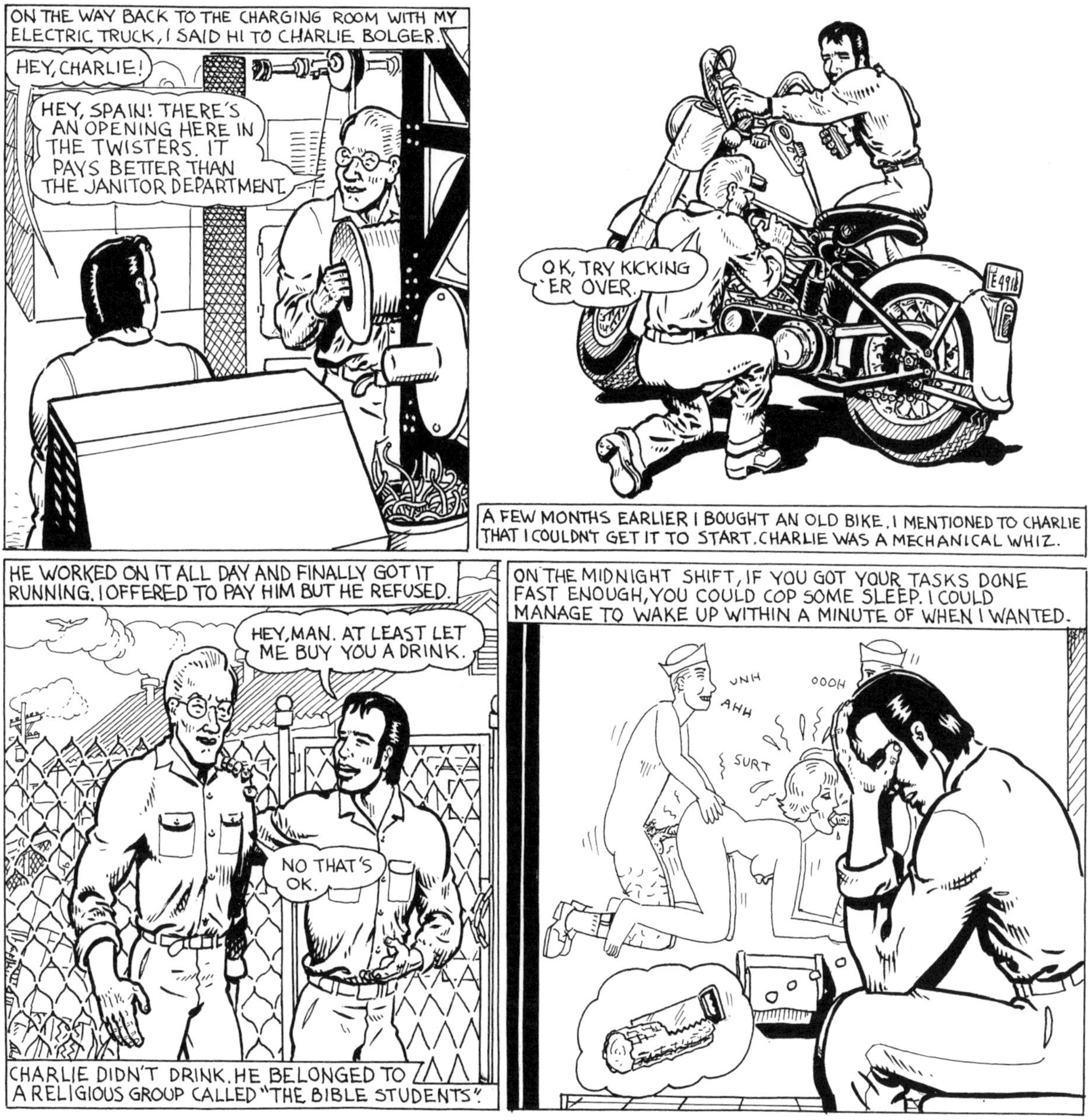
ON THE WAY BACK TO THE CHARGING ROOM WITH MY ELECTRIC TRUCK, I SAID HI TO CHARLIE BOLGER.
HEY, CHARLIE!
HEY, SPAIN! THERE'S AN OPENING HERE IN THE TWISTERS. IT PAYS BETTER THAN THE JANITOR DEPARTMENT.
OK, TRY KICKING 'ER OVER.
A FEW MONTHS EARLIER I BOUGHT AN OLD BIKE. I MENTIONED TO CHARLIE THAT I COULDN'T GET IT TO START. CHARLIE WAS A MECHANICAL WHIZ.
HE WORKED ON IT ALL DAY AND FINALLY GOT IT RUNNING. I OFFERED TO PAY HIM BUT HE REFUSED.
HEY, MAN. AT LEAST LET ME BUY YOU A DRINK.
NO THAT'S OK.
CHARLIE DIDN'T DRINK. HE BELONGED TO A RELIGIOUS GROUP CALLED "THE BIBLE STUDENTS".
ON THE MIDNIGHT SHIFT, IF YOU GOT YOUR TASKS DONE FAST ENOUGH, YOU COULD COP SOME SLEEP. I COULD MANAGE TO WAKE UP WITHIN A MINUTE OF WHEN I WANTED.
UNH
OOOH
AHH
SURT

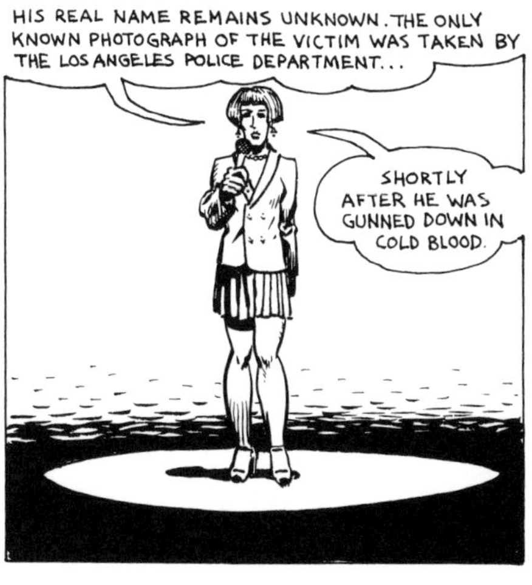
HIS REAL NAME REMAINS UNKNOWN. THE ONLY KNOWN PHOTOGRAPH OF THE VICTIM WAS TAKEN BY THE LOS ANGELES POLICE DEPARTMENT...
SHORTLY AFTER HE WAS GUNNED DOWN IN COLD BLOOD.

Panel from Boots Vol. 1, story by Harry Kamper, art by Spain ©1997 Harry Kamper

that if you let her watch it all she wants, after a while she'll just get sick of it like I did.

You once said, "The thing about the stuff you read about in EC comics was that it was incredible. And somehow everything else you got in the media, you just knew it was bullshit, you just knew that even these people who were conformists weren't really that way, they really weren't these nice people, they were basically as rotten as everybody else. They somehow put on this goody-goody face. That was everything about MAD comics, MAD comics just got through that shit, and Veronica and Archie and all that stuff, hearing the voice of truth out of all the chaos of smarmy niceness."

Did I say that?

Yeah.

[*Laughs.*] That pretty much sums it up, yeah.

Can you elaborate on what you meant by your reference to the conformist aspect of life in the '50s?

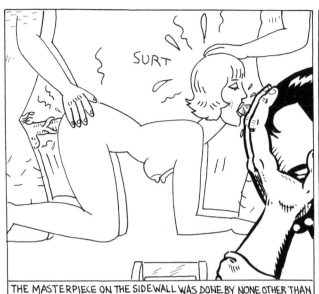

SURT
THE MASTERPIECE ON THE SIDEWALL WAS DONE BY NONE OTHER THAN THE MICHELANGELO OF THE LAVATORY WALL, RON RADETSKY.
BUT ONE MAN TOOK PARTICULAR UMBRAGE TO RON'S DISPLAY OF ARTISTRY. THAT MAN WAS CUSTODIAN ELMER DEDSEL.
SURT
WIPE WIPE WIPE
SUCK
ELMER DEDSEL WAS DETERMINED TO MAKE THE WALLS OF THE BATHROOM STALLS A PLACE OF NOT ONLY PHYSICAL BUT MORAL CLEANLINESS AS WELL.
THE PROBLEM WITH SLEEPING ON THE JOHN FOR ANY LENGTH OF TIME WAS THE RED MARKS FROM YOUR HANDS RESTING ON YOUR FOREHEAD.

Especially in high school. In high school you really got it, and—

That's where you really learned to conform?

Well, no, that's where I learned to rebel. In grammar school, kids are put through that quasi-prison camp routine. And having taught, I can understand why they do that. But I think it doesn't have to be that way. Teaching kids was some sort of karmic comeuppance. I had all these young boys from 8 to about 12, and they'd just love to bust your chops. I would do my best to answer any question they would throw at me. I would just answer them as straight as I could. Even if they were being a wise guy. I mean, at some point you might just have to say, "Everybody in this class knows that that's not a serious question, and you know it too, and so you're just taking up time in the class when we could be doing something that's cool." But that was a rare occasion. I still basically

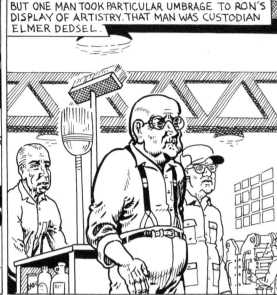

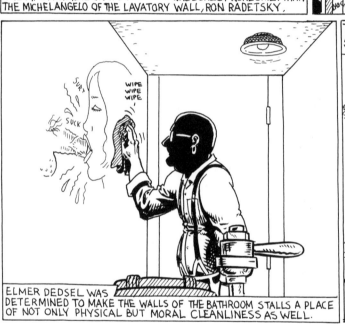

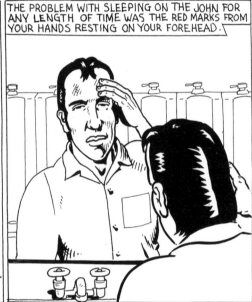

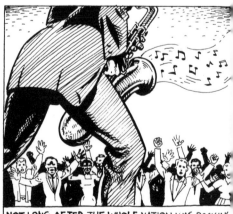

NOT LONG AFTER, THE WHOLE NATION WAS ROCKIN' OUT, AND NOT TOO LONG AFTER THAT, THE WORLD

Panel from "The Discovery of Rock 'N' Roll" in *My True Story* ©1990 Spain

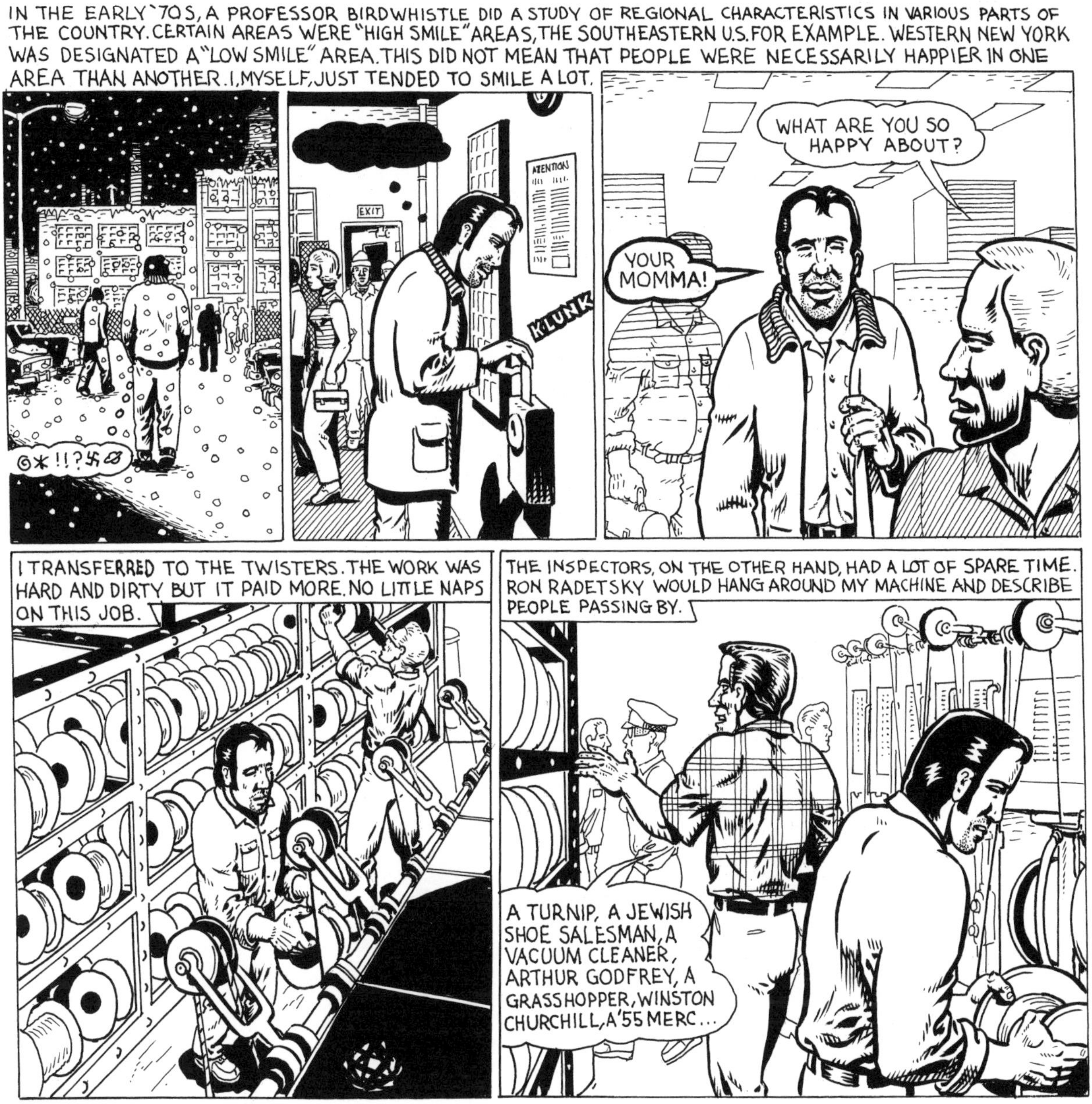
IN THE EARLY '70S, A PROFESSOR BIRDWHISTLE DID A STUDY OF REGIONAL CHARACTERISTICS IN VARIOUS PARTS OF THE COUNTRY. CERTAIN AREAS WERE "HIGH SMILE" AREAS, THE SOUTHEASTERN U.S. FOR EXAMPLE. WESTERN NEW YORK WAS DESIGNATED A "LOW SMILE" AREA. THIS DID NOT MEAN THAT PEOPLE WERE NECESSARILY HAPPIER IN ONE AREA THAN ANOTHER. I, MYSELF, JUST TENDED TO SMILE A LOT.
EXIT
KLUNK
WHAT ARE YOU SO HAPPY ABOUT?
YOUR MOMMA!
I TRANSFERRED TO THE TWISTERS. THE WORK WAS HARD AND DIRTY BUT IT PAID MORE. NO LITTLE NAPS ON THIS JOB.
THE INSPECTORS, ON THE OTHER HAND, HAD A LOT OF SPARE TIME. RON RADETSKY WOULD HANG AROUND MY MACHINE AND DESCRIBE PEOPLE PASSING BY.
A TURNIP, A JEWISH SHOE SALESMAN, A VACUUM CLEANER, ARTHUR GODFREY, A GRASSHOPPER, WINSTON CHURCHILL, A '55 MERC...

sympathize with those kids. I see them as kids who were just like me.

Did you see movies in the '50s?

Oh yeah.

The Wild One *was my favorite—*

That's right, *The Wild One*. I remember seeing it with my parents. My parents asked me if I thought what the bikers did was good. My enthusiastic response was that it was. It wasn't the answer they were looking for.

Did you respond to Brando because he spit in the face of hypocrisy and convention as embodied in those simple townspeople?

There's something about the assuredness they have, in the way they expect you to accept your place as a cog in a productive system, which is not necessarily acting in your interests, or anybody else's, for that matter. It's really an insult to your intelligence that they think you're too dull to realize that what they're claiming to be true is just not true. You can see it all around you. You can see that liberty and justice for all isn't even a pretention with those who represent the law. The Pledge of Allegiance to the flag—I don't have any allegiance to a flag. I have an allegiance to the concepts of the United States Constitution, the ideals of freedom, those ideas that are enunciated in the great documents. Those philosophical concepts are rational, optimistic ideas that I feel a strong allegiance to. But I don't feel any allegiance to a flag, and there's not liberty and justice for all. Under God?

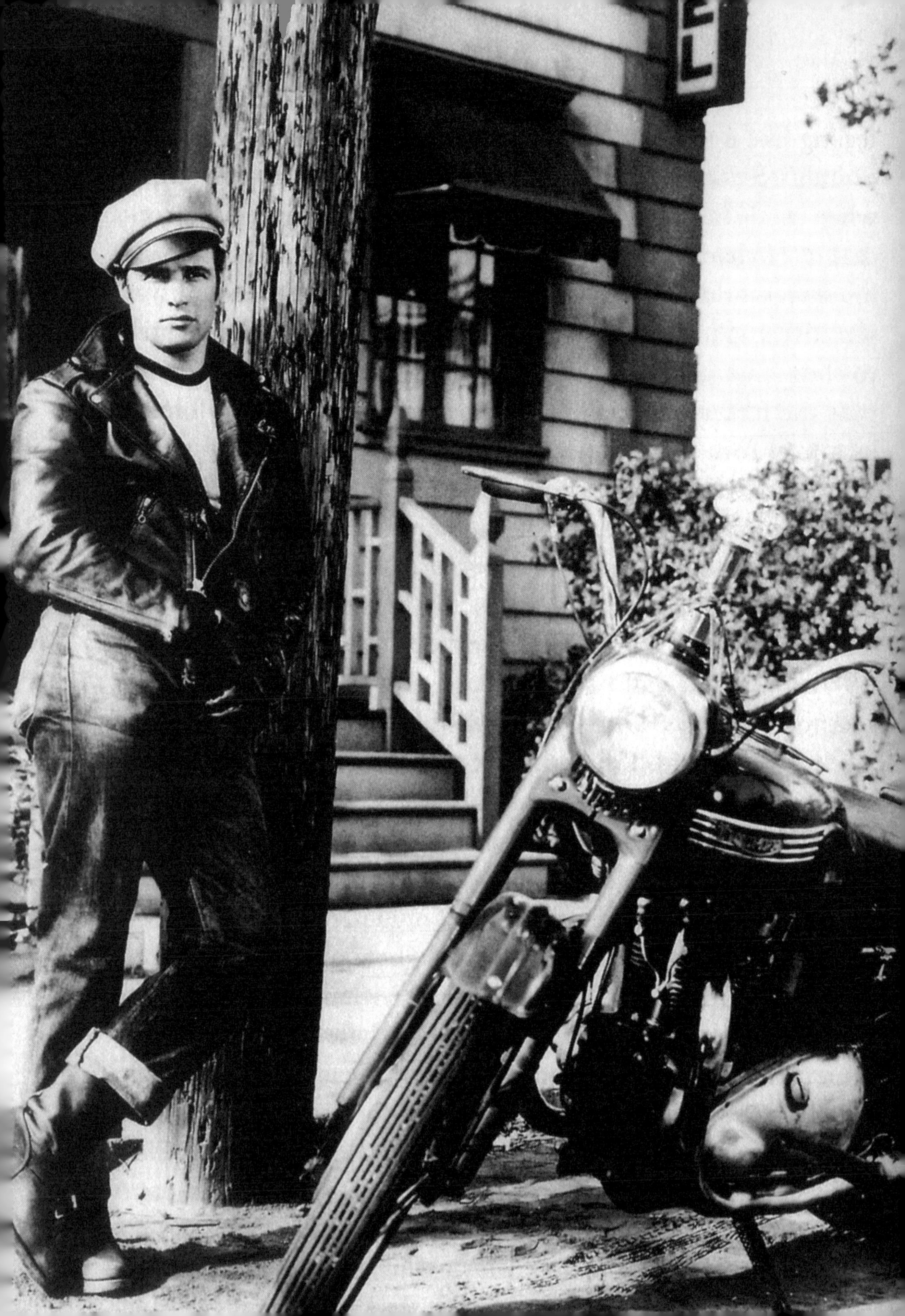
EL

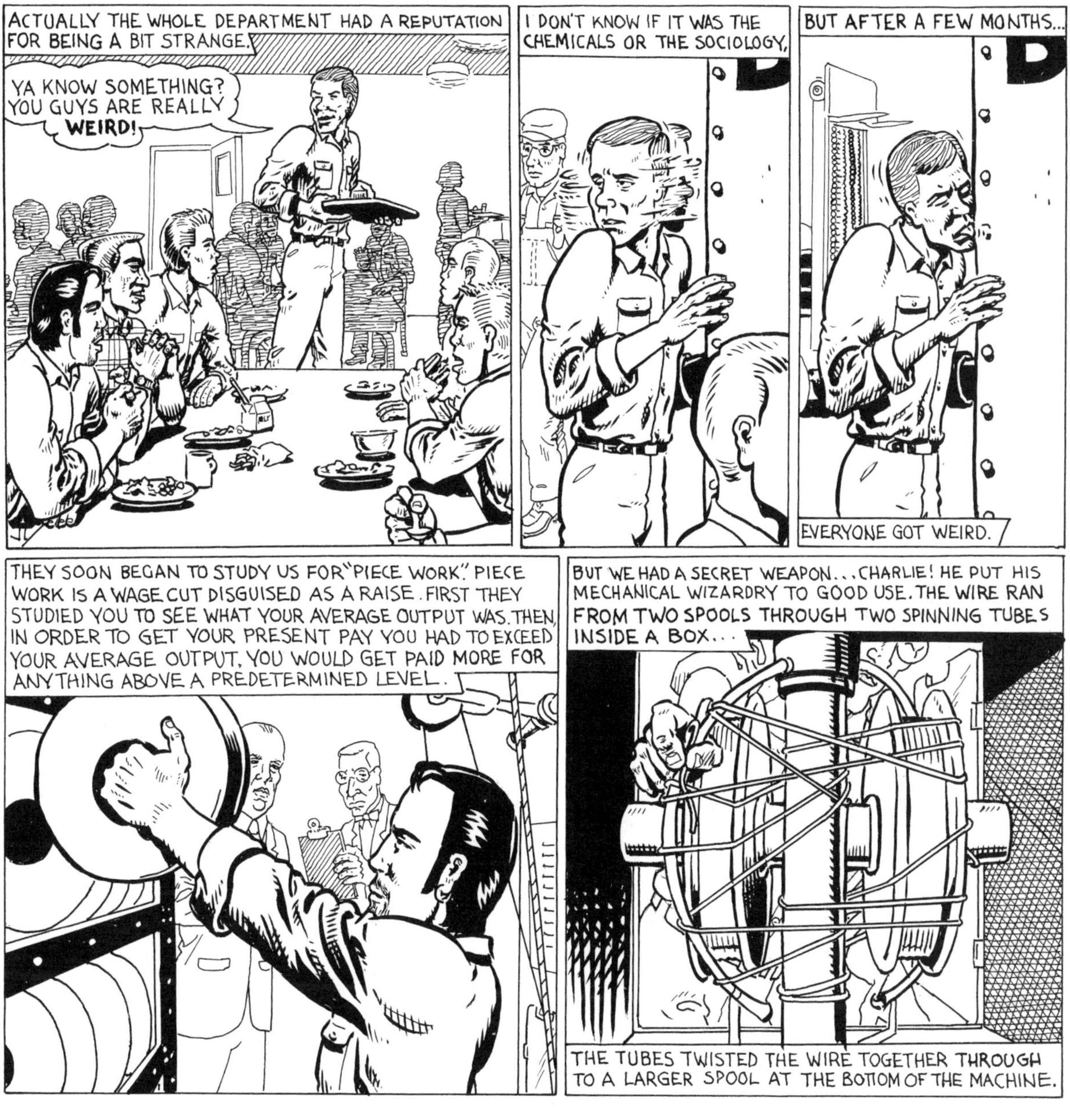
ACTUALLY THE WHOLE DEPARTMENT HAD A REPUTATION FOR BEING A BIT STRANGE.
YA KNOW SOMETHING? YOU GUYS ARE REALLY WEIRD!
I DON'T KNOW IF IT WAS THE CHEMICALS OR THE SOCIOLOGY,
BUT AFTER A FEW MONTHS...
EVERYONE GOT WEIRD.
THEY SOON BEGAN TO STUDY US FOR "PIECE WORK." PIECE WORK IS A WAGE CUT DISGUISED AS A RAISE. FIRST THEY STUDIED YOU TO SEE WHAT YOUR AVERAGE OUTPUT WAS. THEN, IN ORDER TO GET YOUR PRESENT PAY YOU HAD TO EXCEED YOUR AVERAGE OUTPUT. YOU WOULD GET PAID MORE FOR ANYTHING ABOVE A PREDETERMINED LEVEL.
BUT WE HAD A SECRET WEAPON...CHARLIE! HE PUT HIS MECHANICAL WIZARDRY TO GOOD USE. THE WIRE RAN FROM TWO SPOOLS THROUGH TWO SPINNING TUBES INSIDE A BOX...
THE TUBES TWISTED THE WIRE TOGETHER THROUGH TO A LARGER SPOOL AT THE BOTTOM OF THE MACHINE.

Why is it the government's place to promote religion? Look around the world at places where religious fervor is intense, like Algeria or Northern Ireland or the Bible Belt here, where they have all those kid-on-kid massacres. That whole thing spits in the face of the separation of church and state. Instead of the good-natured intelligence that has characterized the best in the American spirit, you have the cult of the flag, which has come to symbolize, especially among its adherents, unquestioning obeisance to authority.

Would your conception of liberty and justice for all include economic equality?

Yeah, definitely, right. I think that most people who have a good balance between productive, fulfilling work and pleasure are basically happy. I think people get loaded all the time as a substitute for therapy. They are people who are trying to work something out. While things can and should be set up so that everyone has the material basis for a decent life, including work at decent wages, access to means of improving their skills, etc., some sort of opportunity has to be made to provide circumstances where even the fucked-up can be useful too… I think everybody, whatever their ideology, wants to see a society of the useful rather than a society of the useless. And I think that there is a strong impulse in people to want to be useful. But the fact of

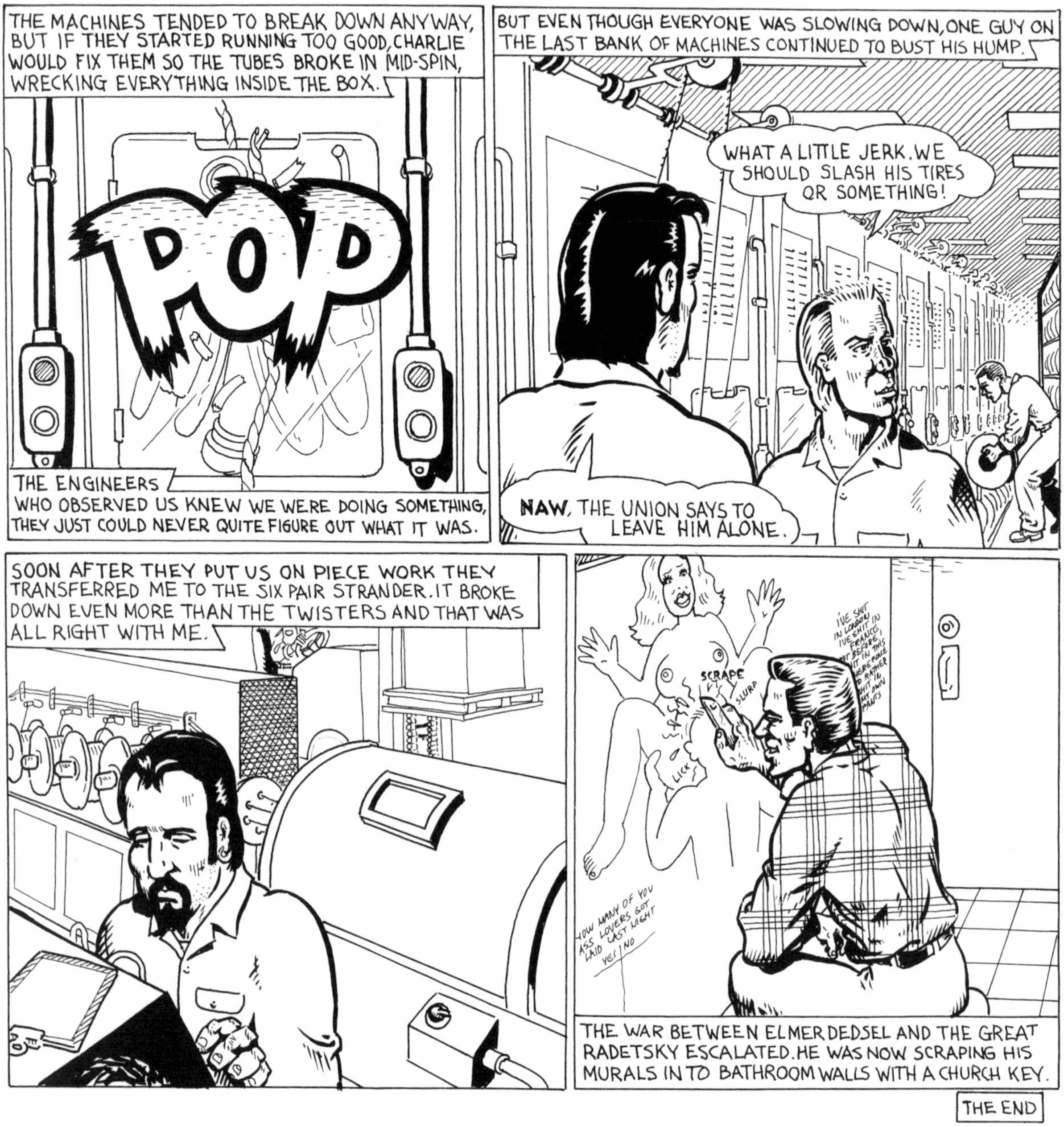
THE MACHINES TENDED TO BREAK DOWN ANYWAY, BUT IF THEY STARTED RUNNING TOO GOOD, CHARLIE WOULD FIX THEM SO THE TUBES BROKE IN MID-SPIN, WRECKING EVERYTHING INSIDE THE BOX.
POP
THE ENGINEERS WHO OBSERVED US KNEW WE WERE DOING SOMETHING, THEY JUST COULD NEVER QUITE FIGURE OUT WHAT IT WAS.
BUT EVEN THOUGH EVERYONE WAS SLOWING DOWN, ONE GUY ON THE LAST BANK OF MACHINES CONTINUED TO BUST HIS HUMP.
WHAT A LITTLE JERK. WE SHOULD SLASH HIS TIRES OR SOMETHING!
NAW, THE UNION SAYS TO LEAVE HIM ALONE.
SOON AFTER THEY PUT US ON PIECE WORK THEY TRANSFERRED ME TO THE SIX PAIR STRANDER. IT BROKE DOWN EVEN MORE THAN THE TWISTERS AND THAT WAS ALL RIGHT WITH ME.
SCRAPE
SLURP
LICK
THE WAR BETWEEN ELMER DEDSEL AND THE GREAT RADETSKY ESCALATED. HE WAS NOW SCRAPING HIS MURALS IN TO BATHROOM WALLS WITH A CHURCH KEY.
THE END

the matter is the capitalist system cannot and does not want to create jobs for everybody. We've strayed off from comics into this politics, but it's a prime motivating factor for my work. I don't want to be a mainstream cartoonist. I don't want to have to be a mouthpiece for what I consider unjust. I'll do commercial work to make bread, but the great thing about doing underground comics is the fact that we can just say it as we see it.

THE STUDENT

What kind of a student were you in high school? You went to jail when you were 16.

Well, actually I just spent an afternoon in the can. I don't want to over-dramatize.

Did you… live by yourself after that?

No, I stayed home and graduated high school. There were certain subjects that I was really absorbed with, history and art. I had to do a term paper for American history, and I started reading about Hannibal. I started reading everything I could find about him, about the Punic Wars, about Hannibal's father… to this day I can run down battles, give you historical dates… it was just something that I found utterly fascinating. And I was always good enough so I could pass. I'm sorry I didn't take more math, because a lot of that stuff seems more interesting to me now. But I was able to get along, pass, get a high school diploma. But there were certain things

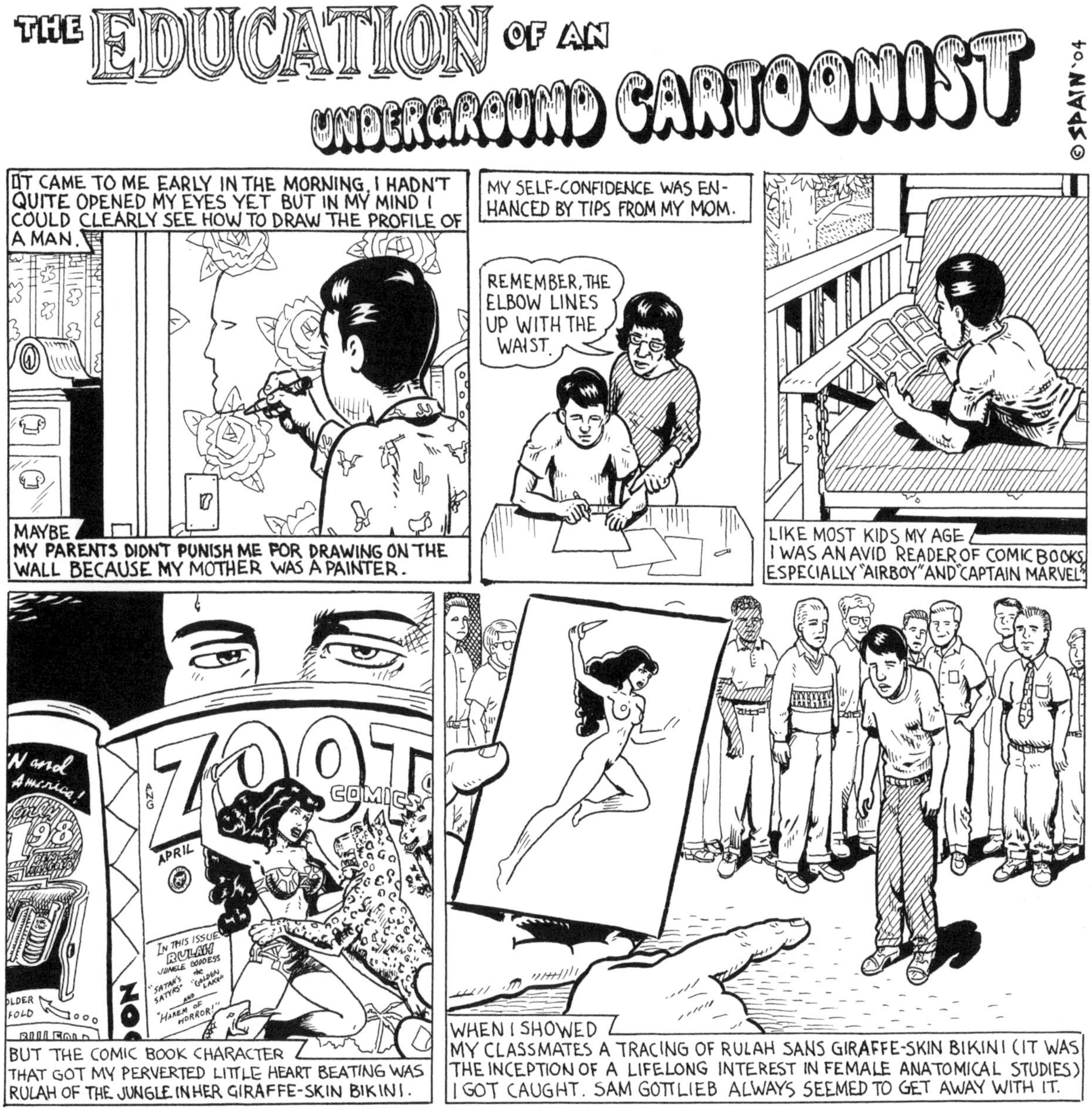
THE EDUCATION OF AN UNDERGROUND CARTOONIST
© SPAIN '04
IT CAME TO ME EARLY IN THE MORNING, I HADN'T QUITE OPENED MY EYES YET BUT IN MY MIND I COULD CLEARLY SEE HOW TO DRAW THE PROFILE OF A MAN.
MAYBE
MY PARENTS DIDN'T PUNISH ME FOR DRAWING ON THE WALL BECAUSE MY MOTHER WAS A PAINTER.
MY SELF-CONFIDENCE WAS ENHANCED BY TIPS FROM MY MOM.
REMEMBER, THE ELBOW LINES UP WITH THE WAIST.
LIKE MOST KIDS MY AGE
I WAS AN AVID READER OF COMIC BOOKS ESPECIALLY "AIRBOY" AND "CAPTAIN MARVEL".
ZOOT COMICS
APRIL
IN THIS ISSUE RULAH JUNGLE GODDESS "SATAN'S SATYRS" the "GOLDEN LAKE" AND "HAREM OF HORROR!"
N and America!
98
FOLD
BUT THE COMIC BOOK CHARACTER
THAT GOT MY PERVERTED LITTLE HEART BEATING WAS RULAH OF THE JUNGLE IN HER GIRAFFE-SKIN BIKINI.
WHEN I SHOWED
MY CLASSMATES A TRACING OF RULAH SANS GIRAFFE-SKIN BIKINI (IT WAS THE INCEPTION OF A LIFELONG INTEREST IN FEMALE ANATOMICAL STUDIES) I GOT CAUGHT. SAM GOTTLIEB ALWAYS SEEMED TO GET AWAY WITH IT.

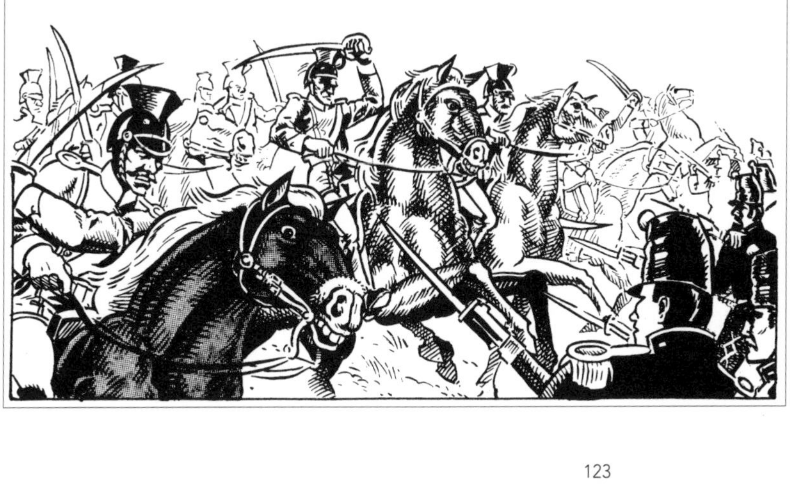

that really intrigued me, and I had some good teachers. I had a teacher in eighth grade, her name was Miss Whetstone, and she was red-haired, and she had eyes that bulged out of her head. And she was known as a no-nonsense teacher… the frightening visage of this woman with these eyes that popped out of her head with this red hair. You knew, when you saw her in action a few times, that when you went to her class, you behaved. But she was also a very

Panel from "1871" in *My True Story* ©1986 Spain

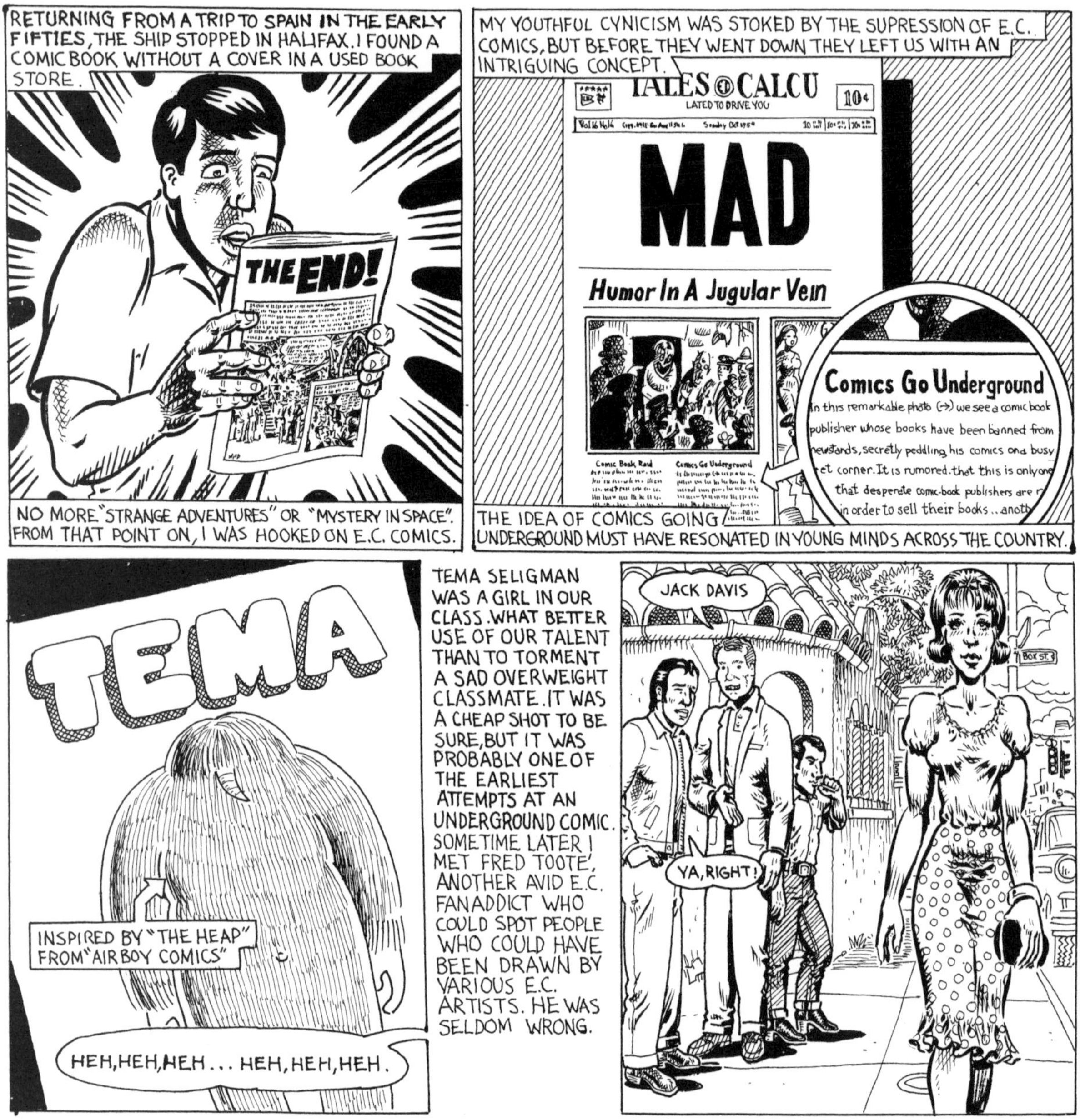
RETURNING FROM A TRIP TO SPAIN IN THE EARLY FIFTIES, THE SHIP STOPPED IN HALIFAX. I FOUND A COMIC BOOK WITHOUT A COVER IN A USED BOOK STORE.
THE END!
NO MORE "STRANGE ADVENTURES" OR "MYSTERY IN SPACE". FROM THAT POINT ON, I WAS HOOKED ON E.C. COMICS.
MY YOUTHFUL CYNICISM WAS STOKED BY THE SUPRESSION OF E.C. COMICS, BUT BEFORE THEY WENT DOWN THEY LEFT US WITH AN INTRIGUING CONCEPT.
TALES CALCU
LATED TO DRIVE YOU
10¢
MAD
Humor In A Jugular Vein
Comics Go Underground
In this remarkable photo (→) we see a comic book publisher whose books have been banned from newstands, secretly peddling his comics on a busy
et corner. It is rumored that this is only one
that desperate comic-book publishers are
in order to sell their books .. anot
THE IDEA OF COMICS GOING UNDERGROUND MUST HAVE RESONATED IN YOUNG MINDS ACROSS THE COUNTRY.
TEMA
INSPIRED BY "THE HEAP" FROM "AIRBOY COMICS"
HEH, HEH, HEH ... HEH, HEH, HEH.
TEMA SELIGMAN WAS A GIRL IN OUR CLASS. WHAT BETTER USE OF OUR TALENT THAN TO TORMENT A SAD OVERWEIGHT CLASSMATE. IT WAS A CHEAP SHOT TO BE SURE, BUT IT WAS PROBABLY ONE OF THE EARLIEST ATTEMPTS AT AN UNDERGROUND COMIC.
SOMETIME LATER I MET FRED TOOTE', ANOTHER AVID E.C. FANADDICT WHO COULD SPOT PEOPLE WHO COULD HAVE BEEN DRAWN BY VARIOUS E.C. ARTISTS. HE WAS SELDOM WRONG.
JACK DAVIS
BOX ST.
YA, RIGHT!

compassionate woman who was very serious about her students learning. She would give us mimeographed sheets of sentences to dissect… I can do this…

You mean diagram?

Diagram the sentences, right, that's what it is, diagram. And to this day, I can do them. If you give me a sentence, I can diagram it. Every day, man, you just had to do it, and she didn't want to hear that you couldn't do it. But she was a woman who would actually talk to you. "How come you guys have that hair style?" But on the other hand, despite her genuine compassion, you just knew that you couldn't cut up in her class.

I was fortunate to have people like that, who brought to your attention the fact that there is an alternative to hanging on the corner, staring dully and drunkenly into the void. These poor kids, you see them, and nobody did that for them. Learning about the world is a pleasure, it's not something that you should have to be whipped into as a kid or as an adult. And so that's the sort of thing I tried to get across to the kids in my class, and my daughter… well, I try to impart that to her, even though I can still feel my resentment of what seemed to me then and now as mindless regimentation… What can I tell you?

I understand.

Didn't you join the bike gang right after high school?

No, I went to art school for three years.

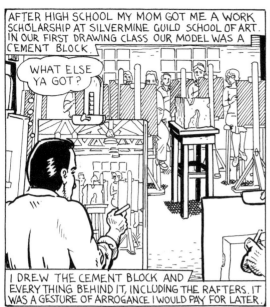

AFTER HIGH SCHOOL MY MOM GOT ME A WORK SCHOLARSHIP AT SILVERMINE GUILD SCHOOL OF ART. IN OUR FIRST DRAWING CLASS OUR MODEL WAS A CEMENT BLOCK.

WHAT ELSE YA GOT?

I DREW THE CEMENT BLOCK AND EVERYTHING BEHIND IT, INCLUDING THE RAFTERS. IT WAS A GESTURE OF ARROGANCE. I WOULD PAY FOR LATER.

ART SCHOOL OPENED UP NEW VISTAS FOR ME. I LEARNED TO BROADEN MY APPRECIATION OF WHAT WAS WORTH SEEING, BUT AS MUCH AS I LIKED TO LOOK AT ABSTRACT ART I GOT NO PLEASURE DOING IT.

I CAN DIG IT!

FOR ME, THE MAIN KICK OF MAKING IMAGES WAS WHAT IT HAD ALWAYS BEEN; TO MAKE A FLAT SURFACE APPEAR THREE DIMENSIONAL.

I HAD IMAGINED MYSELF TO BE SOMETHING OF A HOT SHOT. BUT FOR ALL MY BRAVADO, THE MOTHERFUCKERS HAD A WAY OF GETTING TO YOU.

BUT IT'S SMF ILLUSTRATION

AFTER ALMOST THREE YEARS, WHAT LITTLE OUTPUT I PRODUCED HAD TAKEN A TURN FOR THE WEIRD.

PERHAPS IT WAS THE PORTRAIT OF MYSELF DEAD THAT PROMPTED THEM TO SEND ME TO A SHRINK.

HER ANALYSIS WAS QUICK AND TO THE POINT.

YOU HATE IT HERE, DON'T YOU?

BLAH, BLAH BLAH...UNH YAH!

I LEFT SCHOOL IMMEDIATELY. TO THIS DAY, THE DAY I LEFT ART SCHOOL WAS THE HAPPIEST DAY OF MY LIFE.

Let me just skip back. You attended the Silvermine Guild School of Art of New Canaan, Conn.? What is the Silvermine Guild School of Art?
It was an art school in Connecticut that… one of the people who started it was John Vassos, the guy who designed the Lucky Strike logo. At the time I didn't realize that. He was one of the prominent guys in industrial design… so there were a lot of good teachers there. But of course it was the time when Abstract Expressionism was dominant. The work I did in the commercial art class was appreciated, but the fine arts course was a different story.
Why did you choose that school?
My mother just figured if he stays in the neighborhood, he'll probably end up in jail, so here, he had something going for him…
Send him to Connecticut. [Laughs.]
So I'll send him to Connecticut. That's where people are nice and nobody gets drunk. So I went to Connecticut. In Buffalo, there were no drugs in my neighborhood at that time. When I was a kid, nobody smoked grass, but in Connecticut, man, there was everything, even heroin. But I didn't touch it. I was serious about getting an education.
Did you revel in your freedom?
Well, it wasn't much freedom compared to Buffalo, because I was living out in the country, I didn't have any car, and I didn't have any bread, so I just kind of… I was just at that age I didn't really know how to hit up on girls…
Did you get a job in high school? Did

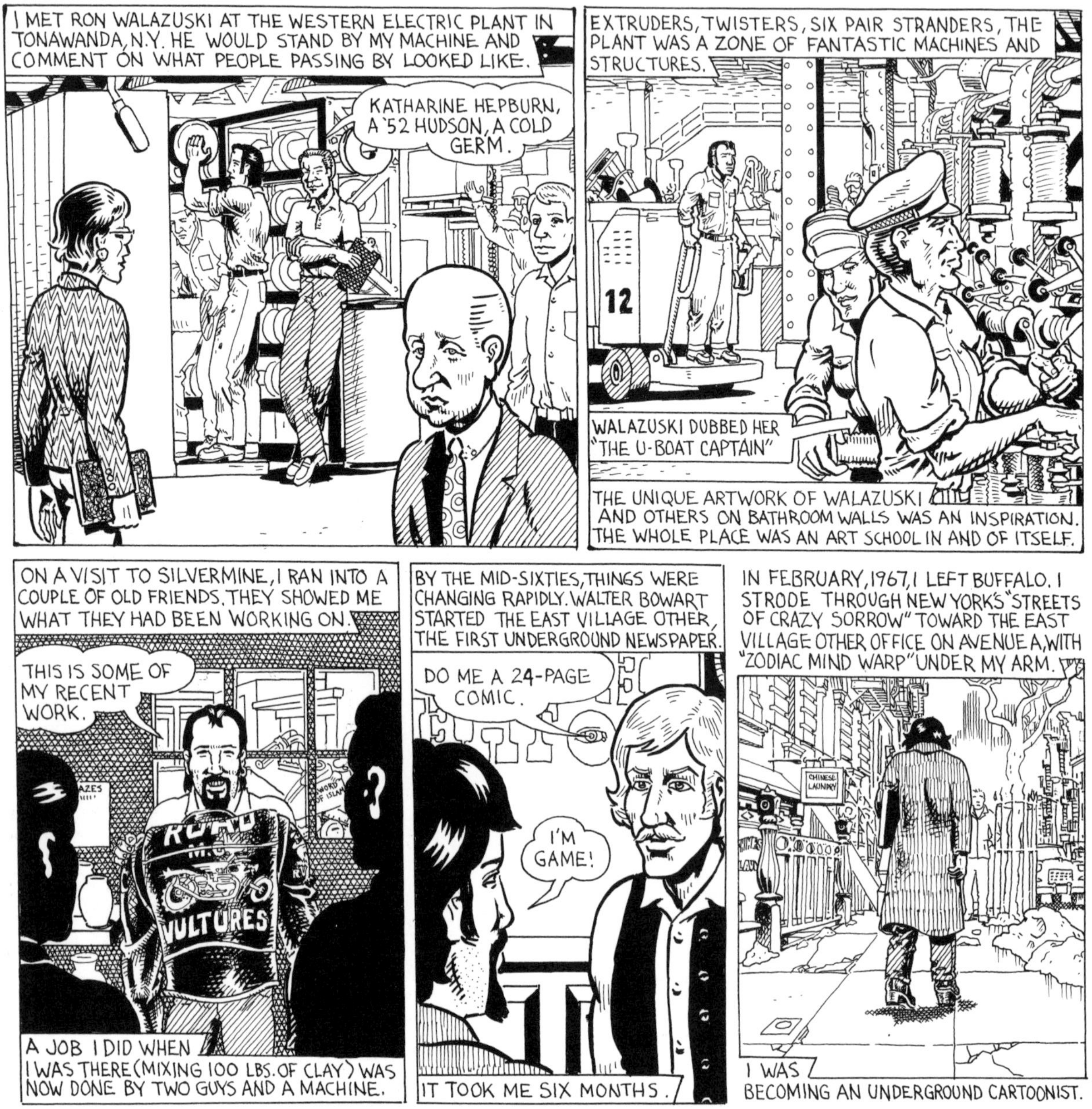
I MET RON WALAZUSKI AT THE WESTERN ELECTRIC PLANT IN TONAWANDA, N.Y. HE WOULD STAND BY MY MACHINE AND COMMENT ON WHAT PEOPLE PASSING BY LOOKED LIKE.
KATHARINE HEPBURN, A '52 HUDSON, A COLD GERM.
EXTRUDERS, TWISTERS, SIX PAIR STRANDERS, THE PLANT WAS A ZONE OF FANTASTIC MACHINES AND STRUCTURES.
12
WALAZUSKI DUBBED HER "THE U-BOAT CAPTAIN"
THE UNIQUE ARTWORK OF WALAZUSKI AND OTHERS ON BATHROOM WALLS WAS AN INSPIRATION. THE WHOLE PLACE WAS AN ART SCHOOL IN AND OF ITSELF.
ON A VISIT TO SILVERMINE, I RAN INTO A COUPLE OF OLD FRIENDS. THEY SHOWED ME WHAT THEY HAD BEEN WORKING ON.
THIS IS SOME OF MY RECENT WORK.
VULTURES
A JOB I DID WHEN I WAS THERE (MIXING 100 LBS. OF CLAY) WAS NOW DONE BY TWO GUYS AND A MACHINE.
BY THE MID-SIXTIES, THINGS WERE CHANGING RAPIDLY. WALTER BOWART STARTED THE EAST VILLAGE OTHER, THE FIRST UNDERGROUND NEWSPAPER.
DO ME A 24-PAGE COMIC.
I'M GAME!
IT TOOK ME SIX MONTHS.
IN FEBRUARY, 1967, I LEFT BUFFALO. I STRODE THROUGH NEW YORK'S "STREETS OF CRAZY SORROW" TOWARD THE EAST VILLAGE OTHER OFFICE ON AVENUE A, WITH "ZODIAC MIND WARP" UNDER MY ARM.
CHINESE LAUNDRY
I WAS BECOMING AN UNDERGROUND CARTOONIST.

you work?

Yeah. I had a paper route. I was an usher… my old man had a gas station, for a while I worked… so I made enough money to have…

Did you date in high school?

Yeah, right, I did, a little bit of dating. But still… it kind of takes you a while to understand how to hang out with girls, and how to approach them in the right way. I'm kind of a crude dude, so it took me a while to figure it out.

Yes. To learn that ritual.

Yes.

Was sex a verboten subject in your family? What was your parents'—

Yeah, I don't think it was generally talked about. When I was 16, my old man told me about the clap, that you could get the clap, and you should wear condoms.

ART SCHOOL EXPERIENCES

Tell me a little bit more about the Silvermine Guild School. You were there for approximately two—

Three years. I split a couple weeks before the end of my third year.

What did you learn there? Was it a good experience?

It was a good experience all in all, because I got to do things. I got to do sculpture, I got to do oil painting, I got to do drawing… well, I was always doing a lot of drawing, but it was a depressing experience for me, for various reasons. One of the things was, I was always a hotshot as an artist. I could think of myself

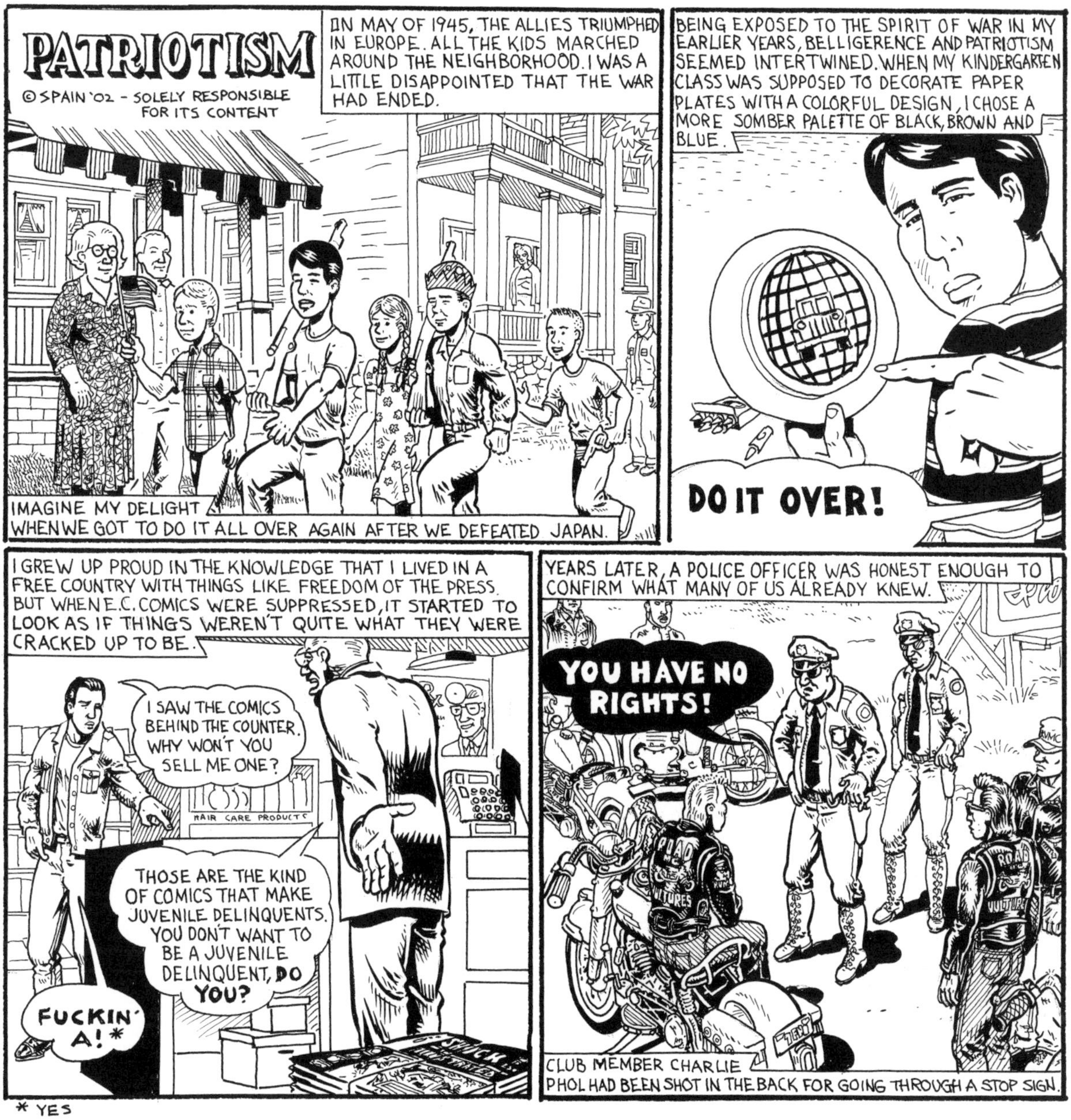
PATRIOTISM
©SPAIN '02 - SOLELY RESPONSIBLE FOR ITS CONTENT
IN MAY OF 1945, THE ALLIES TRIUMPHED IN EUROPE. ALL THE KIDS MARCHED AROUND THE NEIGHBORHOOD. I WAS A LITTLE DISAPPOINTED THAT THE WAR HAD ENDED.
IMAGINE MY DELIGHT WHEN WE GOT TO DO IT ALL OVER AGAIN AFTER WE DEFEATED JAPAN.
BEING EXPOSED TO THE SPIRIT OF WAR IN MY EARLIER YEARS, BELLIGERENCE AND PATRIOTISM SEEMED INTERTWINED. WHEN MY KINDERGARTEN CLASS WAS SUPPOSED TO DECORATE PAPER PLATES WITH A COLORFUL DESIGN, I CHOSE A MORE SOMBER PALETTE OF BLACK, BROWN AND BLUE.
DO IT OVER!
I GREW UP PROUD IN THE KNOWLEDGE THAT I LIVED IN A FREE COUNTRY WITH THINGS LIKE FREEDOM OF THE PRESS. BUT WHEN E.C. COMICS WERE SUPPRESSED, IT STARTED TO LOOK AS IF THINGS WEREN'T QUITE WHAT THEY WERE CRACKED UP TO BE.
I SAW THE COMICS BEHIND THE COUNTER. WHY WON'T YOU SELL ME ONE?
HAIR CARE PRODUCTS
THOSE ARE THE KIND OF COMICS THAT MAKE JUVENILE DELINQUENTS. YOU DON'T WANT TO BE A JUVENILE DELINQUENT, DO YOU?
FUCKIN' A!*
YEARS LATER, A POLICE OFFICER WAS HONEST ENOUGH TO CONFIRM WHAT MANY OF US ALREADY KNEW.
YOU HAVE NO RIGHTS!
ROAD VULTURES
CLUB MEMBER CHARLIE PHOL HAD BEEN SHOT IN THE BACK FOR GOING THROUGH A STOP SIGN.
* YES

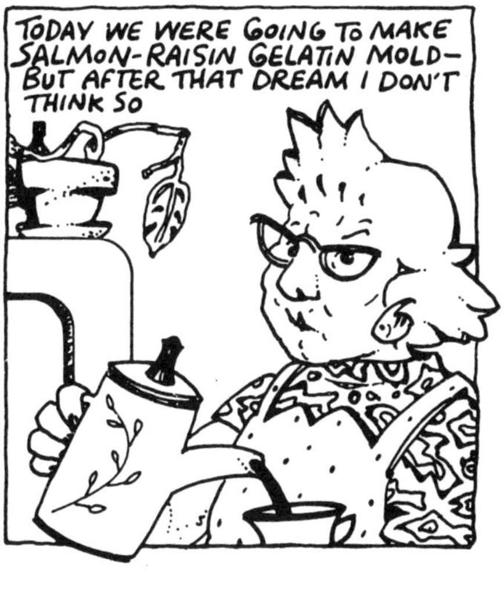
TODAY WE WERE GOING TO MAKE SALMON-RAISIN GELATIN MOLD— BUT AFTER THAT DREAM I DON'T THINK SO

Panel from "Aunt Mary's Kitchen" in *National Lampoon* Vol. 2, #25 (August 1980) by M.K. Brown ©1980 NL Communications, Inc.

as the best artist on the horizon. And even in art school, I thought of myself as the best, except maybe for M.K. Brown, who was in my class. She was the one person whose work I saw as being as good, if not better, than mine. But draftsmanship was not held in high esteem, so that was difficult for me, and I was the one who made those determinations as to what was good or bad. Drawing was always something that I could retreat to, and I found myself in a situation where people who had a different philosophy were judging my work. If somebody could correct my work, and make it better, in my eyes, fine, but to them, my work was too tight. It is tight, but that's the way I like it.

You once said, "When I was in art school, it was the period of trying to figure out what was going on, also coming into contact with anarchist books. I started picking up books and reading all this different stuff." It sounds

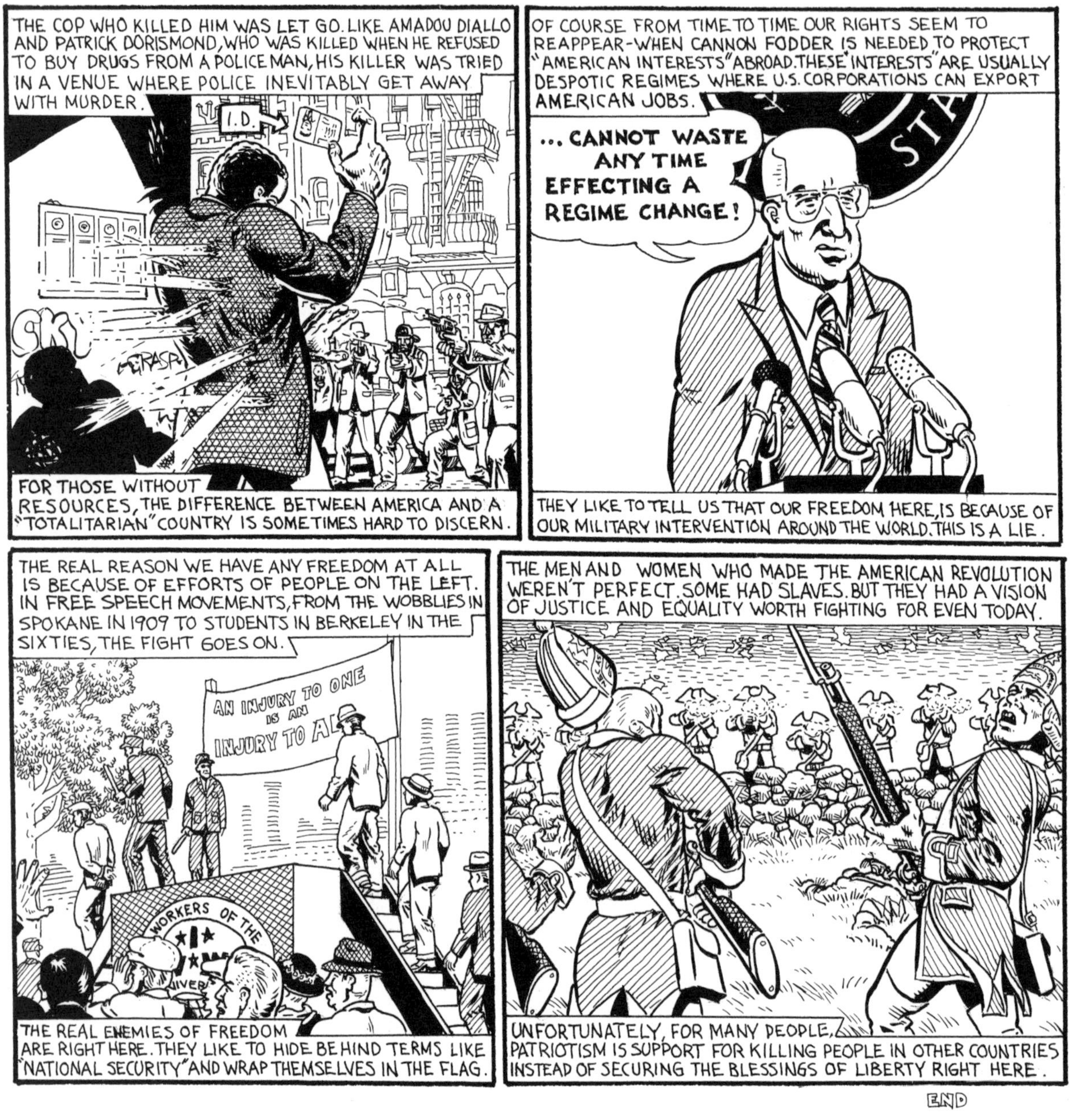
THE COP WHO KILLED HIM WAS LET GO. LIKE AMADOU DIALLO AND PATRICK DORISMOND, WHO WAS KILLED WHEN HE REFUSED TO BUY DRUGS FROM A POLICEMAN, HIS KILLER WAS TRIED IN A VENUE WHERE POLICE INEVITABLY GET AWAY WITH MURDER.
I.D.
FOR THOSE WITHOUT RESOURCES, THE DIFFERENCE BETWEEN AMERICA AND A "TOTALITARIAN" COUNTRY IS SOMETIMES HARD TO DISCERN.
OF COURSE FROM TIME TO TIME OUR RIGHTS SEEM TO REAPPEAR-WHEN CANNON FODDER IS NEEDED TO PROTECT "AMERICAN INTERESTS" ABROAD. THESE "INTERESTS" ARE USUALLY DESPOTIC REGIMES WHERE U.S. CORPORATIONS CAN EXPORT AMERICAN JOBS.
... CANNOT WASTE ANY TIME EFFECTING A REGIME CHANGE!
THEY LIKE TO TELL US THAT OUR FREEDOM HERE, IS BECAUSE OF OUR MILITARY INTERVENTION AROUND THE WORLD. THIS IS A LIE.
THE REAL REASON WE HAVE ANY FREEDOM AT ALL IS BECAUSE OF EFFORTS OF PEOPLE ON THE LEFT. IN FREE SPEECH MOVEMENTS, FROM THE WOBBLIES IN SPOKANE IN 1909 TO STUDENTS IN BERKELEY IN THE SIXTIES, THE FIGHT GOES ON.
AN INJURY TO ONE IS AN INJURY TO A
WORKERS OF THE
THE REAL ENEMIES OF FREEDOM ARE RIGHT HERE. THEY LIKE TO HIDE BEHIND TERMS LIKE "NATIONAL SECURITY" AND WRAP THEMSELVES IN THE FLAG.
THE MEN AND WOMEN WHO MADE THE AMERICAN REVOLUTION WEREN'T PERFECT. SOME HAD SLAVES. BUT THEY HAD A VISION OF JUSTICE AND EQUALITY WORTH FIGHTING FOR EVEN TODAY.
UNFORTUNATELY, FOR MANY PEOPLE, PATRIOTISM IS SUPPORT FOR KILLING PEOPLE IN OTHER COUNTRIES INSTEAD OF SECURING THE BLESSINGS OF LIBERTY RIGHT HERE.
END

like you really started broadening your horizons, or at least educating your own intuitive ideas with concrete…

Yeah. The art school was pretty much art. After a while, they had a course survey of Western civilization that was pretty good. But I just got into philosophy by reading.

A little Kierkegaard, a little Gramsci…

Yeah, right. And Hegel and Kant, poring through all that stuff.

This was more or less on your own?

Yeah. I had a lot of time on my hands, although there was never a dull moment.

And in the midst of all this I was doing a lot of artwork. But at some point I just couldn't do any more artwork there. I finally started doing weird comic-book covers, things like… one was a bed with a dish and a rag and a severed hand and a knife. I started doing these things that disturbed them, so they sent me to a shrink. She said, "You really don't like it here. You really miss being home." And I said, "Jeez, that's right." I had never thought of that. So I just split.

You said you left a few weeks before the third year.

Yeah.

Did that jeopardize your academic status? You didn't give a shit?

I didn't give a shit, and don't, that's right. [*Laughs.*] My academic standing is not really a primary concern.

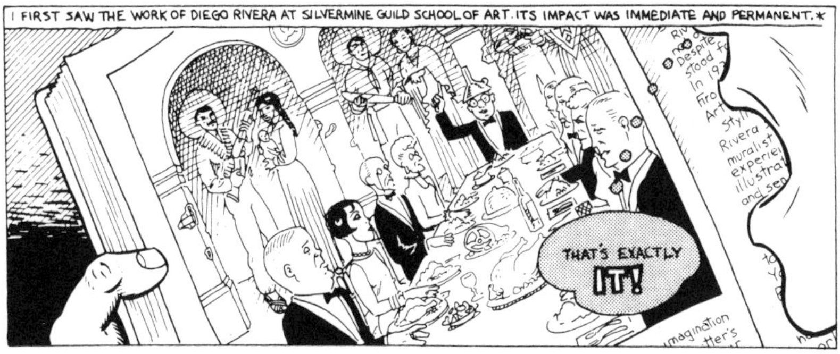
I FIRST SAW THE WORK OF DIEGO RIVERA AT SILVERMINE GUILD SCHOOL OF ART. ITS IMPACT WAS IMMEDIATE AND PERMANENT.*
THAT'S EXACTLY IT!

SEVEN YEARS

When you attended the Silvermine Guild School of Art, you were probably between 18 and 21?
18 and 20, yeah.
The first strip that I know you did was Zodiac Mindwarp *for the* East Village Other. *When you attended the Silvermine Guild School, that must have been between approximately '58 to '60, and I can't imagine you did this strip before about '65.*
Zodiac Mindwarp, I did it in… it came out in '67.
So there's seven years between the time you attended the Guild School of Art and the time you actually had your first strip published. I want to explore what you were doing in those seven years, and how your interest in comics finally culminated in doing that work.
Well, I always wanted to be a cartoonist. That seemed to be my first love. There was something about art school, they were able to insinuate this disdainful attitude towards things like comics, and towards popular forms of art. Even though I tried to fight it, it seemed to infect me. So I did a lot of painting. By the time I got out of art school, I was fairly depressed, but after getting out of art school, I perked up again and did a whole bunch of painting, and continued to do art work. I've always drawn, as a kid, as a teenager… I was one of those people who drew in the margins of their notebooks and on their pads and on anything I could get a hold of. I got just as much of an art education working at Western Electric for five years as I got at the Silvermine Guild School of Art. During that period, I worked in a plant for about five years.
What kind of plant?
We made telephone wire. It was a Western Electric plant. And there were a lot of good artists there, some amazing artists.
What was your job?
I had various jobs. I was a janitor at one point, I worked on these different machines, twisters, standers… the plant was an amazing place. Janitor was actually the best job, because you got to see all the surreal machines, and all this different wire being processed through the extruders and the spinners and all sorts of things. There were a lot of interesting people there.
You went back to Buffalo as soon as you got out of school?
Right, yeah.
And you got a job at the plant pretty quickly?
I got a job fairly quickly, yeah. After a few months. I worked with my dad a little bit, but… I got a job at Western Electric, and went through the various departments…
How did you feel about working there?
I enjoyed it. A lot of it was tedious, but there were a lot of good artists there. There are a lot of good stories that I could tell about working there.
Were you unionized?
Yeah. There was a good union there, CWUA, that stuck up for me. You had to fuck up the same way three times to get fired, and I never fucked up the same way more than once.
So you could fuck up three different ways and not get fired?
You could fuck up twice the same way, the third time you were out. I was actually rather creative in the ways I fucked up, but I would never do the same thing twice.

THE ROAD VULTURES

Tell me what your life was like during that period, both in terms of how your interest in comics coalesced, as well as what else you were doing?
Well, at the time I was riding motorcycles. I had different bikes, and I ended up joining the Road Vultures.
Now, explain how you joined the Road Vultures; what kind of a bike did you get? How did you get into that milieu?
Well, Buffalo is a great party town.

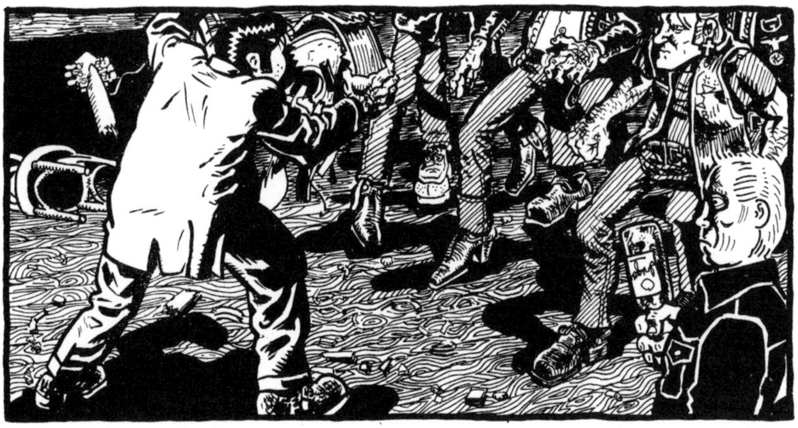

ABOVE
Panel from "Mexico and Me" in *My True Story*
©1992 Spain

RIGHT
Panel from "Evening at the Country Club" in *Zap #6*
©1973 Spain

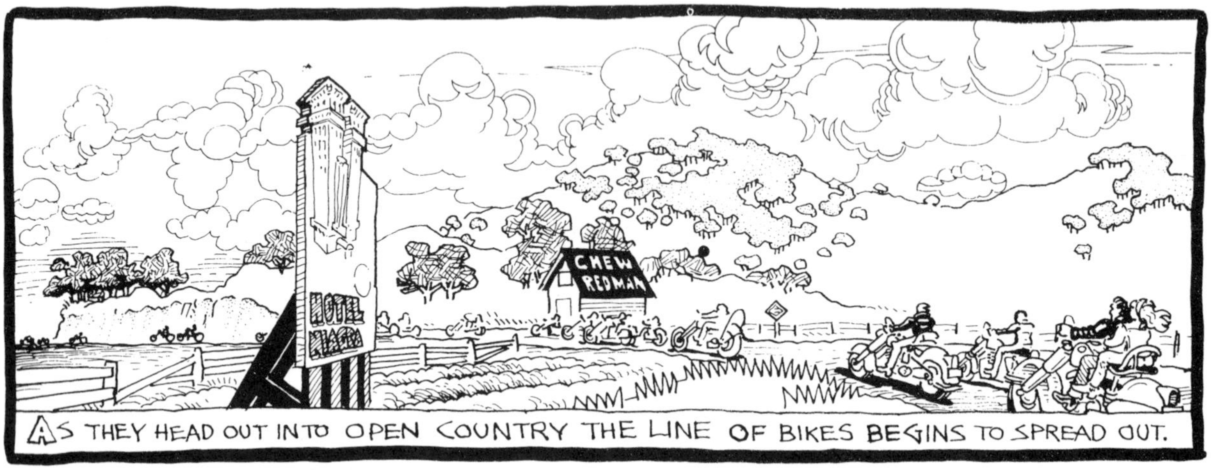
CHEW REDMAN
AS THEY HEAD OUT INTO OPEN COUNTRY THE LINE OF BIKES BEGINS TO SPREAD OUT.

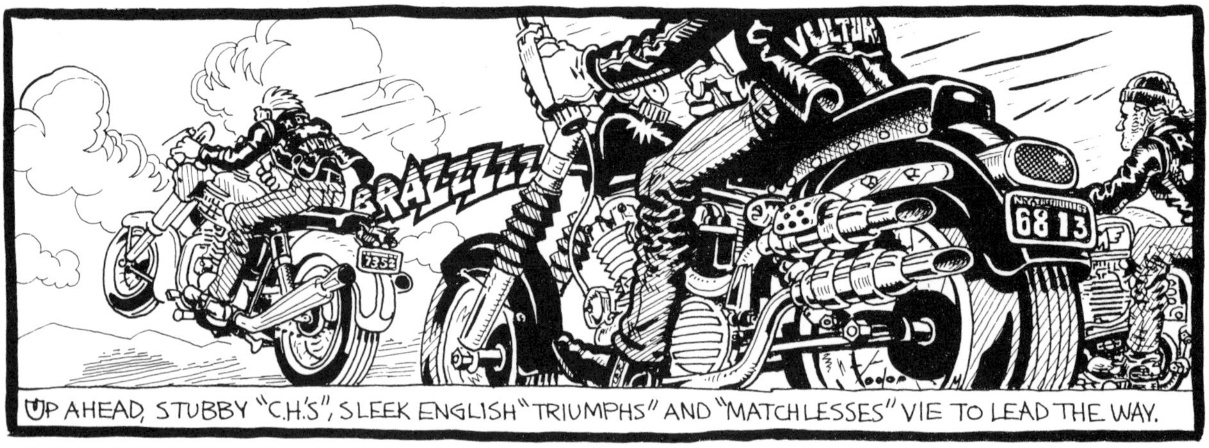
68 13
UP AHEAD, STUBBY "C.H.'S", SLEEK ENGLISH "TRIUMPHS" AND "MATCHLESSES" VIE TO LEAD THE WAY.

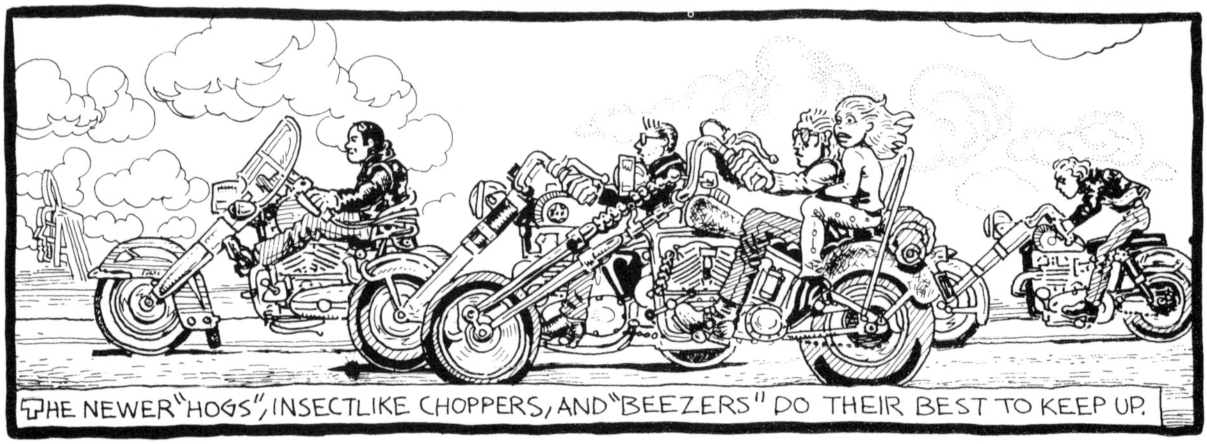
THE NEWER "HOGS", INSECTLIKE CHOPPERS, AND "BEEZERS" DO THEIR BEST TO KEEP UP.

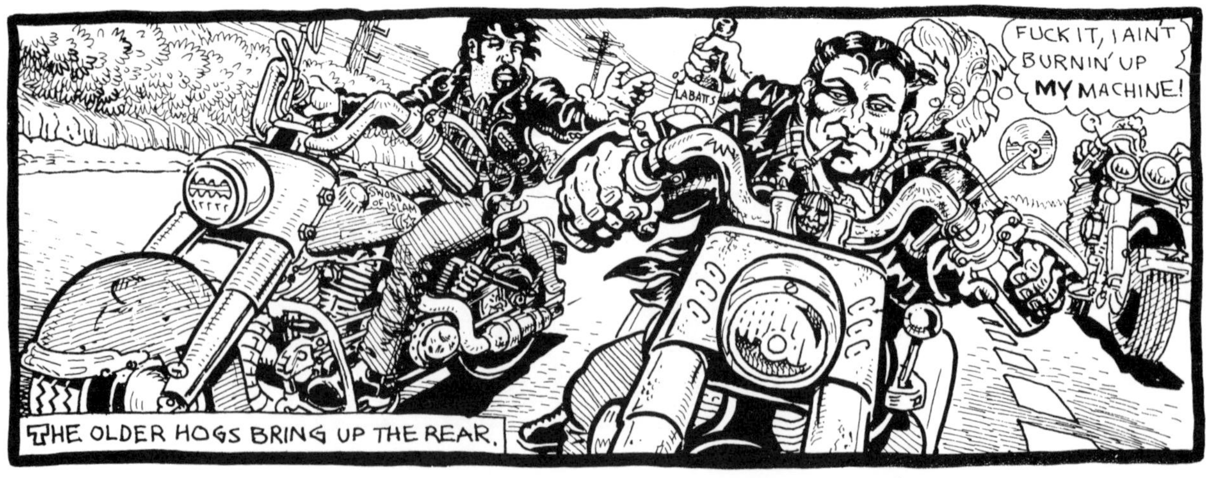
LABATTS
SWORD OF ISLAM
FUCK IT, I AINT BURNIN' UP **MY** MACHINE!
THE OLDER HOGS BRING UP THE REAR.

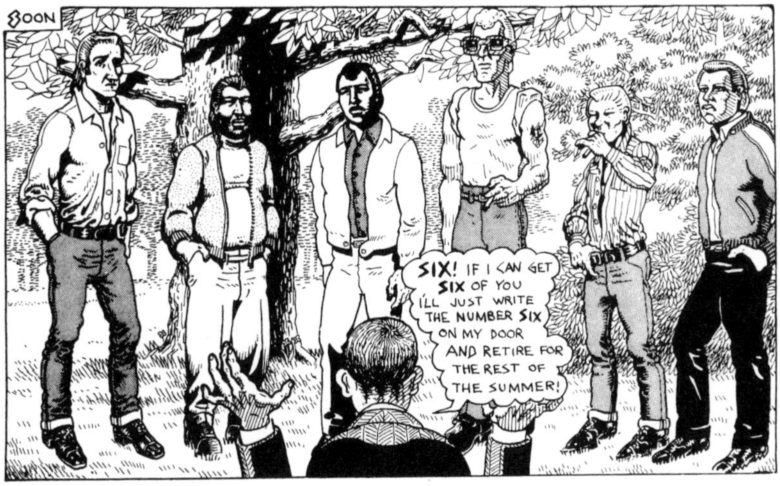
SIX! IF I CAN GET SIX OF YOU I'LL JUST WRITE THE NUMBER SIX ON MY DOOR AND RETIRE FOR THE REST OF THE SUMMER!

Every time I go back there, all the bars are jumping, and there's bands and people dancing; especially at the end of the '50s and in the early '60s, Buffalo really had a great blues scene. There were people from different neighborhoods that were into this scene, and they would get to know each other, sometimes even on good terms. A lot of times you'd get into fights with other neighborhoods, but you'd usually end up drinking with these guys that you had fights with last week. I was already working at Western Electric, it was the spring, and I saw these motorcycles takin' off and I had some money saved in the bank. I said, "I want one." I had a friend who had a motorcycle. His dad taught him how to ride. His dad stopped riding when he drove a bike in between these two trees and skinned off the side of both of his hands. At that point he figured it was time to stop. So his dad had taught him. He was a big blues buff like me. John Biye, a Cajun guy from Louisiana. He taught me how to ride. Some time later, a guy I knew, a guy who had a motorcycle, got jumped and beat up. A whole bunch of us, at least so I thought, went down to this bar to find the ones who had beat him up. I walked into the bar with two other guys, and we assumed that there were a whole bunch of guys behind us, but there weren't.

You mean you thought friends of yours were backing you up?

Yes, we thought there was a whole bunch of us behind us, but when we looked around, we were three guys in this hostile bar. I was fighting five guys, and I kept on fighting even when they knocked me down, and some guy kicked me in the head. At that point I just curled up in a little ball, and let them beat on me. There wasn't anything else I could do. It was amazing how little it hurt. I mean, when you're getting kicked in the head, that hurts, but it's amazing how resilient the human body is—and how much a leather jacket protects you, actually.

A padded motorcycle jacket, right.

But when the Road Vultures heard about it, they thought that that really showed class. They went down to the bar to find those guys, who were long gone by that time. You had to strike for the club, hang around for a certain amount of time, and then they'd vote on you, whether they wanted you in. So I got in in two weeks, and became a Road Vulture.

Well, you've got a number of comics stories that harken back to that period, or even before, and I wanted to know how truly autobiographical these stories are. You did the stories in the '70s, so I'm kind of skipping around here a little, but the first story that I wanted to ask you about was "Dessert," which I think was supposed to have taken place in 1954, which would have made you 14.

Yeah.

In which case it hardly seems likely you were actually involved in that story.

Yeah, we went through this brief period of rolling fags; our neighborhood went through cycles of crime, and this was one of them.

Were you involved in this, or did you only hear about this?

Well, no, I was… well, I guess the statute of limitations has run out. Yeah, sure.

You were a participant?

Yeah.

So you were 14 when you were involved in sexually abusing and beating up a gay guy. Were the other kids older? In the story it certainly looks like they're closer to 18.

Yeah. Well, they were kind of a mature 14. By the time we got to be 18, all that stuff was considered beneath us.

I see. So rolling fags was one of your activities.

For a short time. But anyone approaching us, even on a non-sexual basis, did so at their peril. In 1954… the thing that surprised me back then was that a lot of police were sympathetic to gays.

Huh! That strikes me as… almost contradictory.

Uh, yeah.

I would've thought the police would probably have approved of that activity.

You would think that they would, but no, a lot of police, even in Buffalo, aren't morons.

Another story that I'm curious whether it was autobiographical or not, is titled "How I Almost Got Stomped Through 'The Still of the Night' by the Five Satins," which describes someone attending a concert and sitting in the chair of a black guy's girlfriend, and the black guy comes up and basically says, "That's where my girlfriend sits,"

LEFT
Page from "Field Meet" in *My True Story* ©1974 Spain

ABOVE
Panel from "Dessert" in *My True Story* ©1976 Spain

and the guy says, "I'll get up when she gets here,"and he says, "No, you're going to get up now," and he says, "Yeah, well, why don't you just go fuck yourself?" And he finds himself facing 30 black guys. Was that you?

That's completely autobiographical, yeah.

That was you?

That was me.

That was supposed to be '55, so you were 15 at the time?

Yeah.

So you were a real tough guy?

Well, I certainly fancied myself as that.

You got into a lot of fights…

I got into some, yeah.

You must have been something of an anomaly in the underground scene; I don't imagine most of the underground artists were the kind of guys to get into fights.

It's ironic that they thought that comic books were causing juvenile delinquency, when most juvenile delinquents didn't read comics, or much of anything. I remember a guy from my neighborhood reading *Studs Lonigan*, but he was unusual. I used to read science fiction. But reading wasn't… or even going to college, I think there was one guy who went to college, but most guys didn't go to college. The black guys in my neighborhood were more into higher education than the white guys.

Were the Road Vultures… I mean, was that a fairly violent way of life? Or is that exaggerated?

You'd find a bar to hang out, and everything would be cool for a while. But after a while, guys would get bored, and somebody would always eventually come in and get things going. I mean, you didn't have to look for fights, because somebody always wanted to give you a hard time, because you had long hair, or you had an earring, or something like that. They ended up getting their asses kicked. So there were two ways you could be a nonconformist. You could be a nonconformist and just adopt a Buddha-like attitude of accepting all kinds of abuse, or you could be a Road Vulture.

I assume you read Hunter Thompson's Hell's Angels.

I read parts of it. I never got through the whole book.

I was going to ask you if you thought that was a pretty accurate depiction of a biker gang.

Yeah, the parts I read were pretty plausible. It's interesting that the incident that the movie *The Wild One* was based on was some sort of minor unruliness that took place in Hollister, the Road Vultures had a far bloodier episode in Sherman, N.Y., where somebody lost an eye… at least one guy did time because of that incident.

Were you there at the time?

No, I wasn't. This was before my time.

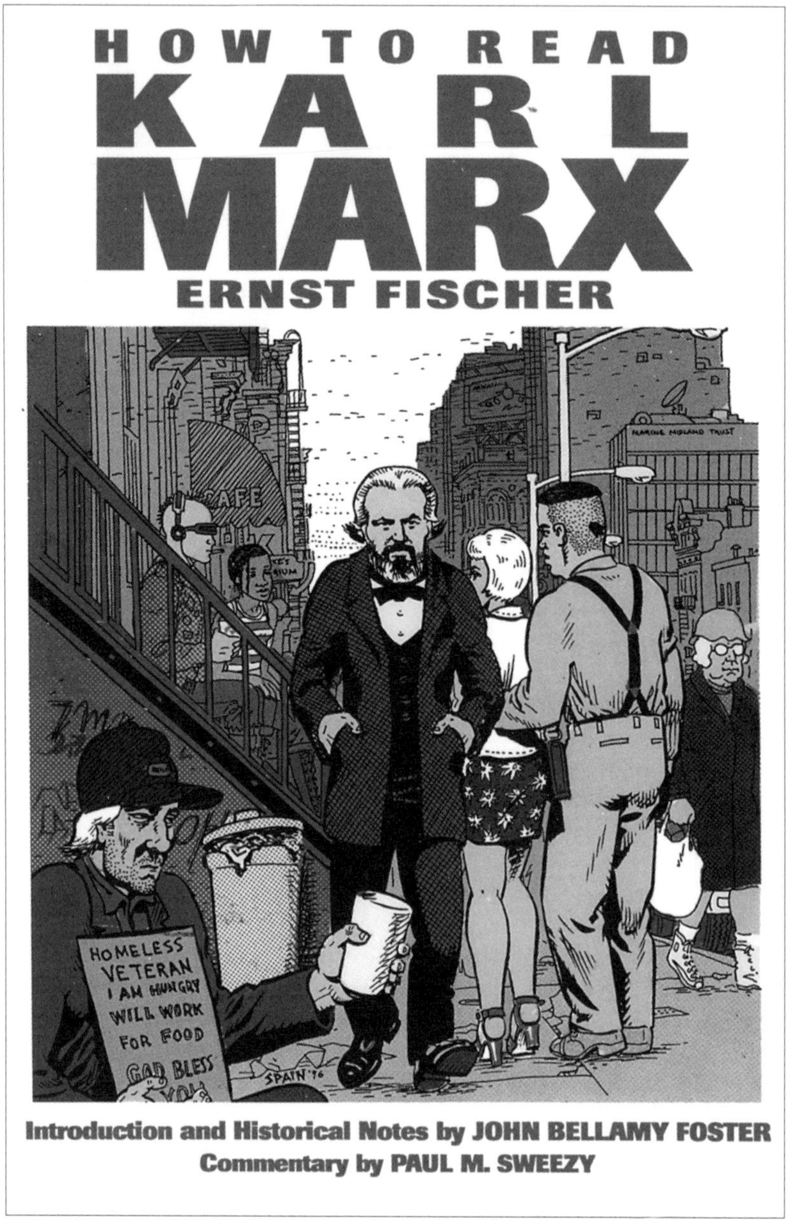
HOW TO READ
KARL MARX
ERNST FISCHER
CAFE
HOMELESS
VETERAN
I AM HUNGRY
WILL WORK
FOR FOOD
GOD BLESS
SPAIN '96
Introduction and Historical Notes by JOHN BELLAMY FOSTER
Commentary by PAUL M. SWEEZY

ABOVE
Cover art by Spain ©1996 *Monthly Review Press*

RIGHT
Panel is from "The Peerless Power of the Silver Surfer" in *Fantastic Four* #55 (October 1966): which was written by Stan Lee, penciled by Jack Kirby and inked by Joe Sinnott ©1966 Marvel Characters, Inc.

How many Road Vultures were there?
Oh, somewhere around 20. So we pretty much kept to ourselves, and—
Can you give me an idea of the social routine? Would you all get together Fridays or Saturdays?
Yeah, we'd have a club meeting once a week, and we'd hang out, depending on what bars would let us in. There was one bar that always let us in, the Silver Sails, that was run by Ma, who would always serve us. It was down by the Niagara River, at the end of the Erie Canal, and we could always count on Ma to let us in. And some weekends would be dead, and sometimes you could go in there on a Tuesday night and the place would be jumping, so that was where we'd hang out in the winter, and then when spring happened, there were all sorts of things you could do—go for rides to different places, and various field meets, and motorcycle events.
I don't want to sound naive, but was there any political dimension to joining the Road Vultures?
Well—
Or did you just want to kick ass?
Well, there were two phases of the Road Vultures. I used to read *The Weekly People*, which was the official organ of the Socialist Labor Party. The format of *The Weekly People* was set around 1911. It had very large pages. When I rolled it out, it was hard not to notice, and it had a great logo, the arm and hammer logo, a muscular arm wielding a hammer with block lettering across "The Weekly People." You could always get into a discussion by just pulling out that paper and sitting there, somebody would always give me an argument about it, and then if you refuted their arguments, they would complain that you're always coming around here with these socialist arguments, and you could tell them, "Well, I was just sitting here reading my paper and you came in here and started bothering me, so stop whining." I used to argue a lot, and they would tell me things like, "Them Negroes, they move into your neighborhood and you know how they are, they're always drinking and causing crime and they're dirty and they're loud, and we don't want people like that around." I always assumed that prejudice was fairly ingrained.

Then something happened that shed a different light on things. They used to have a big field meet in Cuba Lake, it was in what they call the southern tier of New York. What happened was there was always this big dance the night before, and there were a lot of college guys who hung out in that town. There might have been a university or some college around there. It was as though there was an invisible line drawn down the middle of the dance floor, and the bikers would be on one side, and the college guys would be on the other side. This one time, there were these black guys there, maybe about five or six guys, and evidently the college guys had been giving these black guys a hard time. When the black guys saw us, they were really glad to see us. It was like these long-lost brothers. The Road Vultures took these guys around, and made sure that they had plenty of drinks and everything like that, and made sure that these college guys didn't mess with them, took good care of them. And it was the same guys that would make these know-nothing arguments…
Can you elaborate on the social dynamics there? Because I assume the Road Vultures didn't take them in or protect them because they were all a bunch of good liberals.
We were outcasts. There was a certain solidarity with outcasts. It's funny about people. It's funny about people's prejudices. What I suspect is, when I look back upon it, I just think that a lot of these guys were putting me on. You know, some guys were really rabid racists, other guys were not racists at all, and even sympathetic to black people being people who were at the bottom of society like we were, so… There was definitely a cultural affinity at that time. There was this one black bike club who always won the uniform prize. If you're on the road for a few hours, you get pretty dirty, and these guys would roll into town, get some hotel room, and fix themselves up and put on these snazzy uniforms, and just all roll into the field meet, and would inevitably win a prize.

BACK INTO COMICS

What was your interest in comics and art at that time? I mean, did you have much of one?
Oh, yeah, I drew continuously. At the plant they ended up putting me behind a machine that was always breaking down. They were putting us on time study to put us on piece work, which is in reality a wage reduction. Whenever they would watch us, we would just work slower, and I worked slower than anybody else. And they ended up putting me on a machine that was always breaking down. So I had plenty of time to do drawings. In fact, there was one boss who would chide me if I didn't draw him a dirty picture every day. He was on the midnight shift, and if I didn't draw him a

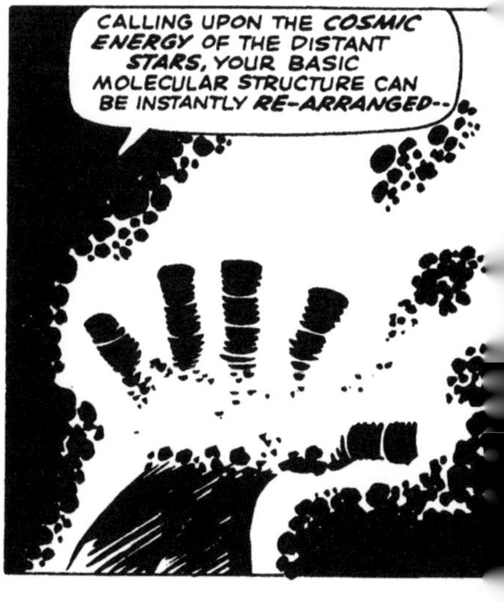
CALLING UPON THE COSMIC ENERGY OF THE DISTANT STARS, YOUR BASIC MOLECULAR STRUCTURE CAN BE INSTANTLY RE-ARRANGED--

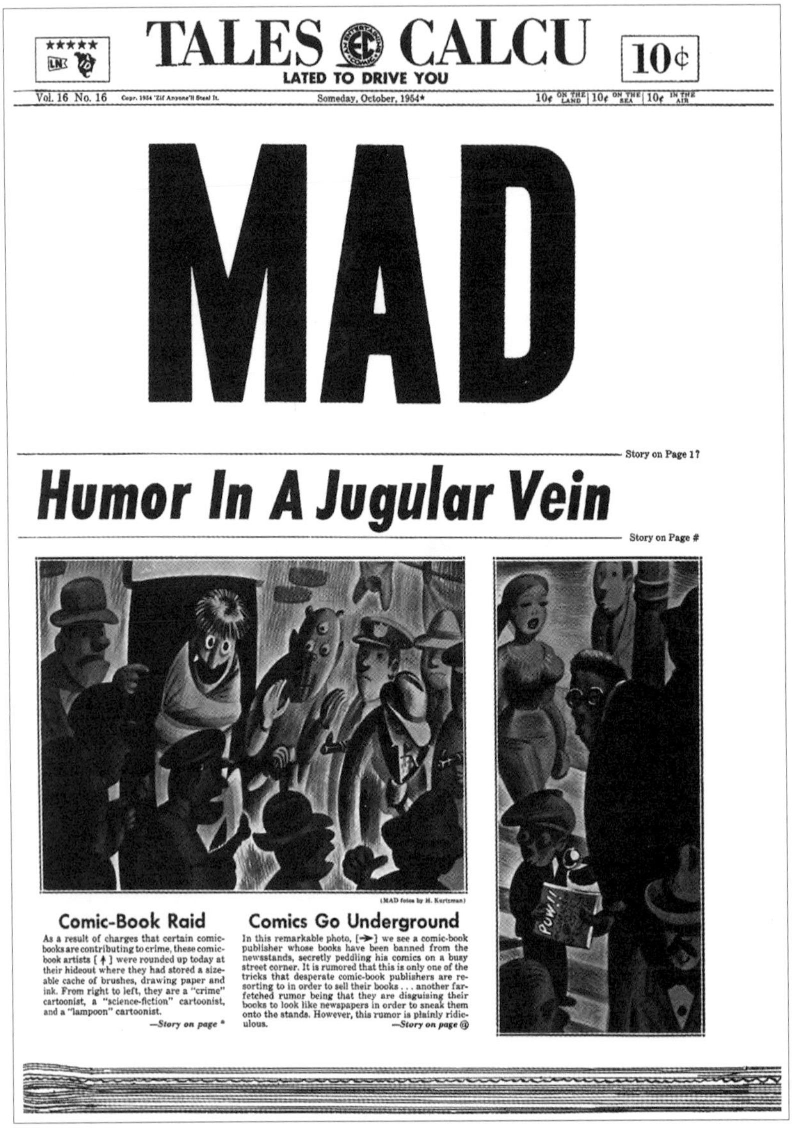

TALES CALCU
LATED TO DRIVE YOU
10¢
Vol. 16 No. 16
Copr. 1954 'Zif Anyone'll Steal It.
Someday, October, 1954*
10¢ ON THE LAND | 10¢ ON THE SEA | 10¢ IN THE AIR
MAD
Story on Page 1?
Humor In A Jugular Vein
Story on Page #
(MAD fotos by H. Kurtzman)
Comic-Book Raid
As a result of charges that certain comic-books are contributing to crime, these comic-book artists [↑] were rounded up today at their hideout where they had stored a size-able cache of brushes, drawing paper and ink. From right to left, they are a "crime" cartoonist, a "science-fiction" cartoonist, and a "lampoon" cartoonist.
—Story on page *
Comics Go Underground
In this remarkable photo, [➔] we see a comic-book publisher whose books have been banned from the newsstands, secretly peddling his comics on a busy street corner. It is rumored that this is only one of the tricks that desperate comic-book publishers are re-sorting to in order to sell their books . . . another far-fetched rumor being that they are disguising their books to look like newspapers in order to sneak them onto the stands. However, this rumor is plainly ridic-ulous.
—Story on page @
POW!!

fuck picture, he would say, "Where are those pictures? I want to see something here." So I got plenty of practice to improve my chops.

So the '60s were starting to gear up, and in Buffalo the bikers merged in with the beatniks and the college crowd, and it became a big party scene. People started getting into Marvel Comics. There seemed to be some sort of psychedelic subtext; it's hard to put your finger on it. I'm sure other people have mentioned this, there was something that resonated. I remember reading *The Fantastic Four*, and it was the first time that I picked up a comic book every time it came off the stand since I was a kid. So there was this feeling it was coming back. When they suppressed comics, there were a bunch of us who were EC fans, and there was that cover of *MAD* where they were leading the underground cartoonists off in chains, and there was something about that that really resonated. There was this girl in our class, kind of a heavyset girl, her name was Tema, and me and a friend did a strip about her. It was called *Tema*, and it was written in letters like *The Heap*. Nasty guys that we were, we put out this strip to terrorize her. We thought of ourselves as underground cartoonists.

Cover of *MAD* #16 (October 1964) by Harvey Kurtzman

Talking to different guys, you'd get a feeling that the idea of underground cartoonists just resonated across the country. Guys I knew would have dreams that they'd walk into some place, and they would see some EC comics that they hadn't seen before. And I would have those dreams, too. When they suppressed EC comics, I went to every bookstore I knew and bought up every EC that I could find. At some point they actually started charging $3 for them.

It was a funny, mixed feeling about it. It was an indication that we weren't the only guys who felt these were great, but on the other hand, you had to pay more for them. You used to be able to get them for a nickel. Suddenly they were charging you—even 50 cents was fine. When they wanted $3 for them, we thought they were going overboard.

So anyway, there was this sense out there. This friend of mind, Fred Tooté, a guy I did a bunch of strips about in *Blab!*, was one of them. There was this core of EC fanatics in my neighborhood. There was a sense that something would happen, and suddenly there was this feeling around 1965 that comics were going to come back. At some point, in '65, I dropped out, I quit work, I had some money saved up, and I went down to the Lower East Side [in New York City] and tried to flood places that would accept my work.

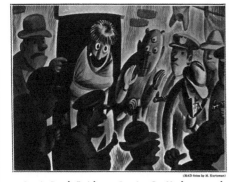

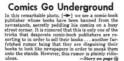

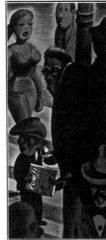

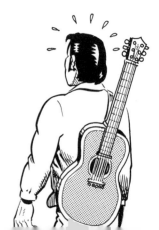